MARKETING 91/92

Thirteenth Edition

Annual Editions
A Library of Information from the Public Press

Editor

John E. Richardson
Pepperdine University

Dr. John E. Richardson is Associate Professor of Management in the School of Business and Management at Pepperdine University. He is president of his own consulting firm and has consulted with organizations such as Bell and Howell and Dayton-Hudson, as well as with various service, nonprofit, and franchise organizations. Dr. Richardson is a member of the American Marketing Association, the American Management Association, the Society for Business Ethics, and Beta Gamma Sigma honorary business fraternity.

Cover illustration by Mike Eagle

The Dushkin Publishing Group, Inc.
Sluice Dock, Guilford, Connecticut 06437

The Annual Editions Series

Annual Editions is a series of over fifty volumes designed to provide the reader with convenient, low-cost access to a wide range of current, carefully selected articles from some of the most important magazines, newspapers, and journals published today. Annual Editions are updated on an annual basis through a continuous monitoring of over 200 periodical sources. All Annual Editions have a number of features designed to make them particularly useful, including topic guides, annotated tables of contents, unit overviews, and indexes. For the teacher using Annual Editions in the classroom, an Instructor's Resource Guide with test questions is available for each volume.

VOLUMES AVAILABLE

Africa
Aging
American Government
American History, Pre-Civil War
American History, Post-Civil War
Anthropology
Biology
Business and Management
Business Ethics
Canadian Politics
China
Comparative Politics
Computers in Education
Computers in Business
Computers in Society
Criminal Justice
Drugs, Society, and Behavior
Early Childhood Education
Economics
Educating Exceptional Children
Education
Educational Psychology
Environment
Geography
Global Issues
Health
Human Development
Human Resources
Human Sexuality

Latin America
Macroeconomics
Management
Marketing
Marriage and Family
Microeconomics
Middle East and the Islamic World
Money and Banking
Nutrition
Personal Growth and Behavior
Psychology
Public Administration
Race and Ethnic Relations
Social Problems
Sociology
Soviet Union and Eastern Europe
State and Local Government
Third World
Urban Society
Violence and Terrorism
Western Civilization,
  Pre-Reformation
Western Civilization,
  Post-Reformation
Western Europe
World History, Pre-Modern
World History, Modern
World Politics

Library of Congress Cataloging in Publication Data
Main entry under title: Annual Editions: Marketing. 1991/92.
    1. Marketing—Addresses, essays, lectures. 2. Marketing—Social aspects—Addresses, essays, lectures. 3. Marketing management—Addresses, essays, lectures. I. Title: Marketing.
HF5415.A642   658.8'005   73-78578
ISBN 1-56134-003-0

Thirteenth Edition

Manufactured by The Banta Company, Harrisonburg, Virginia 22801

Editors/ Advisory Board

EDITOR

John E. Richardson
Pepperdine University

ADVISORY BOARD

Joseph M. Bearson
Eckerd College

John L. Beisel
Pittsburg State University

Joseph Bonnici
Valdosta State College

Steve Brown
Arizona State University

Gertrude A. Butera
State University of New York
Alfred

Robert Coker
Christopher Newport College

Howard W. Combs
Radford University

William H. Eldridge
Kean College of New Jersey

Cleveland Gilcreast
Merrimack College

Marsha Griffin
Alabama A & M University

George Joyce
University of Texas
Tyler

Sandra L. Lueder
Southern Connecticut State
University

Martin D. Martin
Western Carolina University

G. H. G. McDougall
Wilfried Laurier University

Taylor Meloan
University of Southern California

Terry Paul
Ohio State University

David L. Ralph
Pepperdine University

Darlene B. Smith
Loyola College

David Snepenger
Montana State University

Rajendra Srivastava
University of Texas
Austin

Jerald L. Weaver
State University of New York
Brockport

STAFF

Ian A. Nielsen, Publisher
Brenda S. Filley, Production Manager
Roberta Monaco, Editor
Addie Kawula, Administrative Editor
Cheryl Nicholas, Permissions Editor
Diane Barker, Editorial Assistant
Lisa Holmes-Doebrick, Administrative Coordinator
Charles Vitelli, Designer
Shawn Callahan, Graphics
Meredith Scheld, Graphics
Libra A. Cusack, Typesetting Supervisor
Juliana Arbo, Typesetter

To the Reader

In publishing ANNUAL EDITIONS we recognize the enormous role played by the magazines, newspapers, and journals of the *public press* in providing current, first-rate educational information in a broad spectrum of interest areas. Within the articles, the best scientists, practitioners, researchers, and commentators draw issues into new perspective as accepted theories and viewpoints are called into account by new events, recent discoveries change old facts, and fresh debate breaks out over important controversies.

Many of the articles resulting from this enormous editorial effort are appropriate for students, researchers, and professionals seeking accurate, current material to help bridge the gap between principles and theories and the real world. These articles, however, become more useful for study when those of lasting value are carefully *collected, organized, indexed,* and *reproduced* in a *low-cost format*, which provides easy and permanent access when the material is needed. That is the role played by *Annual Editions.* Under the direction of each volume's *Editor*, who is an expert in the subject area, and with the guidance of an *Advisory Board*, we seek each year to provide in each *ANNUAL EDITION* a current, well-balanced, carefully selected collection of the best of the public press for your study and enjoyment. We think you'll find this volume useful, and we hope you'll take a moment to let us know what you think.

The 1990s are proving to be an exciting and challenging time for the American business community. Recent dramatic social, economic, and technological changes have become an important part of the present marketplace. These changes—accompanied by increasing domestic and foreign competition—are leading a wide array of companies and industries toward the realization that better marketing must become a top priority now to assure their future success.

How does the marketing manager respond to this growing challenge? How does the marketing student apply marketing theory to real world practice? Many reach for *The Wall Street Journal*, *Business Week*, *Fortune*, and other well-known sources of business information. There, specific industry and company strategies are discussed and analyzed, marketing principles are often reaffirmed by real occurrences, and textbook theories are supported or challenged by current events.

The articles reprinted in this edition of *Annual Editions: Marketing* have been carefully chosen from numerous different public press sources to provide current information on marketing in the world today. Within these pages you will find articles that address marketing theory and application in a wide range of industries, from automobiles to health care, and computers to transportation. In addition, the selections reveal how several firms interpret and utilize marketing principles in their daily operations and corporate planning.

The volume contains a number of features designed to be useful to marketing students, researchers, and professionals. These include the *industry/company guide*, which is particularly helpful when seeking information about specific corporations; a *topic guide* to locate articles on specific marketing subjects; the *table of contents abstracts*, which summarize each article and highlights key concepts; a *glossary* of 122 key marketing terms; and a comprehensive *index*.

The articles are organized into four units. Selections that focus on similar issues are concentrated into subsections within the broader units. Each unit is preceded by an overview that provides background for informed reading of the articles, emphasizes critical issues, and presents *challenge questions* that focus on major themes throughout the selections.

This is the thirteenth edition of *Annual Editions: Marketing*. Since its first edition in the mid-1970s, the efforts of many individuals have contributed toward its success. We think this is by far the most useful collection of material available for the marketing student. We're anxious to know what you think. What are your opinions? What are your recommendations? Please take a moment to complete and return the article rating form on the last page of this volume. Any book can be improved, and this one will continue to be, annually.

John E. Richardson
Editor

Contents

Unit 1

Marketing in the 1990s and Beyond

Eighteen selections organized within four subsections examine the current and future status of marketing, the marketing concept, marketing ethics, and the utilization of marketing strategies in industries and social organizations.

The concepts in bold italics are developed in the article. For further expansion please refer to the Topic Guide, the Index, and the Glossary.

The concepts in bold italics are developed in the article. For further expansion please refer to the Topic Guide, the Index, and the Glossary.

Unit 2

Research, Markets, and Consumer Behavior

Fourteen selections, organized within three subsections, provide an analysis of consumer demographics and life-styles, the growth and maturation of markets, and the need for market research and planning.

The concepts in bold italics are developed in the article. For further expansion please refer to the Topic Guide, the Index, and the Glossary.

Unit 3

Developing and Implementing Marketing Strategies

Nineteen selections, organized within four subsections—product, price, distribution, and promotion—analyze factors that affect the development and implementation of marketing strategies.

The concepts in bold italics are developed in the article. For further expansion please refer to the Topic Guide, the Index, and the Glossary.

The concepts in bold italics are developed in the article. For further expansion please refer to the Topic Guide, the Index, and the Glossary.

Unit 4

Global Marketing

Six selections discuss the increasing globalization of
markets, trends in world trade, and increasing foreign
competition.

The concepts in bold italics are developed in the article. For further expansion please refer to the Topic Guide, the Index, and the Glossary.

Topic Guide

This topic guide suggests how the selections in this book relate to topics of traditional concern to students and professionals involved with the study of marketing. It is useful for locating articles that relate to each other for reading and research. The guide is arranged alphabetically according to topic. Articles may, of course, treat topics that do not appear in the topic guide. In turn, entries in the topic guide do not necessarily constitute a comprehensive listing of all the contents of each selection.

TOPIC AREA	TREATED IN:	TOPIC AREA	TREATED IN:
Advertising	3. Stalking the New Consumer 8. How to Handle Customers' Gripes 9. Guiding Principles for Improving Customer Service 16. Marketing and Its Discontents 17. Some Food Labels Aren't on the Level 18. Children's Advertising Grow Up 22. New Species for Study 23. Focus Groups Emerging 24. A Symphony of Demographic Change 25. Downscale Consumers 27. "Real" Consumers Just Aren't Normal 29. U.S. Companies Go for the Gray 31. Cueing the Consumer 33. Seize Tomorrow's Markets 34. Enduring Brands Hold Their Allure 37. Sales Lost Their Vim? 42. As Retailers' Sales Crop Up Everywhere 43. Manage by Walking Around—Outside 49. What's Right, What's Wrong With Each Medium 50. Advertising: In Dire Straits 51. Ads of the '80s	**Consumer Demographics/ Consumer Behavior (cont'd)**	13. Service Marketing 16. Marketing and Its Discontents 18. Children's Advertising Grows Up 19. How to Hunt for the Best Source 20. Market Research the Japanese Way 21. The Selling of Life-Styles 22. New Species for Study 24. A Symphony of Demographic Change 25. Downscale Consumers 26. Different Folks, Different Strokes 27. "Real" Consumers Just Aren't Normal 28. Meet Jane Doe 29. U.S. Companies Go for the Gray 30. Beyond Consumer Decision Making 31. Cueing the Consumer 32. Shoppers' Blues 34. Enduring Brands Hold Their Allure 38. The Fine Art of Positioning 39. Middle-Price Brands Come Under Siege 44. Real Service 46. The (Un)Malling of America 47. Revamped Retail 48. Home Depot's Do-It-Yourself Powerhouse 49. What's Right, What's Wrong With Each Medium 50. Advertising: In Dire Straits 52. Strategic Options for Global Market Players
Competition	2. Marketing in an Age of Diversity 4. What Consumers Want in the 1990s 6. King Customer 9. Guiding Principles for Improving Customer Service 13. Service Marketing 15. An Ethical Base for Marketing Decision Making 34. Enduring Brands Hold Their Allure 37. Sales Lost Their Vim? 38. The Fine Art of Positioning 39. Middle-Price Brands Come Under Siege 41. How to Compete on Price 42. As Retailers' Sales Crop Up Everywhere 47. Revamped Retail 48. Home Depot's Do-It-Yourself Powerhouse 49. What's Right, What's Wrong With Each Medium 52. Strategic Options for Global Market Players 53. Global Competitors 54. Beware the Pitfalls of Global Marketing	**Distribution Planning and Strategies**	2. Marketing in an Age of Diversity 33. Seize Tomorrow's Makrets 43. Manage by Walking Around—Outside 44. Real Service 45. Retail Revolution 46. The (Un)Malling of America 50. Advertising: In Dire Straits 57. Distribution: The Key to Success Overseas
		Economic Environment	2. Marketing in an Age of Diversity 4. What Consumers Want in the 1990s 6. King Customer 15. An Ethical Base for Marketing Decision Making 24. A Symphony of Demographic Change 25. Downscale Consumers 28. Meet Jane Doe 43. Manage by Walking Around—Outside 45. Retail Revolution 53. Global Competitors
Consumer Demographics/ Consumer Behavior	1. Portrait of a Changing Consumer 2. Marketing in an Age of Diversity 3. Stalking the New Consumer 4. What Consumers Want in the 1990s 7. Service = Survival 8. How to Handle Customers' Gripes 9. Guiding Principles for Improving Customer Service 10. Sure Ways to Annoy Consumers 11. Customer Satisfaction 12. What Is Good Service?	**Exporting**	52. Strategic Options for Global Market Players 53. Global Competitors 54. Beware the Pitfalls of Global Marketing 56. Myth and Marketing in Japan

TOPIC AREA	TREATED IN:	TOPIC AREA	TREATED IN:
Focus Group	1. Portrait of a Changing Consumer 14. Nonprofits Learn How-To's of Marketing 23. Focus Groups Emerging 32. Shoppers' Blues 33. Seize Tomorrow's Markets 37. Sales Lost Their Vim?	**Marketing Planning and Strategies**	1. Portrait of a Changing Consumer 4. What Consumers Want in the 1990s 7. Service = Survival 11. Customer Satisfaction 14. Nonprofits Learn How-To's of Marketing 17. Some Food Labels Aren't on the Level 20. Market Research the Japanese Way 27. "Real" Consumers Just Aren't Normal 33. Seize Tomorrow's Markets 35. Strengthen Brands With 8 Essential Elements 36. Masters of Innovation 37. Sales Lost Their Vim? 41. How to Compete on Price 42. As Retailers' Sales Crop Up Everywhere 47. Revamped Retail 54. Beware the Pitfalls of Global Marketing
Franchising	39. Middle-Price Brands Come Under Siege 45. Retail Revolution 47. Revamped Retail		
Global Markets	7. Service = Survival 20. Market Research the Japanese Way 34. Enduring Brands Hold Their Allure 40. Marketing the Premium Product 52. Strategic Options for Global Market Players 53. Global Competitors 54. Beware the Pitfalls of Global Marketing 55. Hitting for Singles 57. Distribution: The Key to Success Overseas	**Marketing Research**	1. Portrait of a Changing Consumer 3. Stalking the New Consumer 4. What Consumers Want in the 1990s 5. Marketing Myopia 7. Service = Survival 14. Nonprofits Learn How-To's of Marketing 16. Marketing and Its Discontents 18. Children's Advertising Grows Up 19. How to Hunt for the Best Source 20. Market Research the Japanese Way 21. The Selling of Life-Styles 22. New Species for Study 23. Focus Groups Emerging 25. Downscale Consumers 32. Shoppers' Blues 33. Seize Tomorrow's Markets 36. Masters of Innovation 43. Manage by Walking Around—Outside 45. Retail Revolution 50. Advertising: In Dire Straits 52. Strategic Options for Global Market Players 54. Beware the Pitfalls of Global Marketing 56. Myth and Marketing in Japan
Innovation	3. Stalking the New Consumer 4. What Consumers Want in the 1990s 16. Marketing and Its Discontents 20. Market Research the Japanese Way 34. Enduring Brands Hold Their Allure 36. Masters of Innovation 40. Marketing the Premium Product 47. Revamped Retail 51. Ads of the '80s 53. Global Competitors 54. Beware the Pitfalls of Global Marketing 55. Hitting for Singles		
Market Share	2. Marketing in an Age of Diversity 6. King Customer 17. Some Food Labels Aren't on the Level 39. Middle-Price Brands Come Under Siege 49. What's Right, What's Wrong With Each Medium	**Mass Marketing**	2. Marketing in an Age of Diversity 3. Stalking the New Consumer 12. What Is Good Service? 13. Service Marketing 21. The Selling of Life-Styles 29. U.S. Companies Go for the Gray 39. Middle-Price Brands Come Under Siege 45. Retail Revolution
Marketing Concept	5. Marketing Myopia 6. King Customer 7. Service = Survival 8. How to Handle Customers' Gripes 9. Guiding Principles fo Improving Customer Service 10. Sure Ways to Annoy Consumers 11. Customer Satisfaction 16. Marketing and Its Discontents 20. Market Research the Japanese Way 33. Seize Tomorrow's Markets 46. The (Un)Malling of America 47. Revamped Retail 48. Home Depot's Do-It-Yourself Powerhouse	**New Product Introductions**	22. New Species for Study 23. Focus Groups Emerging 27. "Real" Consumers Just Aren't Normal 33. Seize Tomorrow's Markets 34. Enduring Brands Hold Their Allure 36. Masters of Innovation 50. Advertising: In Dire Straits 51. Ads of the '80s 55. Hitting for Singles
Marketing Ethics & Social Responsibility	4. What Consumers Want in the 1990s 15. An Ethical Base for Marketing Decision Making 16. Marketing and Its Discontents 17. Some Food Labels Aren't on the Level 18. Children's Advertising Grows Up	**Non-profit (Non-business Marketing)**	14. Nonprofits Learn How-To's of Marketing 19. How to Hunt for the Best Source

TOPIC AREA	TREATED IN:	TOPIC AREA	TREATED IN:
Packaging	16. Marketing and Its Discontents 27. "Real" Consumers Just Aren't Normal 31. Cueing the Consumer 33. Seize Tomorrow's Markets 34. Enduring Brands Hold Their Allure 35. Strengthen Brands With 8 Essential Elements 37. Sales Lost Their Vim? 45. Retail Revolution 54. Beware the Pitfalls of Global Marketing 56. Myth and Marketing in Japan	**Psychographics (cont'd)**	21. The Selling of Life-Styles 22. New Species for Study 49. What's Right, What's Wrong With Each Medium 50. Advertising: In Dire Straits
Personal Selling	10. Sure Ways to Annoy Consumers 13. Service Marketing 15. An Ethical Base for Marketing Decision Making 16. Marketing and Its Discontents 29. U.S. Companies Go for the Gray 33. Seize Tomorrow's Markets 44. Real Service 48. Home Depot's Do-It-Yourself Powerhouse	**Public Relations**	14. Nonprofits Learn How-To's of Marketing 33. Seize Tomorrow's Markets 50. Advertising: In Dire Straits
Price Planning and Strategy	9. Guiding Principles for Improving Customer Service 15. An Ethical Base for Marketing Decision Making 39. Middle-Price Brands Come Under Siege 40. Marketing the Premium Product 42. As Retailers' Sales Crop Up Everywhere 54. Beware the Pitfalls of Global Marketing 56. Myth and Marketing in Japan	**Retailing**	3. Stalking the New Consumer 20. Market Research the Japanese Way 29. U.S. Companies Go for the Gray 32. Shoppers' Blues 40. Marketing the Premium Product 41. How to Compete on Price 42. As Retailers' Sales Crop Up Everywhere 45. Retail Revolution 46. The (Un)Malling of America 47. Revamped Retail 48. Home Depot's Do-It-Yourself Powerhouse 50. Advertising: In Dire Straits
Product Planning and Development	4. What Consumers Want in the 1990s 21. The Selling of Life-Styles 23. Focus Groups Emerging 26. Different Folks, Different Strokes 33. Seize Tomorrow's Markets 34. Enduring Brands Hold Their Allure 36. Masters of Innovation 38. The Fine Art of Positioning 39. Middle-Price Brands Come Under Siege 40. Marketing the Premium Product 41. How to Compete on Price 52. Strategic Options for Global Market Players 55. Hitting for Singles 56. Myth and Marketing in Japan	**Sales Promotion**	3. Stalking the New Consumer 29. U.S. Companies Go for the Gray 44. Real Service 50. Advertising: In Dire Straits
		Services Marketing	1. Portrait of a Changing Consumer 4. What Consumers Want in the 1990s 6. King Customer 7. Service = Survival 9. Guiding Principles for Improving Customer Service 10. Sure Ways to Annoy Consumers 11. Customer Satisfaction 12. What Is Good Service? 13. Service Marketing 21. The Selling of Life-Styles 23. Focus Groups Emerging 32. Shoppers' Blues 33. Seize Tomorrow's Markets 41. How to Compete on Price 43. Manage by Walking Around—Outside 48. Home Depot's Do-It-Yourself Powerhouse
Promotion Planning and Development	1. Portrait of a Changing Consumer 3. Stalking the New Consumer 25. Downscale Consumers 34. Enduring Brands Hold Their Allure 42. As Retailers' Sales Crop Up Everywhere 50. Advertising: In Dire Straits 54. Beware the Pitfalls of Global Marketing	**Target Marketing**	3. Stalking the New Consumer 12. What Is Good Service? 13. Service Marketing 16. Marketing and Its Discontents 24. A Symphony of Demographic Change 25. Downscale Consumers 26. Different Folks, Different Strokes 28. Meet Jane Doe 29. U.S. Companies Go for the Gray 33. Seize Tomorrow's Markets 38. The Fine Art of Positioning 40. Marketing the Premium Product 45. Retail Revolution 49. What's Right, What's Wrong With Each Medium 50. Advertising: In Dire Straits 51. Ads of the '80s
Psychographics	1. Portrait of a Changing Consumer 4. What Consumers Want in the 1990s 7. Service = Survival 13. Service Marketing		

INDUSTRY/COMPANY GUIDE

This guide was prepared to provide an easy index to the many industries and companies discussed in detail in the 57 selections included in *Marketing 91/92*. It should prove useful when researching specific interests.

INDUSTRIES

COMPANIES AND DIVISIONS

Marketing in the 1990s and Beyond

- **Changing Perspectives (Articles 1-4)**
- **The Marketing Concept (Articles 5-11)**
- **Services and Social Marketing (Articles 12-14)**
- **Marketing Ethics and Social Responsibility (Articles 15-18)**

If we want to know what a business is we must start with its purpose. . . . There is only one valid definition of business purpose: to create a customer. What business thinks it produces is not of first importance—especially not to the future of the business or to its success. What the customer thinks he is buying, what he considers 'value' is decisive—it determines what a business is, what it produces, and whether it will prosper.

—Peter Drucker, *The Practice of Management*

When Peter Drucker penned these words in 1954, American industry was just awakening to the realization that marketing would play an important role in the future success of businesses. The ensuing years have seen an increasing number of firms in highly competitive areas—particularly in the consumer goods industry—adopt a more sophisticated customer orientation and an integrated marketing focus.

The dramatic economic and social changes of the last decade have stirred companies in an even broader range of industries—from banking and air travel to communications—to the realization that marketing will provide them with their cutting edge. Demographic and life-style changes have splintered mass, homogeneous markets into many markets, each with different needs and interests. Deregulation has made once-protected industries vulnerable to the vagaries of competition. Vast and rapid technological changes are making an increasing number of products and services obsolete. Intense international competition and the growth of truly global markets have caused many firms to look well beyond their national boundaries.

Indeed, it appears that during the 1990s marketing will take on a new significance—and not just within the industrial sector. Social institutions of all kinds, which had thought themselves exempt from the pressures of the marketplace, are also beginning to recognize the need for marketing in the management of their affairs. Colleges and universities, charities, museums, symphony orchestras, and even hospitals are beginning to give attention to the marketing concept—to provide what the consumer wants to buy.

The selections in this unit are grouped into four areas. Their purposes are to provide current perspectives on marketing, discuss differing views of the marketing concept, analyze the use of marketing by social institutions and nonprofit organizations, and examine the ethical and social responsibilities of marketing.

The lead article of the first subsection, "Portrait of a Changing Consumer," prognosticates some important demographic, economic and life-style changes that marketers need to incorporate into future marketing strategies. "Marketing in an Age of Diversity," covers the importance of companies endeavoring to be market driven as they compete in newly diversifying markets. The last two articles in this section provide significant clues about salient approaches and issues that marketers of products and services in the 1990s need to address.

The seven selections addressing the marketing concept include Levitt's now classic "Marketing Myopia," which first appeared in the *Harvard Business Review* in 1960. This version includes the author's retrospective commentary, written in 1975, in which he discusses the uses and misuses that have been made of the article. "King Customer," "Service = Survival," "How to Handle Customers' Gripes," "Guiding Principles for Improving Customer Service," and "Customer Satisfaction" describe key ingredients of customer satisfaction with guidelines and principles for handling customer complaints and improving customer service. In contrast, "Sure Ways to Annoy Consumers," reflects some of the sure "turnoffs" that consumers have in regard to dubious sales practices and poor service treatment.

In the Services and Social Marketing subsection, the first article provides a helpful look at focusing service on the particular needs of diverse consumers (younger consumers, older consumers, and minorities). The second article, "Service Marketing: Image, Branding, and Competition," provides some helpful insight as to why the marketing of services necessitates the development of a positive image. The last article in this section covers some effective ways to apply marketing to the nonprofit agencies.

In the final grouping, the articles take a careful look at the strategic process and practice of incorporating ethics and social responsibility into the marketplace. The first article in this subsection, "An Ethical Base for Marketing Decision Making," provides a conceptual base for combining social responsibility, ethics, and marketing strategy. "Marketing and Its Discontents," describes how marketing's "excesses" and "expertness" often solicits signif-

icant consumer criticism. The last two articles in this section exemplify how questionable labeling practices and advertising to children have recently come under attack.

Looking Ahead: Challenge Questions

There is little doubt that dramatic changes are occurring in the marketing of products and services. What social and economic trends do you believe are most significant today, and how do you think these will affect marketing in the 1990s?

Levitt suggests that, as times change, the marketing concept must be reinterpreted. Given the varied perspectives of the other articles in this unit, what do you think this reinterpretation will entail?

How and where are marketing strategies being used by social institutions and nonprofit organizations? What problems are unique to social marketers?

Given the present competitive business arena, is it possible for marketers to behave ethically in the environment and both survive and prosper? What suggestions would you make that could be incorporated into the marketing strategy for firms that want to be both ethical and successful?

In the article "Marketing and Its Discontents," Steven H. Star describes some marketing "excesses" (shoddy products, deceptive or objectionable advertising, misleading packaging, questionable selling practices, and emphasis on tawdry values). What examples of marketing "excesses" have you encountered? How did you deal with these "excesses"?

Portrait of a Changing Consumer

Ken Dychtwald and Greg Gable

Ken Dychtwald is the chairman and CEO of Age Wave, Inc., Emeryville, Cal. Greg Gable is the director of media projects at Age Wave, Inc.

> *Marketers must recognize the changes in their customer base and change their strategies to fit the new situation.*

The marketplace is changing. People are living longer, healthier, and more productive lives, and we are likely to see further expansions of life expectancy. At the same time, fewer babies are being born, causing a shrinkage in the number and relative proportion of the young in our society. The baby boomers are leaving youth and migrating into middle age. By the year 2000 they will have filled the 35-to-54-year-old age bracket. As a result, spending power is becoming increasingly concentrated in the hands of a more mature consumer base. The clear and unmistakable implication is that business is about to face a larger, more powerful mass of mature consumers as we enter the 1990s and beyond.

The American marketplace has always been predominantly youth-focused. As we have seen, for the past 43 years much of this focus has been on the baby boomers. While some companies missed out on the opportunities of this period, many marketers were able to track the boomers very well as they have moved through each stage of youth and young adulthood. Others were lucky enough to have products or services in the market at the right time to meet the needs of this huge consumer group.

Now, the baby boomers are migrating out of the well-mapped territory of youth and into the new and somewhat uncharted landscape of middle and older age. To remain successful, consumer marketing must change its focus to follow them.

To meet the demands of the maturing marketplace, businesses will next need to know how consumers are likely to live their lives as they face the inevitable milestones of aging. The trillion-dollar question is obvious: What kind of middle-aged and mature consumers does the future hold?

CONSUMER MARKETPLACE 2000

We believe that there is sufficient information about the nature of middle and older age, and about the enduring characteristics of the mass of baby boom consumers moving into those ages, that some predictive description about the future can—and should—be made.

Based on our exhaustive analysis and upon our own in-depth understanding of baby boomers, cohort effects, lifestage factors and the maturing of America, and upon years of research, focus group studies, the collective experience of staff, advisors, futurists, business analysts, and outside consultants, we have come to believe that there very well may be some essential psychological and social characteristics of the emerging 35-54 year old segment that will color their behavior and drive the marketplace in the coming decades.

What follows are snapshots of ten such characteristics. These snapshots are not meant to be exhaustive. Rather, we see these preliminary descriptions as a starting point that may help to focus the range of questions that need to be asked about this emerging market in the coming years, and that can lead business to create strategies and tactics that will profit from the changes ahead. This snapshot represents a predictive first-cut at what clearly needs to be an on-going analysis of this newly emerging market segment.

1. The concerns and perspectives of middle age and maturity will become dominant.

As the center of the consumer marketplace shifts upward to accommodate the new mass of people in their middle years, the characteristics of middle age will dominate the entire consumer marketplace.

Self-Assessment. Middle age is, typically, a period of self-assessment, the time of the "mid-life crisis." People in their early 40s have passed a halfway point, and they often find themselves reviewing their lives. In some cases this mid-life review period acts as a precursor to major changes in work (such as a job change or even retirement), in personal relationships (such as renewed commitments, divorce, or remarriage), and in habits (especially health-related habits). Sometimes a mid-life crisis is less explicit and simply underlies more subtle shifts in attitudes. Big retrospective questions may arise—What's the point of it all? What have I accomplished? What can I do in the years I have left?

Relationship issues will continue to be hot topics among middle-aged boomers, and in fact, they may become even hotter. We can expect a boom in the public discussion of mid-life personal-relationship issues, with numerous books, magazine articles, and TV shows devoted to this topic. There will also be an explosion of new lifestyles in response to the changed roles of men and women, including increases in mid-life divorces, and second, and third marriages. The overall picture will be one of diversity and flexibility, as the baby boomers face the challenges of middle age with their usual unwillingness to fall back on the traditional authority of habit and their interest in finding their own customized solutions.

Responsibilities. In general, middle age is a period when personal and social responsibilities are at their peak.

Family. All family relationships intensify and middle-aged men and women often find themselves "sandwiched" between the needs of two generations. Because the baby boomers have had their children much later in life than their parents did, it will become common for parents of school-age children to be in their 30s and 40s rather than just their 20s and 30s.

And with the continued growth of the senior population, many adult children will be caring not only for their school-age youngsters, but for their aging parents as well. To date, most of this elder care has been provided by women. Research shows that more than 90 percent of the middle-aged adults who are caring for their parents are women. In 1986, for the first time in the history of our country, the average woman could expect to spend more years caring for her mother than for her children. The pressure for men to be involved in the care of older parents will increase as women continue to join the work force, as marriage rates drop, and divorce rates rise, and as family responsibilities are shared more evenly.

Work. At work, people in middle age and approaching retirement are reaching the pinnacles of their careers. Psychologists describe a sense of "generativity" that accompanies middle age, an interest in assisting others and passing on accumulated wisdom to the next generation. At work, generativity is apparent in the middle-aged worker's role as mentor and supervisor.

In middle age, workers often come to the realization that they are closer to the end of their career or work life than they are to the beginning. In their 40s and 50s, people typically develop diminishing expectations for future work-related accomplishments. They may come to feel their youthful aspirations are now unattainable. They may decide to make a career change when faced with what seems like a dead end in their current job. People may all benefit from the change. Volunteerism, for example, rises in middle and older age. People in early middle age typically begin to think about and plan for retirement, and may embark on new leisure pastimes with a passion.

Intimacy and Personal Relationships. Sociologists and psychologists describe interpersonal relationships during early middle age as predominantly "instrumental" rather than "intimate." People at this stage of life are busy getting things done at work, in the community, and at home. They are, in other words, managers. The instrumental/intimate dichotomy tends to reverse as people grow into their 50s and 60s. In these years, many are faced with empty nests, diminishing demands of work, and retirement. They often begin to share their feelings more openly with spouses and friends. Romance shoots to the surface of their priorities as it often hasn't since adolescence.

Psychologists say that during the 20s and 30s men and women can become locked into traditional sex roles because of parenthood. As their children set out on their own, they become less confined by these roles and often break free of them in mid life. For example, men may become more willing to talk about their feelings and more interested in their personal and home lives. Women may become more interested in asserting their independence in work, at home, and in their personal relationships.

2. In middle age, the baby boomers will retain many of their cohort characteristics, including their tendency to delay traditional markers of maturity, their diversity, their distrust of authority, their educational attainment, and their entanglement with the media and marketing arms of business.

What makes a generation different from its parents before it and its children after it are the major historical events they encounter, such as wars, depressions, major technological advances and social and cultural revolutions. This is especially true of those events that accompany a generation's youth, when individuals form important and long-lasting attitudes about life. Sociologists and psychologists call these *cohort effects*.

For example, one of the most dramatic areas where cohort effects are apparent in the consumer marketplace is in a generation's attitude towards the making and managing of money. Consider the differences in attitude between the baby boomers and their parents and grandparents: most generations form their attitudes about making and managing money in the years when they first start working. They then tend to hold that viewpoint for the rest of their lives. For consumer markets, their *attitude* about spending is just as important as how much money they have. For example, yesterday's elders began working during the Depression. Their point of view on money is very conservative. They believe it is essential to save for that inevitable rainy day. Many of our current misconceptions about older consumers are based on our perceptions about this cohort of older adults. On the other hand, the parents of the baby boomers, those people today in their 50s and 60s, were influenced by the Depression, but also by the boom period following World War II. Their attitude and behavior towards money is typically less restrained: they prefer to save some and spend some.

The baby boom generation, in contrast, developed their attitudes towards making and managing money during the prosperous post-war period. More typical of this generation is this attitude: "if you have no money in the bank, but at least two credit cards that are not over the limit, then you are doing great." For example, today 80 percent of baby boomers have credit cards, and more than a third of those charged $1000 in the last 12 months.

Beyond this generation's orientation toward spending, other factors color their consumer style as well. For our purposes here, it would be impossible to review all the unique traits and characteristics of this generation, but we believe that there are five key ones substantial enough that they will be carried into middle and older age to affect this group's future consumer behavior. They are:

• **Delay of Traditional Markers of Maturity.** As a group, baby boomers have stayed in school longer than previous generations (because proportionally more of them were going to college), waited longer to start careers, waited longer to get married, waited longer to buy homes, and waited longer to have children. In 1986 when the boomers started turning 40, analysts remarked that boomers seemed to be delaying their mid-life crises as well. It might be said in general that *baby boomers are taking longer to grow up*.

• **Diversity of Lifestyles.** The 1960s, 1970s, and especially the 1980s were notable for the changes in lifestyles that they fostered. During this period, we have seen one of the single most important revolutions of our time, the dramatic rise in the number and stature of women in the work force, and a change in the roles of men and women and the ways they relate, both personally and professionally; we have seen a dramatic change in racial integration and attitudes towards race relations; we have seen the development of openly gay and lesbian lifestyles; we have seen an increase in the number of unmarried but cohabiting relationships; we have seen a rise in the divorce rate, and a rise in the number of people in second, third, even fourth marriages; we have seen the sexual revolution loosen and change our attitudes about sex, sexuality and sexual fulfillment; we have seen a change in attitudes towards work and careers that is marked by a new independence and sense of individuality; we have seen a rise in the number of people who are self-employed, and a rising interest in job and career changes. It is likely that much of this proclivity for social diversity will persist in the years ahead.

• **Skepticism and Distrust of Authority.** One of the dominant themes of the last 30 years has been a pronounced distrust of government and authority. In its political form it reflects the lingering effects of the

Vietnam War and Watergate. In subtle ways it affects this generation's attitudes towards commercialism, traditionalism, influence, and even work. The evidence is apparent in their occasional disdain and criticism of the mass media and the advertising that supports it, their non-traditional approach to family and work, their unwillingness to accept pat answers or unsubstantiated claims, their interest in consumer activism, their cynicism, their apparent disinterest in politics, and their increased interest in consumer activism, their cynicism, their apparent disinterest in politics, and their increased interest in entrepreneurial pursuits. We will undoubtedly see a change in the willingness of consumers to accept product endorsements from non-expert "influentials," as their increasing cynicism leads them to question the authority of the spokesperson, as well as to doubt the veracity of paid endorsements. Their distrust of authority, combined with their willingness to experiment will mean their loyalty to brands will become increasingly fleeting and subject to change.

• **Education.** This is the most educated generation in our history. Their higher level of education bears on their attitudes toward work and the kinds of work for which they are qualified. Education also has a dramatic bearing in the marketplace. It has increased their willingness to demand product information, increased their skepticismn, made them less brand loyal and more rational in their purchasing decisions. Additionally, they now have years of experience applying their education in the marketplace.

• **Self Absorption and Entanglement with the Media and Marketing Industries.** Unlike any other generation before it, the baby boom has grown up being talked about, and talking about, itself. Whether or not the baby boom wanted to be thought of as a group apart from others, the business community has had good reason to concentrate its attention upon these 76 million like-minded consumers: their sheer size. By targeting the boomers time and time again, America's business helped to generate this generation's own self-awareness, their sense of style, and their sense of self. And in an **unending feedback loop, as this generation's sense of self increased, so did marketers' ability to target them exclusively. It wasn't always that a product represented the choice of a new generation—this generation represented the choice of many businesses. The baby boom generation is entangled with the mass media and the marketing arms of American businesses: they are media- and**

> *"We now have a choice between growing old as we always have, with two or three decades of old age tagged on at the end, or of taking those extra years and cycling them throughout every part of life."*

advertising-fluent and demand excellence, high production values, entertainment, relevance, information and empathy from both.

3. Middle-aged and maturing consumers will be embarking upon "cyclic lifestyles" and will defy the age markets traditionally associated with maturity.

One of the greatest impacts that extended longevity has on lifestyle is its effect on our attitude toward the latter half of life. With 28 years added to our life expectancy during the last century, we now have a choice between growing old as we always have, with two or three decades of old age tagged on at the end, or of taking those extra years and cycling them throughout every part of life. Extended life and the expectation of health and vigor in later life lead many people to reconsider the appropriate lifestyle they should lead now.

Family. For example, when the average life expectancy was 45 to 55 years, we spent nearly every moment of our adult years raising our children. As a result, we have come to think of our adult family roles as being primarily that of parent. As recently as one century ago, by the time the last child was grown and ready to leave home, one or both of the parents had already passed away. Now, most of us will have more years of adult life *after* the children have grown and have left home than we had when we were raising them. As a result, the role of parenting will fade in the overall architecture of family life, and the importance of mature friendship, companionship and social compatibility will rise as core elements of mid- and late-life marital relationships.

Education. In the past, education was geared to preparing the young for their lifetime careers. We are now coming to think of learning as an ongoing, lifelong process. An incredible increase in continuing education is already upon us, and will only increase as more people reach late middle age and their early years of maturity. As people continue to learn in the middle and later years, they will be more inclined to try new products and services. Education and the spirit of learning it engenders will work as an antidote to brand loyalty and consumer rigidity.

Work. We have thought of work as the job we perform essentially nonstop from our early 20s until we either retire or die. We expect to expand and enlarge our abilities in the early years of our careers, reaching a peak in the late 40s or early 50s, and then winding down to a halt during the remaining decades. We will soon find ourselves cycling in and out of several different careers throughout our lives, each interspersed with periods of rest, recreation, retraining and personal reflection. Some older men and women will hit their career stride for the first time when others are retiring, as, for example, when some women return to the workforce in their 40s following childrearing.

Leisure. We have thought of leisure as rest from work and as something we could enjoy for extended periods only during early childhood or old age. Now we are beginning to envision leisure as an ongoing element of our adult years with regular time taken away from work for recreation and personal growth.

The travel business will experience enormous changes. Leisure travel is already booming, accounting today for more than $181 billion annually. And leisure is one sector of the American economy that responds to the marketplace with remarkable plasticity. It isn't surprising that the travel industries have already begun to reflect the changing shape of the American population and the values that come with it. Today already, 80 percent of luxury travel in America is purchased by people over 55. For them, convenience, access and experiences, rather than cost, may be the main issues.

In the future, mature travelers will be looking for travel that is more individualized, intimate, unusual, stimulating, and challenging. As leisure becomes more fully integrated into our lives, we will be seeing a wave of travelers who are more interested in exotic travel and in cultural information, and who are more willing to trek, to backpack, to get wet—in short, to do whatever is necessary to have that exotic experience.

Community Service. We are already seeing the rise in community service that a longer healthier life makes possible. Through membership organizations like AARP, and volunteer activities in community institutions like hospitals and senior centers, communities around the country have already benefited from the expanding interest in community service among the maturing population. Middle age is also typically a period when donations and charity rise, another indication of people's increased sense of involvement and responsibility in their communities.

Already, indications of the emergence of a cyclic lifestyle are upon us. Increasing numbers of men and women are marrying later in life and choosing to delay parenting until they have established careers and financial stability. For women, the average age of first marriages has risen to its highest point (23 years old) in the nation's history. For men, it has reached the highest point (26 years old) since 1900. Divorce and remarriage rates remain high. More than 50 percent of all marriages end in divorce, and 80 percent of divorced people remarry, making "serial monogamy" the norm rather than the exception. It is becoming increasingly common for middle-aged and older people to go back to school; the average age of evening students has soared to 38. Today, 45 percent of all undergraduate students are over 25. The average American now changes jobs every three years; nearly 14 percent of American corporations offer some form of paid sabbatical from work. Only about 27 percent of Americans want to stop working completely at retirement age, and more than 60 percent hope to keep working either full- or part-time. Finally, the Rand Corporation predicts that by the year 2020, the average worker will need to be retrained up to 13 times in his or her lifetime.

4. The new middle-aged will seek ways to balance work, family, and recreation.

Our self identity, how we define ourselves, is diversifying. And while work has and will remain an important element of our identity, the work-driven "yuppie" image we have become accustomed to in the last 10 years will be replaced. In large part, our obsession with the yuppie mystique may simply have been another reflection of our obsession with baby boomers. As they entered their 20s and 30s and work became a central issue in their lives, the yuppie motif made sense.

Taking a longer view, the part that work plays in our lives is diminishing significantly. During the past century, the amount of time we spent working has dropped by almost half. Today the average

American works less than 14 percent of the hours that he or she lives. For a typical full-time worker, the year's 365 days include 104 weekend days, 10 holidays, 10 sick days, and 10 days of vacation, adding up to 134 days outside of work. The protestant ethic is giving way to the ethic of balance and diversity. In this new approach, instead of identifying leisure primarily as a means of promoting and enhancing work, we are increasingly viewing a more even blend of work and leisure as the optimal lifestyle arrangement.

Boomers are likely to emphasize this notion of balance in their attitudes toward work, home, and recreation. They are just as likely, for example, to define themselves as mothers and fathers, wind-surfers and skiers, as to talk about themselves as accountants and lawyers, carpenters and secretaries.

The urge to create such a "balance" between work and recreation is not a pipe dream. Already many of the wheels have been set in motion to change the structure of work. And increasingly, the pressures of parenting, and an increasing demand for older workers as the labor pool of younger workers diminishes will cause changes in the work environment. In addition to the vast increase in company training programs that help employees move in and out of various job tracks and thus promote career diversity, an increasing number of companies are allowing employees to take personal sabbaticals to pursue their own interests.

The new American ideal may become a combination of successful work and free time, a sense of personal well-being, and the freedom and wisdom to fill one's life with productive, fulfilling and expressive activities.

One consequence of an expanding effort to create this balance will be that the home regains a prominence in our lives that it has not held since the 1950s. In ten years, three-quarters of the boomers will be married, the majority will have children, and two-thirds will be homeowners. The middle-aging of the baby boom assures that we are becoming a generation of homebodies. We should expect a renewed emphasis **on the home as an oasis from the stress of work. A reemphasis on the family will be apparent because of the sheer numbers of households made up of married couples with children.**

But finding ways and time to enjoy home life will remain challenging. Today, both parents in most married-couple households with children are in the labor force. This kind of couple outnumbers two-earner couples without children by two to one.

> "In ten years, three-quarters of the boomers will be married, the majority will have children, and two-thirds will be homeowners. The middle-aging of the baby boom assures that we are becoming a generation of homebodies."

From now until the turn of the century, this lifestyle will grow. Households composed of middle-aged married couples with children will grow by roughly 40 percent, while households of married couples grow by only 13 percent. Marketers who can make it easier for people to enjoy the time they spend at home will find middle-aged consumers lining up at their doors (or, more likely, flooding them with telephone and mail orders).

5. People in middle age will become increasingly concerned with health and wellness.

Two forces are converging to create an increasing interest in health and wellness: age and predisposition. In middle and older age, maintenance of health is a crucial concern. In addition, the well-educated baby boom generation carries with it a predisposed interest in health promotion, and substantial knowledge about the role of personal behavior in health maintenance.

Lifelong Wellness. Nutrition and exercise will remain hot topics. Fitness habits, once instilled, are usually long-lasting. They are relatively well-instilled in the baby boom generation now and are not likely to diminish with age. But watch for different emphases in the kind of exercise undertaken. Walking for exercise is a trend that still has great growth potential. Approximately 25 million Americans exercise by walking. Of this group, more than 60 percent are women, 28 percent are over 55, and they cover an average of ten miles a week.

Healthfood crazes are only beginning. There is a substantial rise in the interest in healthful diets, sometimes driven by health problems (high blood pressure or diabetes), but often driven simply by age. In the past few years we have seen two substantial nutrition crazes that have been largely age-driven: the calcium craze and the oatbran craze. Both have promised to stave off substantial, largely age-related health problems. There will be an increasing interest in low-fat, low-salt, and low-sugar foods as consumers become more savvy. Staying lean and reducing the risk of heart disease are motivating a revolution. As reported in a February 1988 article "Quest for Fake Fat" in *U.S. News and World Report,* "Spurred by an estimated $2 billion in annual sales for truly tasty fat substitutes, the food marketing war of the 1990s will be under way, making the low fat, Lean Cuisine, diet-soda, light-beer revolution of the 1980s look like small potatoes." Today, fitness foods are the fast growing segment of the $300 billion retail-food industry.

Interest in exercise and fitness is already high among the baby boom generation. For example, baby boomers are more likely to belong to healthclubs (17 percent of this group are healthclub members, compared to only 8 percent of nonboomers), and more likely to participate in exercise classes and to engage in a variety of sports. Twenty-six percent of boomers say that they jog regularly, 29 percent enjoy bicycling, and 23 percent report that they do calisthenics. The proportion of baby boomers who regularly swim, dance, bicycle, jog, ski, and participate in team sports is twice that of the rest of the population.

The boomers' skepticism and distrust, coupled with their high level of education, mean that they will continue to take an assertive role in maintaining their health. They will be interested in food ingredients. They'll demand detailed information from their health-care providers, and they will seek out information on health-relative topics.

Today, the middle- and older-aged populations use a disproportionately high amount of health care services and products, including prescription and over-the-counter pharmaceuticals and institutional services. As their numbers increase, so too will their use of these products and services.

Vitality and Youth Maintenance. The baby boom created a youth crazed society, and the baby boomers are not likely to give up their youthful lifestyles easily. As they move into middle age, they will do whatever they can to delay the aging process. In the process, they'll redefine what middle age means: middle age will now be more vigorous and active, more casual, more

attractive, and sexier—in short, more "youthful."

Baby boomers will take every advantage of anti-aging products for hair, skin and vitality that keep themselves looking "good." Vitamins, nutritional products, "lite" healthy foods, personal care and cosmetics products and services will boom. Middle-aged boomers will be willing to spend on health: for healthy foods, on clubs, on exercise equipment, spas, and retreats, and on healthy and beauty-related products and services like designer glasses, hair-replacement treatments, skin care, and plastic surgery.

Perhaps the area of greatest concern pertaining to physical aging is the health and appearance of the skin. Throughout the body, cells liquify and disappear, to be replaced by fat, scar tissue, or droplets of liquid. As cells disappear, the body's tissues shrink, causing the skin to become dry and thin. It also tends to lose its elasticity due to changes in the structure of the body's collagen. In addition, the loss of elastic collagen fibers and of underlying muscle mass lead to wrinkling.

In the years ahead, the cosmetics industry will experience the biggest boom in its history. Cosmetics manufacturers will increasingly target the mature market. Mature Americans today already spend 40 percent more on average on health and personal care products. As they expand in number, they will comprise a tremendous growth market for these industries. The market for products for maturing men has also begun to boom. For example, the sale of men's skin-care products is already showing a 16 percent annual growth rate.

Physical Abilities. In general, health in middle age is still good. But people at this stage of life begin to face some of the inevitabilities of aging, including the possibility of developing chronic illnesses such as cardiovascular disease, arthritis, and diabetes.

Some changes in physiology may be beginning. Eyesight, hearing, taste, stamina, and strength, for example, may diminish somewhat. Weight control may become an issue, and people may begin slight changes in lifestyle to account for physiological changes. They may choose sports that are less stressful on their joints (for instance, swimming, bicycling, and walking instead of jogging), avoid night driving, sit farther back in movie theaters, and look for larger-print books and magazines. They may select looser, more comfortable clothes; choose quieter restaurants in order to hear the conversation better; and purchase audio equipment with improved high-frequency responses. they are more likely to avoid doing heavy lifting or heavy yard work in order to prevent back and muscle strain.

Arthritis is far more common in middle and older aged people than in younger groups. Increasing stiffness and loss of dexterity in the fingers can pose a constant and annoying problem to many older people. Medicine bottles, food containers, cutlery, computer keyboards, appliance controls, and purse clasps will need to be redesigned to better accommodate these changes. Similarly, clothing manufacturers will use more Velcro tabs and will switch to larger buttons, eliminating the small buttons and tiny snaps that can be difficult for some hands to manipulate.

Food designers need to be aware of the changes that take place in our sensitivity to taste as we mature. The average person loses 64 percent of his or her taste buds between the ages of 30 and 80. The average 30-year-old has 245 taste buds on each little bump (papilla) on the tongue. By the time that person reaches 80, he or she will have only 88. As a result, it becomes harder to discriminate among the four basic taste sensations: sweet, bitter, sour, and salty. Sweet buds diminish the most, and sour, the least.

Because of these significant taste changes, all of our foods will have to be, in a sense, redesigned to offer enjoyable flavorings to less capable palates. This will present an interesting challenge to food manufacturers and restaurants, especially in light of the various food sensitivities and nutritional needs the more mature eater might also have.

Ultimately, all products will have to adapt themselves to accommodate physiological changes, as will the communications that promote those products and services. For example, our eyes begin to change in our mid-40s. The lenses start to thicken and become more yellow. Its surface becomes less even. The pupil becomes smaller, and the muscles that control its opening and closing become increasingly slow to respond. These changes can make it difficult for a person to see quick-moving images— yet the production tempo of today's television programming and especially advertising relies on quick pace. In addition, the yellow film that forms over the eye with age tends to change color perception—for instance, light blue, pink, and salmon, seen as very distinct shades through the eyes of a young art director, may be hard to differentiate by the middle- and older-aged consumer, just as black, gray, dark

> *"Ultimately, all products will have to adapt themselves to accommodate physiological changes, as will the communications that promote those products and services."*

blue, and brown begin to seem increasingly similar. Thus, an advertisement or container that seems very striking to a young designer may miss the mark with the middle-aged or mature people for whom the product is targeted. In the future, publishers and ad agencies will use more contrasting colors and will steer clear of overly cluttered pages. Type sizes will also grow larger. Mature people often have difficulty seeing in low light, and their range of vision tends to be more narrow than that of younger people. As a result, they may not be as quick to see landmarks, exit signs over doors, items on high shelves, overhead direction signs in airports, high billboards, overhead freeway signs, or elevator floor numbers.

Unlike problems with vision, which are fairly obvious to other people, partial deafness is not so evident. Today, over 30 million Americans have hearing problems of varying degrees. Hearing loss manifests itself in a number of important ways. For example, it may become increasingly hard to isolate significant sounds from background noise. Designing sound for effective communications needs to consider this requirement for an "uncluttered" aural environment. High frequencies tend to be harder to hear as we age, musical mixes need to accommodate the change.

6. Men and women are becoming increasingly similar in the marketplace.

As the baby boomers grow older, three psycho-social factors are converging that will diminish some of the traditional distinctions between men and women as consumers.

Lifestage Factors. We described earlier how psychologists and sociologists who study lifestage note an increasing "androgeny" of middle age. Women who have been heavily involved in childrearing may explore new outwardly directed interests, such as career or community involvement. Men may find themselves expanding their interest in interpersonal relationships, personal reflection and exploration.

Work. The phenomenal historical shift that has brought women increasingly into the work force, and now increasingly into positions of equal stature and pay, has caused ripples in nearly every aspect of society from education, to marriage, to child-rearing, to the financial structure of family wealth. This revolution, however, is still in its early stages. As women continue to expand their role in the workforce, social changes will accompany them. In the marketplace, businesses will increasingly find themselves faced with the converged attitudes, expectations and buying habits of a more androgenous male/female.

Home and Family. Baby boomers are already breaking down many of the traditional male and female role distinctions of the past and will continue the trend.

Middle age used to be a period dominated by the style, structure, and needs of the traditional nuclear family with its traditional male-female roles. But this has changed: for example, 75 percent of baby boomers say they believe that an "equal marriage" is preferable to the traditional model. Studies show that a substantial number of husbands do as much cooking and cleaning as their wives do. Twenty-one percent of women working full-time say that their husbands do the same amount of cooking; 34 percent report sharing housecleaning equally; 38 percent share food shopping equally; and 45 percent share child care equally.

Baby boomers of both sexes are more likely to describe themselves as oriented equally toward family and career. A survey by DuPont of its 100,000 employees showed that the number of men interested in moving from full-time to part-time work to free their time for other activities almost doubled between 1985 and 1988, from 18 percent to 33 percent.

With these life-stage and cohort factors combined, we can expect to see middle-aged baby-boom men and women become increasingly similar in the range of product choices they make. Marketers would be wise to target men more actively for household products, and women for such items as cars and electronic equipment like stereos and VCRs.

7. Seasoned consumers evaluate their choices based on years of consumer ex-perience and product trials. They will seek and recognize quality above all else.

Because of their greater experience, middle-aged and mature consumers are likely to be more thoughtful purchasers than younger buyers and will be less inclined to follow fads or to buy on impulse. A man who has bought ten cars has a more critical eye than someone who has bought only one, and he is more likely to look for things that are not evident to the novice buyer. Someone buying their 100th business suit is likely to understand much better what it is they are looking for than when they bought their first suit. Middle-aged and mature consumers aggressively evaluate all products and services, including, foods, packaged goods, durables, financial services, health services, entertainment and dining out.

Baby boomers will add to their years of shopping experience their high level of education and their consumerist attitudes. Aging baby boomers will be unlikely to take things on face value.

The old argument that mature consumers are more "brand loyal" needs to be completely rethought. Brand loyalty is less likely in a consumer who believes their decisions are made on point by point assessment of product attributes. Studies, like Yankelovich, Clancy, Shulman's "Senior Monitor," indicate that middle-aged and older consumers are neither brand loyal nor uninterested in coupons and other pricing promotions for encouraging new product trial. Almost 75 percent of the 1,000 people aged 55 surveyed by the Center for Mature Consumers Studies said they would use coupons, and 57 percent said they would switch brands because of them. In addition, nearly 50 percent said they bought things they didn't plan to because of "special sales." As a result, the fight for market share will intensify.

Seasoned consumers want information that will allow them to take charge of their purchasing decision. They want to play an active role as consumers and expect to be treated accordingly. Sales messages need to be based on facts, not just on emotions.

Ratcheting. By middle age, consumer expectations and buying habits have typically "ratcheted up." A consumer who has already graduated to a luxury car is less likely to be interested in an economy model in the future. Consumers who have become accustomed to buying the choicest cuts of meats and the fanciest produce are not as likely to shop for specials. Consumers are very hesitant to move down a notch, once they have ratcheted up, as moving down may indicate "failure" or loss of status.

8. Convenience and comfort will become increasingly important consumer issues.

Maturity prefers and often demands privilege, convenience, and comfort. For example, as mentioned earlier, people in middle age are striving to strike a balance between work and recreating. Their time becomes a precious asset which they will do (and pay) anything to conserve. Expect to see changing patterns of consumption—a shift away from household chores (cooking, cleaning, washing, sewing, and child care) and the products that accompany them, and toward convenience services such as food services (restaurants, catering, prepared foods), home maintenance services, and day care. Similarly, products that are redesigned with convenience in mind, will benefit from the shift.

Home deliveries of everything from pizza to furniture and health care services will be making a comeback, as thoughtful merchants and service providers look for ways to attract and assist the older shopper. For example, New York's Doctors on Call and Washington, D.C.'s Geodan Medical House Calls, Inc., are bringing back the old-fashioned house calls at a cost of $50 per visit. Physicians with Doctors on Call visit more than 50,000 patients per year. If needed, the company will even bring traveling labs to the patient's door for blood and urine samples, X-rays, EKGs, and ultrasound.

Several innovative drug and grocery stores are designing convenience-oriented shopping systems. Customers call up products on a specially designed television screen (or at home in the case of interactive cable systems) and, simply by pushing a button, send the product to the checkout stand or have it delivered to their home. Should a drugstore customer need assistance in making a selection, a pharmacist or nurse will be available to answer any questions.

Increasingly, products will be packaged together with services that appeal to these more demanding expectations. Service warranties on cars that include pick-up, delivery, and the use of a loaner would appeal to the two-earner couple with money to spend, but no time to spend at the mechanic. Home delivery will boom. Other services will expand, including banking services that accommodate for work schedules (after 6 p.m. and weekend ser-

> "One key psychological difference between the young and the mature is a profound sense among middle-aged and mature consumers of their vulnerability, and an awareness of the risks associated with almost every decision they make."

vice), no hassle, no waiting car rentals, and home maintenance contracts that come with the purchase of new homes.

As people look for ways to find leisure in small bites, easy access to leisure activities will become increasingly important. Getaway retreats near urban centers will boom, weekend trips will boom, vacation homes will become increasingly popular.

In the 50+ market, comfort becomes a key psychological need not just out of increased expectations (though that certainly is important) but also out of physical need. Simply put, as we age, we become more interested in being comfortable. One of the most telling manifestations of this need is reflected in the increasing interstate "gray migration" that is taking place throughout America, as retirees move south and west to warmer, more comfortable climates.

But the desire to be comfortable goes far beyond relocation to a warmer climate. As we age, we come to feel that we have had enough hassles. We feel less inclined to confirm ourselves to products that were not designed with ease of use in mind. At the same time, we are less concerned with showing off; we are less impressed by what looks good and more by what feels good.

9. Middle-aged consumers will be looking for ways to increase their sense of control.

One key psychological difference between the young and the mature is a profound sense among middle-aged and mature consumers of their vulnerability, and an awareness of the risks associated with almost every decision they make. As they face the inevitability of growing older, the diminishing of some physical capacities, the potential loss of income due to impending retirement, and the deaths of friends or family members, people may begin to develop what is best described as a sense of loss of control. By the time they have reached mid-life and beyond, consumers have more at risk, both physically and financially, they have less time to repair costly accidents or losses.

For example, 50-year-olds would be less likely to pack a backpack and hit the road for the summer, though they may have the time, the energy and the interest in doing so. Instead, they would be concerned with safety, they would want to know that medical facilities were available, that their home was being watched and maintained during their absence, and that easy, regular methods of communication were available to them in case of emergencies.

Financial security is even more to the point. Middle-aged and mature consumers have spent years working hard for what they have, and they are at a point in their lives when they want to feel financially secure. Knowing that they might not get a second chance to accumulate these hard-earned resources, they are more inclined to take risks and try new things only with the credible promise of trusted authorities or institutions, and ideally with a complete money-back guarantee. They will be unlikely to respond to user testimonials from unknown consumers or to store displays that spur impulse buying but are not associated with any clear positive benefits. They will be very careful how they manage their assets, and they will listen very carefully to product claims that promote security and increase their sense of control.

10. The middle-aged and maturing consumers will be increasingly interested in purchasing "experiences" rather than "things."

By the time consumers reach their mid-40s, they have spent considerable time accumulating things. While they will still be making purchases, in general these consumers are more interested in purchasing products and services only insofar as they create a desirable experience or enrich the quality in their lives. This characteristic will be apparent in two areas. First having the money to travel, to learn and to explore new areas of their lives, consumers in the second half of life will have as their goals enrichment, satisfaction, personal well-being, and self-fulfillment. Exotic travel, education, health and wellness, social activities—all will benefit as experience, rather than thing, related.

Second, when evaluating purchasing decisions for products or services, they will be more keenly interested in the experiences that accompany that product or service. For example, a younger car buyer may be very impressed with the way a car looks, or with the status that it offers. But an older buyer is certain to be interested in the experience of driving that car: does it drive well? is it comfortable? is it quiet? is it safe? They'll want to know how they will feel driving the car.

In addition, the baby-boom generation, which once exalted anti-materialism, is likely to meet maturity with a renewed interest in expanding the experiential side of their lives. Look for an increasing interest in continuing education in general.

As marketers have long been aware, the desire for experiences can also be applied to things. Consider, as an example, the changing American bathroom. Once a utilitarian space set aside for a few basic activities, the bathroom recently has become a new home recreation center that includes hot tubs, whirlpool baths, exercise equipment, "environmental chambers" with steam, heat, and soft music. Purchasing bathroom fixtures is less utilitarian today, and increasingly experience oriented. The rise of gourmet kitchens reflects a similar trend. The kitchen has become the new hub of family life. Purchasing a new kitchen may have less to do in the future with creating a utilitarian space that has the necessary products to get a job done, than it will with creating an enjoyable experience.

Researchers have already noted a new interest in experiences among the mature population that has changed some of their attitudes towards how they spend their time and money. It seems that the me generation's concentration on self has trickled up, leading mature consumers to an interest in their own fulfillment. They show every indication of a growing and committed interest in spending on products and services that enhance their enjoyment of life. With increased discretionary income available to them, these new consumers are interested in a certain amount of self-indulgence.

According to Dr. James Ogilvy, "the success of the industrial revolution has satisfied most of the demand for tangible goods like housing, clothing, and cars. . . . The growth of our economy is no longer driven by the desires of consumers to accumulate goods. It is driven by the consumer's quest for vivid experiences." According to Ogilvy, "The experience industry cultivates through education, broadens through travel, allows escape through entertainment, heals through psychotherapy, numbs through drugs and alcohol, edifies through religion, informs through reading, and enraptures through art."

*Beyond mass production and
mass marketing to designer
jeans and designer genes*

Marketing in an Age of Diversity

Regis McKenna

*Regis McKenna is chairman of Regis McKenna Inc.,
a Palo Alto headquartered marketing company that
advises some of America's leading high-tech companies.
He is also a general partner of Kleiner Perkins Caufield
& Byers, a technology venture-capital company. His
book,* The Regis Touch *(Addison-Wesley), was published in 1985.*

Spreading east from California, a new individual-
ism has taken root across the United States. Gone is
the convenient fiction of a single, homogeneous market. The days of a uniformly accepted view of the
world are over. Today diversity exerts tremendous influence, both economically and politically.

Technology and social change are interdependent.
Companies are using new flexible technology, like
computer-aided design and manufacturing and software customization to create astonishing diversity
in the marketplace and society. And individuals tem-
porarily coalescing into "micromajorities" are making use of platforms—media, education, and the
law—to express their desires.

In the marketing world, for example, the protests
of thousands of consumers, broadcast by the media as

an event of cultural significance, was enough to force
Coca-Cola to reverse its decision to do away with
"classic" Coke. On the political scene, vociferous
minorities, sophisticated in using communication
technology, exert influence greatly disproportionate
to their numbers: the Moral Majority is really just another minority—but focused and amplified. When we
see wealthy people driving Volkswagens and pickup
trucks, it becomes clear that this is a society where
individual tastes are no longer predictable; marketers cannot easily and neatly categorize their customer base.

Over the last 15 years, new technology has spawned
products aimed at diverse, new sectors and market
niches. Computer-aided technologies now allow
companies to customize virtually any product, from

designer jeans to designer genes, serving ever narrower customer needs. With this newfound technology, manufacturers are making more and more high-quality products in smaller and smaller batches; today 75% of all machined parts are produced in batches of 50 or fewer.

Consumers demand—and get—more variety and options in all kinds of products, from cars to clothes. Auto buyers, for example, can choose from 300 different types of cars and light trucks, domestic and imported, and get variations within each of those lines. Beer drinkers now have 400 brands to sample. The number of products in supermarkets has soared from 13,000 in 1981 to 21,000 in 1987. There are so many new items that stores can demand hefty fees from packaged-foods manufacturers just for displaying new items on grocery shelves.

Deregulation has also increased the number of choices—from a flurry of competing airfares to automated banking to single-premium life insurance that you can buy at Sears. The government has even adapted antitrust laws to permit companies to serve emerging micromarkets: the Orphan Drug Act of 1983, for instance, gives pharmaceutical companies tax breaks and a seven-year monopoly on any drugs that serve fewer than 200,000 people.

Diversity and niches create tough problems for old-line companies more accustomed to mass markets. Sears, the country's largest retailer, is trying to reposition its products, which traditionally have appealed to older middle-class and blue-collar customers. To lure younger, style-minded buyers, Sears has come up with celebrity-signature lines, fashion boutiques, and a new line of children's clothing, McKids, playing off McDonald's draw. New, smaller stores, specialty catalogs, and merchandise tailored to regional tastes are all part of Sears's effort to reach a new clientele—and without alienating its old one.

Faced with slimmer profits from staples like detergents, diapers, and toothpaste, and lackluster results from new food and beverage products, Procter & Gamble, the world's largest marketer, is rethinking what it should sell and how to sell it. The company is now concentrating on health products; it has high hopes for a fat substitute called "olestra," which may take some of the junk out of junk food. At the same time that P&G is shifting its product thinking, it also is changing its organization, opening up and streamlining its highly insular pyramidal management structure as part of a larger effort to listen and respond to customers. Small groups that include both factory workers and executives work on cutting costs, while other teams look for new ways to speed products to market.

In trying to respond to the new demands of a diverse market, the problem that giants like Sears and P&G face is not fundamental change, not a total turnabout in what an entire nation of consumers wants. Rather, it is the fracturing of mass markets. To contend with diversity, managers must drastically alter how they design, manufacture, market, and sell their products.

Marketing in the age of diversity means:

☐ More options for goods producers and more choices for consumers.

☐ Less perceived differentiation among similar products.

☐ Intensified competition, with promotional efforts sounding more and more alike, approaching "white noise" in the marketplace.

☐ Newly minted meanings for words and phrases as marketers try to "invent" differentiation.

☐ Disposable information as consumers try to cope with information deluge from print, television, computer terminal, telephone, fax, satellite dish.

☐ Customization by users as flexible manufacturing makes niche production every bit as economic as mass production.

☐ Changing leverage criteria as economies of scale give way to economies of knowledge—knowledge of the customer's business, of current and likely future technology trends, and of the competitive environment that allows the rapid development of new products and services.

☐ Changing company structure as large corporations continue to downsize to compete with smaller niche players that nibble at their markets.

☐ Smaller wins—fewer chances for gigantic wins in mass markets, but more opportunities for healthy profits in smaller markets.

The Decline of Branding, the Rise of 'Other'

In today's fractured marketplace, tried-and-true marketing techniques from the past no longer work for most products—particularly for complex ones based on new technology. Branding products and seizing market share, for instance, no longer guarantee loyal customers. In one case after another, the old, established brands have been supplanted by the rise of "other."

Television viewers in 1983 and 1984, for instance, tuned out the big three broadcasters to watch cable and independent "narrowcast" stations. Last year, the trend continued as the big three networks lost 9% of their viewers—more than six million people. Small companies appealing to niche-oriented viewers attacked the majority market share. NBC responded by buying a cable television company for $20 million.

No single brand can claim the largest share of the

gate array, integrated circuit, or computer market. Even IBM has lost its reign over the personal computer field—not to one fast-charging competitor but to an assortment of smaller producers. Tropicana, Minute Maid, and Citrus Hill actually account for less than half the frozen orange juice market. A full 56% belongs to hundreds of mostly small private labels. In one area after another, "other" has become the major market holder.

IBM's story of lost market share bears elaboration, in large part because of the company's almost legendary position in the U.S. business pantheon. After its rise in the personal computer market through 1984, IBM found its stronghold eroding—but not to just one, huge competitor that could be identified and stalked methodically. IBM could no longer rely on tracking the dozen or so companies that had been its steady competition for almost two decades. Instead, more than 300 clone producers worldwide intruded on Big Blue's territory. Moreover, IBM has faced the same competitive challenge in one product area after another, from supercomputers to networks. In response, IBM has changed how it does business. In the past, IBM wouldn't even bother to enter a market lacking a value of at least $100 million. But today, as customer groups diversify and markets splinter, that criterion is obsolete. The shift in competition has also prompted IBM to reorganize, decentralizing the company into five autonomous groups so decisions can be made closer to customers.

Similar stories abound in other industries. Kodak dominated film processing in the United States until little kiosks sprang up in shopping centers and ate up that market. Twenty years ago, the U.S. semiconductor industry consisted of 100 companies; today there are more than 300. In fact, practically every industry has more of every kind of company catering to the consumer's love of diversity—more ice cream companies, more cookie companies, more weight loss and exercise companies. Last year, enterprising managers started 233,000 new businesses of all types to offer customers their choice of "other."

The False Security of Market Share

The proliferation of successful small companies dramatizes how the security of majority market share—seized by a large corporation and held unchallenged for decades—is now a dangerous anachronism. In the past, the dominant marketing models drew on the measurement and control notions embedded in engineering and manufacturing. The underlying mechanistic logic was that companies could measure everything, and anything they could measure, they could control—including customers.

Market-share measurements became a way to understand the marketplace and thus to control it. For example, marketers used to be able to pin down a target customer with relative ease: if it were a man, he was between 25 and 35 years old, married, with two-and-a-half children, and half a dog. Since he was one of so many measurable men in a mass society, marketers assumed that they could manipulate the market just by knowing the demographic characteristics.

But we don't live in that world anymore, and those kinds of measurements are meaningless. Marketers trying to measure that same "ideal" customer today would discover that the pattern no longer holds; that married fellow with two-and-a-half kids could now be divorced, situated in New York instead of Minnesota, and living in a condo instead of a brick colonial. These days, the idea of market share is a trap that can lull businesspeople into a false sense of security.

Managers should wake up every morning uncertain about the marketplace, because it is invariably changing. That's why five-year plans are dangerous: Who can pinpoint what the market will be five years from now? The president of one large industrial corporation recently told me, "The only thing we know about our business plan is that it's wrong. It's either too high or too low—but we never know which."

In the old days, mass marketing offered an easy solution: "just run some ads." Not today. IBM tried that approach with the PC JR., laying out an estimated $100 million on advertising—before the product failed. AT&T spent tens of millions of dollars running ads for its computer products.

In sharp contrast, Digital Equipment Corporation spent very little on expensive national television ad-

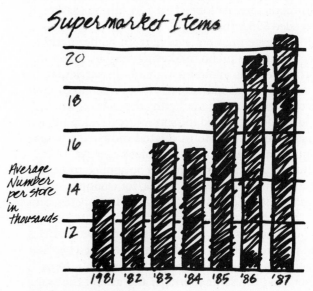

Supermarket Items

Average Number per store in thousands

Source: Food Marketing Institute

Today's consumers have 60% more product variety in the supermarket than they did in 1981.

vertising and managed to wrest a healthy market position. Skipping the expensive mass-advertising campaigns, DEC concentrated on developing its reputation in the computer business by solving problems for niche markets. Word of mouth sold DEC products. The company focused its marketing and sales staffs where they already had business and aimed its message at people who actually make the decision on what machines to buy. DEC clearly understood that no one buys a complex product like a computer without a reliable outside reference—however elaborate the company's promotion.

Niche Marketing: Selling Big by Selling Small

Intel was in the personal computer business two years before Apple started in Steve Jobs's garage. The company produced the first microprocessor chip and subsequently developed an early version of what became known as the hobby computer, sold in electronics hobby stores. An early Intel advertisement in *Scientific American* showed a junior high school student using the product. Intel's market research, however, revealed that the market for hobbyists was quite small and it abandoned the project. Two years later, Apple built itself on the hobbyist market. As it turned out, many of the early users of personal computers in education, small business, and the professional markets came from hobbyists or enthusiasts.

I recently looked at several market forecasts made by research organizations in 1978 projecting the size of the personal computer market in 1985. The most optimistic forecast looked for a $2 billion market. It exceeded $25 billion.

Most large markets evolve from niche markets. That's because niche marketing teaches many important lessons about customers—in particular, to think of them as individuals and to respond to their special needs. Niche marketing depends on word-of-mouth references and infrastructure development, a broadening of people in related industries whose opinions are crucial to the product's success.

Infrastructure marketing can be applied to almost all markets. In the medical area, for example, recognized research gurus in a given field—diabetes, cancer, heart disease—will first experiment with new devices or drugs at research institutions. Universities and research institutions become identified by their specialties. Experts in a particular area talk to each other, read the same journals, and attend the same conferences. Many companies form their own scientific advisory boards designed to tap into the members' expertise and to build credibility for new technology and products. The word of mouth created

Frozen Concentrate

Private label other 56%

Minute Maid 27%

Tropicana 8%

Citrus Hill 9%

Data: Coca-Cola Foods BCI Holdings, A.C. Nielsen Co.

The "big" brands aren't so big after all. "Other" is the market leader.

by infrastructure marketing can make or break a new drug or a new supplier. Conductus, a new superconductor company in Palo Alto, is building its business around an advisory board of seven top scientists from Stanford University and Berkeley.

Represented graphically, infrastructure development would look like an inverted pyramid. So Apple's pyramid, for instance, would include the references of influential users, software designers who create programs, dealers, industry consultants, analysts, the press, and, most important, customers.

Customer focus derived from niche marketing helps companies respond faster to demand changes. That is the meaning of today's most critical requirement—that companies become market driven. From the board of directors down through the ranks, company leaders must educate everyone to the singular importance of the customer, who is no longer a faceless, abstract entity or a mass statistic.

Because niche markets are not easily identified in their infancy, managers must keep one foot in the technology to know its potential and one foot in the market to see opportunity. Tandem Computers built its solid customer base by adapting its products to the emerging on-line transaction market. Jimmy Treybig, president and CEO, told me that the company had to learn the market's language. Bankers don't talk about MIPS (millions of instructions per second) the way computer people do, he said; they talk about transactions. So Tandem built its products and marketing position to become the leading computer in the transaction market. Not long ago, Treybig was on a nationwide tour visiting key customers. "Guess who was calling on my customers just a few days ahead of me," he said. "John Akers"—chairman of IBM.

Many electronics companies have developed

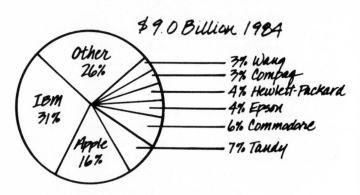

PC Market Share
(By Factory Revenue, U.S. only)

$9.0 Billion 1984

Other 26%
IBM 31%
Apple 16%

3% Wang
3% Compaq
4% Hewlett-Packard
4% Epson
6% Commodore
7% Tandy

Source: Future Computing, Inc. 1986

IBM led the market then...

teams consisting of software and hardware development engineers, quality control and manufacturing people, as well as marketing and sales—who all visit customers or play key roles in dealing with customers. Convex Computer and Tandem use this approach. Whatever method a company may use, the purpose is the same: to get the entire company to focus on the fragmented, ever-evolving customer base as if it were an integral part of the organization.

The Integrated Product

Competition from small companies in fractured markets has even produced dramatic changes in how companies define their products. The product is no longer just the thing itself; it includes service, word-of-mouth references, company financial reports, the technology, and even the personal image of the CEO.

As a result, product marketing and service marketing, formerly two distinct fields, have become a single hybrid. For example, Genentech, which manufactures a growth hormone, arms its sales force with lap-top computers. When a Genentech salesperson visits an endocrinologist, the physician can tie into a data base of all the tests run on people with characteristics similar to his or her patients. The computer represents an extended set of services married to the original product.

Or take the example of Apple Computer and Quantum Corporation, which recently announced a joint venture offering online interactive computer services for Apple Computer users. In addition to a long list of transaction services that reads like a television programming guide, Apple product service, support, and even simple maintenance will be integrated into the

product itself. Prodigy, a joint venture between IBM and Sears, will soon offer IBM and Apple users access to banking, shopping, the stock market, regional weather forecasts, sports statistics, encyclopedias of all kinds—and even direct advice from Sylvia Porter, Howard Cosell, or Ask Beth.

In consumer products, service has become the predominant distinguishing feature. Lands' End promotes its catalog-marketed outdoorsy clothes by guaranteeing products unconditionally and promising to ship orders within 24 to 48 hours. Carport, near Atlanta, offers air travelers an ultradeluxe parking service: it drives customers to their gates, checks their bags, and, while they are airborne, services, washes, and waxes their cars. "Macy's by Appointment" is a free shopping service for customers who are too busy or too baffled to make their own selections.

With so much choice backed by service, customers can afford to be fickle. As a result, references have become vital to product marketing. And the more complex the product, the more complex the supporting references. After all, customers who switch toothpaste risk losing only a dollar or so if the new choice is a dud. But consumers buying a complete phone system or a computer system or any other costly, long-term and pervasive product, cannot afford to take their investments lightly. References become a part of the product—and they come in all kinds of forms. Company financial reports are a kind of reference. A person shopping for an expensive computer wants to see how profitable the company is; how can the company promise maintenance service if it's about to fold? Even the CEO's personality can

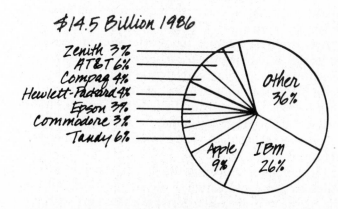

PC Market Share
(By Factory Revenue, U.S. only)

$14.5 Billion 1986

Zenith 3%
AT&T 6%
Compaq 4%
Hewlett-Packard 4%
Epson 3%
Commodore 3%
Tandy 6%

Other 36%
Apple 9%
IBM 26%

Source: Future Computing, Inc. 1986

...but now it's been eclipsed by clone companies it can't identify or stalk.

make a sale. Customers who see Don Petersen of Ford splashed across a magazine cover—or Apple's John Sculley or Hewlett-Packard's John Young—feel reassured that a real person stands behind the complex and expensive product.

In this complicated world, customers weigh all these factors to winnow out the products they want from those they don't. Now more than ever, marketers must sell every aspect of their businesses as important elements of the products themselves.

The Customer As Customizer

Customer involvement in product design has become an accepted part of the development and marketing processes in many industries. In technologically driven products, which often evolve slowly as discoveries percolate to the surface, the customer can practically invent the market for a company.

Apple's experience with desktop publishing shows how companies and customers work together to create new applications—and new markets. Apple entered the field with the Macintosh personal computer, which offered good graphics and easy-to-use features. But desktop publishing didn't even exist then; it wasn't on anyone's pie chart as a defined market niche, and no one had predicted its emergence.

Apple's customers made it happen; newspapers and research organizations simply started using Macintosh's unique graphics capability to create charts and graphs. Early users made do with primitive software and printers, but that was enough to spark the imagination of other developers. Other hardware and software companies began developing products that could be combined with the Macintosh to enhance the user's publishing power. By visiting and talking to customers and other players in the marketplace, Apple began to realize desktop publishing's potential.

As customers explored the possibilities presented by the technology, the technology, in turn, developed to fit the customers' needs. The improved software evolved from a dynamic working relationship between company and customers, not from a rigid, bureaucratic headquarters determination of where Apple could find an extra slice of the marketing pie.

Technological innovation makes it easier to involve customers in design. For example, Milliken, the textile manufacturer, provides customers with computer terminals where they can select their own carpet designs from thousands of colors and patterns. Electronics customers, too, have assumed the role of product designer. New design tools allow companies

like Tandem and Convex to design their own specialty chips, which the integrated-circuit suppliers then manufacture according to their specifications. Similarly, American Airlines designs its own computer systems. In cases like these, the design and manufacturing processes have been completely separated. So semiconductor companies—and many computer companies—have become raw-materials producers, with integration occurring all the way up the supply line.

The fact that customers have taken charge of design opens the door for value-added resellers, who integrate different materials and processes. These people are the essence of new-age marketers: they add value by understanding what happens in a doctor's office or a travel agency or a machine-tool plant and customize that service or product to the customer's needs. To capitalize on market changes, companies should follow these examples and work directly with customers—even before products hit the drawing boards.

The Evolution of Distribution

It's nearly impossible to make a prediction on the basis of past patterns. Perhaps many big institutions founded on assumptions of mass marketing and market share will disappear like dinosaurs. Or they'll evolve into closely integrated service and distribution organizations.

In fact, tremendous innovation in distribution channels has already begun in nearly every industry. Distribution channels have to be flexible to survive. As more flows into them, they have to change. Grocery stores sell flowers and cameras. Convenience stores rent out videos. And television offers viewers direct purchasing access to everything from diamonds to snowblowers to a decent funeral.

To get products closer to customers, marketers are distributing more and more samples in more ways. Today laundry detergent arrives in the mail, magazines enfold perfume-doused tear-outs, and department stores offer chocolate samples. Software companies bind floppy disk samples into magazines or mail out diskettes that work only until a certain date, giving customers the chance to test a product before buying.

Every successful computer retailer has not only a showroom but also a classroom. The large computer retailers are not selling to just off-the-street traffic. Most of their volume now comes from a direct sales force calling on corporate America. In addition, all have application-development labs, extensive user-training programs and service centers—and some have recently experimented with private labeling their own computer product brands. The electronics community talks more and more about design centers—places where customers can get help customizing products and applications.

Today the product is an experience. As customers use it, they grow to trust it—and distribution represents the beginning of that evolving relationship. That's why computer companies donate their systems to elementary schools: schools are now a distribution channel for product experience.

Goliath plus David

Besides making changes in distribution channels, big corporations will also have to forge new partnerships with smaller companies. IBM, for example, already has ties to 1,500 small computer-service companies nationwide, offering help for IBM mid-sized machine owners. Olivetti makes personal computers for AT&T. All over the world, manufacturers are producing generic computer platforms; larger companies buy these, then add their own service-oriented, value-adding applications.

This approach seems almost inevitable considering what we know about patterns of research and development. Technological developments typically originate with basic research, move to applied research, to development, then to manufacturing and marketing. Very few U.S. companies do basic research; universities and various public and private labs generally shoulder that burden. Many big companies do applied R&D while small companies concentrate on development. Basic and applied research means time and money. Consider the cases of two seminal inventions—antibiotics and television—the first of which took 30 years and the second 63 years from idea to the market.

Perhaps because of their narrow focus, small companies realize more development breakthroughs than larger ones. For example, the origins of recombinant DNA technology go back to the mid-1950s; it took Genentech only about six years to bring the world's first recombinant DNA commercial product to market.

A 1986 study by the Small Business Administration showed that 55% of innovations have come from companies with fewer than 500 employees, and twice as many innovations per employee come from small companies than from large ones. This finding, however, does not indicate that large companies are completely ineffective developers. Rather, the data

suggest that small, venture-capitalized companies will scramble to invent a product that the market does not yet want, need, or perhaps even recognize; big companies will wait patiently for the market to develop so they can enter later with their strong manufacturing and marketing organizations.

The Japanese have shown us that it's wise to let small companies handle development—but only if large companies can somehow share that wisdom before the product reaches the market. From 1950 to 1978, Japanese companies held 32,000 licensing agreements to acquire foreign technology—mostly from the United States—for about $9 billion. In essence, the Japanese simply subcontracted out for R&D—and then used that investment in U.S. knowledge to dominate one market after another.

If orchestrated properly, agreements between large and small companies can prove mutually beneficial. When Genentech developed its first product, recombinant DNA insulin, the company chose not to compete against Eli Lilly, which held over 70% of the insulin market. Instead, Genentech entered into a licensing agreement with Lilly that put the larger company in charge of manufacturing and marketing the products developed by the smaller company. Over time, Genentech built its own manufacturing company while maintaining its proprietary product.

This model worked so well that it has shaped the fortunes of Silicon Valley. Of the 3,000 companies there, only a dozen hold places on the lists of America's largest corporations. Most of the companies are small developers of new products. Like the Japanese, large U.S. companies are now subcontracting development to these mostly high-tech startups. In the process, they are securing a critical resource—an ongoing relationship with a small, innovative enterprise.

Giant companies can compete in the newly diversifying markets if they recognize the importance of relationships—with small companies, within their own organizations, with their customers. Becoming market driven means abandoning old-style marketshare thinking and instead tying the uniqueness of any product to the unique needs of the customer. This approach to marketing demands a revolution in how businesspeople act—and even more important, in how they think. These changes are critical to success, but they can come only gradually, as managers and organizations adapt to the new rules of marketing in the age of diversity. As any good marketer knows, even instant success takes time.

STALKING THE NEW CONSUMER

AS MARKETS FRACTURE, P&G AND OTHERS SHARPEN 'MICRO MARKETING'

In 15,000 supermarkets and drugstores in all 50 states, shoppers pushing carts down aisles are serenaded by music interspersed with commercials for Crest, Ivory shampoo, and Pepto-Bismol. In the lunchroom of Central High School in Knoxville, Tenn., the Chicago Bulls' Michael Jordan looks down at teenagers from a giant poster, at the bottom of which are ads for Scope and Head & Shoulders. At state fairs, staffers at Pampers' mobile Baby Care Centers change 80,000 diapers a year. And all across the country, fans of *The Wizard of Oz* will see a spot for Downy when they pop a tape into their VCRs.

Radio spots in supermarkets? Ads on videotapes? Welcome to the brave new world of marketing, Procter & Gamble-style. If it all sounds a little strange, well, as Dorothy said to Toto: "I have a feeling we're not in Kansas anymore."

Life used to be much simpler. Mass marketers such as Procter & Gamble Co. would cook up innovative but fairly utilitarian products and advertise them on network TV. All the housewives between the ages of 18 and 34 watching *Search for Tomorrow* or *The Edge of Night* would see the ads and rush out to buy disposable diapers and dish detergent. The commercials were boring, but they saturated the airwaves and repeated the products' names over and over. Supermarkets stocked their shelves, and consumers came and bought.

Things don't work quite that way anymore. Real product innovations are rare. And most women 18 to 34 aren't sitting at home watching the soaps. They're in college, or they're working as lawyers, cab drivers, or lathe operators. A 15-year-old boy may be doing the family shopping. Many customers are single, many are old, many don't speak English, and some can't even read. Few of them are watching dull, name-dropping ads.

Supermarkets have changed, too. Retailers are no longer willing to give manufacturers miles of shelf space to park their soap or canned beans. They're more interested in selling high-margin items such as their own flowers or store-baked cookies. They need incentives to squeeze a product in somewhere.

'MOSAIC.' The wonderful post-World War II mass market has shattered into millions of pieces. "The mythological homogeneous America is gone. We are a mosaic of minorities," says Joel D. Weiner, senior vice-president for marketing services at Kraft USA. "All companies will have to do more stratified or tailored or niche marketing."

At Procter & Gamble, the change has been particularly tough to accept. The huge consumer-products company practically invented mass marketing, pioneering such classic techniques as couponing and radio and TV advertising. But now, even this grandfather of the business is feeling its way to a whole new type of marketing. The closely watched but notoriously tight-lipped company is using new information and technologies to pinpoint its customers and figure out what motivates them. It is experimenting with new, targeted media to reach them. It's using sophisticated promotions, specialized messages, better ads, and customized products to motivate them. It is learning to become a micro marketer.

HOW TO BE A MICRO MARKETER

KNOW YOUR CUSTOMERS
Consumer-goods companies are using high-tech techniques to find out who their customers are—and aren't. By linking that knowledge with data about ads and coupons, they can fine-tune their marketing

MAKE WHAT THEY WANT
In an age of diversity, products must be tailored to individual tastes. So where once there were just Oreos, now there are Fudge Covered Oreos, Oreo Double Stufs, and Oreo Big Stufs, too

USE TARGETED AND NEW MEDIA
Companies aiming for micro markets are advertising on cable TV and in magazines to reach special audiences. And they're putting their messages on walls in high-school lunchrooms, on videocassettes, and even on blood-pressure monitors

USE NON MEDIA
Marketers are sponsoring sports, festivals, and other events to reach local or ethnic markets. Latino events such as Carnaval Miami are hot. So are sports ranging from golf to hydroplane racing

REACH CUSTOMERS IN THE STORE
Consumers make most buying decisions while they're shopping. So marketers are putting ads on supermarket loudspeakers, shopping carts, and in-store monitors.

SHARPEN YOUR PROMOTIONS
Couponing and price promotions are expensive and often harmful to a brand's image. Thanks to better data, some companies are using fewer, more effective promotions. One promising approach: Aiming coupons at a competitor's customers

WORK WITH RETAILERS
Consumer-goods manufacturers must learn to "micro market" to the retail trade, too. Some are linking their computers to the retailers', and some are tailoring their marketing and promotions to an individual retailer's needs

DATA: BW

> Rather than make one boffo ad, micro marketers spread their bets on many efforts that pay off in small increments

P&G is hardly alone. All U. S. consumer-goods companies have been struggling in recent years to meet the new marketing challenges of the 1980s. "Maybe you have to come up with a new definition of a mass marketer," says Marv Solomon, vice-president for marketing services at Warner-Lambert Co., which has cut its ad spending on network TV for its brands, including Listerine, Trident, and Schick. Instead, it is experimenting with everything from direct mail to cable TV to putting ads on blood-pressure monitors in pharmacies.

Micro marketing is vastly more complex than mass marketing. Rather than wagering big bucks in hopes of producing one boffo TV ad that will quickly boost sales, micro marketers spread their bets on lots of different efforts, each of which may pay off in small increments. Much of the resulting variety of methods and media is still experimental, and it's often hard to tell exactly how well each is working. But the little things do seem to be adding up.

P&G noticed, for example, that vacuum brick-packs of ground coffee were popular in the South, so it repackaged its Folgers brand for those markets. That was part of a general revamping that included a new ad image and targeted promotions. Result: Folgers coffee rocketed to 32% of the total U. S. market last year, from 24% in 1982. Overall, seven of P&G's nine U. S. consumer divisions hit record unit volumes in the fiscal year ended June 30. With improving margins at home and soaring results overseas (page 58), the company reported net earnings of $1.2 billion, up 18%, on revenues of $21.4 billion, up 11%.

Nowhere has the shattering of the mass market been more apparent than in TV advertising. Even during prime time, the networks' share of the audience has plummeted during the past decade from 92% to 67%, according to A. C. Nielsen Co. And their daytime share has fallen to 57%, from 78%. At the same time, the average price of a choice 30-second prime-time spot has shot up 85%, to $185,000. To make matters worse, 35% of all network ads are now only 15 seconds long, so more messages are cluttering the airwaves. All that adds up to less effective advertising. "It is much, much more difficult for us as advertisers to reach our audience—and more expensive," says one food-company executive.

BITTER PILL. For P&G management that grew up in a world where network television was the only medium that mattered, those changes have been disconcerting. "They knew that every week they would have three minutes on *As the World Turns,* and that was chiseled in granite," says one former P&Ger. "It has been a very tough pill to swallow to say it just isn't working."

But it isn't. The loss of the old verities of media and marketing cost P&G dearly. Mired in low-growth markets and battered by a series of unsuccessful new-product forays, trouble overseas, and loss of market share to newly aggressive competitors, P&G suffered a startling earnings decline in 1985—its first since 1953. There was talk that the Cincinnati colossus had feet of clay—that it was too big, too bureaucratic, and too sclerotic to respond to a rapidly shifting marketplace.

Lately, though, P&G has been proving the naysayers wrong. It has become one of the biggest sponsors of such ad alternatives to the networks as cable and syndicated TV, as well as spending heavily on radio, specialized magazines, and other media.

While much of that shift is the result of rising costs, it also reflects a growing desire to target the company's ads and chase the audiences that are deserting the networks. For example, P&G buys ad time on health-related cable TV shows to trumpet the benefits of its low-saturated-fat Puritan oil. And it now has six different campaigns aimed at Crest toothpaste buyers—including kids,

blacks, and Hispanics. P&G also spends some $61 million a year to advertise to target audiences on syndicated TV shows. This summer, for instance, it is advertising such brands as Clearasil acne medicine to teens on *Endless Summer with The Beach Boys,* a series of concert shows.

Other marketers are doing much the same. At Best Foods, the CPC International Inc. unit that sells Hellmann's, Mazola, and other brands, cable accounts for about 10% of all media spending. "We can't be successful only appealing to the 70% watching network TV," says Robert J. Gillespie, Best's president. Since September, H. J. Heinz Co.'s Ore-Ida Foods Inc. unit has spent almost half the ad budget for its Steakumm sandwich meats on MTV in order to reach teens. That has helped the brand reverse several years of market-share declines. "We found this audience not through ABC, NBC, or CBS, but through MTV," says Anthony J. F. O'Reilly, chief executive of Heinz. "As the dozens of cable channels begin to define their own audiences, people with products for those audiences will go that way."

'EXOTICA.' Many already have. In all, ad spending on both syndication and cable is expected to rise 25% this year, compared with only 1% for the networks. And one major ad agency, DDB Needham Worldwide Inc., has even told its clients to put 25% of their total ad budgets into cable, up from only 5% five years ago.

P&G has also been plowing a lot of money and effort into what one network executive sniffily calls "media exotica." These new ad beasts include Point-of-Purchase Radio Corp., which offers 48 minutes of music interspersed with 12

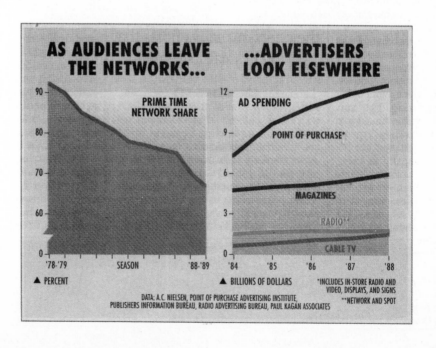

One coupon specialist has data on product usage, hobbies, and travel habits for 25 million households

minutes of ads—all played over a supermarket's loudspeakers. By one estimate, two-thirds of all buying decisions are made in the store, so companies are trying to reach shoppers at that crucial moment. Besides radio, they're putting up signs, installing computerized information kiosks, and beaming ads to video screens on shopping carts.

And as the networks lose viewers to the VCR, P&G is just following along onto videocassettes. P&G's Scope, Pepto-Bismol, Head & Shoulders, and Crest now provide half the ads on Home Video Pre-

view. This startup distributes 70,000 free 35-minute videotapes each month previewing movies that will soon be available for rental. P&G's Downy and MGM/UA Home Video have just begun a joint promotion of a 50th anniversary video of *The Wizard of Oz*. Besides TV ads and a $5 tape rebate tied to the purchase of Downy, the campaign includes an ad for the fabric softener on the cassette.

P&G is also a big spender on the experimental media offered by Whittle Communications. Whittle has created advertising wallboards that it hangs in such places as high schools, beauty parlors, and dentists' offices. It also places free magazines called *Special Reports* in doctors' waiting rooms. And it is the creator of Channel One, an ad-supported news broadcast for schools. Despite strong opposition in some states, Whittle says the 12-minute telecast will be offered to high schools nationwide next spring. Whittle has become one of Procter's biggest media vendors after the three networks—although there are signs that P&G has growing

doubts about the effectiveness of Whittle's products.

HYDROPLANING. P&G is also using local promotions and event sponsorship to reach special markets. There's the Pampers Baby Care Center, and there are such things as Pepto-Bismol chili cooking contests, sing-in-the-shower contests sponsored by Coast soap, and the Crisco American Pie Contest. And its Jif peanut butter and Pringles potato chips sponsor a 30-foot hydroplane that is competing in 10 races this summer.

P&G is also stepping up its marketing efforts aimed at Hispanics, blacks, and the elderly. It advertises heavily on Spanish-language TV and has become a major sponsor of local Hispanic events. At Carnaval Miami last March, for instance, 14 of the company's brands helped put on entertainment ranging from a beauty contest to a block party, and consumers lined up for free samples of P&G products.

RETAIL DETAIL. Besides coming up with

THANKS TO THE CHECKOUT SCANNER, MARKETING IS LOSING SOME MYSTERY

Half the money I spend on advertising is wasted, and the trouble is, I don't know which half.
—William H. Lever
founder of Lever Brothers Ltd.

What makes a shopper buy a particular brand of dog food or detergent? It seems like a simple enough question. Yet, despite billions of dollars spent every year to advertise and promote packaged goods, companies have never been entirely sure how effective each marketing tool really is.

That's finally beginning to change. The installation of checkout scanners in most of the nation's supermarkets has brought with it an avalanche of data, more timely and specific than any available before. Though most marketers are only beginning to exploit this information, they are getting a better feel for exactly what a price cut, coupon blitz, store display, or discount to the retailer actually does for sales and profits.

WEEKLY REPORTS. Instead of receiving monthly or bimonthly reports with at best a regional breakdown of how a brand is doing in its category, marketers now get weekly data for every item and size, sometimes down to the individual store. This creates endless possibilities for investigation. How often should a coupon be used, and does it work better in Des Moines than in Dallas? Is one size

easier to sell to retailers than another?

So far, marketers have gotten furthest in examining the effectiveness of promotions such as displays and newspaper ads. The three sellers of scanner data—Control Data's SAMI, Dun & Bradstreet's A. C. Nielsen, and Information Resources Inc.—all track such information along with product sales. Using such data, Nestlé Foods Corp. learned that a combination of store displays and newspaper ads resulted in huge volume increases for its Quik chocolate drink.

Warner-Lambert Co. found that in some instances, store displays were far more effective than newspaper ads or price promotions, and its sales force now focuses on persuading supermarkets to provide such displays. Ore-Ida Foods Inc. priced a frozen-food brand below a key rival's, but it turned out that retailers were pocketing the difference and providing the competition with more merchandising support. When weekly chain-by-chain scanner and promotion data revealed the problem, Ore-Ida decided to boost its prices and use the extra margin to pay for promotional efforts such as bigger newspaper ads.

FRUSTRATION. Most marketers haven't gotten as far using scanner data to analyze the effects of TV advertising and consumer promotions such as cou-

pons. Nielsen, SAMI, and IRI all supply some of that data. But a system to provide reliable nationwide information linking which TV ads individual households watch with what they buy is still under construction. Eventually, packaged-goods companies hope such "single source" data will allow them to hone their marketing even more finely. If they know how effective specific commercials or coupon programs are, they can decide whether they are worth the trouble and expense.

In the meantime, they are trying to figure out how to make better use of the reams of information they already have. After some early optimism, most big manufacturers are frustrated by their slow progress. The data still have glitches, and there's not enough software available for analyzing them. "The information preceded clients' ability to handle it," says SAMI head Steven A. Wilson. "They can't absorb the amount of information we're imposing on them." Adds Brian M. Shea, Ore-Ida's marketing research manager: "The promise is there to do all this linking, but I haven't seen it yet."

Still, that hasn't stopped packaged-goods marketers from continuing their push to use scanner data. If that information ultimately gives them the answer to Lever's conundrum, it will be worth the wait.

Zachary Schiller in New York

P&G GOES GLOBAL BY ACTING LIKE A LOCAL

Pink diapers for girls and blue ones for boys? The idea prompted snickers at first, but no one's laughing now. The sex-typed diapers are a hit on three continents. Their universal success is also the latest sign that Procter & Gamble Co. has learned a lot about marketing overseas.

P&G wasn't always so nimble abroad. For years, it was something of an Ugly American, taking products developed for the U.S. market and trying to push them into foreign markets with American-style marketing and ads. Such efforts to standardize worldwide marketing techniques were fashionable in the early 1980s, under the banner of "global marketing." But P&G has learned that the trick to going global is acting like a local.

BIG LOSSES. Take P&G's experiences in Japan. A homogeneous society, Japan remains in many ways a classic mass market. Still, for P&G, it is a fragment of the worldwide market, and one for which it has carefully tailored its marketing. But it learned to do so only after some bitter lessons—and more than $200 million in losses from its arrival in 1971 to 1987. "P&G had a very hard time accepting that Japan was not going to be like the U.S.," says an American marketing executive in Tokyo.

P&G won an early lead in disposable diapers after introducing Pampers in Japan in 1977, for example. But it quickly lost market share when competitors Uni-Charm Corp. and Kao Corp. introduced fitted, thin diapers that won over mothers who had resisted disposables. "We really didn't understand the consumer," says Edwin L. Artzt, P&G's vice-chairman, who acknowledges that P&G was slow to improve its bulky, rectangular Pampers.

Now, things have turned around dramatically. P&G's sales in Japan grew 40%, to $1 billion, in the fiscal year ended June 30. Overall international profits grew by 37%, to $417 million. Says S&G's Artzt: "We want to be the No. 1 consumer-products company in Japan." To help reach that goal, P&G has hired more Japanese staff and attuned its ways to local styles. "It's more Japanese than some Japanese companies," says Noriko Sakoh, an analyst at SBCI Securities (Asia) Ltd.

TALKING DIAPERS. For example, P&G's ads now prominently mention the company's name as well as the product's. That's something P&G's ads in the U.S. rarely do, but such corporate identification is important to the Japanese. And while a U.S. ad might show a diaper absorbing a cup of liquid, a popular Pampers ad in Japan used an indirect approach: A talking diaper promised toddlers that the brand wouldn't leak or cause diaper rash. P&G finally introduced a superabsorbent thin diaper, and then it surprised rivals with the pink and blue Pampers. After sinking to less than 10% of the market, P&G's share is up to 20.5%, challenging Kao for the No. 2 spot.

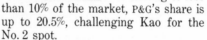

P&G'S FOREIGN BOOM
SALES $8,400*
$417*
EARNINGS**
FOREIGN RESULTS AS SHARE OF TOTAL
▲ PERCENT   *MILLIONS OF DOLLARS
**1987 AND 1989 EARNINGS EXCLUDE SPECIAL CHARGES
DATA: COMPANY REPORTS; KIDDER, PEABODY & CO.

Worldwide, P&G is rolling out new products more quickly, partly because it has built strong local operations that are closer to the market. "P&G used to be bloody slow," says Michael R. Angus, chairman of Unilever PLC, P&G's global archrival. "They were so thorough, the world changed between the origination of an idea and the product actually appearing on shelves."

P&G now tries to develop what Artzt calls "big edge" products, with a technology that can be applied worldwide but in forms tailored to local needs. Its Japanese sanitary pad, Whisper, for example, is smaller and thinner than its U.S. counterpart, Always. "We've made it right for the Japanese woman, and we've made it right for the American woman," Artzt says. P&G's foreign performance has been so torrid that there is even talk that Artzt, who is in charge of international, could become P&G's next chief executive. The very idea speaks volumes about the globalization of the Cincinnati colossus.

By Zachary Schiller in Cincinnati and Ted Holden in Tokyo, with Mark Maremont in London

new tools for reaching smaller groups of customers, consumer-products companies are finding new ways to figure out just who it is they want to reach. Most mass marketers have long relied on fairly blunt tools to give them a rough picture of who was likely to buy their products. They segmented the market by demographics—age, sex, income, and so on—and later by psychographics, which classified people by attitudes and values. But all such systems were approximations, abstract methods to group still-anonymous consumers into big clumps.

More recently, packaged-goods companies have been coming a little closer to the direct-marketing techniques used so effectively by banks, airlines, and hotels, which collect customers' names, addresses, and details of what they have bought in the past. If the sellers of soap and spaghetti sauce could get that sort of data, they could see what ads and promotions worked best at keeping current customers and at luring new ones.

Now, although the progress is still slow, they are getting some of those data and figuring out how to use them (box). "The marketing battleground is shifting at an extremely rapid pace to the information battleground," says Don Peppers, executive vice-president for business development at Lintas:USA, a New York ad agency with a large base of packaged-goods clients.

Weapons for that battle are becoming quite sophisticated. Computerized Marketing Technologies Inc., for example, sends out millions of detailed consumer questionnaires. As a result, CMT now has data on the product usage, hobbies, travel habits, and other facts for 25 million households. It mails coded coupons three times a year to 15 million households and can deliver different coupons to different consumers. For some two dozen products, "we know who are current users, who are competitive users, and who are nonusers," says Gary R. Blau, CMT's managing partner.

That's especially useful information. Since markets for products such as soap and food are scarcely growing, packaged-goods companies can get bigger only by luring customers from the other guy. But because most coupons—80% to 85%—are redeemed by current users of the product, they aren't much help in doing that. Now, CMT can send out coupons for one product to regular users of a competing brand. Anything that can make coupons more effective will be a big relief to consumer-goods companies, which typically spend 25% of their marketing budgets on consumer promotions.

Since P&G has always been a by-the-numbers sort of marketer, it's not surprising that it is working hard to use new technology to make its promotions more effective. In the past, P&G had to judge the effectiveness of an ad campaign, coupon drop, or other promotion on the basis of how many cases a retailer bought, even if many of them just went into inventory for sale later. Now, by using the weekly sales data that are available from supermarket scanners, "P&G is able to get a better idea of consumers' response to the promotion," notes Greg Goff, former Crest brand manager. The company can look at which sizes to push, how it does against the competition at different prices, and what combination of newspaper feature ads and store displays is most effective.

PAPERLESS COUPONS. That's just the beginning, though. Procter has also started a joint venture with Donnelley Marketing and CheckRobot Inc. called Advanced Promotion Technologies Inc. APT's Vision System can automatically deduct instant refunds from a customer's tab. Or it can print out coupons right at the check-out counter to influence brand choices on the next shopping trip—with the type determined by what the shopper has just bought.

And later this summer, APT will begin testing a frequent-shopper program at a Des Moines supermarket chain. Shoppers will use a "smart card" with a computer microchip to record their purchases. A shopper who buys a brand from P&G or another participating marketer such as Kraft General Foods, Campbell Soup, Del Monte, or Ralston Purina will win points toward catalog merchandise. Since holders of these smart cards supply information about themselves, retailers and manufacturers will be able to build data bases on consumers, figuring out who the best customers are.

Of course, all the sharp marketing in the world won't make much difference if a product doesn't appeal to its audience. Many companies are finding that one of the most effective ways to target specific groups of consumers is with the products themselves. Using the strength of existing brand names, they're tweaking core products into a wide array of line extensions aimed to please ever-narrower tastes or needs. From 1947 to 1984, for example, P&G sold only one type of Tide. Now, there are four additional varieties of the detergent, including Liquid Tide and Tide with Bleach. Downy fabric softener spent its first 23 years alone. Since 1984, however, it has gotten three siblings.

As manufacturers refine their consumer marketing techniques, they are also start-ing to cooperate much more closely with retailers. "Today, to get to the consumer, you have to do it together," says Joseph W. Masse, vice-president for sales at Warner-Lambert's Consumer Health Products Group. Besides focusing their efforts on precise target groups of consumers, packaged-goods companies are tailoring their marketing to an individual retailer's needs. As P&G Chief Executive John G. Smale recently told company managers: "The major retailers around the world are moving toward cooperative alliances with a select few suppliers. We must be one of them."

SHELVING FEES. In mass marketing's heyday, the retailer was a passive conduit. The manufacturer could dictate the amount and type of shelf space and display a product received in a store, because its powerful brands and powerful advertising pulled consumers in. But as the market has fragmented, the manufacturers' power over retailers has waned. These days, the stores dictate how much or how little space they'll give a product, and they're demanding a

---

> 'P&G has gone from a vendor that was maybe the least desirable to deal with to the most desirable'

---

growing list of fees and discounts to do so (BW—Aug. 7). Such trade promotions ate up 44% of a typical marketing budget in 1988, up from 34% in 1980, according to Donnelly Marketing, and they're hurting margins, too. Now, partly in an effort to break out of this trade-promotion trap, P&G is starting to micro market to its retailers, too.

When it comes to trade relations, perhaps no company had more to learn than high-handed P&G. A few years ago, Jack Shewmaker, then president of Wal-Mart Stores Inc., wanted to talk to P&G's Smale. After several fruitless phone calls, an irate Shewmaker gave up. P&G had snubbed a huge retailer. And why did Shewmaker want Smale? Just to tell him that Wal-Mart wanted to give P&G an award as vendor of the year.

If P&G didn't exactly deserve the award then, it may now. In the past year, P&G has moved a dozen officials to Arkansas to develop a joint strategy with the big Bentonville-based retailer. Can both companies use the same number to identify an item, eliminating a need to reticket each shipping container when it arrives? Can P&G adapt its up-and-down pricing to Wal-Mart's everyday-low-price approach?

P&G now receives daily data by satellite on Wal-Mart's Pampers sales and forecasts and ships orders automatically. As a result, Wal-Mart can maintain smaller inventories and still cut the number of times it runs out of Pampers. And P&G has increased its proportion of on-time deliveries to 99.6% from 94%. "P&G has gone from a vendor that was maybe the least desirable to deal with to the most desirable to deal with," says the now retired Shewmaker.

The results have been astonishing. Procter's volume at Wal-Mart grew by more than 40%, or by more than $200 million, in the fiscal year ended June 30. P&G's approach to Wal-Mart seems likely to spread to its relations with other retailers as the company scraps its separate sales efforts at each division in favor of teams that handle top retail accounts. P&G's new attitude toward the trade is "a 180-degree turnaround from five or seven years ago," says a merchandiser at a major supermarket chain.

Other manufacturers also hope that tailoring their marketing plans to the needs of individual retailers will reduce the pressure for ever-greater trade promotions. Warner-Lambert, for example, has been sending more experienced marketing managers out from headquarters into the field, where they work closely with retailers. The marketers have been showing retailers how to boost sales by playing up Listerine's endorsement by the American Dental Assn. as a plaque fighter. As a result, Warner-Lambert, which used to give retailers trade allowances of 28% to 30% off the wholesale price of Listerine, now gives up only half as much.

For all its efforts, P&G is still often slammed for its too-cautious, by-the-book ways. "P&G is always P&G," says Rich George, a former P&G marketer. "You might be able to tip the boulder a bit, but it's still a boulder." Nevertheless, P&G is clearly questioning some of its fundamental principles. And if it comes up with enough innovative answers, it may well become the wizard of packaged goods again.

Zachary Schiller in Cincinnati

WHAT CONSUMERS WANT IN THE 1990s

Aging is in, fitness fanaticism is going out, and with casual sex on the wane, people are looking for other kinds of thrills. Have you tried ecotourism?

Anne B. Fisher

BEEN WATCHING much prime-time TV lately? Have you noticed what has happened to commercials? Suddenly all those highly polished, career-obsessed men and women, who through most of the Eighties worked hard, played hard, and seemed bent on raising self-absorption to an art, are disappearing. In their place Adland is giving us a picture of American life straight out of W. C. Fields's worst nightmare: adorable kiddies, cuddly puppy dogs, and sentiment galore.

Take Kellogg's new Raisin Bran commercials. A 30-ish mother and her two small children are eating the stuff in their kitchen when the phone rings. It's dad, away on a business trip, also eating Raisin Bran in his hotel room. "I just thought we could have breakfast together," he says. Then an avuncular voice-over intones cozily, "The American family is alive and well. And eating Kellogg's Raisin Bran." The spot ends with the slogan, "Health food for the American family." WARNING: Repeated exposure to this commercial and its ilk may induce an overwhelming urge to groan, "Oh, puh-*leeze.*"

If it sometimes seems they've banned saccharine from the products and coated the ads with it instead, be assured that this is no illusion: Hammering on the heartstrings will be the predominant theme in consumer marketing for the 1990s. That's because in the next decade the largest, best-educated, and most affluent bunch of consumers in history—the generation born between 1945 and 1965—will turn 35, 40, even (gasp!) 50.

Geoffrey Greene of the research firm

Data Resources points out that in 1980, 42% of U.S. disposable income belonged to household heads between 35 and 54 years old; in 1989 that percentage rose to 47%, and in 2000 it will reach 55%. While real household income will most likely increase for all Americans during the Nineties, that huge 35 to 54 crowd will see their peak earning years. "So the number of affluent consumers will grow," notes Greene, "and many of them will be in the most intensely home-focused stage of the life cycle, settling down, raising children. For marketers in the Nineties, home will be where the action is."

Certainly marketers must beware of overlooking a remarkably vigorous, diverse, and well-to-do group—consumers over 50. Barbara Feigin of Grey Advertising's Strategic Services says, "They feel advertisers are ignoring them." Likewise, the baby-bust generation, that relatively small cohort now age 18 to 25, will be in such demand in the labor force that they will enjoy considerable purchasing power. The best marketing strategies will touch every point in the demographic spectrum. But as always, the baby-boomers will be so numerous that they will strongly influence the tastes and mores of everyone else.

How best to pitch products and services to well-off homebodies in the Nineties? Smart marketers will have to address, in varying degrees, five fundamental issues: time, quality, health, the environment, and home.

■ **TIME.** "Time will be the currency of the Nineties," says Feigin of Grey Advertising. Reason: the ubiquity of the two-career family. Convenience will be para-

mount, particularly in foods, and woe to the purveyor of comestibles whose product can't be quickly popped from freezer or fridge to microwave and ready to eat in a flash. Fresh, ready-made meals will be available in most big grocery stores, and ever more restaurants will deliver elaborate feasts to your doorstep: Just wait till the tots are asleep, add candles and wine, and serve.

Nobody will want to waste time standing in the checkout line, so supermarkets are being designed to make shopping quicker. A&P, ShopRite, and Publix will be experimenting with do-it-yourself automated checkouts. Kroger tested an automated system that let shoppers check themselves out by running their purchases through an electronic scanner and then paying the computer with a special cash card. "The technology worked fine," says a Kroger official, "but we found that people really missed seeing a human face at the checkout counter." Kroger is therefore looking at different ways to speed things up. Each department—floral, bakery, ready-made meals, and so on—has its own express checkout. A customer who just wants to run in and grab something for dessert doesn't have to get anywhere near the shopper who is laying in a month's supply of vittles and paying with an out-of-state check.

The disappearance of mom as an all-day unpaid laborer also means that kids, especially teenagers, are making more grown-up purchasing decisions than ever before. "If you were a kid 20 years ago, chances are your mom wouldn't let you anywhere near the washing machine," says Feigin. "Now mothers are so pressed for time, they're *hoping* the children will do their own laundry. And kids have a say in choosing almost

REPORTER ASSOCIATE *William E. Sheeline*

every household item, whether it's a box of detergent or a new VCR. They are a kind of hidden force in the marketplace."

Margaret Regan, a consultant with Towers Perrin Foster & Crosby, has done research on flexible-benefit plans for corporate clients and found that what employees say they really want is not better dental coverage or more vacation time, but somebody to run ordinary errands to places like the post office and the bank. "In the Nineties there will be a huge market for quotidian services," says Regan. "Business has to rise to the challenge."

The market for care of the elderly will grow apace. A 1987 study by the American Association of Retired Persons showed that seven million U.S. households included someone personally taking care of an older relative and that 55% of those caregivers also held jobs. As the population ages, the time crunch will become more widespread and acute. Notes Regan: "The grown daughter, who traditionally has cared for her aging parents, is in the work force now. People are going to need innovative, compassionate solutions, and with time generally scarcer than money, they'll be willing to pay for them."

■ **QUALITY.** With time at a premium and errands a problem, people balk at buying anything that will need much servicing or repair. But demands for quality go beyond merely wanting things to work right. Yankelovich Clancy Shulman, the consumer research firm, has discovered what senior vice president Susan Hayward calls "a major shift in consumer values" that emerged in the late Eighties and seems likely to continue through the next ten years. "The Eighties were intensely competitive. Everybody wanted to be a winner." As early as 1986, however, Yankelovich researchers began to notice a difference. Says Hayward: "Each consumer began to question whether consumption was really the road to happiness."

Of course, people aren't about to stop buying things. But instead of more and glitzier, they will want fewer and more durable. Thus, the latest trend is nontrendiness, which Yankelovich has dubbed neotraditionalism. Status, until lately defined as grabbing all the glittering prizes, now means, Hayward says, "what makes sense for me." If the Eighties were a Ferrari Testarossa, the Nineties will be something else entirely—perhaps a Jeep Cherokee, perhaps a Volvo station wagon.

■ **HEALTH.** We won't soon see the end of oat bran mania. Consumers are so preoccupied with health that in a survey of shoppers, over half said a new product should be allowed on supermarket shelves *only* if it contained little cholesterol, little fat, and few calories. Beverage Marketing Corp., a New York firm that predicts what people will drink, expects that the fastest-growing beverage category in the Nineties will continue to be bottled water.

As a selling point, health is often connected with home. Kellogg's "Health food for the American family" makes that link tidily and will be widely imitated. Some home-and-health pairings are a bit puzzling. Campbell's Home Style tomato soup, aimed at higher-income consumers, contains massive amounts of vitamin C, which you probably don't recall grandma stirring into the pot.

The fitness fanaticism of the Eighties—a trend that at times showed all the zeal and kindly tolerance of a secular Spanish Inquisition—will mellow considerably. It will be all right to soften a bit around the edges. The boom in exercise equipment is over, and fewer ads will feature sweaty amateur athletes pushing themselves to the edge of collapse. Hayward of Yankelovich says, "The baby-boomers will fight the physical aging process as long as they can, which is great news for cosmetics companies. But once they finally give up, aging will become chic. Gray hair will be fashionable." Hayward notes that the women's clothing industry has already suffered a few rude shocks, including the dismal failure of the reintroduced miniskirt, from Woodstock-generation customers who are feeling their age.

■ **ENVIRONMENT.** Remember Earth Day? Well, its 20th anniversary—April 22, 1990—will get heavy worldwide attention, and many consumer markets experts say the Nineties will be the Earth Decade. A Gallup poll reveals that 76% of Americans think of themselves as "environmentalists," and businesses of all kinds are responding. Predicts Joel Makower, a syndicated columnist and co-author of a forthcoming book called *The Green Consumer*: "In the Nineties terms like 'environment-friendly' will come to be as widely used, overused, and abused as 'natural' and 'light' have been in the Eighties."

Environment fervor will give rise to whole new industries. One of these, still in its infancy but growing fast, is the low-environmental-impact travel business, sometimes called ecotourism. The idea is to gain an appreciation of undeveloped areas, which are disappearing fast, without harming them. A popular journey offered by Breakaway Adventure Travel of Cambridge, Massachusetts, takes small groups of tourists deep into the Amazonian rain forest, where they live for six days with indigenous tribespeople—an experience, Breakaway's brochure notes, "previously only available to hardcore explorers, anthropologists, and missionaries." The cost: $1,595 per person, not including air fare to Caracas.

Wildland Journeys, a Seattle ecotourism enterprise growing 20% a year, runs some trips that are even more redolent of the Peace Corps than Breakaway's are, including one that takes groups of 14 adventurers on two-week treks to Peru (at about $1,900 a head, air fare included) to clean up the hiking trails around the ruins at Machu Picchu. The Audubon Society, which offers trips to all parts of the world (latest destinations include Alaska, Antarctica, Indonesia, and Scandinavia), encourages sightseers to abide by a seven-point code of ethics: no littering, no bothering the animals, no snickering at local folkways, and so on. Audubon travel manager Margaret Mullaly says, "People want to feel assured, especially in fragile areas, that they won't be hurting the environment." Nearly 1,000 travelers signed on for Audubon trips in 1989, twice as many as in 1988.

The ecotourism business isn't only about conservation. Kurt Kutay, a co-founder of Wildland Journeys, says most of his customers are mainly after adventure. Arnold Brown, who ponders the future for the New York consulting firm Weiner Edrich Brown, believes the Nineties will see a marked increase in consumers' appetite for thrills. "As people become more financially secure, they tend to look around for a bit of excitement," he says, "and let's face it, with all the fear of AIDS and so on, one major source of excitement has been curtailed." By his reckoning, rock-climbing expeditions and white-water rafting trips are nudging aside love affairs as the pulse quickeners of the future. This is happy news for marketers of such items as backpacks, life jackets, and Swiss army knives, but the rest of us may be excused a little wistfulness.

■ **HOME.** In a more domesticated society, many technological innovations in the Nineties will make staying home more fun. So-called smart television (FORTUNE, November 20) will read the TV listings and record programs you might want to watch later—editing out the commercials—while also scanning databases for information of interest, answering the telephone, playing compact discs, and running other appliances around the house. This innovation will be so expensive at first that demand may be slow off the mark. Not to worry: Greene at Data Resources predicts that home entertainment will be "the single strongest growth market of the Nineties" and that competition will drive prices down in a hurry.

Some of the most salutary advances of

this home-centered decade will be in the design and construction of houses. Many homes will soon *do* more. Electronic and fiber-optic technology will bring sophisticated monitoring systems—lighting controls and motion detectors, for example—plus cable TV in most rooms and sensor-activated fire sprinklers similar to the kind now found only in stores and office buildings.

The next few years will also bring innovations aimed at making new housing more affordable. Researchers at the Lawrence Berkeley Laboratory at the University of California are among those studying ways to cut costs. Much of the cost of construction labor, for example, could be eliminated by building components of a house— say, entire rooms with doors and windows installed—in factories, and then hauling the components to the construction site for final assembly. Such techniques have been widely discussed for decades, but until now most of the progress has been outside the U.S. "The Europeans do a lot of component-housing manufacture, which is very cost-effective, and the U.S. will be moving in that direction," says Berkeley researcher Brandt Andersson. "We haven't changed the way we build houses in centuries. It's time for a fresh look."

At least one developer has begun applying such thinking to the problem of how to house the elderly. Coastal Colony Corp. of Manheim, Pennsylvania, sells factory-built cottages complete with carpeting, appliances, and whatever roofing and siding the customer chooses. They are intended primarily for families with an elderly relative who wants to live nearby without losing too much independence. Coastal Colony will install a cottage in a family's backyard, and if the family moves, the cottage can move too. A two-bedroom unit, installed, costs about $33,000.

"So far we've focused on this as a solution to elderly people's needs," says Ed Guion, Coastal Colony's president. "But because modular housing is easily expandable, it could be great for first-time home buyers too. They could add rooms as their families grow." The market for brand-new houses at $33,000 each could be sizable. If this catches on, other homebuilders will have to compete, and home buyers will be the winners.

UNDERLYING all the changes in consumers' concerns, and as important as all of them, will be a markedly changed inner sense. The Nineties will see what consumer-marketing consulting firm FCB/Leber Katz in New York calls "the end of the myth of Me." Narcissism is out, and so is dog-eat-dog ambition. At the same time Americans will seek a sense of moral stability. According to futurist Arnold Brown, "people are searching for absolute values and a sure grasp of right and wrong."

Brown sees "a return to the eternal verities," a groundswell of longing for some permanent, transcendent set of values. Consider that M. Scott Peck's *The Road Less Traveled*, a book billed as offering "spiritual inspiration," has been on the New York *Times* best-seller list for an astonishing 324 weeks. Brown foresees a renewal of interest in religion. You might well wonder how marketers of consumer goods can contrive to capitalize on the hope that God is not dead. But consider Kleenex tissues' new slogan: "Kleenex says Bless You." Anyone who doubts the trend need only peek into any church in midtown Manhattan—former hotbed of Eighties materialism—on a Sunday morning. The pews and choir lofts are filling up with persons bearing a suspicious resemblance to investment bankers and other fast-track types, often with babies in tow.

The Nineties will be a far less cynical decade than the Eighties. Yes, we will still care what things cost. But we will seek to value only those things—family, community, earth, faith—that will endure.

Marketing myopia
(With Retrospective Commentary)

*Shortsighted managements often
fail to recognize that in
fact there is no such
thing as a growth industry*

Theodore Levitt

**At the time of the article's publication,
Theodore Levitt was lecturer in business
administration at the Harvard Business
School. Now a full professor there, he is
the author of several books, including
The Third Sector: New Tactics for a
Responsive Society *(1973)* and Market-
ing for Business Growth *(1974)*.**

*How can a company ensure its con-
tinued growth? In 1960 "Marketing
Myopia" answered that question in a
new and challenging way by urging
organizations to define their industries broadly to take advantage of
growth opportunities. Using the
archetype of the railroads, Mr. Levitt
showed how they declined inevitably
as technology advanced because they
defined themselves too narrowly. To
continue growing, companies must
ascertain and act on their customers' needs and desires, not bank on
the presumptive longevity of their
products. The success of the article
testifies to the validity of its message.
It has been widely quoted and anthol-
ogized, and HBR has sold more than
265,000 reprints of it. The author of 14
subsequent articles in HBR, Mr. Levitt
is one of the magazine's most prolific
contributors. In a retrospective commentary, he considers the use and
misuse that have been made of "Marketing Myopia," describing its many
interpretations and hypothesizing
about its success.*

Every major industry was once a
growth industry. But some that are
now riding a wave of growth enthusiasm are very much in the shadow of
decline. Others which are thought of
as seasoned growth industries have
actually stopped growing. In every
case the reason growth is threatened, slowed, or stopped is *not* because the market is saturated. It is because there has been a failure of management.

Fateful purposes: The failure is at the
top. The executives responsible for
it, in the last analysis, are those
who deal with broad aims and policies. Thus:

☐
The railroads did not stop growing
because the need for passenger and
freight transportation declined. That
grew. The railroads are in trouble today not because the need was filled by
others (cars, trucks, airplanes, even
telephones), but because it was *not*
filled by the railroads themselves. They
let others take customers away from
them because they assumed themselves
to be in the railroad business rather
than in the transportation business.
The reason they defined their industry wrong was because they were rail-
road-oriented instead of transporta-
tion-oriented; they were product-oriented instead of customer-oriented.

☐
Hollywood barely escaped being totally
ravished by television. Actually, all
the established film companies went
through drastic reorganizations. Some
simply disappeared. All of them got
into trouble not because of TV's inroads but because of their own myopia. As with the railroads, Hollywood defined its business incorrectly.
It thought it was in the movie business when it was actually in the entertainment business. "Movies" implied
a specific, limited product. This produced a fatuous contentment which
from the beginning led producers to
view TV as a threat. Hollywood
scorned and rejected TV when it
should have welcomed it as an opportunity—an opportunity to expand the
entertainment business.

Today TV is a bigger business than
the old narrowly defined movie business ever was. Had Hollywood been
customer-oriented (providing entertainment), rather then product-oriented (making movies), would it have
gone through the fiscal purgatory that
it did? I doubt it. What ultimately
saved Hollywood and accounted for its
recent resurgence was the wave of new
young writers, producers, and directors
whose previous successes in television
had decimated the old movie companies and toppled the big movie
moguls.

There are other less obvious examples
of industries that have been and are
now endangering their futures by im-
properly defining their purposes. I
shall discuss some in detail later and
analyze the kind of policies that lead
to trouble. Right now it may help to
show what a thoroughly customer-oriented management *can* do to keep a
growth industry growing, even after
the obvious opportunities have been

exhausted; and here there are two examples that have been around for a long time. They are nylon and glass—specifically, E. I. duPont de Nemours & Company and Corning Glass Works.

Both companies have great technical competence. Their product orientation is unquestioned. But this alone does not explain their success. After all, who was more pridefully product-oriented and product-conscious than the erstwhile New England textile companies that have been so thoroughly massacred? The DuPonts and the Cornings have succeeded not primarily because of their product or research orientation but because they have been thoroughly customer-oriented also. It is constant watchfulness for opportunities to apply their technical know-how to the creation of customer-satisfying uses which accounts for their prodigious output of successful new products. Without a very sophisticated eye on the customer, most of their new products might have been wrong, their sales methods useless.

Aluminum has also continued to be a growth industry, thanks to the efforts of two wartime-created companies which deliberately set about creating new customer-satisfying uses. Without Kaiser Aluminum & Chemical Corporation and Reynolds Metals Company, the total demand for aluminum today would be vastly less.

Error of analysis: Some may argue that it is foolish to set the railroads off against aluminum or the movies off against glass. Are not aluminum and glass naturally so versatile that the industries are bound to have more growth opportunities than the railroads and movies? This view commits precisely the error I have been talking about. It defines an industry, or a product, or a cluster of know-how so narrowly as to guarantee its premature senescence. When we mention "railroads," we should make sure we mean "transportation." As transporters, the railroads still have a good chance for very considerable growth. They are not limited to the railroad business as such (though in my opinion rail transportation is potentially a much stronger transportation medium than is generally believed).

What the railroads lack is not opportunity, but some of the same managerial imaginativeness and audacity that made them great. Even an amateur like Jacques Barzun can see what is lacking when he says:

"I grieve to see the most advanced physical and social organization of the last century go down in shabby disgrace for lack of the same comprehensive imagination that built it up. [What is lacking is] the will of the companies to survive and to satisfy the public by inventiveness and skill." [1]

Shadow of obsolescence

It is impossible to mention a single major industry that did not at one time qualify for the magic appellation of "growth industry." In each case its assumed strength lay in the apparently unchallenged superiority of its product. There appeared to be no effective substitute for it. It was itself a runaway substitute for the product it so triumphantly replaced. Yet one after another of these celebrated industries has come under a shadow. Let us look briefly at a few more of them, this time taking examples that have so far received a little less attention:

☐

Dry cleaning—This was once a growth industry with lavish prospects. In an age of wool garments, imagine being finally able to get them safely and easily clean. The boom was on.

Yet here we are 30 years after the boom started and the industry is in trouble. Where has the competition come from? From a better way of cleaning? No. It has come from synthetic fibers and chemical additives that have cut the need for dry cleaning. But this is only the beginning. Lurking in the wings and ready to make chemical dry cleaning totally obsolescent is that powerful magician, ultrasonics.

☐

Electric utilities— This is another one of those supposedly "no-substitute"

1. Jacques Barzun, "Trains and the Mind of Man," *Holiday*, February 1960, p. 21.

products that has been enthroned on a pedestal of invincible growth. When the incandescent lamp came along, kerosene lights were finished. Later the water wheel and the steam engine were cut to ribbons by the flexibility, reliability, simplicity, and just plain easy availability of electric motors. The prosperity of electric utilities continues to wax extravagant as the home is converted into a museum of electric gadgetry. How can anybody miss by investing in utilities, with no competition, nothing but growth ahead?

But a second look is not quite so comforting. A score of nonutility companies are well advanced toward developing a powerful chemical fuel cell which could sit in some hidden closet of every home silently ticking off electric power. The electric lines that vulgarize so many neighborhoods will be eliminated. So will the endless demolition of streets and service interruptions during storms. Also on the horizon is solar energy, again pioneered by nonutility companies.

Who says that the utilities have no competition? They may be natural monopolies now, but tomorrow they may be natural deaths. To avoid this prospect, they too will have to develop fuel cells, solar energy, and other power sources. To survive, they themselves will have to plot the obsolescence of what now produces their livelihood.

☐

Grocery stores—Many people find it hard to realize that there ever was a thriving establishment known as the "corner grocery store." The supermarket has taken over with a powerful effectiveness. Yet the big food chains of the 1930s narrowly escaped being completely wiped out by the aggressive expansion of independent supermarkets. The first genuine supermarket was opened in 1930, in Jamaica, Long Island. By 1933 supermarkets were thriving in California, Ohio, Pennsylvania, and elsewhere. Yet the established chains pompously ignored them. When they chose to notice them, it was with such derisive descriptions as "cheapy," "horse-and-buggy," "cracker-barrel storekeeping," and "unethical opportunists."

The executive of one big chain announced at the time that he found it "hard to believe that people will drive for miles to shop for foods and sacrifice the personal service chains have perfected and to which Mrs. Consumer is accustomed." [2] As late as 1936, the National Wholesale Grocers convention and the New Jersey Retail Grocers Association said there was nothing to fear. They said that the supers' narrow appeal to the price buyer limited the size of their market. They had to draw from miles around. When imitators came, there would be wholesale liquidations as volume fell. The current high sales of the supers was said to be partly due to their novelty. Basically people wanted convenient neighborhood grocers. If the neighborhood stores "cooperate with their suppliers, pay attention to their costs, and improve their service," they would be able to weather the competition until it blew over. [3]

It never blew over. The chains discovered that survival required going into the supermarket business. This meant the wholesale destruction of their huge investments in corner store sites and in established distribution and merchandising methods. The companies with "the courage of their convictions" resolutely stuck to the corner store philosophy. They kept their pride but lost their shirts.

Self-deceiving cycle: But memories are short. For example, it is hard for people who today confidently hail the twin messiahs of electronics and chemicals to see how things could possibly go wrong with these galloping industries. They probably also cannot see how a reasonably sensible businessman could have been as myopic as the famous Boston millionaire who 50 years ago unintentionally sentenced his heirs to poverty by stipulating that his entire estate be forever invested exclusively in electric streetcar securities. His posthumous declaration, "There will always be a big demand for efficient urban transportation," is no consolation to his heirs who sustain life by

pumping gasoline at automobile filling stations.

Yet, in a casual survey I recently took among a group of intelligent business executives, nearly half agreed that it would be hard to hurt their heirs by tying their estates forever to the electronics industry. When I then confronted them with the Boston streetcar example, they chorused unanimously, "That's different!" But is it? Is not the basic situation identical?

In truth, *there is no such thing* as a growth industry, I believe. There are only companies organized and operated to create and capitalize on growth opportunities. Industries that assume themselves to be riding some automatic growth escalator invariably descend into stagnation. The history of every dead and dying "growth" industry shows a self-deceiving cycle of bountiful expansion and undetected decay. There are four conditions which usually guarantee this cycle:

1
The belief that growth is assured by an expanding and more affluent population.
2
The belief that there is no competitive substitute for the industry's major product.
3
Too much faith in mass production and in the advantages of rapidly declining unit costs as output rises.
4
Preoccupation with a product that lends itself to carefully controlled scientific experimentation, improvement, and manufacturing cost reduction.

I should like now to begin examining each of these conditions in some detail. To build my case as boldly as possible, I shall illustrate the points with reference to three industries—petroleum, automobiles, and electronics—particularly petroleum, because it spans more years and more vicissitudes. Not only do these three have excellent reputations with the general public and also enjoy the confidence of sophisticated investors, but their managements have become known for progressive thinking in areas like financial control, product research, and

management training. If obsolescence can cripple even these industries, it can happen anywhere.

Population myth

The belief that profits are assured by an expanding and more affluent population is dear to the heart of every industry. It takes the edge off the apprehensions everybody understandably feels about the future. If consumers are multiplying and also buying more of your product or service, you can face the future with considerably more comfort than if the market is shrinking. An expanding market keeps the manufacturer from having to think very hard or imaginatively. If thinking is an intellectual response to a problem, then the absence of a problem leads to the absence of thinking. If your product has an automatically expanding market, then you will not give much thought to how to expand it.

One of the most interesting examples of this is provided by the petroleum industry. Probably our oldest growth industry, it has an enviable record. While there are some current apprehensions about its growth rate, the industry itself tends to be optimistic.

But I believe it can be demonstrated that it is undergoing a fundamental yet typical change. It is not only ceasing to be a growth industry, but may actually be a declining one, relative to other business. Although there is widespread unawareness of it, I believe that within 25 years the oil industry may find itself in much the same position of retrospective glory that the railroads are now in. Despite its pioneering work in developing and applying the present-value method of investment evaluation, in employee relations, and in working with backward countries, the petroleum business is a distressing example of how complacency and wrongheadedness can stubbornly convert opportunity into near disaster.

One of the characteristics of this and other industries that have believed very strongly in the beneficial consequences of an expanding population, while at the same time being indus-

2. For more details see M. M. Zimmerman, *The Super Market: A Revolution in Distribution* (New York, McGraw-Hill Book Company, Inc., 1955), p. 48.

3. Ibid., pp. 45–47.

tries with a generic product for which there has appeared to be no competitive substitute, is that the individual companies have sought to outdo their competitors by improving on what they are already doing. This makes sense, of course, if one assumes that sales are tied to the country's population strings, because the customer can compare products only on a feature-by-feature basis. I believe it is significant, for example, that not since John D. Rockefeller sent free kerosene lamps to China has the oil industry done anything really outstanding to create a demand for its product. Not even in product improvement has it showered itself with eminence. The greatest single improvement—namely, the development of tetraethyl lead—came from outside the industry, specifically from General Motors and DuPont. The big contributions made by the industry itself are confined to the technology of oil exploration, production, and refining.

Asking for trouble: In other words, the industry's efforts have focused on improving the *efficiency* of getting and making its product, not really on improving the generic product or its marketing. Moreover, its chief product has continuously been defined in the narrowest possible terms, namely, gasoline, not energy, fuel, or transportation. This attitude has helped assure that:

○
Major improvements in gasoline quality tend not to originate in the oil industry. Also, the development of superior alternative fuels comes from outside the oil industry, as will be shown later.
○
Major innovations in automobile fuel marketing are originated by small new oil companies that are not primarily preoccupied with production or refining. These are the companies that have been responsible for the rapidly expanding multipump gasoline stations, with their successful emphasis on large and clean layouts, rapid and efficient driveway service, and quality gasoline at low prices.

Thus, the oil industry is asking for trouble from outsiders. Sooner or later,

in this land of hungry inventors and entrepreneurs, a threat is sure to come. The possibilities of this will become more apparent when we turn to the next dangerous belief of many managements. For the sake of continuity, because this second belief is tied closely to the first, I shall continue with the same example.

Idea of indispensability: The petroleum industry is pretty much persuaded that there is no competitive substitute for its major product, gasoline—or if there is, that it will continue to be a derivative of crude oil, such as diesel fuel or kerosene jet fuel.

There is a lot of automatic wishful thinking in this assumption. The trouble is that most refining companies own huge amounts of crude oil reserves. These have value only if there is a market for products into which oil can be converted—hence the tenacious belief in the continuing competitive superiority of automobile fuels made from crude oil.

This idea persists despite all historic evidence against it. The evidence not only shows that oil has never been a superior product for any purpose for very long, but it also shows that the oil industry has never really been a growth industry. It has been a succession of different businesses that have gone through the usual historic cycles of growth, maturity, and decay. Its overall survival is owed to a series of miraculous escapes from total obsolescence, of last-minute and unexpected reprieves from total disaster reminiscent of the Perils of Pauline.

Perils of petroleum: I shall sketch in only the main episodes.

First, crude oil was largely a patent medicine. But even before that fad ran out, demand was greatly expanded by the use of oil in kerosene lamps. The prospect of lighting the world's lamps gave rise to an extravagant promise of growth. The prospects were similar to those the industry now holds for gasoline in other parts of the world. It can hardly wait for the underdeveloped nations to get a car in every garage.

In the days of the kerosene lamp, the

oil companies competed with each other and against gaslight by trying to improve the illuminating characteristics of kerosene. Then suddenly the impossible happened. Edison invented a light which was totally nondependent on crude oil. Had it not been for the growing use of kerosene in space heaters, the incandescent lamp would have completely finished oil as a growth industry at that time. Oil would have been good for little else than axle grease.

Then disaster and reprieve struck again. Two great innovations occurred, neither originating in the oil industry. The successful development of coal-burning domestic central-heating systems made the space heater obsolescent. While the industry reeled, along came its most magnificent boost yet—the internal combustion engine, also invented by outsiders. Then when the prodigious expansion for gasoline finally began to level off in the 1920s, along came the miraculous escape of a central oil heater. Once again, the escape was provided by an outsider's invention and development. And when that market weakened, wartime demand for aviation fuel came to the rescue. After the war the expansion of civilian aviation, the dieselization of railroads, and the explosive demand for cars and trucks kept the industry's growth in high gear.

Meanwhile, centralized oil heating—whose boom potential had only recently been proclaimed—ran into severe competition from natural gas. While the oil companies themselves owned the gas that now competed with their oil, the industry did not originate the natural gas revolution, nor has it to this day greatly profited from its gas ownership. The gas revolution was made by newly formed transmission companies that marketed the product with an aggressive ardor. They started a magnificent new industry, first against the advice and then against the resistance of the oil companies.

By all the logic of the situation, the oil companies themselves should have made the gas revolution. They not only owned the gas; they also were the only people experienced in handling, scrubbing, and using it, the only people experienced in pipeline technology and transmission, and they understood heating problems. But, partly because they knew that natural gas would compete with their own sale of heating oil, the oil companies poohpoohed the potentials of gas.

The revolution was finally started by oil pipeline executives who, unable to persuade their own companies to go into gas, quit and organized the spectacularly successful gas transmission companies. Even after their success became painfully evident to the oil companies, the latter did not go into gas transmission. The multibillion dollar business which should have been theirs went to others. As in the past, the industry was blinded by its narrow preoccupation with a specific product and the value of its reserves. It paid little or no attention to its customers' basic needs and preferences.

The postwar years have not witnessed any change. Immediately after World War II the oil industry was greatly encouraged about its future by the rapid expansion of demand for its traditional line of products. In 1950 most companies projected annual rates of domestic expansion of around 6% through at least 1975. Though the ratio of crude oil reserves to demand in the Free World was about 20 to 1, with 10 to 1 being usually considered a reasonable working ratio in the United States, booming demand sent oil men searching for more without sufficient regard to what the future really promised. In 1952 they "hit" in the Middle East; the ratio skyrocketed to 42 to 1. If gross additions to reserves continue at the average rate of the past five years (37 billion barrels annually), then by 1970 the reserve ratio will be up to 45 to 1. This abundance of oil has weakened crude and product prices all over the world.

Uncertain future: Management cannot find much consolation today in the rapidly expanding petrochemical industry, another oil-using idea that did not originate in the leading firms. The total United States production of petrochemicals is equivalent to about 2% (by volume) of the demand for all petroleum products. Although the petrochemical industry is now expected to grow by about 10% per year, this will not offset other drains on

the growth of crude oil consumption. Furthermore, while petrochemical products are many and growing, it is well to remember that there are nonpetroleum sources of the basic raw material, such as coal. Besides, a lot of plastics can be produced with relatively little oil. A 50,000-barrel-per-day oil refinery is now considered the absolute minimum size for efficiency. But a 5,000-barrel-per-day chemical plant is a giant operation.

Oil has never been a continuously strong growth industry. It has grown by fits and starts, always miraculously saved by innovations and developments not of its own making. The reason it has not grown in a smooth progression is that each time it thought it had a superior product safe from the possibility of competitive substitutes, the product turned out to be inferior and notoriously subject to obsolescence. Until now, gasoline (for motor fuel, anyhow) has escaped this fate. But, as we shall see later, it too may be on its last legs.

The point of all this is that there is no guarantee against product obsolescence. If a company's own research does not make it obsolete, another's will. Unless an industry is especially lucky, as oil has been until now, it can easily go down in a sea of red figures—just as the railroads have, as the buggy whip manufacturers have, as the corner grocery chains have, as most of the big movie companies have, and indeed as many other industries have.

The best way for a firm to be lucky is to make its own luck. That requires knowing what makes a business successful. One of the greatest enemies of this knowledge is mass production.

Production pressures

Mass-production industries are impelled by a great drive to produce all they can. The prospect of steeply declining unit costs as output rises is more than most companies can usually resist. The profit possibilities look spectacular. All effort focuses on production. The result is that marketing gets neglected.

John Kenneth Galbraith contends that just the opposite occurs.[4] Output is so prodigious that all effort concentrates on trying to get rid of it. He says this accounts for singing commercials, desecration of the countryside with advertising signs, and other wasteful and vulgar practices. Galbraith has a finger on something real, but he misses the strategic point. Mass production does indeed generate great pressure to "move" the product. But what usually gets emphasized is selling, not marketing. Marketing, being a more sophisticated and complex process, gets ignored.

The difference between marketing and selling is more than semantic. Selling focuses on the needs of the seller, marketing on the needs of the buyer. Selling is preoccupied with the seller's need to convert his product into cash, marketing with the idea of satisfying the needs of the customer by means of the product and the whole cluster of things associated with creating, delivering, and finally consuming it.

In some industries the enticements of full mass production have been so powerful that for many years top management in effect has told the sales departments, "You get rid of it; we'll worry about profits." By contrast, a truly marketing-minded firm tries to create value-satisfying goods and services that consumers will want to buy. What it offers for sale includes not only the generic product or service, but also how it is made available to the customer, in what form, when, under what conditions, and at what terms of trade. Most important, what it offers for sale is determined not by the seller but by the buyer. The seller takes his cues from the buyer in such a way that the product becomes a consequence of the marketing effort, not vice versa.

Lag in Detroit: This may sound like an elementary rule of business, but that does not keep it from being violated wholesale. It is certainly more violated than honored. Take the automobile industry.

---

4. *The Affluent Society* (Boston, Houghton Mifflin Company, 1958), pp. 152-160.

Here mass production is most famous, most honored, and has the greatest impact on the entire society. The industry has hitched its fortune to the relentless requirements of the annual model change, a policy that makes customer orientation an especially urgent necessity. Consequently the auto companies annually spend millions of dollars on consumer research. But the fact that the new compact cars are selling so well in their first year indicates that Detroit's vast researches have for a long time failed to reveal what the customer really wanted. Detroit was not persuaded that he wanted anything different from what he had been getting until it lost millions of customers to other small car manufacturers.

How could this unbelievable lag behind consumer wants have been perpetuated so long? Why did not research reveal consumer preferences before consumers' buying decisions themselves revealed the facts? Is that not what consumer research is for—to find out before the fact what is going to happen? The answer is that Detroit never really researched the customer's wants. It only researched his preferences between the kinds of things which it had already decided to offer him. For Detroit is mainly product-oriented, not customer-oriented. To the extent that the customer is recognized as having needs that the manufacturer should try to satisfy, Detroit usually acts as if the job can be done entirely by product changes. Occasionally attention gets paid to financing, too, but that is done more in order to sell than to enable the customer to buy.

As for taking care of other customer needs, there is not enough being done to write about. The areas of the greatest unsatisfied needs are ignored, or at best get stepchild attention. These are at the point of sale and on the matter of automative repair and maintenance. Detroit views these problem areas as being of secondary importance. That is underscored by the fact that the retailing and servicing ends of this industry are neither owned and operated nor controlled by the manufacturers. Once the car is produced, things are pretty much in the dealer's inadequate hands. Illustrative of Detroit's arm's-length attitude is the fact that, while servicing holds enormous sales-stimulating, profit-building opportunities, only 57 of Chevrolet's 7,000 dealers provide night maintenance service.

Motorists repeatedly express their dissatisfaction with servicing and their apprehensions about buying cars under the present selling setup. The anxieties and problems they encounter during the auto buying and maintenance processes are probably more intense and widespread today than 30 years ago. Yet the automobile companies do not *seem* to listen to or take their cues from the anguished consumer. If they do listen, it must be through the filter of their own preoccupation with production. The marketing effort is still viewed as a necessary consequence of the product, not vice versa, as it should be. That is the legacy of mass production, with its parochial view that profit resides essentially in low-cost full production.

What Ford put first: The profit lure of mass production obviously has a place in the plans and strategy of business management, but it must always *follow* hard thinking about the customer. This is one of the most important lessons that we can learn from the contradictory behavior of Henry Ford. In a sense Ford was both the most brilliant and the most senseless marketer in American history. He was senseless because he refused to give the customer anything but a black car. He was brilliant because he fashioned a production system designed to fit market needs. We habitually celebrate him for the wrong reason, his production genius. His real genius was marketing. We think he was able to cut his selling price and therefore sell millions of $500 cars because his invention of the assembly line had reduced the costs. Actually he invented the assembly line because he had concluded that at $500 he could sell millions of cars. Mass production was the *result* not the cause of his low prices.

Ford repeatedly emphasized this point, but a nation of production-oriented business managers refuses to hear the great lesson he taught. Here is his operating philosophy as he expressed it succinctly:

"Our policy is to reduce the price, extend the operations, and improve the article. You will notice that the reduction of price comes first. We have never considered any costs as fixed. Therefore we first reduce the price to the point where we believe more sales will result. Then we go ahead and try to make the prices. We do not bother about the costs. The new price forces the costs down. The more usual way is to take the costs and then determine the price; and although that method may be scientific in the narrow sense, it is not scientific in the broad sense, because what earthly use is it to know the cost if it tells you that you cannot manufacture at a price at which the article can be sold? But more to the point is the fact that, although one may calculate what a cost is, and of course all of our costs are carefully calculated, no one knows what a cost ought to be. One of the ways of discovering . . . is to name a price so low as to force everybody in the place to the highest point of efficiency. The low price makes everybody dig for profits. We make more discoveries concerning manufacturing and selling under this forced method than by any method of leisurely investigation." [5]

Product provincialism: The tantalizing profit possibilities of low unit production costs may be the most seriously self-deceiving attitude that can afflict a company, particularly a "growth" company where an apparently assured expansion of demand already tends to undermine a proper concern for the importance of marketing and the customer.

The usual result of this narrow preoccupation with so-called concrete matters is that instead of growing, the industry declines. It usually means that the product fails to adapt to the constantly changing patterns of consumer needs and tastes, to new and modified marketing institutions and practices, or to product developments in competing or complementary industries. The industry has its eyes so firmly on its own specific product that it does not see how it is being made obsolete.

5. Henry Ford, *My Life and Work* (New York, Doubleday, Page & Company, 1923), pp. 146-147.

The classical example of this is the buggy whip industry. No amount of product improvement could stave off its death sentence. But had the industry defined itself as being in the transportation business rather than the buggy whip business, it might have survived. It would have done what survival always entails, that is, changing. Even if it had only defined its business as providing a stimulant or catalyst to an energy source, it might have survived by becoming a manufacturer of, say, fanbelts or air cleaners.

What may some day be a still more classical example is, again, the oil industry. Having let others steal marvelous opportunities from it (e.g., natural gas, as already mentioned, missile fuels, and jet engine lubricants), one would expect it to have taken steps never to let that happen again. But this is not the case. We are now getting extraordinary new developments in fuel systems specifically designed to power automobiles. Not only are these developments concentrated in firms outside the petroleum industry, but petroleum is almost systematically ignoring them, securely content in its wedded bliss to oil. It is the story of the kerosene lamp versus the incandescent lamp all over again. Oil is trying to improve hydrocarbon fuels rather than develop *any* fuels best suited to the needs of their users, whether or not made in different ways and with different raw materials from oil.

Here are some things which nonpetroleum companies are working on:

☐
Over a dozen such firms now have advanced working models of energy systems which, when perfected, will replace the internal combustion engine and eliminate the demand for gasoline. The superior merit of each of these systems is their elimination of frequent, time-consuming, and irritating refueling stops. Most of these systems are fuel cells designed to create electrical energy directly from chemicals without combustion. Most of them use chemicals that are not derived from oil, generally hydrogen and oxygen.

☐
Several other companies have advanced models of electric storage batteries designed to power automobiles. One of these is an aircraft producer that is working jointly with several electric utility companies. The latter hope to use off-peak generating capacity to supply overnight plug-in battery regeneration. Another company, also using the battery approach, is a medium-size electronics firm with extensive small-battery experience that it developed in connection with its work on hearing aids. It is collaborating with an automobile manufacturer. Recent improvements arising from the need for high-powered miniature power storage plants in rockets have put us within reach of a relatively small battery capable of withstanding great overloads or surges of power. Germanium diode applications and batteries using sintered-plate and nickel-cadmium techniques promise to make a revolution in our energy sources.

☐
Solar energy conversion systems are also getting increasing attention. One usually cautious Detroit auto executive recently ventured that solar-powered cars might be common by 1980.

As for the oil companies, they are more or less "watching developments," as one research director put it to me. A few are doing a bit of research on fuel cells, but almost always confined to developing cells powered by hydrocarbon chemicals. None of them are enthusiastically researching fuel cells, batteries, or solar power plants. None of them are spending a fraction as much on research in these profoundly important areas as they are on the usual run-of-the-mill things like reducing combustion chamber deposit in gasoline engines. One major integrated petroleum company recently took a tentative look at the fuel cell and concluded that although "the companies actively working on it indicate a belief in ultimate success . . . the timing and magnitude of its impact are too remote to warrant recognition in our forecasts."

One might, of course, ask: Why should the oil companies do anything different? Would not chemical fuel cells, batteries, or solar energy kill the present product lines? The answer is that they would indeed, and that is precisely the reason for the oil firms having to develop these power units before their competitors, so they will not be companies without an industry.

Management might be more likely to do what is needed for its own preservation if it thought of itself as being in the energy business. But even that would not be enough if it persists in imprisoning itself in the narrow grip of its tight product orientation. It has to think of itself as taking care of customer needs, not finding, refining, or even selling oil. Once it genuinely thinks of its business as taking care of people's transportation needs, nothing can stop it from creating its own extravagantly profitable growth.

'Creative destruction': Since words are cheap and deeds are dear, it may be appropriate to indicate what this kind of thinking involves and leads to. Let us start at the beginning—the customer. It can be shown that motorists strongly dislike the bother, delay, and experience of buying gasoline. People actually do not buy gasoline. They cannot see it, taste it, feel it, appreciate it, or really test it. What they buy is the right to continue driving their cars. The gas station is like a tax collector to whom people are compelled to pay a periodic toll as the price of using their cars. This makes the gas station a basically unpopular institution. It can never be made popular or pleasant, only less unpopular, less unpleasant.

To reduce its unpopularity completely means eliminating it. Nobody likes a tax collector, not even a pleasantly cheerful one. Nobody likes to interrupt a trip to buy a phantom product, not even from a handsome Adonis or a seductive Venus. Hence, companies that are working on exotic fuel substitutes which will eliminate the need for frequent refueling are heading directly into the outstretched arms of the irritated motorist. They are riding a wave of inevitability, not because they are creating something which is technologically superior or more sophisticated, but because they are satisfying a powerful customer need. They are also eliminating noxious odors and air pollution.

Once the petroleum companies recognize the customer-satisfying logic of what another power system can do, they will see that they have no more choice about working on an efficient, long-lasting fuel (or some way of delivering present fuels without bothering the motorist) than the big food chains had a choice about going into the supermarket business, or the vacuum tube companies had a choice about making semiconductors. For their own good the oil firms will have to destroy their own highly profitable assets. No amount of wishful thinking can save them from the necessity of engaging in this form of "creative destruction."

I phrase the need as strongly as this because I think management must make quite an effort to break itself loose from conventional ways. It is all too easy in this day and age for a company or industry to let its sense of purpose become dominated by the economies of full production and to develop a dangerously lopsided product orientation. In short, if management lets itself drift, it invariably drifts in the direction of thinking of itself as producing goods and services, not customer satisfactions. While it probably will not descend to the depths of telling its salesmen, "You get rid of it; we'll worry about profits," it can, without knowing it, be practicing precisely that formula for withering decay. The historic fate of one growth industry after another has been its suicidal product provincialism.

Dangers of R&D

Another big danger to a firm's continued growth arises when top management is wholly transfixed by the profit possibilities of technical research and development. To illustrate I shall turn first to a new industry—electronics—and then return once more to the oil companies. By comparing a fresh example with a familiar one, I hope to emphasize the prevalence and insidiousness of a hazardous way of thinking.

Marketing shortchanged: In the case of electronics, the greatest danger which faces the glamorous new companies in this field is not that they do not pay enough attention to research and development, but that they pay *too much* attention to it. And the

fact that the fastest growing electronics firms owe their eminence to their heavy emphasis on technical research is completely beside the point. They have vaulted to affluence on a sudden crest of unusually strong general receptiveness to new technical ideas. Also, their success has been shaped in the virtually guaranteed market of military subsidies and by military orders that in many cases actually preceded the existence of facilities to make the products. Their expansion has, in other words, been almost totally devoid of marketing effort.

Thus, they are growing up under conditions that come dangerously close to creating the illusion that a superior product will sell itself. Having created a successful company by making a superior product, it is not surprising that management continues to be oriented toward the product rather than the people who consume it. It develops the philosophy that continued growth is a matter of continued product innovation and improvement.

A number of other factors tend to strengthen and sustain this belief:

1
Because electronic products are highly complex and sophisticated, managements become top-heavy with engineers and scientists. This creates a selective bias in favor of research and production at the expense of marketing. The organization tends to view itself as making things rather than satisfying customer needs. Marketing gets treated as a residual activity, "something else" that must be done once the vital job of product creation and production is completed.
2
To this bias in favor of product research, development, and production is added the bias in favor of dealing with controllable variables. Engineers and scientists are at home in the world of concrete things like machines, test tubes, production lines, and even balance sheets. The abstractions to which they feel kindly are those which are testable or manipulatable in the laboratory, or, if not testable, then functional, such as Euclid's axioms. In short, the managements of the new glamour-growth companies tend to favor those business activities which lend them-

selves to careful study, experimentation, and control—the hard, practical realities of the lab, the shop, the books.

What gets shortchanged are the realities of the *market*. Consumers are unpredictable, varied, fickle, stupid, shortsighted, stubborn, and generally bothersome. This is not what the engineer-managers say, but deep down in their consciousness it is what they believe. And this accounts for their concentrating on what they know and what they can control, namely, product research, engineering, and production. The emphasis on production becomes particularly attractive when the product can be made at declining unit costs. There is no more inviting way of making money than by running the plant full blast.

Today the top-heavy science-engineering-production orientation of so many electronics companies works reasonably well because they are pushing into new frontiers in which the armed services have pioneered virtually assured markets. The companies are in the felicitous position of having to fill, not find markets; of not having to discover what the customer needs and wants, but of having the customer voluntarily come forward with specific new product demands. If a team of consultants had been assigned specifically to design a business situation calculated to prevent the emergence and development of a customer-oriented marketing viewpoint, it could not have produced anything better than the conditions just described.

Stepchild treatment: The oil industry is a stunning example of how science, technology, and mass production can divert an entire group of companies from their main task. To the extent the consumer is studied at all (which is not much), the focus is forever on getting information which is designed to help the oil companies improve what they are now doing. They try to discover more convincing advertising themes, more effective sales promotional drives, what the market shares of the various companies are, what people like or dislike about service station dealers and oil companies, and so forth. Nobody seems as interested in probing deeply into the basic human needs that the industry might be trying to satisfy as in probing into the basic properties of the raw material that the companies work with in trying to deliver customer satisfactions.

Basic questions about customers and markets seldom get asked. The latter occupy a stepchild status. They are recognized as existing, as having to be taken care of, but not worth very much real thought or dedicated attention. Nobody gets as excited about the customers in his own backyard as about the oil in the Sahara Desert. Nothing illustrates better the neglect of marketing than its treatment in the industry press.

The centennial issue of the *American Petroleum Institute Quarterly*, published in 1959 to celebrate the discovery of oil in Titusville, Pennsylvania, contained 21 feature articles proclaiming the industry's greatness. Only one of these talked about its achievements in marketing, and that was only a pictorial record of how service station architecture has changed. The issue also contained a special section on "New Horizons," which was devoted to showing the magnificent role oil would play in America's future. Every reference was ebulliently optimistic, never implying once that oil might have some hard competition. Even the reference to atomic energy was a cheerful catalogue of how oil would help make atomic energy a success. There was not a single apprehension that the oil industry's affluence might be threatened or a suggestion that one "new horizon" might include new and better ways of serving oil's present customers.

But the most revealing example of the stepchild treatment that marketing gets was still another special series of short articles on "The Revolutionary Potential of Electronics." Under that heading this list of articles appeared in the table of contents:

○
"In the Search for Oil"
○
"In Production Operations"
○
"In Refinery Processes"

○
"In Pipeline Operations"

Significantly, every one of the industry's major functional areas is listed, *except* marketing. Why? Either it is believed that electronics holds no revolutionary potential for petroleum marketing (which is palpably wrong), or the editors forgot to discuss marketing (which is more likely, and illustrates its stepchild status).

The order in which the four functional areas are listed also betrays the alienation of the oil industry from the consumer. The industry is implicitly defined as beginning with the search for oil and ending with its distribution from the refinery. But the truth is, it seems to me, that the industry begins with the needs of the customer for its products. From that primal position its definition moves steadily backstream to areas of progressively lesser importance, until it finally comes to rest at the "search for oil."

Beginning & end: The view that an industry is a customer-satisfying process, not a goods-producing process, is vital for all businessmen to understand. An industry begins with the customer and his needs, not with a patent, a raw material, or a selling skill. Given the customer's needs, the industry develops backwards, first concerning itself with the physical *delivery* of customer satisfactions. Then it moves back further to *creating* the things by which these satisfactions are in part achieved. How these materials are created is a matter of indifference to the customer, hence the particular form of manufacturing, processing, or what-have-you cannot be considered as a vital aspect of the industry. Finally, the industry moves back still further to *finding* the raw materials necessary for making its products.

The irony of some industries oriented toward technical research and development is that the scientists who occupy the high executive positions are totally unscientific when it comes to defining their companies' overall needs and purposes. They violate the first two rules of the scientific method —being aware of and defining their companies' problems, and then devel-

oping testable hypotheses about solving them. They are scientific only about the convenient things, such as laboratory and product experiments.

The reason that the customer (and the satisfaction of his deepest needs) is not considered as being "the problem" is not because there is any certain belief that no such problem exists, but because an organizational lifetime has conditioned management to look in the opposite direction. Marketing is a stepchild.

I do not mean that selling is ignored. Far from it. But selling, again, is not marketing. As already pointed out, selling concerns itself with the tricks and techniques of getting people to exchange their cash for your product. It is not concerned with the values that the exchange is all about. And it does not, as marketing invariably does, view the entire business process as consisting of a tightly integrated effort to discover, create, arouse, and satisfy customer needs. The customer is somebody "out there" who, with proper cunning, can be separated from his loose change.

Actually, not even selling gets much attention in some technologically minded firms. Because there is a virtually guaranteed market for the abundant flow of their new products, they do not actually know what a real market is. It is as if they lived in a planned economy, moving their products routinely from factory to retail outlet. Their successful concentration on products tends to convince them of the soundness of what they have been doing, and they fail to see the gathering clouds over the market.

Conclusion

Less than 75 years ago American railroads enjoyed a fierce loyalty among astute Wall Streeters. European monarchs invested in them heavily. Eternal wealth was thought to be the benediction for anybody who could scrape a few thousand dollars together to put into rail stocks. No other form of transportation could compete with the railroads in speed, flexibility, durability, economy, and growth potentials.

As Jacques Barzun put it, "By the turn of the century it was an institution, an image of man, a tradition, a code of honor, a source of poetry, a nursery of boyhood desires, a sublimest of toys, and the most solemn machine—next to the funeral hearse—that marks the epochs in man's life." [6]

Even after the advent of automobiles, trucks, and airplanes, the railroad tycoons remained imperturbably self-confident. If you had told them 60 years ago that in 30 years they would be flat on their backs, broke, and pleading for government subsidies, they would have thought you totally demented. Such a future was simply not considered possible. It was not even a discussable subject, or an askable question, or a matter which any sane person would consider worth speculating about. The very thought was insane. Yet a lot of insane notions now have matter-of-fact acceptance—for example, the idea of 100-ton tubes of metal moving smoothly through the air 20,000 feet above the earth, loaded with 100 sane and solid citizens casually drinking martinis—and they have dealt cruel blows to the railroads.

What specifically must other companies do to avoid this fate? What does customer orientation involve? These questions have in part been answered by the preceding examples and analysis. It would take another article to show in detail what is required for specific industries. In any case, it should be obvious that building an effective customer-oriented company involves far more than good intentions or promotional tricks; it involves profound matters of human organization and leadership. For the present, let me merely suggest what appear to be some general requirements.

Visceral feel of greatness: Obviously the company has to do what survival demands. It has to adapt to the requirements of the market, and it has to do it sooner rather than later. But mere survival is a so-so aspiration. Anybody can survive in some way or other, even the skid-row bum. The trick is to survive gallantly, to feel

the surging impulse of commercial mastery; not just to experience the sweet smell of success, but to have the visceral feel of entrepreneurial greatness.

No organization can achieve greatness without a vigorous leader who is driven onward by his own pulsating *will to succeed.* He has to have a vision of grandeur, a vision that can produce eager followers in vast numbers. In business, the followers are the customers.

In order to produce these customers, the entire corporation must be viewed as a customer-creating and customer-satisfying organism. Management must think of itself not as producing products but as providing customer-creating value satisfactions. It must push this idea (and everything it means and requires) into every nook and cranny of the organization. It has to do this continuously and with the kind of flair that excites and stimulates the people in it. Otherwise, the company will be merely a series of pigeonholed parts, with no consolidating sense of purpose or direction.

In short, the organization must learn to think of itself not as producing goods or services but as *buying customers,* as doing the things that will make people *want* to do business with it. And the chief executive himself has the inescapable responsibility for creating this environment, this viewpoint, this attitude, this aspiration. He himself must set the company's style, its direction, and its goals. This means he has to know precisely where he himself wants to go, and to make sure the whole organization is enthusiastically aware of where that is. This is a first requisite of leadership, for *unless he knows where he is going, any road will take him there.*

If any road is okay, the chief executive might as well pack his attaché case and go fishing. If an organization does not know or care where it is going, it does not need to advertise that fact with a ceremonial figurehead. Everybody will notice it soon enough.

Retrospective commentary

Amazed, finally, by his literary success, Isaac Bashevis Singer reconciled an attendant problem: "I think the moment you have published a book, it's not any more your private property. . . . If it has value, everybody can find in it what he finds, and I cannot tell the man I did not intend it to be so." Over the past 15 years, "Marketing Myopia" has become a case in point. Remarkably, the article spawned a legion of loyal partisans—not to mention a host of unlikely bedfellows.

Its most common and, I believe, most influential consequence is the way certain companies for the first time gave serious thought to the question of what businesses they are really in.

The strategic consequences of this have in many cases been dramatic. The best-known case, of course, is the shift in thinking of oneself as being in the "oil business" to being in the "energy business." In some instances the payoff has been spectacular (getting into coal, for example) and in others dreadful (in terms of the time and money spent so far on fuel cell research). Another successful example is a company with a large chain of retail shoe stores that redefined itself as a retailer of moderately priced, frequently purchased, widely assorted consumer specialty products. The result was a dramatic growth in volume, earnings, and return on assets.

Some companies, again for the first time, asked themselves whether they wished to be masters of certain technologies for which they would seek markets, or be masters of markets for which they would seek customer-satisfying products and services.

Choosing the former, one company has declared, in effect, "We are experts in glass technology. We intend to improve and expand that expertise with the object of creating products that will attract customers." This decision has forced the company into a much more systematic and customer-sensitive look at possible markets and users, even though its stated strategic object has been to capitalize on glass technology.

6. Jacques Barzun, "Trains and the Mind of Man," *Holiday,* February 1960, p. 20.

Deciding to concentrate on markets, another company has determined that "we want to help people (primarily women) enhance their beauty and sense of youthfulness." This company has expanded its line of cosmetic products, but has also entered the fields of proprietary drugs and vitamin supplements.

All these examples illustrate the "policy" results of "Marketing Myopia." On the operating level, there has been, I think, an extraordinary heightening of sensitivity to customers and consumers. R&D departments have cultivated a greater "external" orientation toward uses, users, and markets—balancing thereby the previously one-sided "internal" focus on materials and methods; upper management has realized that marketing and sales departments should be somewhat more willingly accommodated than before; finance departments have become more receptive to the legitimacy of budgets for market research and experimentation in marketing; and salesmen have been better trained to listen to and understand customer needs and problems, rather than merely to "push" the product.

A mirror, not a window

My impression is that the article has had more impact in industrial-products companies than in consumer-products companies—perhaps because the former had lagged most in customer orientation. There are at least two reasons for this lag: (1) industrial-products companies tend to be more capital intensive, and (2) in the past, at least, they have had to rely heavily on communicating face-to-face the technical character of what they made and sold. These points are worth explaining.

Capital-intensive businesses are understandably preoccupied with magnitudes, especially where the capital, once invested, cannot be easily moved, manipulated, or modified for the production of a variety of products—e.g., chemical plants, steel mills, airlines, and railroads. Understandably, they seek big volumes and operating efficiencies to pay off the equipment and meet the carrying costs.

At least one problem results: corporate power becomes disproportionately lodged with operating or financial executives. If you read the charter of one of the nation's largest companies, you will see that the chairman of the finance committee, not the chief executive officer, is the "chief." Executives with such backgrounds have an almost trained incapacity to see that getting "volume" may require understanding and serving many discrete and sometimes small market segments, rather than going after a perhaps mythical batch of big or homogeneous customers.

These executives also often fail to appreciate the competitive changes going on around them. They observe the changes, all right, but devalue their significance or underestimate their ability to nibble away at the company's markets.

Once dramatically alerted to the concept of segments, sectors, and customers, though, managers of capital-intensive businesses have become more responsive to the necessity of balancing their inescapable preoccupation with "paying the bills" or breaking even with the fact that the best way to accomplish this may be to pay more attention to segments, sectors, and customers.

The second reason industrial products companies have probably been more influenced by the article is that, in the case of the more technical industrial products or services, the necessity of clearly communicating product and service characteristics to prospects results in a lot of face-to-face "selling" effort. But precisely because the product is so complex, the situation produces salesmen who know the product more than they know the customer, who are more adept at explaining what they have and what it can do than learning what the customer's needs and problems are. The result has been a narrow product orientation rather than a liberating customer orientation, and "service" often suffered. To be sure, sellers said, "We have to provide service," but they tended to define service by looking into the mirror rather than out the window. They *thought* they were looking out the window at the customer, but it was

actually a mirror—a reflection of their own product-oriented biases rather than a reflection of their customers' situations.

A manifesto, not a prescription

Not everything has been rosy. A lot of bizarre things have happened as a result of the article:

☐
Some companies have developed what I call "marketing mania"—they've become obsessively responsive to every fleeting whim of the customer. Mass production operations have been converted to approximations of job shops, with cost and price consequences far exceeding the willingness of customers to buy the product.

☐
Management has expanded product lines and added new lines of business without first establishing adequate control systems to run more complex operations.

☐
Marketing staffs have suddenly and rapidly expanded themselves and their research budgets without either getting sufficient prior organizational support or, thereafter, producing sufficient results.

☐
Companies that are functionally organized have converted to product, brand, or market-based organizations with the expectation of instant and miraculous results. The outcome has been ambiguity, frustration, confusion, corporate infighting, losses, and finally a reversion to functional arrangements that only worsened the situation.

☐
Companies have attempted to "serve" customers by creating complex and beautifully efficient products or services that buyers are either too risk-averse to adopt or incapable of learning how to employ—in effect, there are now steam shovels for people who haven't yet learned to use spades. This problem has happened repeatedly in the so-called service industries (financial services, insurance, computer-based services) and with American companies selling in less-developed economies.

"Marketing Myopia" was not intended as analysis or even prescription; it was intended as manifesto. It did not pretend to take a balanced position. Nor was it a new idea—Peter F. Drucker, J.B. McKitterick, Wroe Alderson, John Howard, and Neil Borden had each done more original and balanced work on "the marketing concept." My scheme, however, tied marketing more closely to the inner orbit of business policy. Drucker—especially in *The Concept of the Corporation* and *The Practice of Management*—originally provided me with a great deal of insight.

My contribution, therefore, appears merely to have been a simple, brief, and useful way of communicating an existing way of thinking. I tried to do it in a very direct, but responsible, fashion, knowing that few readers (customers), especially managers and leaders, could stand much equivocation or hesitation. I also knew that the colorful and lightly documented affirmation works better than the tortuously reasoned explanation.

But why the enormous popularity of what was actually such a simple pre-existing idea? Why its appeal throughout the world to resolutely restrained scholars, implacably temperate managers, and high government officials, all accustomed to balanced and thoughtful calculation? Is it that concrete examples, joined to illustrate a simple idea and presented with some attention to literacy, communicate better than massive analytical reasoning that reads as though it were translated from the German? Is it that provocative assertions are more memorable and persuasive than restrained and balanced explanations, no matter who the audience? Is it that the character of the message is as much the message as its content? Or was mine not simply a different tune, but a new symphony? I don't know.

Of course, I'd do it again and in the same way, given my purposes, even with what more I now know—the good and the bad, the power of facts and the limits of rhetoric. If your mission is the moon, you don't use a car. Don Marquis's cockroach, Archy, provides some final consolation: "an idea is not responsible for who believes in it."

KING CUSTOMER

AT COMPANIES THAT LISTEN HARD AND RESPOND FAST, BOTTOM LINES THRIVE

Early one afternoon in late 1988, Premier Industrial Corp. got a call from the manager of a Caterpillar Inc. tractor plant in Decatur, Ill. A $10 electrical relay had broken down, idling an entire assembly line. A sales representative for Premier, a distributor of industrial parts, located a replacement at the company's Los Angeles warehouse and rushed it to a plane headed for St. Louis. By 10:30 that night, a Premier employee had delivered the part, and the line was up and running. "You can't build tractors if you can't move the line," says Vern Jourdan, a Caterpillar purchasing analyst. "They really saved us a whole lot of money."

Such service costs Premier a bundle, but it pays off. Premier can charge up to 50% more than competitors for every one of the 250,000 mundane industrial parts it stocks, and its return on equity was a healthy 27.8% on sales of $596 million in 1989. Says cofounder and Chairman Morton L. Mandel: "To us, customer service is the main event."

Like Mandel, lots of U.S. managers are talking about customer service these days. They figure that companies can score big gains in sales and profits by satisfying customers first. But Mandel and other managers aren't just talking about service with a smile and money-back guarantees. They're talking about organizing entire companies—from research to manufacturing, from information systems to pay incentives—around giving customers what they want. Say Roger A. Enrico, president of PepsiCo Worldwide Beverages: "If you are totally customer-focused and you deliver the services your customers want, everything else will follow."

JUST A FAD? Some zealous executives and management gurus have already labeled the 1990s the Decade of the Customer. Publishers are churning out books with such titles as *The Service Advantage* and *Customer Satisfaction Guaranteed*. Consulting firm McKinsey & Co. reports that its customer-service work has tripled in the past three years, and consultant Bain & Co. has developed a model for measuring the dollar-and-cents value of retaining customers through better service.

This sudden flare-up of enthusiasm suggests that "customer focus" could become just another boardroom fad with few long-term results. And many consumers would laugh at the idea that banks, car dealers, and airlines are offering better service. Even the champions of this new approach wonder if companies are really catching on to the idea. "More top managers are recognizing they have to be customer-focused," says James M. Hulbert, a marketing professor at Columbia Business School. "But they don't always recognize the way the organization has to change."

Still, many executives realize that they had better move from jargon to action. For encouragement, they point to American Express, Nordstrom, and American Airlines, which have built profits on a sophisticated appreciation of customer needs.

Paying attention to the customer isn't exactly a new concept. Back in the 1950s, General Motors Corp. helped write the book on consumer satisfaction by designing cars for every lifestyle and pocketbook. This was a breakthrough for an industry that had been largely driven by production needs ever since Henry Ford promised any color car as long as it was black. GM rode its insights into customers' needs to a 52% share of the U.S. car market in 1962.

But with a booming economy, a rising population, and virtually no foreign competition, many U.S. companies had it too easy. Through the 1960s and into the 1970s, many could sell just about anything they could produce. With customers seemingly satisfied, management concentrated on cutting production costs and making splashy acquisitions.

To manage these growing behemoths, chief executives turned to strategic planners for help. The MBAs helped create centralized bureaucracies that focused on winning market share—not on getting in touch with remote customers. "Markets came to be defined as aggregations of competitors, not customers," says Frederick E. Webster Jr., a marketing professor at Dartmouth College's Amos Tuck School of Business Administration. Later, the wave of hostile takeovers forced managers to placate Wall Street with short-term results, and customers came to matter even less.

TO THE RESCUE. The Japanese were the first to recognize the problem. In the 1970s, they started to rescue customers from their limbo of so-so merchandise and take-it-or-leave-it service. They built loyalty in the U.S. by assiduously uncovering and accommodating customer needs. In 1973, for example, Toyota Motor Corp. opened a design center in Southern California to fine-tune its cars for American tastes. In Palo Alto, Sony Corp.'s Video Technology Center developed a new approach to editing videotape for CBS that cost much less than competing systems. Sony's innovation won it an Emmy award.

When American companies saw former customers driving Toyotas stacked with Panasonic boxes, it dawned on them that it might be time to change their ways. Ford Motor Co. was one of the companies most hurt by Japanese competition. In 1980, its U.S. market shared had plummeted to 17.2% from 23.5% in 1978. But Ford has benefited from following Japan's lead. Says Chairman Donald E. Petersen: "If we aren't customer-driven, our cars won't be, either."

With the chairman adamant about the need to listen to customers, other Ford employees had to take it seriously

as well. Ray A. Ablondi Jr., Ford's recently retired head of customer research, convened a focus group of car buyers in California in 1980. At that session, he recalls, "the general feeling was we had let them down." Even worse, "people of college age said, 'I don't own a Ford. I don't know anybody who owns a Ford. I have never been in a Ford.' "

EARLY RESULTS. The news shook Ford into action. To develop the Taurus and Sable models, design engineers invited more consumers than ever before to evaluate prototypes. One result: When consumers complained that they were scuffing their shoes because the rear seats lacked foot room, Ford sloped the floor underneath the front seats, widened the space between the seat-adjustment tracks, and made the tracks out of smooth plastic instead of metal. Buyers have rewarded Ford for such efforts by making it the best-selling nameplate in California for the past five years.

Now, Ford surveys some 2.5 million customers a year and regularly invites owners to meet engineers and dealers to discuss quality problems. It has also designed a software system that makes it easier for executives and engineers to use customer-satisfaction data. One example of Ford's greater responsiveness: Even though Chairman Petersen and Design Vice-President John J. Telnack wanted to ditch the boxy Lincoln Town Car in the mid-1980s, the company kept the sedan after surveys showed that older drivers still love it. In January, the revamped Town Car won *Motor Trend* magazine's Car of the Year award.

Ford still has a way to go, though. While it takes the Japanese four years to design and launch a new car, the Taurus will have been on the road 10 years before a new model is introduced that incorporates additional consumer input. And Ford's customer follow-through still doesn't match Nissan's. Every customer who buys or services a vehicle at a Nissan Motor Corp. dealership gets a call from an outside research firm to see how they were treated.

Ford's decade-long effort shows how tough it is to transform a company into an operation obsessed with pleasing customers at every stage. Hyatt President Thomas J. Pritzker says there's a

fallacy that customer service can just be turned on: "Management has to set a tone and then constantly push, push, push."

A lot of U.S. executives may have no choice about making the effort. Demand for many consumer products is growing at only the same slow rate as the population. And technological advances have resulted in a slew of products of similar quality, which makes it tough for companies to stand out, while price competition has resulted in margin-killing battles for market share.

Creative changes in service can make the difference. Extra service enables Armstrong World Industries Inc. to charge higher prices for floor tiles and Weyerhaeuser Co.'s wood-products division to command premiums for its commodity two-by-fours. Weyerhaeuser enhanced its service by developing a computer system for retail home centers and lumber yards so buyers can custom-design decks and shelving. "There's hard evidence that perceived-service firms can charge 10% more for their products than competitors," says Michelle A. Yakovac, a manager of quality positioning at GTE Telephone Operations Inc., which markets local phone service in 31 states.

Since the mid-1980s, the top managers of Du Pont Co. have been trying to better adapt the company's technological achievements to customer needs. According to Du Pont Chairman Edgar S. Woolard Jr., the biggest problem has been getting researchers and manufacturing employees to think more about customers as they develop new materials. One of Woolard's policies: having Du Pont technicians spend more time in customers' plants to figure out new applications for Du Pont products. That sounds like a simple idea, but it took Du Pont a long time to get it. As a result, says David M. McAndrews, director of industrial polymers, "we were walking away from a lot of business."

NEW SHOES. Du Pont's efforts paid off at Reebok International Ltd. Until late 1987, Du Pont just sold adhesives to the shoe industry. Then, a Du Pont salesman in Korea asked Reebok officials how Du Pont could help them further. The result: Du Pont polymer technicians incorporated flexible plastic tubes developed for the auto industry into the soles of Reebok's new ERS lines. The tubes give the sneakers more bounce, and the success of the ERS lines helped Reebok's 1989 net earnings rebound by 27% after a 17% decline in 1988. "[Du Pont] helped us in amazing ways," says Paul Litchfield, Reebok's advanced-technologies manager.

Some smaller companies with fewer management layers are finding that personal relationships between senior executives and customers can help, too. Detroit Diesel Corp., a maker of truck engines, lost money for years as a division of General Motors. Then, in 1987, former race-car driver Roger S. Penske bought a majority stake. Penske, a former Detroit Diesel distributor and a customer through his truck-leasing business, requires all managers and distributors to call or visit four customers a day. He also invited employees from some 40 independent distributorships to visit Detroit Diesel's new warehouse in Canton, Ohio. These customers suggested 250 changes that helped the warehouse cut delivery time for engine parts from five days to three. Emergency orders take less than 24 hours. Now, Detroit Diesel makes money—$21 million in operating profits last year on $971 million in sales. Market share for heavy-duty truck engines has gone from 3% in 1987 to nearly 6% in 1989.

NITTY-GRITTY. Smaller companies can also be nimbler at applying technologies that help customers. Everex Systems Inc., a 1983 startup in Fremont, Calif., sells its personal computers to wholesalers and dealers through a system it calls Zero Response Time. Phone orders are reviewed every two hours so the factory can adjust assembly to match demand. "It has worked out well," says Paul D. Zoerb, president of Micro Strategies Inc., a computer dealer in Alameda, Calif. "I can be very responsive to my customers, and I don't have to have cash tied up in inventory," Everex's profits more than doubled in the year ended July, 1989, to $21.25 million, on a 41% sales increase, to $377.3 million.

A successful policy of customer focus has to start with a strong commitment from top executives. But for all the inspirational work by CEOs, the nitty-gritty of satisfying customers often falls to sales clerks and factory workers.

Marriott Corp., for one, knows that workers who deal directly with customers can make or break a marketing program. For years, Marriott's room-service business didn't live up to its potential. But after initiating a 15-minute-delivery guarantee for breakfast in 1985, Marriott's breakfast business—the biggest portion of its room-service revenue—jumped 25%. Marriott got employees to devise better ways to deliver the meals on time, including having deliverers carry walkie-talkies so they can receive instructions more quickly.

To learn more about service, executives are putting in stints at the front lines. At Xerox Corp., executives spend one day a month taking complaints from customers about machines, bills, and service. At Hyatt hotels, senior executives—including President Pritzker—put in time as bellhops.

A more substantive change than dressing executives in uniforms is to give employees power to solve customer problems on the spot. Montgomery Ward Chairman Bernard F. Brennan has authorized 7,700 sales clerks to approve checks and handle merchandise-return problems—functions that once were reserved for store managers. "Customers would get frustrated when the manager wasn't around," says Brennan.

To reward good service, Montgomery Ward and other companies are linking performance reviews and bonuses to customer-satisfaction rating. Until 1987, GTE Telephone Operations in Irving, Tex., a $12.5 billion unit of GTE Corp., gave customer-satisfaction and quality measurements only a 15% weighting in compensation evaluations for managers. GTE has since boosted the customer-service weighting to 35%.

As the gospel of customer focus spreads, more companies will try to convince employees, investors, and themselves that the customer really does come first. That doesn't mean everything will go smoothly, though. Nordstrom Inc. has a great reputation for service, but it has recently agreed to pay millions to employees who claim they were overworked. And many store owners are talking customer focus without following through. Consultant Carol A. Farmer believes

many retailers say to themselves: "Of course we want to give better service—but not if it costs us anything," In Farmer's opinion, "putting a piano player in the atrium because it works for Nordstrom and putting a senior-citizen greeter at the front door because it works for Wal-Mart" is not the answer.

COMPROMISE. Indeed, many retailers still don't seem to have a good grasp of their customers' needs. Sears, Roebuck & Co., which has been struggling to reverse the sagging fortunes of its 850-store merchandising group, doesn't honor any credit cards but its own. Management argues that outside credit cards don't generate enough business. That sounds reasonable, but it's not convenient for Sears customers. In February, recognizing that it might be losing business from holders of Visa, MasterCard, and American Express cards, Sears compromised. As of Mar. 1, those customers can receive on-the-spot approval for a Sears charge card.

Promising customers more than a company can deliver can be disastrous, too. Florida Power & Light Co., which had been selling itself as a master of quality control for the better part of the 1980s, incurred the wrath of consumers last Christmas when it failed to supply enough power during a statewide freeze. "When I start pumping up people's service expectations and don't deliver, I end up giving worse service than if I had never said anything at all," says venture capitalist William H. Davidow, co-author of *Total Customer Service.*

Leading Edge Products Inc. learned that lesson the hard way. The maker of IBM PC clones, which was plucked out of Chapter 11 last November by Daewoo Telecom Co., was the one to beat several years ago. Besides low price, the company offered a 15-month guarantee—12 months more than the competition. But after an ill-conceived diversification drained cash and management attention, it couldn't fill orders. And when its machines acted up, consumers couldn't get help. Leading Edge "was a victim of their own marketing success," says Robert Orbach, director of business development at 47th Street Photo in New York. "They couldn't live up to the expectations they set."

COSTLY MISTAKES. As the battle for happy customers heats up, even companies renowned for their service will struggle. IBM is desperately trying to stay on top of its customers' needs in an era of global competition. One way it is doing this is through new working partnerships with customers. The company recently teamed up with Shearson Lehman Hutton Inc., for instance, to design software that speeds overnight processing of stock trades. But with the market full of rivals that can design sophisticated systems for clients, IBM has yet to make its new customer focus pay off in renewed profit growth.

Mail-order guru L.L. Bean Inc. is another example of the mistakes even a customer-focused company can make. In 1988, dissatisfied customers returned $82 million worth of goods. That represented 14% of Bean's total sales—and $2 million in return freight charges.

In response, the company scaled back its annual revenue-growth plans to around 5% from 25%. Then, since about 65% of the returns involved wrong sizes, employees recommended updating the size information in catalogs and in order-takers' computers. Bean is also retraining 3,200 employees in techniques that boost customer service and quality.

It seems so simple. Businesses exist to serve customers and should bend over backward to satisfy their needs. But too many companies still don't get it. And in the 1990s, more customers are likely to take the opportunity to reward the ones that do.

By Stephen Phillips in Cleveland and Amy Dunkin in New York, with James B. Treece in Detroit, Keith H. Hammonds in Boston, and bureau reports

Service = Survival

Special attention is the hallmark at Draeger's, a Menlo Park, Calif., grocery store. Here, Richard Draeger, center, a son of the founder, oversees the packing of a customer's *purchases. The store combines the convenience of a modern supermarket with old-fashioned touches such as letting regular customers charge their purchases.*

Joan C. Szabo

Demands of American consumers for high-quality service are higher than ever, and businesses that ignore the new realities of customer satisfaction can jeopardize not only their future sales but also their very survival.

Service has achieved this critical importance in today's complex economy because of factors that include contemporary lifestyles, technology's impact on consumer products, and even global

Free-lance writers Ellen Mansoor Collier, in Houston, and Sylvia Blishak, in Menlo Park, Calif., contributed to this article.

trade. Those factors affect service levels in different ways:

Lifestyles. Married couples that have both work and family responsibilities want hassle-free shopping. Don Shapiro of First Concepts Development Corp., a Burbank, Calif., management-consulting firm in the fields of customer satisfaction and employee motivation, says: "People are working longer but doing more. They want to spend more time with their children, they want to exercise, they want to pursue recreation and culture. They have less free time, and they are more consciously aware of how that time is used. They don't want to use it trying to solve problems with stores and other places where they

spend their money. Their expectations for quality and service have risen dramatically."

Technology. The increased complexities and the widening choices among today's technology-based products and services—many utilizing advanced electronics—make consumers less able to evaluate options, says Warren Blanding, founder and chairman of the Customer Service Institute, an educational and training organization in Silver Spring, Md. "Most buyers don't have the technical knowledge necessary to identify the best choice in such products as electronic equipment, motor vehicles, or office machines," Blanding says. "So they want reassurance that support and service will be available if problems arise." He offers this maxim: "Service is the product."

Trends In Global Trade. As foreign companies launch or acquire U.S. subsidiaries in the retail, hotel, food, and other industries, they introduce service standards that make them tough competitors for American firms. Karl Albrecht, a management consultant and author of *At America's Service*, says, "American service industries of all kinds are ripe for invasion." He cites a leading example: "The Japanese have shown that they can focus resources and talent on virtually any industry they choose. So far, they have chosen mostly manufacturing industries. But now they are moving aggressively into banking and financial services. . . . They are nibbling away at the retail sector and the hotel industry, and we can expect them soon in the restaurant business. . . . The Japanese cultural penchant for catering to the individual in a courteous and deferential way . . . is legendary."

The increasing importance of rising expectations among customers has special implications for small businesses. "Providing top-notch service is the only inexpensive way small companies have

Recognizing the growing demand for customer satisfaction can boost a small business above the ranks of its competitors; ignoring it can jeopardize a company's future.

to really distinguish themselves from their competitors and lift themselves above the pack," says John Tschohl, a customer-service expert and president of the Better Than Money Corp., a Bloomington, Minn., consulting firm. He also points out that the challenge is greater for small businesses: "Customers expect small firms to be closer to them and to deliver better service."

Companies that lose customers because they have not recognized changing consumer attitudes on quality service will pay a high price. The American Management Association says that 65 percent of the average company's business comes from its present, satisfied customers. The Customer Service Institute estimates that it costs five times as much to acquire a new customer as it costs to service an existing one.

CSI's research also shows that a business that each day for a year loses just one customer spending $50 a week will find its sales reduced by $949,000 for the following year. The toll is higher, of course, for the loss of higher-spending customers. (See the chart.)

There's also the danger of a multiplier effect. The Technical Assistance Research Programs Institute (TARP), a research firm in Washington, says its studies indicate that 91 percent of unhappy customers will never again buy from the offending company and will let their dissatisfaction be known to at least nine other people.

But the multiplier effect can have positive results. Ron Zemke of Minneapolis, a consultant and author on customer service, writes: "Research shows that companies that hit on winning service formulas are profitable, grow in market share, and inspire a lot of highly positive word-of-mouth commentary among the people they satisfy."

In his latest book, *The Service Edge: 101 Companies That Profit From Customer Care* (NAL Books, New York), Zemke says: "Today's consumers are willing to pay a premium to have their basic needs met in a timely and efficient manner, and they'll be pleasantly surprised if they're treated with a little dignity and respect in the bargain."

And how does a business reach such levels of customer satisfaction? The principal avenues are aggressive efforts to determine customers' wants and needs, a staff trained and motivated to deliver on those wishes, and active follow-up that includes efforts to obtain customers' appraisals of service quality.

Draeger's, a grocery store in Menlo Park, Calif., is an example of a business with a growing base of customers willing to pay extra for top service. The store enjoyed a 57 percent growth in sales over the past three years by combining the convenience of a modern supermarket with old-fashioned service. Even though its prices are higher than those of its competitors, Draeger's continues to expand its customer base.

Owner Frank Draeger says the key to his successful operation is "taking the drudgery out of shopping" by responding to needs expressed by its customers. The store has a gourmet delicatessen, an old-fashioned butcher shop, a flower stand, an imported-foods section, and racks of upscale wines.

In addition, Draeger's packs box lunches for customers on their way to events such as San Francisco Giants baseball games or Stanford University football games. The store also sells prepared meals that customers can pick up after work and reheat at home. What's more, Draeger's not only sells party supplies but also offers the services of a party coordinator to help busy customers put the supplies to best use.

Customer loyalty extends beyond the store's Menlo Park shopping area. Draeger's fans across the country regularly send in their orders for meat, fruit baskets, cheeses, and wines.

A decidedly old-fashioned touch at Draeger's is the system of letting customers pay later for their purchases. A regular customer who arrives in the checkout line without cash or a checkbook, for example, can charge the cost of the groceries—no credit application required—and expect an invoice in a few days requesting payment within 30 days. The store also has its own credit card—which does require a credit application—and statements are sent monthly.

Draeger says the store maintains its reputation for service through its selection of managers: "If a manager doesn't have the inner conviction about excellent service, we find that we can't always instill it—so we have to choose service-minded people."

In following up on their pledges to provide excellent service, some businesses have developed powerful incentives. Norrell Temporary Services, in Atlanta, promises clients that they don't have to pay if they are disappointed with the performance of Norrell's temporary employees. Moreover, that commitment holds even if the reason for the dissatisfaction does not surface for several weeks. Bea Ruffin, Norrell's vice president of marketing, says

What Customers Look For

In a research project on quality service, the Marketing Science Institute of Cambridge, Mass., asked customers of a wide range of service businesses, such as banking and appliance repair, what factors they considered most important in assuring their satisfaction with a product or a service.

The researchers found that these were the most important characteristics of quality service from the customers' viewpoints:

● **Reliability.** It topped the list of what customers expect of quality service. They want companies to perform the desired service dependably, accurately, and consistently. A major source of customer dissatisfaction is an unkept promise. Don't make promises you can't keep.

● **Responsiveness.** Companies should be helpful and provide prompt service. A business that answers or responds to telephone calls quickly meets this expectation.

● **Assurance.** A company's employees should be knowledgeable and courteous, customers say, and should convey confidence in the service they provide.

● **Empathy.** Customers want companies to provide individualized attention and to listen to them.

● **Tangibles.** Physical facilities and equipment should be attractive and clean, and employees should be well-groomed.

that the promise of satisfaction is one of the reasons that "our rate of sales growth in the last five years has outstripped the average rate of growth for the temporary-employment industry as a whole."

The Visible Changes chain of hair salons, based in Houston, opened its doors with a strong commitment to quality service already in place. "We gave away haircuts for six weeks," says John McCormack, cofounder of the chain, "not because our hairdressers couldn't cut hair or because they weren't experienced, but because we felt the haircuts weren't up to our quality standards." Then, when quality reached the required level, customers willingly paid $15, and Visible Changes was on its way to success.

John and Maryanne McCormack, who are husband and wife as well as business partners, now own 16 Visible Changes salons with a total gross of $20 million a year, and their accomplishment spotlights the "people" factor in providing customer satisfaction. "The first step is setting standards," John McCormack says. "Then make sure everyone in the company understands those standards. Finally, reward people for achieving your standards and goals. If you reward your associates for superior performance, then your customers are going to get the service you ultimately wish to deliver."

The company holds motivational classes designed to build employees' service-oriented attitudes and enhance their confidence. In addition to six weeks of training, stylists take 12 advanced classes a year.

Complaints are recorded and reviewed by the individual salon managers. An employee named in three or more complaints within two weeks must meet with John McCormack at corporate headquarters in Houston. "Usually it's a personal problem," he says. "I give them time off to work things out."

A system of incentives and rewards is designed to make the stylists employed at Visible Changes feel and act like entrepreneurs, each with his or her own clientele. Those whose services are requested by repeat customers receive extra rewards. A stylist who doesn't achieve a 65 percent request rate within six months is asked to leave the firm.

McCormack describes the people factor this way: "If you take care of your employees, they will take care of your customers. There is not one company in America that has a problem as long as they have happy employees. If you don't have your people on your side, how can they help your business succeed?"

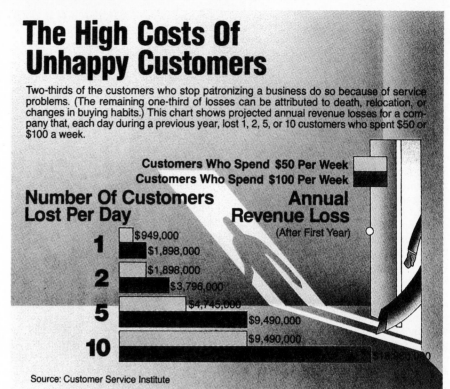

The High Costs Of Unhappy Customers

Two-thirds of the customers who stop patronizing a business do so because of service problems. (The remaining one-third of losses can be attributed to death, relocation, or changes in buying habits.) This chart shows projected annual revenue losses for a company that, each day during a previous year, lost 1, 2, 5, or 10 customers who spent $50 or $100 a week.

Customers Who Spend $50 Per Week
Customers Who Spend $100 Per Week

Number Of Customers Lost Per Day

Annual Revenue Loss (After First Year)

	Customers Who Spend $50 Per Week	Customers Who Spend $100 Per Week
1	$949,000	$1,898,000
2	$1,898,000	$3,796,000
5	$4,745,000	$9,490,000
10	$9,490,000	

Source: Customer Service Institute

CHART: DALE GLASGOW

Karl Albrecht, writing in *At America's Service*, describes the employees' role this way: "Firms that embrace a customer-service philosophy see their organization as an inverted pyramid. Who's on top? Customers, of course. Every facet of the company is dedicated to supporting them and ensuring that their needs, expectations, and problems are dealt with satisfactorily.

"Next come supervisors, middle managers, and, finally—at the bottom—senior executives. This organization scheme, when implemented successfully, makes each level of management support the next, and everybody supports the customer."

Unfortunately, he adds, too many companies limit their service-improvement programs to "let's round up the employees and make them better people by giving them smile training."

Mini Maid Services, with franchises in 24 states, demonstrates the effectiveness of one of the most critical elements of quality service—the follow-up. Leone Ackerly, president and chief executive officer, reports that every customer is contacted the day after receiving service, and all comments, whether favorable or unfavorable, are recorded. This information is fed back to the employees who performed the service. "We're very quick to compliment and rarely criticize," Ackerly says.

Strong personal involvement by top management is also a critical factor in developing service-oriented attitudes among employees. "I motivate by example," Ackerly says. "Our Mini Maids and team leaders all know that the CEO knows what she's talking about—she's done it herself. Service quality starts with me and goes down to each franchisee and Mini Maid."

When he founded University National Bank & Trust Co. in Palo Alto, Calif., Chairman Carl Schmitt said he wanted to create an institution that provided customers with a high level of personal attention. The bank performs services such as sending messengers to pick up deposits, arranging after-hours appointments for business managers too busy to get to the bank during regular hours, free shoe shines for customers, and notifying customers of overdrafts instead of bouncing their checks and imposing penalties.

To maintain its service-based operation, the bank looks for experienced employees and uses its entire staff as recruiters. Says Vice President Ann Sonnenberg: "Existing employees get a referral fee for introducing successful new hires—people they may have worked with elsewhere who were outstanding. Our goal is to hire genuinely nice people who are very capable and enjoy helping others."

An unusual way of building team spirit is the monthly Statement Day. Chairman Schmitt explains: "Everybody, including me, gathers on the third floor of the bank on the first day of the month to stuff statements into envelopes. This makes it possible to provide our customers with a special service—a statement arriving by mail on the second or third of the month. And it gives us a feeling of teamwork."

And in accord with the experts' contention that outstanding service improves a company's bottom line, University Bank reports that its return-on-assets ratio is 75 percent higher than the state average.

Service-oriented companies such as University Bank recognize an aspect of service that many firms overlook. As Warren Blanding of the Customer Service Institute points out, it is important to realize that customer service is an investment in future sales: "The current sale has already been made. You have convinced the customer to come into your shop or office and buy your product or service. But the way that first transaction is handled is the key to future business. One of the biggest single problems in customer service is the reluctance of managers to look on customer service as a marketing strategy. Too many see it as an after-sale service, something relating back to the previous sale rather than ahead to the next one.

"The customer makes a decision on the quality of service on the basis of the actions of the person handling the transaction, but that person often cannot control the level of service. When a customer sees a long line at a check-out stand and returns the product to the shelf rather than waiting to buy it, that's not the cashier's fault; that's inept management control of resources.

"If a manager gets a complaint that a service giver had alienated a customer through poor performance or even impoliteness, the first question that manager should ask is whether that service giver has been provided with the necessary resources to keep customers satisfied."

Managers also must realize that from the customer viewpoint, perhaps dozens of things can go wrong—from improper recording at the outset to late delivery on the other end. And a single mistake can alienate a customer. Blanding urges businesses to remember that "the missing link" in service is usually "the customer point of view." Think about it this way, he advises: "The secret of good service is to do things for a customer the way that customer would do them if given the opportunity."

Don Shapiro of First Concepts Development Corp. says that a business that is determined to improve service standards must begin with a firm commitment not only to achieve a much higher level of customer satisfaction but also

---

A Scorecard For Service

Customers of Wendy's, the fast-food chain, receive a scorecard on which they can evaluate the service they have received. The points covered, slightly modified for general use, can work as a good guide for any small business that wants to audit its own service or survey its own customers.

The scorecard asks, "How would you rate us?" The rating scale ranges from 5 for excellent to 1 for poor.

The scorecard covers these points:

- Your overall experience on this occasion
- Quality
- Value for money
- Accuracy of order (inside)
- Accuracy of order (pickup)
- Service (courtesy, helpfulness, appearance)
- Greeting
- Speed of service
- Comfort and atmosphere
- Cleanliness

The final question asks how many times the customer has been in a Wendy's in the past month. The rating card also tells customers that if they are not satisfied after bringing any matter to the attention of a local manager, they are invited to telephone company President Ron Kirstien.

---

to "consistently deliver this level of satisfaction even if it means lower profits in the short run."

Shapiro, who founded his company after working in restaurant, retail, and manufacturing jobs, tells business owners that achieving and maintaining a high level of customer satisfaction is related to "everything that everyone does in your organization. Every department, every function—management and nonmanagement, from the janitor to the chief executive officer—affects the customer decision on where to buy.

"One of the first recommendations I make to clients is that every employee spend time with customers every year—maybe a day and a half as a rule, but longer for higher-ups.

"Customer contact can make a big change in attitudes. Take the example of a sales representative who files an order, only to be told by the warehouse manager that it can't be filled the way

---

the customer wants it. The sales rep should be able to instruct the manager: 'You tell the customer, eyeball-to-eyeball, that you can't do it.' An amazing thing happens when you do that. The manager starts seeing his function through the eyes of the customer, who sees the world a lot differently than the seller. It opens up a whole new world of reality."

Shapiro has this warning to businesses eager to improve customer satisfaction: "Examine your service policies to see if they are based on the actions of your problem customers, probably 1 percent of your total, who commit abuses and dishonest acts, or are they based on the actions of the 99-plus percent who are good, honest people?"

Some stores generate enormous customer good will by accepting returned merchandise with no questions asked, he says, even if the store knows, for example, that the daughter of the woman bringing back an evening gown wore it to her high-school prom over the weekend. Other stores, Shapiro says, will make it as difficult as possible for a customer to return something. "Now which of these stores is more likely to win customer loyalty?" he asks.

Paul Hawken of Smith & Hawken, a mail-order house with a nationwide clientele for its garden tools, says a liberal return policy is more than a matter of good will; it's a measure of a company's confidence in its own products.

He points out in his book *Growing A Firm* that his company allows a customer to return "any product, anytime, for any reason—or no reason." Hawken says: "The most frugal thing we can do is be certain our products are of the highest quality. If it should cost us so much to replace products that we have to go out of business, then we should go out of business. A no-holds-barred return policy is the litmus test for quality."

Shapiro agrees with Blanding and other experts that one of the most critical areas is follow-up. That means not only prompt, effective service when a customer has a problem with a new product or service, Shapiro says, but also such things as routine calls to determine whether the customer is satisfied. "The customer expects the worst," he says. "Anything a business does of a positive nature to follow up on a sale exceeds customer expectations and is a strong plus for a business. Don't wait for problems to develop."

And don't assume that the absence of complaints means customers are satisfied; in fact, a business receiving few or no complaints courts trouble if it finds that situation reassuring. Albrecht warns: "A lot of research shows that most people don't complain. So you may have a very large dissatisfaction index and totally miss it if you don't engage in active investigation."

John Goodman, president of TARP, the Washington research firm, encourages businesses to set up feedback channels that include a toll-free, 800 telephone number. "It is very low-risk," he says. "If you don't get many calls, then you don't incur very much cost. And we find that each minute you spend on one of these calls is probably going to more than pay for itself in terms of enhanced profits and sales."

A recent TARP study, he reports, showed that 54 to 70 percent of customers who complain will do business with the target company again if the complaint is resolved satisfactorily. When customers felt there was a rapid resolution, the figure soars to 95 percent.

Sometimes, listening to customers can trigger massive changes in an organization. BellSouth Corp. was reacting to customer input when it decided in 1985 to try to recombine its business services and its equipment sales and maintenance operations, which had been scattered into separate subsidiaries as part of the original Bell System divestiture plan.

The Atlanta-based telecommunications company found that customers were confused and irritated because they had to deal with different organizations for each different need. Many wanted to go back to the old days, before the court-ordered break-up, when business customers could handle everything with one call to the telephone operating company.

That, essentially, is what BellSouth has done, with the Federal Communications Commission's permission. On Jan. 1, it restored "one-stop shopping" for business customers, becoming the first of the Bell companies to recombine its services and equipment sales and maintenance staff completely under the FCC's new rules. "We took this step because customers have told us time and again over the past five years that this is what they wanted," says Jere Drummond, senior vice president-marketing for BellSouth.

BellSouth's decision to reintegrate, which took four years to implement, was an outgrowth of what the company calls its "Customer First" strategy. That strategy includes almost continual measurements of the satisfaction levels of the large, midsized, and small businesses and the residential customers it serves within its nine-state area.

Major customers are contacted in person or by mail every year. Some 2,000 midsized and small businesses are surveyed randomly each month. Still another survey, called the Telephone Service Attitude Measurement, tells the company each month what's on the minds of some 35,000 residential and business users with one or two telephone lines.

"We promise customers that we will do everything possible to provide faultless service and to stand behind the service we provide," explains Drummond. "We judge our performance by their standards, and one of those standards is being easy to do business with."

Companies of all sizes are adopting a similar philosophy, consultant Ron Zemke says, and the service situation throughout American business can be summed up this way: "Today more and more organizations than ever before have taken up the challenge of providing superior service to their customers. They are listening, responding, and taking new, even novel approaches to creating and managing high-quality service.... Granted, the battle to eradicate mundane, lackadaisical, ineffective service is far from over. But we are finally getting a handle on how it should be waged."

HOW TO HANDLE CUSTOMERS' GRIPES

Complainers can shoot down a company faster than you can say "I'm sorry." But GE, Coca-Cola, Johnson & Johnson, and others are turning them into loyal buyers.

Patricia Sellers

FRED JEROME survived a frequent flier's nightmare. Boarding a 9:30 Pan Am shuttle in New York one morning, he expected to arrive in Boston in plenty of time for a full afternoon of business meetings. However, Logan Airport was blanketed in fog and the pilot circled for two hours before landing in Hartford, Connecticut, to refuel.

"No one will be permitted to leave the plane," the pilot announced, frustrating passengers who wished to switch to a rental car or use a telephone. When the pilot said he was returning to LaGuardia, some rose in fury, yelling, "You can't do that! I've got to get to Boston!" He relented and finally landed in Boston about 4 P.M. Jerome caught a flight home and arrived in New York at 6:30 P.M. His day was shot and he was steamed.

What should a company do for angry customers? According to those who have tackled the issue: just about anything it can. Studies show customers tell twice as many people about bad experiences as good ones, so complainers left unhappy can send a company's image crashing. Simply listening to complaints tremendously boosts brand loyalty—that is, a customer's tendency to buy again (see chart). "The key is getting customers to complain to the company," says John Goodman, president of Technical Assistance Research Programs, a Washington, D.C., consulting firm that has been studying corporate complainers for the past decade.

The firm used buying patterns, profit margins, and dozens of other factors to develop an economic model that calculates the return on company dollars invested in units that handle complaints and inquiries. The average return for makers of consumer durables like washing machines and refrigerators is 100%. In other words, if manufacturers spend $1 million, they get $2 million in benefits. For banks it is as much as 170%. The payoff can be even higher in retailing, where top-quality service is essential for keeping customers. Maryanne Rasmussen, vice president of worldwide quality at American Express, says, "The formula I use is: Better complaint handling equals higher customer satisfaction equals higher brand loyalty equals higher profitability."

THE GROWING EVIDENCE that customer happiness shows up on the bottom line is one reason such companies as GE, Coca-Cola, and British Airways are investing millions of dollars to improve complaint handling. Programs include toll-free 800-number telephone systems, intensive staff training, liberal refund policies, and even booths where irate customers can vent their anger—on videotape. The challenge of these damage-control techniques: to turn a company critic into a loyal supporter.

Pan Am's response to Fred Jerome was a case study of how *not* to handle complaints. At the end of Jerome's nine-hour odyssey, a Pan Am representative advised him to complain to the customer service department at the airline's New York headquarters. Jerome, executive vice president of the Scientists' Institute for Public Information, a nonprofit group that assists journalists, went to the headquarters only to be told

that Pan Am's LaGuardia Airport office handles complaints about the shuttle. The first person he tried to contact at the airport didn't return his call. He finally reached a representative who told him in a computer-like tone: "We are not responsible for delays caused by the weather."

Jerome, 49, expressed his frustration by writing a column entitled "Hijacked to Hartford" for the New York *Times*. The piece drew some 20 letters and calls from other annoyed air travelers. John M. Siefert, a vice president of the Eastern Air Lines shuttle, sent Jerome a sympathy letter, offering him a free New York–Boston flight. Jerome declined. "I would have been happy with an apology from Pan Am," he says. Pan Am says it wrote to Jerome. He says he still has not heard from the airline and now will fly the Pan Am shuttle only as a last resort.

In the airline industry, the correlation between customer contentment and profitability is strong. The U.S. Department of Transportation received 44,845 complaints last year, more than three times the number for 1986 (flight delays and cancellations are No. 1). The grievances that get to Transportation come mostly from travelers who turn to the government because they are dissatisfied with the airlines' responses. Continental, Eastern, and Pan Am, which lost a combined total of $714.4 million in 1987, often rank near the top of the Transportation Department's monthly tallies of airlines that attract the most consumer complaints (see table). Relatively few gripes come from fliers on American, Delta, and Piedmont, which happen to be among the healthiest U.S. airlines. Dan Smith, direc-

REPORTER ASSOCIATE *Karen Nickel*

tor of consumer and industry affairs at the International Airline Passengers Association in Dallas, says these carriers satisfy unhappy customers by "giving a full explanation if they can't comply with a request."

British Airways is flying high partly because of Chief Executive Sir Colin Marshall's fixation with customer service. Marshall, 54, spent his early career as a steward on a cruise ship. Since taking charge at British Airways four years ago, he has tried to give unhappy passengers royal treatment—or at least the chance to complain. In London, disgruntled travelers can tape their grievances as soon as they get off

UNHAPPY CUSTOMERS WHO BUY AGAIN

54% Complaint resolved

19% Complaint not resolved

9% Complaint not made

the plane in the airline's new Video Point booths. Customer service managers view the videos and respond to complaints.

In August, British Airways gave full refunds averaging $3,200 to 63 passengers on a Concorde flight from London, because a technical problem left customers bound for Miami and Washington grounded in New York. After passing out letters of apology, the airline chartered planes to fly the passengers to their destinations. "We'd rather spend money and keep customers satisfied than initiate five or six complaints," says John Lewis, vice president of customer services. That philosophy pays off. In the fiscal year that ended March 31, British Airways posted one of the largest net incomes of all international airlines, $189 million on revenues of $7 billion. Six years ago it was one of the biggest money losers in the skies.

Companies that want to win over dissatisfied customers must empathize with them and reward them. "Turning away a complainer by telling him, 'It's our policy,' enrages him," says Richard C. Whiteley, president of Forum Corp., a Boston consulting firm that specializes in customer service. "That's the corporate equivalent to your parents saying, 'Because I said so.'" Hechinger Co., a Maryland-based retailer of hardware and home and garden gear, accepts returns of items even when the customer has obviously abused

them. The retailer sends particularly perturbed purchasers a dozen roses. Hechinger posted profits of $41.9 million on sales of $742.2 million last year. Earnings have compounded 29% annually since the company went public 16 years ago.

Neiman Marcus, the Dallas-based specialty retailer, is gracious with gripers too. "We're not just looking for today's sale. We want a long-term relationship with our customers," says Gwen Baum, director of customer satisfaction for the 22-store chain. "If that means taking back a piece of Baccarat crystal that isn't from one of our stores, we'll do it." For most retailers, dishonest customers who return items that they have already used or bought elsewhere account for fewer than 5% of returns. Says Baum: "If you let profit protection or security rule the way you treat customers, satisfaction is bound to suffer."

Customers seem to give companies bonus points if top managers hear them out. Rex McClelland, senior vice president of operations at Delta Air Lines, regularly calls passengers who write to complain. Marriott Chairman J. W. Marriott Jr. reads about 10% of the 8,000 letters and 2% of the 750,000 guest comment cards the company receives each year. When Marriott was president in the late 1960s, some 30,000 hotel guests submitted comment cards each year. He read every one.

AT FIDELITY BANK, a 124-branch institution based in Philadelphia, President Rosemarie B. Greco, a former nun, is devoted to complaint handling. Results have been close to miraculous. When Greco, who joined the bank as a secretary 20 years ago, became president in early 1987, letters from customers poured into her office. "Maybe because I'm a woman they thought I would be more sensitive to their needs," she says. Greco phoned one retired customer who had serious problems with his IRA account statement. "He was beside himself with gratitude," she says. "That taught me an important lesson about letting customers know management is personally involved with their problems."

Fidelity assigned 25 people to visit American Express, L.L. Bean, and ten other companies known for excellent customer service. "We didn't look at any banks. Service is service," says Greco, 42. Fidelity consolidated its complaint-handling systems—one for each of 14 different business segments. Customers with problems involving savings accounts, auto loans, and credit cards now call one telephone number. Clients with major problems write to the office of the president. Greco reads all of those letters, as well as summaries of the bank's other complaints and inquiries, which total around 120 monthly. Today

87% of Fidelity's customers say they are satisfied or highly satisfied with service, vs. 57% in 1986.

Loyalty is especially important to firms that depend on customers to buy again and again. Many companies find the answer in toll-free 800 numbers. When Whirlpool pioneered the service in 1967, "Ralph Nader was attacking big business for not listening to customers," says Gary L. Lockwood, group director for consumer services. "We wanted to show that we listen." At first, 800 numbers were considered a gimmick, but today over half of all companies with more than $10 million in sales

THE AIRLINES THEY LOVE TO HATE

COMPLAINTS per 100,000 passengers	
Continental*	16.9
Eastern*	13.3
Northwest	9.1
Pan Am	9.0
TWA	8.2

use them to handle complaints, inquiries, and orders, according to the American Management Association. AT&T and its rivals rang up around $4.5 billion in revenues last year from more than eight billion 800-number calls.

Coca-Cola installed its 1-800-GET-COKE lines in late 1983 to promote feedback. Roger Nunley, manager of industry and consumer affairs at Coca-Cola USA, says some studies indicated that only one unhappy person in 50 takes time to complain. "The other 49 switch brands, so it just makes good business sense to seek them out," he says. Without the toll-free lines, Coca-Cola might never have understood the depths of its error in trying to replace old Coke with new.

Right after the company launched its reformulated New Coke in 1985, calls on the phone system fizzed from an average of 400 a day to more than 12,000. Nine out of ten were from customers who said they preferred the old cola to the new drink. On the day following old Coke's return as Coca-Cola Classic, 18,000 people called, including thousands who had complained earlier. They wanted to say thank you. Nunley says that consumer "emotion"—his term for brand loyalty—is stronger today for Coke Classic than it was before the episode. And by selling both Cokes and several new colas, the company has increased its U.S. market share to over 40%.

Toll-free phone systems deliver additional benefits. A Technical Assistance Research survey for Coca-Cola showed that a complainer who is denied a request over the phone is 30% more likely to remain brand loyal than a buyer who receives the same message in a letter. That's because a phone conversation is more personal and gives the service representative a chance to explain the company's position and woo the customer back. Not only is answering complaints by phone faster, it usually saves money. American Express spends five to ten times as much replying to a letter as it does answering a complaint over its toll-free lines. The company often ends up having to call the letter writer anyway to get more information about the problem.

Companies must carefully train, monitor, and motivate the folks who field the 800-number calls. At Procter & Gamble, new customer service representatives spend four to five weeks in classrooms learning to diffuse anger as well as to solve problems. Toyota, which touts customer courtesy in its ads, ranks its telephone representatives daily on productivity. American Express used to track only the number of calls each operator handled. Now it evaluates the way they talk to customers too. To show the importance it puts on telephone reps at its customer support center in Colorado Springs, Digital Equipment places them next to windows, where they can peer at Pike's Peak. Managers sit in windowless offices.

The GE answer center in Louisville is the state-of-the-art 800-number operation, according to many customer service experts. Manager N. Powell Taylor developed some of his ideas by visiting Disney University in Florida, which trains employees for Disney World. "Disney has a great reputation for knowing how to make people happy," he says. At Disney, Taylor learned the importance of professional dress (GE male reps wear coats and ties, and women wear dresses and suits), corny motivators (computer screens carry greetings such as "Put a smile in your voice"), and incentives

(GE awards clothing, sporting goods—and trips to Disney World). Taylor and his staff evaluate the service representatives three times a year. If they earn a score of 80%—based on productivity, attitude, attendance, and quality of service—the new goal becomes 85%. Many top reps move to field offices as sales managers.

The five-year-old GE answer center handles three million calls a year and costs more than $8 million to operate. A giant database, which stores 750,000 answers concerning 8,500 models in 120 product lines, "makes every representative an expert," says Taylor. Service reps have fielded some bizarre calls: A submarine off the Connecticut coast needed help fixing a motor, a homeowner wanted to convert a black-and-white TV to color, and technicians on a James Bond film couldn't get underwater lights to work. GE says its people can solve 90% of complaints or inquiries on the first call.

THIS YEAR the answer center will direct some 700,000 callers to GE dealers, 10,000 of which are logged in the center's computers. Surveys indicate that 95% of callers are satisfied with the answer center's service, and complainers often convert into even more loyal buyers. The center produces at least twice the return GE expected. The company probably spends between $2.50 and $4.50 on a typical call—15% are complaints—and reaps two to three times that in additional sales and warranty savings. Says Taylor: "Most businesses don't understand that customer service is really selling."

Good complaint handling at GE, Whirlpool, and other companies has brought the appliance industry a long way. Twenty years ago it was among the worst in responding to complainers. Today, according to the Council of Better Business Bureaus, automakers and auto-services firms leave a lot of customers dissatisfied. But they're working hard to shape up. General Motors operates one of the most sophisticated toll-free systems, and Ford Motor is building an 800-number operation modeled on GE's. Auto dealerships are creating customer re-

lations departments. And compared with five years ago, twice as many car dealers call customers following repairs to find out if everything's okay.

CUSTOMER NEEDS dictate what kind of service companies provide. Johnson & Johnson is consolidating seven 800-number systems into a single one, hoping to make its system more efficient. That means turning its 14 information specialists in areas like baby products and sun care into generalists. Over 14 months experts are giving them 300 hours of coaching on Band-Aids (Wound Management I), dressings and tape (Wound Management II), and 90 other products. J&J has raised the amount reps can refund without higher approval from nothing to $50.

The best—and cheapest—way to keep customers satisfied, of course, is to serve them well from the start. Dinah Nemeroff, director of customer affairs at Citicorp, says: "Our philosophy is that we never recover." Managers there must come up with a "hierarchy of horrors," a list of the five worst things they could do to customers and ways to avoid them. For example, a breakdown of an automatic teller machine is horrible because, as the company's ads once said, "The Citi never sleeps."

Advertising hype can create customer expectations that rise faster than service can improve. Consultant Whiteley of Forum Corp. warns companies not to overpromise because consumers rank reliability as the key ingredient of good service. Delta painted itself into a corner when it vowed, "Delta is ready when you are." So did Holiday Inn with its slogan: "No excuses. Guaranteed." These companies were begging for grumblers and eventually switched to less omnipotent slogans. Of course, the company that does live up to its promises can reap some very tangible benefits. With consumers smarter, choosier, and more demanding than ever before, courting the complainers has become an essential part of business. That it can also be good business is a nice bonus.

Guiding Principles for Improving Customer Service

Richard T. Garfein

Richard T. Garfein is Director of Worldwide Market Research in the Travel Related Services Company of American Express. He is responsible for establishing and maintaining quality standards and guidelines for market research conducted around the world. Dr. Garfein joined American Express in 1978 as a human resources consultant. Since then he has held a variety of human resources and market research positions with the company.

In 1983, Dr. Garfein conducted the original market research that led to American Express' launching of its highly successful Platinum Card. To support the company's global expansion strategy, most of his energies today are devoted to international business units, including Latin America, Australia, Japan, and other key development and implementation of a worldwide customer satisfaction research program designed to measure service quality from the customer's point of view. Many of the lessons learned from that program are described in this article.

Prior to joining American Express, Dr. Garfein served on the faculties of New York University and Brooklyn College, where he taught social psychology and personality. He received his doctorate in social psychology from New York University in 1977.

Customer service is on many people's minds these days. There is more than just a growing sense that service in America leaves much to be desired and, in fact, has gotten worse over the past several years. A recent article in *Time Magazine* said:

> Personal service has become a maddeningly rare commodity in the American marketplace. Flight attendants, salesclerks and bank tellers all seem to have become too scarce and too busy to give consumers much attention.[3]

The good news is that there is a growing awareness of the room for improvement in service quality, and more and more companies are trying to do something about it. There is also a growing realization that service quality can ultimately make or break a company and that customer satisfaction has direct bottom line implications.

Karl Albrecht and Ron Zemke, in their book entitled *Service America!* talk about a "new service imperative":

> This "new service imperative" will mean that the old customer service department will probably fade into obscurity as executives and managers work to transform their entire organizations into customer-driven business entities.[1]

Following are some guidelines for improving customer satisfaction in your organization. Many of these are drawn from empirical evidence obtained in the customer service research program at American Express. At American Express, delivery of the best possible service to customers is a long-standing business priority that receives constant vigilance.

Meet the Customer's Expectations

Did the service exceed, meet, or fall below what the customer expected? This will ultimately determine how satisfied the customer is. Furthermore, if the customer expects more from your company than from the competition, the challenge is even greater. Expectations are usually formed on the basis of four considerations:

1. *Price.* By and large, more is expected of higher priced products and services. For example, more personal attention is expected from a full-service brokerage firm than from a discount brokerage firm. A full-service airline needs to deliver more in the way of amenities than a no-frills airline.
2. *The customer's prior experience with the company.* The irony here is that the better the job your company does, the more the customer will expect of you in the future. It is indeed a mixed blessing that people who *have* previously contacted American Express with a question on their billing statements *expect more* in the future than people who have never contacted the company.

From *The Journal of Services Marketing*, Vol. 2, No. 2, Spring 1988, pp. 37-41. Copyright © 1988 by The Journal of Services Marketing. Reprinted by permission.

3. *The customer's experience with other companies.* For better or for worse, there is no way of avoiding comparisons to one's competitors. The first-time renter from Budget Rent-A-Car will judge Budget on the basis of his or her prior experience with Hertz and Avis. For example, Avis has "rapid return." Does Budget have automated return?

4. *Advertising claims and world-of-mouth.* American Express's new advertising campaign—"membership has its privileges"—emphasizes high-quality service delivery and is bound to raise customer expectations.

Reduce Time

The average leisure time among Americans has decreased from nearly four hours per day in 1973 to 2½ hours in 1985. Clearly, most of us have less time to spend today waiting in lines and on hold.

Obviously, fast service leads to satisfaction and slow service to dissatisfaction. However, the precise nature of this relationship varies with the situation and is an important area of contribution for a market research program (as is shown in Figure 1). For example, Chart E could be used to describe satisfaction with speed of service at a restaurant. There is an optimal timeframe for serving the meal—too fast or too slow is unacceptable. Chart C depicts satisfaction with speed of answering the telephone. According to surveys among Cardmembers who call American Express, satisfaction with its speed of answering the phone remains high until three rings, but then drops off sharply.

Time spent waiting is definitely linked to status in our society. A psychologist described this linkage in a recent *Psychology Today* article titled "Waiting is a Power Game":

> Status dictates who waits. The more important we are, the greater the demand for our time. And since time is limited, its value increases with our perceived importance. Like any valuable commodity, the time of important people must be protected.[2]

The marketing team at American Airlines knows this rule very well. Members of both their frequent flyer program and airline clubs are given "special unlisted reservations phone numbers." The implicit message to these customers is that they are important and their time is valuable. (Ostensibly, they are less likely to get a busy signal or a recorded message when they call.)

Reduce the Number of Contacts. The number of people that a customer needs to speak with to get a question answered or a problem resolved certainly affects satisfaction. Unquestionably, when customers call a company, they are more satisfied when the first person they speak with is able to solve their problem. In many instances, more than one contact is too many. A high number of contacts usually means, for the customer:

- Greater effort expended to take care of something that, in the customer's mind, should have been simple.
- A need to repeat the story over and over again.
- The possibility of getting conflicting messages or instructions.

To the customer these can be very stressful situa-

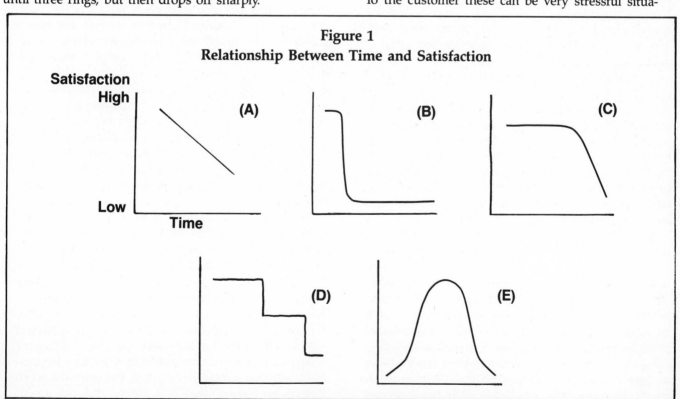

Figure 1
Relationship Between Time and Satisfaction

tions. As a general rule, front-line customer service people should be made as self-sufficient as possible to cut down on the number of referrals.

Give Clear Instructions. Tell the customer precisely what he or she needs to do to get a problem resolved. Very often, Cardmembers call American Express asking that charges for unused airline tickets be removed from their bills. Before the company can do anything, the customer must return the unused ticket to the airline or travel agent. Good service from American Express (meaning fast removal of the charge from the bill) depends upon the clarity of the instructions that the customer service representative gives.

Bridge the Language Gap. There is nothing more annoying to a customer than getting hit with company jargon. Actually, the customer service representative has two basic tasks in bridging the language gap:
• First, interpretation of what it is that the customer is saying
• Second, clear communication back to the customer in the customer's language

High-quality service companies adjust well to varying levels of customer sophistication. For an airline, the ideal is to make both the frequent business traveler and the first-time vacation traveler feel at home.

Make the Customer Feel Valued. Don't make the customer feel like a nuisance. No one seems to do a better job of making the customer feel valued than Marriott. A classic example is the name they gave to their Frequent Traveler Award Program—The Honored Guest Program. The wording of the welcoming letter from J. W. Marriott, Jr., says it all: "We have created Marriott Honored Guest Awards to express our sincere appreciation to our best customers by honoring them and rewarding them with wonderful and exciting travel vacations around the world."

Never Make the Customer Feel at Fault. It's true that the customer isn't always right, but the customer should not be made to feel at fault. The last thing that a customer in a predicament needs to hear is that the predicament was of his or her own making. American Express has found in its research on past due notices that customers do not take kindly to a "guilty until proven innocent approach." It not only leaves a bad taste, but it can lead to reduction in card use and increased attrition.

Never Embarrass the Customer. One of the most delicate customer interactions at American Express is the "authorization voice contact": The customer, when trying to use the American Express card, gets called to the telephone to speak to an American Express representative. In the card business this happens to be a vital checkpoint in the fraud and credit control process, but from the consumer's point of view it is an inherently touchy situation. American Express has found in its customer satisfaction research that the manner in which the situation is handled actually has a greater affect on satisfaction than whether the customer is approved or declined for the charge. This fact underscores the need for tact and sensitivity on the part of the representatives.

Optimize Speed Vs. Personal Attention Trade-Off. While the trade-off between speed and personal attention is inevitable (as anyone who runs a telephone servicing center can tell you), it need not be a zero-sum game. At American Express, Mondays and lunch hours are especially busy telephone periods, which can easily lead to backlogs. A solution to this problem was suggested to management by a quality circle participant in the Phoenix Operations Center: Under normal conditions, telephone representatives handle the call and then do a certain amount of paperwork or online data entry as follow-up. Why not skip the follow-up steps during peak periods (and put them aside for a later shift) and immediately move on to the next call? The idea was implemented by management and has been highly successful.

Technological advances can favorably impact on the speed versus personal attention trade-off. Innovations like express check-out in the lodging industry, automated return in the car rental industry, and automated ticketing machines in the airline industry enable time-conscious consumers to save valuable minutes while freeing desk personnel to spend more time with customers desiring personal attention.

Include quality of service measures as part of employee job performance criteria. Typically, only the most easily measurable aspects of an employee's job get measured. In a telephone servicing center, this might be number of calls handled per day. For years this was the only criterion that American Express measured, but many problems arise under these conditions. The message communicated to employees is to complete their calls quickly, with little regard for tone and manner. To address this problem, American Express added tone and manner ratings to the mix. Employees are told up front that their calls will be randomly monitored. They are given extensive training in telephone technique and familiarized with the criteria on which they are rated. Doing this has greatly enhanced the levels of courtesy, helpfulness, and patience in the minds of customers.

American Express further tries to instill a spirit of delivering the highest quality service through its "great performers" program, which awards employees whose efforts go far beyond the call of duty. For example, a truck driver called one of the telephone representatives in Phoenix, Arizona. He had just left Kansas City, Missouri, on his way home to Decatur, Illinois. He was approximately 70 miles east of Kansas City when his truck broke down in a little town called Odessa, Missouri (in the middle of nowhere). He took his truck to a garage to be fixed, but after the work began, he learned that this garage did not accept

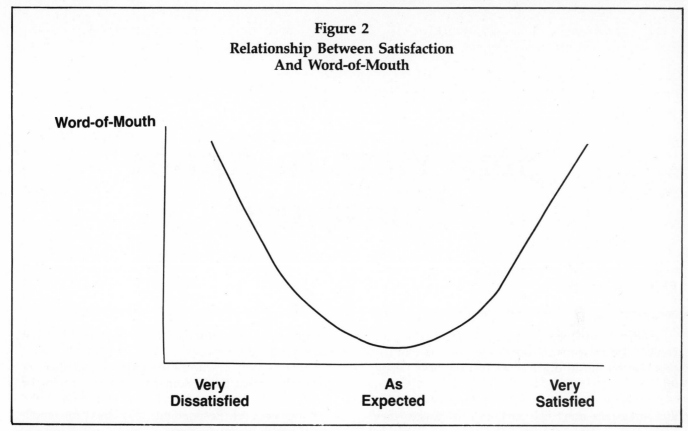

Figure 2
Relationship Between Satisfaction
And Word-of-Mouth

American Express. To make matters worse, he had no cash or other means of payment. In other words, he was stranded. The Phoenix telephone representative contacted the Kansas City Travel Office, and someone from the travel office actually drove the 70 miles and presented the truck driver with $200 in cash and $100 in travelers' checks. Needless to say, he was grateful—and probably told a lot of people about his experience.

It is very often reported in the customer service literature that dissatisfied customers tell more people about their experience than satisfied customers. In contrast, American Express's research reveals a U-shaped curve relationship, where both very satisfied and very dissatisfied customers tell more people than customers in the middle (See Figure 2). Clearly, word also gets spread about good service.

Some Concluding Thoughts

The value of setting up a market research program to measure perceptions of a company's service cannot be emphasized enough. At American Express, members of the management team who initially had to be sold on the idea have come to regard this research program as indispensable. A good program will help you get to know your customer better, show you how to improve service, and ultimately contribute toward your company's long-term growth.

Finally, in this age of diminished consumer loyalties, deregulation, and increased foreign competition, service is more and more becoming the distinguishing factor in customers' deciding among department stores, restaurants, hotels, brokerage firms, and other service companies. Companies able to rise above the fray will be in a much better position over the near and long term.

References

1. Albrecht, K., and R. Zemke, *Service America! Doing Business in the New Economy*, Homewood, Ill.: Dow Jones-Irwin, 1985.

2. Levine, R., "Waiting Is A Power Game," *Psychology Today*, April, 1987.

3. Russel, G., M. Grant, and W. Szonskl, "Pul-eeze! Will Somebody Help Me," *Time*, February 2, 1987.

Sure Ways to Annoy Consumers

David Wessel

Staff Reporter of The Wall Street Journal

Americans are polled ad nauseam about what conveniences, dish soaps and advertising slogans they like best. We set out to discover what really ticks people off.

And the answer came back with unmistakable clarity: Americans don't like anything that wastes their time.

Nearly four of every 10 people surveyed in The Wall Street Journal's "American Way of Buying" survey say that among their top peeves is waiting in long lines while other service windows or cash registers stay closed.

"That does kill me, especially in banks," says Karen Osif of Hopewell, N.J. "The bank tellers are going to lunch while everyone else is trying to get their business done before their lunch hours end."

And don't try suggesting that she use an automated teller machine. She does occasionally, but the mere mention reminds her of another pet peeve: the growing tendency of banks to levy charges for every little service, including imposing a fee each time a customer sticks a card in one of those machines.

As part of the Journal's survey, pollster Peter Hart asked 1,034 consumers—about half of the total sample—to select from a list of 19 items the two or three that most annoy them. A scant 1% of the respondents said "none of the above," confirming that beneath the surface of nearly every seemingly satisfied American consumer a few gripes are lurking.

Three in 10 complain about one of the recent time-consuming innovations in telecommunications: the prerecorded solicitation. "You're holding the line for a machine!" says Paul Overman Sr. of Kansas City, Mo. "As soon as I hear that message, I hang up on them."

And for any kamikaze company that wants to make unwanted sales pitches even more unpopular, here's a hint: Program the computer to dial at supper time.

Getting sales calls during dinner is another thing that drives Americans mad.

Dubious sales practices—like price quotes that are lower than what the customer will end up paying or sale items that are out of stock—also rank high on the get-your-goat list. Respondents also object to complicated health insurance forms.

Then there are the little things—minor annoyances that seldom ruin a day but often wreck the moment. Child-proof caps, for instance, are cited by 12% of those surveyed; the elderly complain about them most often. Twelve percent also grumble about poor instructions on how to assemble or use products. Another 8% cite recorded messages that play over and over as they hold on the phone. Even newspapers aren't immune: Some 7% complain about ink coming off on their hands.

The mailbox of Andy Rooney, the resident grump of television's "60 Minutes," is something of a running poll on Americans' pet peeves. A lot of his letters complain about forms—forms that don't fit in the envelope provided, for instance. But the one gripe Mr. Rooney hears about the most pertains to "the drop-out things in magazines," those loose insert cards that flutter to the floor from almost every magazine.

In the Journal survey, though, only 4% rank those cards as among the most annoying things, dead even with the pens found in banks and stores—the ones that seem always to be out of ink. Other gripes that drew only a few nods in the Journal poll were seat belts that fasten automatically and video stores that never seem to have the tapes one wants. People between 18 and 29 years old, however, were twice as likely as others to complain about the video stores.

In addition to the consumers queried about their peeves, Mr. Hart asked the other half of the sample specifically about service complaints. Cited most of-

Americans' Pet Peeves

Things that bother Americans the most as consumers:

Waiting in line while other windows or registers are closed	36%
Solicitations using prerecorded messages	31
Being quoted one price, then learning real price is higher	24
Getting a sales call during dinner	21
Learning that sale items aren't in stock	20
Dealing with complicated health insurance forms	18
"Urgent" mail that is only trying to sell something	17

Americans' biggest complaints about service:

Staying home for delivery or salespeople who fail to show	40%
Poorly informed salespeople	37
Salesclerks who are on the phone while waiting on you	25
Salesclerks who say, "It's not my department"	25
Salespeople who talk down to you	21
Salesclerks who can't describe how a product works	16

Note: Totals don't add to 100% because each respondent was allowed up to three responses.

Source: Wall Street Journal Centennial Survery

ten—far more than, say, salesclerks who can't speak English or stores that make returns difficult—is the no-show service or delivery person. Overall, 40% of those polled complain about no-shows, but the numbers behind the numbers tell an even more interesting story.

For one thing, substantially more women than men, 46% to 33%, put the no-show at the top of their list, a reflection of just who in the family is most likely to have to cope with such inconveniences. Moreover, working women are even more likely to complain than other women; all told, 52% of them call the no-show their biggest service annoyance.

Close behind in the gallery of consumer villains is the poorly informed sales person. Nearly four in 10 of those polled cite the know-nothing as a chief service peeve; another 16% gripe about a similar irritation: the sales person who can't describe how an item works.

A quarter of them cite salesclerks who talk on the phone while waiting on customers, a gripe that seems somewhat more pronounced in the South than elsewhere in the country. The poll doesn't reveal if that's because Southern salesclerks engage in this practice more often or if Southern customers dislike it more intensely.

A quarter of the respondents also complained about salesclerks who brush off customers saying: "It's not my department." Fans of home shopping by television cite this substantially more often than other consumers, which may help explain why they shop from home.

Restaurants fared surprisingly well. Of the dozen possible complaints about service that were offered to respondents, the two that drew the least response were waiting to get a check at a restaurant and hosts who won't seat customers even though empty tables are available.

In case you were wondering, one of Mr. Rooney's pet peeves is reporters who waste his time by phoning to ask what ticks him off. "Reporters are always calling me and asking what were the 10 worst Christmas presents I ever received," says the commentator, who on that question doesn't comment.

Customer Satisfaction

The Ten Commandments of customer service.

BEVERLY BATTAGLIA, DR. ROBERT LORBER, & DARLENE JAMESON

Beverly Battaglia is President of Battaglia LTD., a consulting firm located in Santa Ana. Robert Lorber is President and Darlene Jameson is Vice President of Lorber Kamai Associates, a company specializing in the strategic design and implementation of productivity improvement systems and customer service programs, located in Long Beach, California.

What do Nordstrom, American Express, Disneyland, McDonald's, Federal Express and IBM have in common? They all know that customer satisfaction pays. The service age is here. Two-thirds of the United States GNP comes from service-related industries. With crowded markets, global competition, similar pricing, and little perceived difference of product quality by the customer, smart companies are attempting to differentiate their products and services from their competition. This is becoming more and more difficult to accomplish, as customers are now more selective, better educated, and thus, have increased their service expectations. Today's customer expects satisfaction and will settle for nothing less than having this expectation met. A recent Forum Corporation survey states that of 80 percent of a company's customers who are satisfied with their product, 60 percent will purchase that product from them again. A trend in the last few years has been that customer service, rather than price or quality of a tangible product was the deciding factor in a customer's satisfaction. However, recent reports show that the concern for both price and quality have increased. In short, companies will have to try even harder to provide perceptive customers with both a quality product and exceptional service in order to maintain their competitive edge. What is the cost of mediocre service? According to the White House Office of Consumer Affairs, 96 percent of unhappy customers do not complain. Rather than complain, ninety percent just go somewhere else according to a Technical Assistance Research Programs survey. Thus, only 4 percent of your customers give you an opportunity to improve your service in order to keep them. The unfortunate thing is that these unhappy customers tell at least nine other people of their experience. Given that it is easier and five times cheaper to keep existing customers than recruiting new ones, it appears that customer satisfaction is not only profitable, it is mandatory for the survival of businesses. The outstanding service companies listed in this article do more than philosophize about good customer service; they develop systems to assure exceptional customer service is actually being provided.

> ## Determine what your customers expect, want or need and compare this to what they are getting.

Here are a list of Ten Commandments, that if followed, can assist your organization in providing improved service to your clients and customers.

1. Turn your organization upside down. Instead of the usual right side up pyramid style organization chart where the front-line people are at the bottom, supporting corporate hierarchy at the top, and customers aren't even included; turn it upside down - putting customers at the top of your organization chart. Everyone else must work for them and corporate must support those employees who are closest to the customer. If you look at the customer in this way, you will probably take a new view of employment practices, training, compensating, and providing the necessary tools to assist in providing customer satisfaction.

2. Increase service accountability. Hold everyone accountable for providing the highest level of customer satisfaction. Include customer service responsibilities in job descriptions and review how employees are doing in this regard, not only when conducting performance reviews, but on an on-going basis. Show that you are interested and *listen.*

3. Identify every customer/employee "touch point". Each time customers and employees touch, you have an opportunity to win or lose with service. Companies who are successful in providing customer satisfaction know this. The Disney organization puts their new employees through extensive orientation and training on dealing with park guests. All employees, ticket takers to street sweepers, are considered to be hosts and hostesses, and are taught how to answer questions, to provide assistance, and to deal with unhappy people

From Orange County *Business to Business*, Vol. 1, No. 2. August 1989, pp. 30-31. Reprinted with permission of Executive Excellence, 8 West Center, Provo, Utah 84601.

because Walt Disney knew the value of these touch points.

4. Determine what your customers expect, want or need, and compare this to what they are getting. Talk to customers, survey them, listen to them. Measure service at every "touch point". Measure speed of response, error-free transactions, client satisfaction. Quantify these survey results and graph them on an on-going basis so that the people involved can see how they are doing. A large financial company uses "Tell the President" questionnaires to calculate customer satisfaction. These questionnaires are tallied, the resulting trends are monitored and the president personally responds to specific concerns. Then the positive and negative comments are posted to give employees feedback on their performance.

5. Service is everybody's business. Involve your employees in setting new goals for service and determining methods of exceeding customer expectations. When people are involved in setting the objectives and standards, they have a greater commitment to meet them. One Southern California home builder recently eliminated a high number of walk-through home inspection items to be fixed (punch list) by taking the time to customer service train and involve sub-contractors in the buyer's walk-through inspection. In three months the number of punch list items dropped 90 percent on the average. One sub-contractor said that it was an eye opening experience—he had never looked at his work in the house from a customer's point of view!

6. Empower your people. The concept of empowering people has been given lip-service for a long time. You need to make it real by giving every "touch point"

employee the authority, responsibility and support to fix customer concerns, problems and create ways to improve service. This means providing all employees with information, training, resources and freedom to use their creativity to satisfy customer needs and expectations.

7. "Over" Communicate. Provide regular, frequent feedback to every employee about their current service performance levels. This can be done verbally, visually or in writing. Most employees need specific, objective information about their performance in order to improve it. Feedback enables them to maintain or improve good performance and change poor performance. Tell everyone satisfied customer stories, and on a regular basis, talk about how you can improve.

8. Pay attention to your internal customers. Some departments provide support services to other employees in your organization and thus, have internal customers. Demand the same high level of service from those support departments as you do from those who work directly with the customer. A client recently complained to us about their administrative services department. They felt the department forgot what their role and mission in the organization was. The service department's attitude was that the client contact departments had to adjust to their schedules and to their operating procedures. Instead of being perceived as efficient and supportive, the service department was viewed as unsupportive, uncooperative, selfish, and a barrier to getting things done in the firm.

9. Pay attention to details. Look at even the smallest opportunities to improve the customers' perceptions of your service. Good customer service is an intangible in

business. It is made up of small fragments which, when fitted together, demonstrate a caring and helpful attitude as perceived by the customer. When you find out what kind of services your customers like and appreciate, then figure out a way to provide them.

10. Recognize your high performers. Share the good news with everyone. Small improvements, when recognized and rewarded, grow into big ones. Providing positive consequences after performance achievement can increase or maintain that desired performance. It's best to remember the old adage of "different strokes for different folks." The better you know your employees and what reinforces them, the more effective your recognition will be. Most of the ideas in the ten commandments are common sense. You probably have heard a number of them before in one way or another. However, our experience has shown that they have not yet become second nature in many organizations. When you can build these concepts into your everyday business operation, you will truly be differentiating your organization from others. Top management must make a conscious decision that excellent customer service is what they want to provide. The enthusiasm for company-wide improvement must be constantly and consistently supported by management. State the customer service policy clearly and frequently. What gets attention, gets done. By sponsoring an environment where employees feel free to take some risk to do the exceptional in customer service, the customers, the management and the company will be the long term winners.

WHAT IS GOOD SERVICE?

Patricia Braus

Patricia Braus is a freelance writer in Rochester, New York.

Everybody talks about good service, but what exactly is it? That depends on the customer. Good service means different things to different people.

Whether people are satisfied with service depends on their expectations, says Cynthia Webster, an associate marketing professor at Mississippi State University. And expectations are shaped by many factors, including age, sex, race, and income.

How do different kinds of people want to be served? Answering the question is not easy. But the effort can pay off with a competitive edge for your company, because the importance of good service is growing every year.

Between 37 and 45 percent of people who are unhappy with the service they receive do not complain, according to the U.S. Office of Consumer Affairs. They simply go elsewhere.

In a society marked by increasing consumer segmentation, the hazards of mass-marketing service will also increase. To prosper, businesses must recognize their diverse customer base and provide customized service to each segment.

RESPECT YOUR ELDERS

A customer's age plays a big role in how he or she looks at service. Cynthia Webster found many age-based differences in service expectations when she surveyed 300 residents of a large southwestern city. Webster asked a variety of questions, such as whether the person expected a dentist's or doctor's office to be clean and neat, and whether they expected a dry cleaner to return clothes promptly.

Age is especially important when consumers look at providers of professional services, such as physicians, attorneys, and dentists, Webster wrote in the spring 1989 *Journal of Services Marketing*. Older people care more than younger people about courtesy, security, and how well a professional knows his or her client. They also care more about a company's name, reputation, and confidentiality than do adults aged 35 to 64. Middle-aged service customers care more about reliability, competence, and access, meaning that the service should be available at convenient hours and easily accessible by telephone.

Webster found that age didn't make a difference in consumers' attitudes toward nonprofessional services such as banking, laundry, dry cleaning, and automobile-related businesses. But other researchers have found that younger and older shoppers do have different expectations for nonprofessional services.

Older consumers are more likely than younger consumers to mention service as a reason for choosing a particular place to shop, according to Impact Resources in Columbus, Ohio. In studies conducted between September 1986 and February 1989, it asked shoppers in 35 major metropolitan markets about the importance of service. It found that 27 percent of 18-to-24-year-olds see service as the main reason for picking a food store, compared with 35 percent of those aged 55 to 64.

Differences in shopping styles also affect the kinds of services older and younger people expect. Older people like to take their time shopping, says Ron Zemke, author of the book *The Service Edge*. But "young people tend to be more concerned with convenience, buying something in a hurry." Zemke, who is the president of Performance Research Associations in Minneapolis, claims that "older people are more concerned with return policies, rest rooms, and easy access."

Older consumers emerged as more thoughtful shoppers in *America's Search for Quality*, a report on consumers in the 1980s sponsored by the Whirlpool Corporation. When Whirlpool asked a sample of Americans to gauge the quality of consumer products and services, older respondents were more concerned than younger people with warranties, having personal experience with a product, and safety considerations. They also cared more about political considerations, such as the environmental impact of a product or whether it was made in America.

Price is also important to older consumers, says Judith Langer, president of Langer Associates in New York City. Her qualitative research indicates that many older customers are more cautious about spending money than their youthful counterparts: "They realize their high earning years are coming to an end."

Campbell Soup Company has found that sometimes the needs of older people and younger people are diametrically opposed. When the company asked customers whether they used recipes that are printed on Campbell's products, the customer's age determined the answer. "People 35 and older wanted the recipe," says Anthony Adams, vice president of marketing research for Campbell. Shoppers under 35 were not interested. "Younger shoppers want a 1-2-3 product," he says.

To please younger shoppers, Campbell is now working to streamline the selection of soups, so shoppers can find what they want as quickly as possible. "After about 45 seconds, we find that consumers just give up," Adams says.

But Campbell's surveys also found that older shoppers enjoy having a personal relationship with a company. To woo them, the company is expanding its toll-free telephone service so anyone can call the company with questions or comments. "People want to have a sense that they're not dealing with a computer," Adams says.

Older people also demand more information about a product's content, particularly the presence of salt, fat, and cholesterol. "The older consumer is sensitive to deception," says Mona Doyle, president of The Consumer Network Inc., a Philadelphia firm that questions supermarket shoppers around the country.

In a recent survey Doyle's firm conducted of 600 people aged 60 to 85, older people were most dissatisfied with automobile salespeople and the transportation and fashion industries. Older women were frustrated by clothing that was designed for younger bodies, or clothing that was too snug in the waist. Both older men and older women were frustrated by automobile dealers who didn't realize the difficulties older people sometimes have in opening car doors, getting in and out of a car, or using a seat belt.

But if mass-marketing service is a mistake, devising one service strategy for all older people is also misguided. "When we look at other age groups, we tend to look in four-year increments," says Judith Langer. "Suddenly, it's 50 to infinity." An affluent 50-year-old in good health with a good job has different service needs than a 75-year-old retiree with limited income in poor health, says Langer. "The old myth was that no one over 50 has money. The new myth is that everyone does."

DO THE RIGHT THING

Race also affects a person's service expectations. Impact Resources found that Asians are least likely to cite service as the reason they chose a retailer. Blacks are most likely to be concerned about service, followed by whites and Hispanics. Only 16 percent of Asians considered service important in choosing a place to shop for children's clothing, compared with 18 percent of Hispanics, 20 percent of whites, and 21 percent of blacks.

Blacks say that certain attitudes can be critical to their feelings about a business. Many blacks are greeted with condescension when they should instead be served, says Eugene Morris, a black man who is president of his own advertising agency in Chicago.

"If I get on an airplane and I'm hanging my bag in first class, the automatic response is, 'That belongs in the back,'" says Morris. "The first thing a black person starts to think, if something goes wrong, is that race is an issue."

Banking can be particularly frustrating for blacks. "Banking is a real problem for minority entrepreneurs," says Al Wellington, president of a 12-year-old marketing research firm in Oaklyn, New Jersey. Wellington says he has never been able to borrow money from a bank. "I'm a graduate of the Wharton School of Business. If I were not black, I would expect to get a line of credit."

Black consumers of luxury items pay attention to the attitude of the salesperson. "Black consumers say they require a certain respect," says Melvin J. Muse, president of the advertising agency Muse Cordero Chen in Los Angeles. He says the sale will hinge, in part, on whether or not businesses offer black customers the respect they want.

"Black consumers also tend to have a real concern about the social consciousness of people selling the products," says Muse. In an eight-state survey of black consumers conducted by his company, Muse found a high degree of sensitivity to issues related to employment practices, investments in South Africa, and other social issues. The Whirlpool study confirms that blacks are more concerned with political and civil rights questions than is the general public. Black consumers support companies whose politics they agree with, says Muse.

TREAT HER KINDLY

Gender also makes a difference in perceptions of service. Webster found that women's expectations of the quality of professional services were generally higher than men's. In particular, women were more likely than men to have high expectations about accuracy in billing, convenient hours of operation, and competent personnel.

Zemke has evidence, however, that women have lower expectations than men in the area of health care. "Women are usually surprised when they're treated well in health care. They usually expect not to be treated well," he says. Men see things differently—in part because they're statistically less likely to need to see a doctor. "They have higher expectations and are more concerned about the bill."

The Whirlpool study found that men, particularly those aged 18 to 24, are most influenced by advertising when making purchase decisions. Women are more concerned with other elements related to service, such as product safety and warranties for the products purchased.

Income also helps to dictate consumer expectations for professional services, says Webster, although it doesn't make a difference in attitudes toward nonprofessional services. Low- and high-income people expect the most from a professional service, while middle-income customers expect less.

Impact Resources found that people with annual household incomes of $50,000 or more are harder to pin down. Service is actually less important to affluent consumers than to others when they shop for health and beauty aids or children's clothing. But don't skimp on service if you want affluent shoppers visiting your men's clothing store. Thirty-two percent of affluent shoppers cite service as a reason for choosing where to shop for men's clothing, Impact Resources found.

Offering services to individuals with different expectations will challenge businesses in the 1990s. But ignoring the differences will be increasingly dangerous to businesses that depend on service. As baby boomers age, and as women and minorities play greater roles in the economy, businesses that mass-market service may find themselves playing a losing game.

Service Marketing: Image, Branding, and Competition

Sak Onkvisit and John J. Shaw

Sak Onkvisit is an associate professor of marketing at San Jose State University. **John J. Shaw** is an associate professor of marketing at Providence College. The authors have published several articles in *Business Horizons*.

The marketing of services requires, even more than does product marketing, a positive image for the service to transform it from a commodity to a product.

Much like product marketing, the effective marketing of a service requires the development of a desirable image. It can even be argued that, because of the intangible nature of services, the creation of a proper image is actually more critical for service marketing than for product marketing. In the market for TV news programs, the package is regularly updated to sustain ratings. A desired image is created by adding a sweater on an anchorperson (Dan Rather as a prime example), changing anchors, and adding female, black, or Hispanic reporters.

This article discusses the relationships among the service image, an individual's image, and final purchase behavior. A key distinction is made between the two levels of service offerings—form and brand. The analysis then probes into ways that a unique image based on salient attributes can transform a commodity item into a branded service. Finally, the paper emphasizes the marketing mix and managerial implications.

SERVICE: COMMODITY OR PRODUCT?

A commodity is an undifferentiated product, and a product is a value-added, differentiated commodity. The distinction between the two is not superficial, and it has significant managerial implications for service marketers. Although services are often treated as commodities, they can be branded and transformed into products. Branding assures buyers of uniform service quality and can provide service marketers with a greater degree of pricing freedom, if the brand image is properly created and promoted. Holiday Inn was first to introduce a branded service to the hotel business on a large scale. By using the brand name to assure travelers of uniform service standards and experience, Holiday Inn was able to transform a commodity into a product. The branding strategy developed is a major contributing reason for the company's tremendous growth. Whenever possible, a service provider should attempt to become a

"power brander" by possessing these four characteristics:

- The company brand is distinctive;
- The company brand is relevant;
- The company brand has a tangible quality;
- The company's most important services are branded and linked.[1]

When services are treated as commodities by companies and consumers, price competition is inevitable. One major reason why airline-fare wars are common is because airlines are in the commodity business. They all offer essentially identical services, locations, and flight times. A distinction exists between product forms (full-service airlines vs. discount airlines); however, the degree of differentiation at the brand level is minimal. Travelers, knowing that airline services are essentially the same, are concerned primarily with flight schedules and fares and much less with airline images. Standardization of services and price sensitivity are evidence of a commodity rather than a product. As a result, airline

Figure 1
Service Forms and Brands of Credit Cards

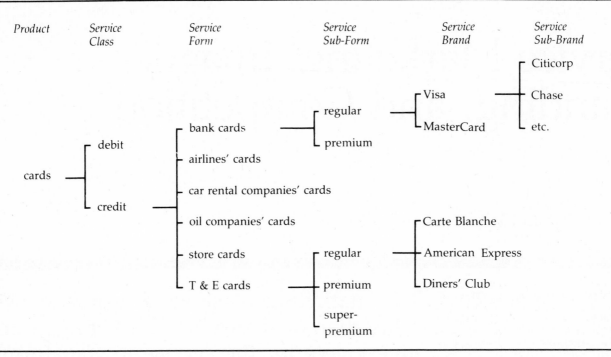

fares are determined by competition instead of distance or costs. The frequent flyer clubs create a brand loyalty that is spurious at best.

However, a service cannot be automatically transformed from a commodity into a product simply by putting a brand name on it. Anything, of course, can be branded, but it makes sense to do so only if the brand can be promoted and differentiated from other competitive brands in a meaningful manner. The saliency concept is thus significant for the branding of a service. A product attribute is salient only when it is sufficiently meaningful and important to a consumer that he recognizes it and includes it in his decision making.

The airline industry provides a good illustration of why it is futile to attempt to create a favorable image based on a non-salient attribute. At one time, airlines fought the "menu wars." However, as American Airlines explained, "that's not the main reason people fly. And if what you do is try to differentiate yourself with something that is really unimportant in the consumer's eye, you may be changing his total image of you in a negative way."[2] What American Airlines has done to create a favorable

image is to select flight attendants, uniforms, interiors, and exteriors to project an image that sets it apart. Its "something special in the air" advertising campaign captures this image.

SERVICE FORM VS. SERVICE BRAND

A service marketer must distinguish between the two basic levels of his offerings. Like the two levels of a product (product form and product brand), there are two distinct service levels: service form and service brand. Although service brands (such as MCI and Allnet) are more readily apparent, it would be an error to ignore the service form category, since each level is capable of generating a unique personality. As a matter of fact, service brand is merely a subset of service form.

The Credit Card Industry

Each service form category can acquire a distinct image. Credit cards

serve as an illustration because they have several service forms that vary in degree of prestige (see **Figure 1**). Bank cards are less exclusive than travel and entertainment cards but are more prestigious than retail store charge cards and those issued by airlines, car rental companies, and oil companies.

For each service form, there are usually a number of service brands (service marks). The two major brands of bank cards are Visa and MasterCard. Among the travel and entertainment cards, American Express is much better known in the United States than the Diners' Club and Carte Blanche brands owned by Citicorp. Internationally, Diners' Club seems to have acquired an edge because of its early presence.

American Express has been successful in segmenting the credit card market and creating new service forms for these segments. As the credit card becomes less of a specialty good and more of a convenience good, and as it moves toward the maturity stage of its product life cycle, a good marketing approach is to use a segmentation strategy. In addition to its regular cards, American Express was the first to introduce premium cards ("gold"

"Although many banks now have their own premium (gold) cards, the images of the Visa and MasterCard brands are so strong that it is difficult for these gold cards to shed the mass market image."

cards). The prestige of such cards allows the company to charge a higher membership fee. In response to bank cards' high interest rates on loans (cash advances), American Express also has introduced a card with revolving credit to supplement its 30-day single payment plan. This new brand, Optima, provides credit at a rate significantly lower than those charged by banks.

When banks began to offer their own "gold" cards, American Express was quick to initiate a new segment by offering the super-premium "platinum" card for its most exclusive group. Interestingly, MasterCard, when advised by American Express that "Gold Card" was its registered trademark, retitled its gold card as the "preferred customer" card. When MasterCard started using "gold card" again by contending that the term was a generic one, American Express filed a complaint alleging "trademark and service mark infringement, false designation of origin, unfair competition, misappropriation, unjust enrichment and dilution."[3]

As stated earlier, the two most prominent brands of bank cards are Visa and MasterCard. Although many banks now have their own premium (gold) cards, the images of the Visa and MasterCard brands are so strong that it is difficult for these gold cards to shed the mass market image. One analyst commented, "If you want to buy an expensive car, you tend to buy a Mercedes or a Cadillac, not a souped-up Honda."[4] Undeniably, brand extension as a strategy has its own merits, but a good case can also be made for the introduction of totally new brands.

Since a great number of banks offer the Visa and MasterCard brands, the banks' own cards are actually competitors. In a mature market, competitive strategy often involves taking

market share away from competing cards. Pavel and Binkley explain that "as long as the demand for bank cards is not fully exhausted, suppliers would probably concentrate on selling bank cards to those who do not have them. But, as saturation is reached, suppliers would have to increase output by taking other suppliers' market share through lower overall prices, lower credit standards, or greater product differentiation."[5]

After intensely pressuring the two major card associations, banks have won the right to reduce the size of the Visa and MasterCard logos on the cards and to display their own corporate logos more prominently. The purpose in this is to attempt to differentiate among banks that offer essentially the same brand. This differentiation at the sub-brand level for bank cards, however, appears to be less than a success. A Visa card is still a Visa card, regardless of which bank issues it. A consumer is not going to turn down a free Visa card issued by a local bank just to have the Citibank logo on his card, especially when Citibank's Visa card carries an annual fee. What matters to the consumer is the Visa card (brand) itself rather than the issuing bank (sub-brand).

The competition between bank cards and travel and entertainment cards is becoming very intense. Bank cards are now accepted by most hotels and restaurants; Visa even states in its advertisements that there are many establishments that do not accept American Express. American Express has fought back by signing up many retail stores (department and specialty stores and even some gas stations) to accept its travel and entertainment card. Apparently, the distinction between these two service forms has become increasingly blurred, and the competition has been

focused at the brand level instead. There is some evidence, however, that "holders of one card (either VISA or MC) are relatively more similar to each other than they are to holders of both cards."[6] In any case, it should also be noted that, for most cardholders, both Visa and MasterCard are virtually indistinguishable, and the fact that a great number of banks offer both cards to their customers does not help clarify the matter.

SINGLE BRAND VS. MULTIPLE BRANDS

Some service providers believe that, since part of what they market is the overall image of the organization, it is difficult to justify having a separate brand to market a separate product. This kind of erroneous thinking promotes inflexibility and can sentence a service marketer to a dying business in an ever-changing world. The existing corporate image may also inhibit a company from expanding into new market segments or new businesses. It is difficult to believe, for example, that Allegis (formerly UAL) would abandon the United Airlines, Hertz, Westin, and Hilton brands in favor of a single brand and an overall corporate image. As a matter of fact, the company decided to abandon the $7 million Allegis name only a few months after its adoption.

The hotel industry can provide a good illustration of the use of a multiple-brand strategy. To overcome the hotel glut, several hotel chains have emphasized their services as a branded product with varying degrees of success. In the 1950s, Hilton was very likely the only well-known brand name in this type of business. Now there are many hotel brands serving a wide variety of lodging segments. At the low end of the lodging segment are such budget chains as Motel 6, Red Roof, Days Inn, Super 8, and Econo Lodge. At the opposite end of the scale are the more prestigious names—Marriott, Hilton, Sheraton, and Hyatt. Hyatt has been very successful in cultivating its quality image, initially for the upper class and more recently for the upper-middle class. To capitalize on its upscale image, Hyatt has extended its brand by adding small European-style hotels under the Park Hyatt name to offer more services at higher rates.

For the mass market, there are several well-known brands: Ramada Inn, Quality Inn, Howard Johnson, and Holiday Inn. All of these middle-market competitors have been trying to trade up by upgrading their images. Marriott and Quality Inn, in contrast, have traded down by entering the low-cost market with Courtyard by Marriott and Comfort Inn respectively. Holiday Inn, in particular, is trying to change its middle-class image and has created several new brands for the various travel segments: Hampton Inn for the budget segment and Crowne Plaza and Embassy Suites (with only suite accommodations) for the upscale business traveler. Because some of these segments overlap, Holiday Inn has had a difficult task of differentiating, especially when both brands are located in the same city or market. In any event, it should not be difficult to see that market segmentation and trading up or down often necessitate using multiple brands, so that the main business of the existing brand will not be affected by the images of new segments.

TANGIBLE SYMBOLS FOR IMAGE CREATION

Since there is generally no objective measure of the quality of a professional service, the client really buys confidence in the company. Among mutual funds, companies such as Vanguard, Fidelity, Dreyfus, and T. Rowe Price have a competitive advantage because investors are more comfortable with those that have brand-name recognition. Given that there are hundreds of funds and that what is at risk is money, investors prefer to stay away

from unknown brands. A well-known mutual fund brand thus provides a degree of confidence and security to investors.

Because a service is inherently abstract, image creation is a difficult task that must be undertaken carefully. By presenting a number of promotional variables, the company may actually create more abstraction and dilute the reality of its service. Service marketers thus should enhance the specific reality and differentiate it from other "realities" by the presentation of tangible clues. The insurance industry makes the intangibility of insurance more easily understood by employing relevant tangible objects (Allstate's good hands, Travelers' umbrella, and Prudential's piece of the rock). A related hypothesis is that consumers use price and physical facilities to judge service quality. To impress clients, lawyers use law books to fill shelf space. These books are basically worthless because most are outdated and can be purchased for a very low price from the estates of deceased lawyers.

Van Doren and Relle define intangible as incapable of being touched, incapable of being defined or determined with certainty, and vague. They explain that the first problem can be solved by providing a physical representation of the service (brochures, offices, sample "end products," and so forth). Certainty can be achieved by using descriptive documentation to spell out precisely the service to be performed. Finally, interpersonal communication—the third-party reference—can be used to overcome vagueness.[7]

George and Berry provide six guidelines for the advertising of services. Three of the guidelines require advertising to provide tangible clues, make the service more easily understood, and contribute to continuity.[8] Brokerage firms provide a good illustration of these guidelines. Dreyfus is easily identifiable because of its lion. Merrill Lynch had its bull, but made the mistake of retiring it. Realizing that a mistake was made, Merrill Lynch fired its advertising agency and quickly brought the bull back. As can

Figure 2
Service Repositioning

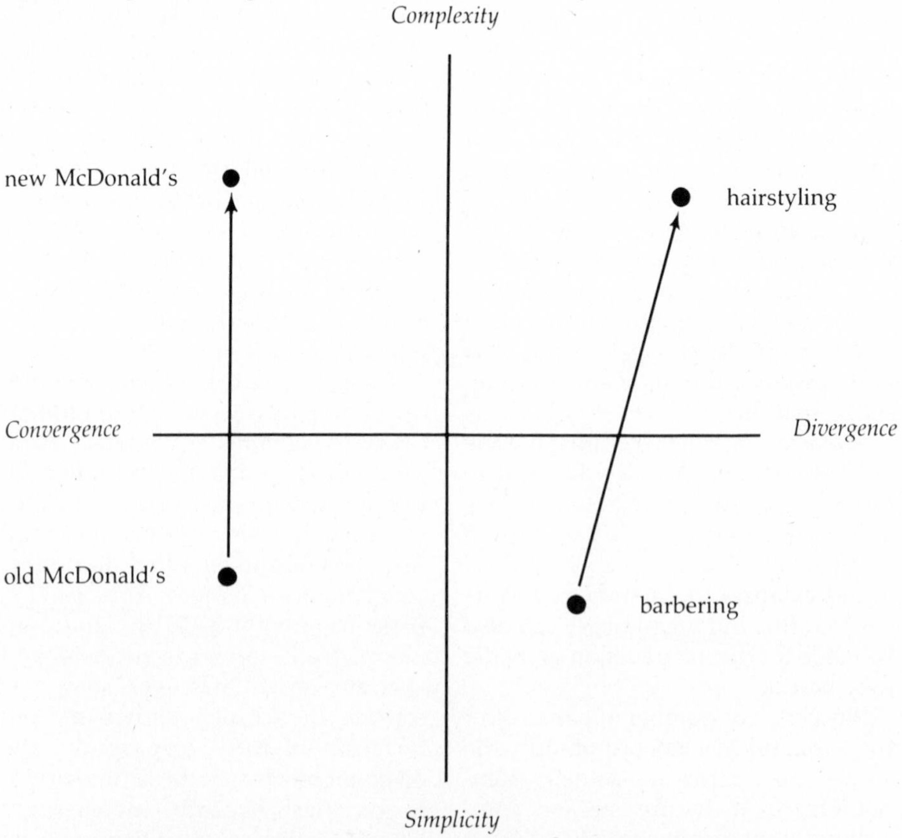

be easily seen, the bull provides a tangible clue, easy comprehension, and continuity.

IMAGE POSITIONING

Because of the intangible, experiential nature of many services, the company needs to help prospective customers get a mental fix on its product. On this score, Federal Express has done exceptionally well by positioning itself as a company that is very reliable.

When the existing image is not favorable, a company or its service should be repositioned. Commercial banks generally have poor images with the public. An unflattering story is told of a man needing a heart transplant who was informed by his doctor that he could choose between a heart of a young, strong athlete or the heart of an old banker. To his doctor's amazement, the patient chose the banker's heart. When asked why, the patient's reasoning was: the banker's heart had never been used. This negative image explains why juries often have no sympathy for bankers and why they are likely to award large sums when bankers are found guilty of misconduct toward their customers. It is thus wise for bankers to find the causes of this negative image and attempt to reposition banks in a more favorable light.

Due to deregulation, banks now must consider the consumer image of other types of financial institutions (savings and loan associations, insurance companies, brokerage firms, and mutual funds) as well as of other banks. According to one study, "S&Ls are still strong in being seen as the better place for a mortgage and are 'moving' toward strength in the more traditional banking services—checking accounts, credit cards, and car financing, among others, while banks are 'moving' away from being a better place for these services."[9]

As can be seen from **Figure 2**, the service image can be repositioned through structural change. The process involves changes (either an increase or a decrease) in complexity and divergence.[10] A service becomes more complex when current service products are enhanced or when new service lines are added. A drastic increase in the number of new products offered by banks is a good example of increased complexity. Complexity decreases when a service marketer's product lines, classes, forms, or brands are reduced.

A service becomes more divergent if it is customized to command higher prices. Divergent services are more difficult to manage, control, and distribute. In contrast, divergence reduction, although promoting inflexibility, results in standardization, economies of scale, and lower costs and prices.

A service company should determine the actual position occupied by its service on a perceptual map based on the two dimensions described. If the position occupied is undesirable or inferior to that of its competitors, the service company should reposition its service by undertaking marketing activities that will move it closer to the ideal position. Barbering (simple haircutting) was placed in jeopardy in the early 1960s because of the Beatles' appearance (and their hairstyle) on the popular scene. Those barbers who have survived were able to reposition themselves as hairstylists who offer more complex and divergent services. McDonald's is less divergent than Burger King because Burger King allows its customers to have the hamburgers "their way." Despite this, McDonald's has been immensely successful by controlling divergence while measurably increasing the complexity of its product lines. In its early years, McDonald's product line consisted primarily of hamburgers, cheeseburgers, Big Macs, french fries, apple pies, milk shakes, and drinks. Since that time, McDonald's has added breakfast, McNuggets, McDLTs, pineapple pies, cookies, and other products.

Much like a product, a service should be endowed with a proper, desirable image. Some services are commodities and, by their nature, have no significant meaning to consumers. Any advertising effort to create images for such products are likely to be fruitless and wasteful. In general, however, services should be converted from commodities into products whenever feasible and practical. To do so requires the identification of a salient attribute that will make branding meaningful.

Many purchases made by consumers are directly influenced by the image an individual has of himself and the image of a product or seller. Since users of consumer services are self-image buyers, a strong and distinct image is essential. Image takes on a greater degree of importance in the service markets, and it should be fully integrated into a firm's marketing programs.

Although the images of service form and service brand can and often do interact with each other, consumers still tend to evaluate each of these elements independently. A service marketer thus must develop a proper image for each service level of the offering in the market. Also at each level, the marketer should determine the position his service occupies on the perceptual map. The idea is to be as close to the ideal position as possible to maximize the image appeal of the service product in the marketplace.

1. Leonard Berry, "Big Ideas in Services Marketing," *Journal of Consumer Marketing*, Spring 1986, p. 47-51.8

2. Gary Knisely, "Service Business is People Dealing with Other People," *Advertising Age*, May 14, 1979.

3. Dan Abramson, "No Settlement Seen in 'Gold Card' Lawsuit," *DM News*, March 15, 1988, p. 2.

4. "A New Marketing Blitz in the War of the Plastic Cards," *Business Week*, July 23, 1984, p. 126, 128.

5. Christine Pavel and Paula Binkley, "Cost and Competition in Bank Credit Cards," *FRB Chicago Economic Perspectives*, March-April 1987, p. 3-13.

6. Douglass K. Hawes, "Profiling Visa and MasterCard Holders: An Overview of Changes—1973 to 1984, and Some Thoughts for Future Research," *Journal of the Academy of Marketing Science*, Spring 1987, p. 62-69.

7. Doris C. Van Doren and Paul B. Relle, "Confronting Intangibility: A Practical Approach," *Journal of Professional Services Marketing*, Spring 1987, p. 31-40.

8. William R. George and Leonard L. Berry, "Guidelines for the Advertising of Services," *Business Horizons*, July-August 1981, p. 52-56.

9. Gary M. Mullet, "Correspondence Analysis: A New Tool for Image Studies," *Journal of Professional Services Marketing*, Spring 1987, p. 83-100.

10. G. Lynn Shostack, "Service Positioning through Structural Change," *Journal of Marketing*, January 1987, p. 34-43.

Nonprofits learn how-to's of marketing

by Kathleen Vyn

Kathleen Vyn is a free-lance writer based in Chicago.

Nonprofit agencies have learned they have to market to stay alive, but the problem now is how to organize for an effective marketing campaign.

For years, nonprofits avoided the word "marketing" because they associated it with corporate insensitivity. But stiff competition for donations (*Marketing News,* Feb. 13) has forced most organizations to develop marketing strategies.

Large nonprofits are more likely to have public relations or communications departments that develop campaigns. Smaller nonprofits, with limited resources, hire marketing consultants or train their volunteer staffs.

Basically, nonprofits do whatever they can afford to do.

"We've seen a dramatic change in the nonprofits' attitude toward marketing in the last 10 years," said Donald Bates, president of The Bates Co. Inc., a PR and marketing firm in New York, whose clients include trade and professional associations and charitable organizations. "Their use of the word is no longer perjorative. Nonprofit organizations now understand that well-handled marketing can become a source of renewal as well as a source of revenue."

But even with that change of heart, said Bates, former vice president of communications for Planned Parenthood Federation of America Inc., a lot of nonprofits claim they're doing marketing when they're not.

"They do soft marketing, which isn't heavily research-based," he said. "Just because you have a good cause doesn't mean you don't have to reach a target audience."

Some nonprofits find that training their volunteers is the best way to organize their marketing efforts.

United Way of America, Alexandria, Va., which has 2,300 local units, develops a marketing strategy and trains its volunteers accordingly, said Anthony DeCristofaro, director of PR and internal communications.

"All of our other groups tie in with our theme," said DeCristofaro. "Our theme now is 'United Way Brings Out the Best in All of Us.' We use lots of tools in marketing United Way, such as home videos, films, and a multi-image slide-show program."

According to Roberta Van Der Voort, United Way's senior vice president of marketing, the organization began its marketing strategy to unite the local units, which have their own boards and raise their own money.

"We were fractionalized," she said, "and if we wanted to expand quickly we had to communicate nationally through ads and the media. We needed a message that would represent us as one group."

United Way put together a volunteer group of experts led by John Akers, chairman of IBM. Focus groups revealed that people didn't know how United Way worked. So the headquarters launched a national TV ad campaign. Each commercial told the story of someone in desperate need of help and how that person received assistance.

United Way was satisfied enough with its marketing to publish a book, *Competitive Marketing,* "about how we do what we do," Van Der Voort said. "It's for other charities. Next month we will be doing a marketing workbook for all of our branches. We're also holding periodic conferences for marketing personnel from local United Ways, including an annual marketing and advertising conference."

Training its personnel in marketing is one of the major aspects of the Association of Junior Leagues, New York, said Liz Quinlan, director of marketing and communications. With 273 separate Junior Leagues in the U.S. and four international units,

marketing/public relations conferences are held several times a year.

"I regard public relations as a support function for marketing," said Quinlan. "Marketing defines the product. Public relations delivers the message. Our position is to train our staff. We meet with our volunteers to discuss marketing and public relations. We rely heavily on our research. The Junior Leagues have always done extensive research for programs to determine community needs. We target everything."

Seven years ago, Quinlan said, the Denver Junior League used Philip Kotler's book on marketing for nonprofits.

"After they studied it, they traveled around the country to train other Junior Leagues," Quinlan said. "As a result of this consciousness raising, marketing has become a buzzword. Sometimes we don't use the term correctly. There's a blurring of terms with public relations, but we rely on the same steps: knowing our public, defining how we can best engage them, and finally research."

New York-based Boys Clubs of America, structured like the Junior Leagues, consists of 592 separate organizations in the U.S., Puerto Rico, and the Virgin Islands.

Its approach to marketing, however, is slightly different.

"I have learned that nonprofit organizations cannot succeed in marketing and communications without paid, professional staff, and a budget for that function," said Jerry Bergman, director of marketing and communications services. "You can do some things through volunteers to help the organization, but marketing on an ongoing basis requires some professional help. I recognize that many nonprofit groups cannot afford their own paid professional marketing and communications personnel."

Groups that rely heavily on volunteers must try to recruit those with the appropriate professional backgrounds,

Reprinted from *Marketing News,* August 14, 1989, pp. 1, 2, published by the American Marketing Association, Chicago, IL 60606.

skills and knowledge, then try to merge their talents with those of the in-house staff so they can work as a team to develop an effective marketing plan, he said.

But Bergman has found that first he has to convince the individual Boys Clubs of the need for marketing.

"Small, rural clubs may not understand the importance of marketing," he said. "They think it's a gimmick—Madison Avenue. We're constantly running workshops, seminars, articles in our national publications to drive home the point.

"We take our marketing very seriously. We offer extensive training for our clubs on topics such as how to be a spokesperson and how to get publicity, etc.," said Bergman. "We know that an organization must create a sense of uniqueness about itself, its message, and its mission."

Some organizations, such as Planned Parenthood Federation of America Inc., are so well-known that they can keep marketing to a minimum.

"We don't have to worry about getting publicity," said Roberta Sinal, media relations specialist. "We're always in the news, especially with the abortion issue in the limelight. But we still create videotapes, which we give to our affiliates. We also do a large number of political ads in response to political issues."

Today the "marketing" department for the organization concerns itself with publications and products.

Like other nonprofits that have many affiliates, the national headquarters for Planned Parenthood in New York offers leadership, marketing, and spokesperson training.

Planned Parenthood does a lot of research, using Harris polls to get information, and has an "advocacy" meeting each year.

"We don't call it marketing, though it does concern marketing," Sinal said. "We don't have any strategy that's set in stone."

The YMCA of the USA has had a continuing marketing campaign since 1981, according to Jan McCormick, director of marketing and communications.

"Before we had a marketing depart-

ment, we used consultants," she said. "When the YMCA headquarters moved from New York to Chicago in May of 1980, the entire marketing office was reorganized into three divisions: corporate communications, public relations, and marketing."

The YMCA does not have enough funding to do extensive research, McCormick said. "Our research is informal. Our instincts have to be pretty good. You make mistakes, but people make mistakes with millions of dollars."

The Independent Sector, a coalition of 650 nonprofit organizations based in Washington, D.C., has found that outside consultants are effective in launching their marketing strategy.

"We're a small organization with limited funds," said John Thomas, vice president of communications.

The group has only a 35-member staff, he said, so having a separate department wouldn't be cost-effective."

"I would love to have a marketing department, but the chances of that are very slim," Thomas said. "Our marketing consultant did help us by showing us how to put our materials forward. He improved our mailing lists by helping us identify who would be most likely to purchase our materials. I'm very pleased with how far we've come in nine years...but I do think that today large nonprofits should have a marketing department. This is the age of marketing. One must put the message across."

Thomas said the Independent Sector began to reach beyond its previous marketing strategies in the last few years.

"For the first seven or eight years, we just concentrated on media relations and member relations," he said, but recently we've been trying to get better known by marketing to nonprofits and doing more fundraising. In the past two years, we've mailed over two million direct mail pieces. We're now marketing to a broader base. We do whatever research is necessary."

Nonprofits that are still a bit marketing-shy experiment with programs under the heading of communications. Last year, the American Red Cross, Washington, D.C., raised $300,000 using cause-related marketing tech-

niques in conjunction with Master-Card International Inc., according to Steve Delphen, development officer.

"Though we've stayed away from marketing as a term and a label for any department, we're just beginning to understand the nuances of how to make marketing strategies help us," he said. "I disagree with people who push marketing for nonprofits. They're just talking about basic communications techniques: research and evaluating results."

The Red Cross combines its needs with that of corporations. The corporation finds that its association with the charity enhances its image, "so we cater to corporate marketing needs and the charity's needs," Delphen said. "Some people don't like it."

And some nonprofits don't like marketing at first, but when they see the results they think differently.

Natel Matschulet, former vice president for marketing and community affairs at Mount Sinai Medical Center, New York, met some resistance when she created the hospital's first marketing department program, but the department continues her work today.

"At first they were not very open to marketing," she said. "But at that time, in 1986, the occupancy rate was down from 96% to 73%. They were resistant to the idea of financing my research. So I explained to them that research is basically a diagnostic procedure. Would you prescribe medicine without first running tests on the patient?"

In this case, the "patient" got better: Mount Sinai's occupancy rate returned to the 96% level as a result of the marketing campaign.

"Most hospitals don't know how to implement marketing techniques," said Matschulet, who is now vice president, director of strategic marketing for Citicorp in New York. "With occupancy rates dropping across the country, everyone is jumping on the marketing bandwagon. However, at most hospitals, they appoint the public affairs director as the marketing head. Though this individual is bright, he or she knows nothing about marketing. Without proper funding, no research is done. They get meager results, then the institution becomes disillusioned with marketing."

AN ETHICAL BASE FOR MARKETING DECISION MAKING

Geoffrey P. Lantos

Geoffrey Lantos is assistant professor of Marketing in the Business Administration Department of Stonehill College. He received his Ph.D. from Lehigh University in 1980.

Dr. Lantos has published in the Journal of the Academy of Marketing Sciences, Journal of Market Research Society, *and* Marketing News. *He has also published several cases on marketing for Christian organizations and has given several presentations on Christian business ethics. An article on teaching ethics in business curricula appeared in* Marketing News. *His book reviews on advertising society appear in several academic and trade journals and in the* Journal of Public Policy and Marketing.

The Need for Ethical Standards

The 1970's and 1980's have witnessed an increased concern about building an ethical foundation upon which to make better business decisions in those areas where the rightness or wrongness of those decisions is open to question. Ethics is the name given to the attempt to think through the moral implications of human actions; business ethics is the study of the morality of business decisions and the determination of standards for those decisions.

A concern for incorporating ethical standards into business decision making is occurring in American business organizations and college business curricula. Never in our history has there been more public discussion of ethics.

In early December of 1985, *U.S. News and World Report* published results of a survey on ethics stating that immorality is on the rise, especially among the young. The concern about eroding moral values was heightened by the questioning of big government and big business at the time of the Watergate scandals. "If we can't trust those entrusted to make decisions in the public interest, who can we trust?" went the public's reasoning.

Today the lack of morals in decision making screams at us from newspaper headlines: brokerage firms defraud banks by check-kiting, banks launder mob money, defense contractors steal from taxpayers by overbilling and gift giving, ad agency personnel get creative on cocaine, and advertisers bring each other to court over false and misleading competitive claims.

Many of these news stories play upon the already entrenched stereotype of "robber baron" capitalists as being greedy, exploitative, and manipulative, an image that has been with us at least since 1867, when Karl Marx wrote *Das Kapital*. During the 1970's and 1980's, picking up on the skeptical, if not hostile, public mood, the media hyped this image, and the vilification of entrepreneurs became a major theme of countless television programs, books, and movies. "Crime in the suites" became a popular topic of TV newscasters, who insinuated that Big Business is the root cause of human suffering. The media and "consumer advocates" presented as solutions more government regulation, marketplace intervention, and public scrutiny. Congressman William Dannenmeyer (R-CA) has noted such tendencies in liberal welfare states: "If it moves, regulate it. If it grows, tax it. If it makes a profit, investigate it."

From *The Journal of Business and Industrial Marketing*, Vol. 2, No. 2, Spring 1987, pp. 11-16. Copyright © 1987 by The Journal of Business and Industrial Marketing. Reprinted by permission.

However, most businesspeople would agree with Max Weber, who wrote in 1904 in *The Protestant Ethic and the Spirit of Capitalism* that the idea that capitalism or free enterprise favors greed is a "kindergarten" notion. Anticapitalists, who argue that significant business decisions need to be made in the public domain in order to ensure the public good, live in a Polyanna Utopian dreamer's world. The capitalist spirit has enabled people to invest their talents in the future—to place them at risk in a burst of creativity. A free market is itself a moral achievement; it is a product of discipline and of the postponement of present satisfaction for future goals. It has enabled people at the bottom of the socioeconomic ladder to become actively responsible for their own destiny, to make freely their own decisions and to cooperate in economic acts with other consenting adults.

Moreover, the idea that businesspeople are unethical to pursue profits is fatally flawed. It derives from the Marxian notion that labor alone creates value; and therefore the profits that the employer makes are derived from the work for which the laborers are not paid. This view fails to note that the capitalist must invest capital in his plant, incur selling costs, and the like. He is certainly entitled to a return on his investment. Additionally, the entrepreneur is the risk taker. Workers receive their wages whether or not the product moves off the shelves. Businesspeople are entitled to a return for the risks they have taken.

The dominant desire of the capitalist spirit has been to create goods and services never seen before, and to do so earlier and more inexpensively than would otherwise have been the case. Of course, the latter has also been the marketer's objective. Yet marketing, as the aspect of business most visible to the public, has taken a disproportionate share of the criticism of our free enterprise way of life. The rekindling of interest in consumerism over the last twenty-five years is evidence of this. Of course, consumerism is not exactly the Communist's plot to bedevil God-fearing, flag-waving American marketers that some businesspeople would have us believe it is. However, it has arisen as a response to the failure of business organizations and marketers to respond to legitimate consumer demands.

Adam Smith in his *Wealth of Nations* stated, "Consumption is the sole end purpose of all production" (i.e., why make goods unless they will be consumed?) "and the interest of the producer ought to be attended to, only so far as

The capitalist spirit has enabled people to invest their talents in the future—to place them at risk in a burst of creativity.

it may be necessary for promoting that of the consumer." This statement suggests that if businesspeople and marketers don't get their act together and truly practice the marketing concept, society has a right to inflict the heavy hand of regulation.

Marketing and Morality

It is reassuring to know that marketing has a very moral purpose: to satisfy human needs and wants and to help people through the exchange process. Good marketing helps to identify deficiencies of current marketplace offerings and to present to the consumer an alternative to correct the deficiency. Marketing, by its nature, coordinates the variables of product, price, place, and promotion to most effectively and efficiently address need deficiencies.

Therefore to make the often heard broad-brush statement to the effect that marketing by its nature is sleazy and unethical is absurd in that it implies a monolithic marketing force. One argument against marketing as an ethical discipline is the fact that it satisfies wants for unessential items in life. Harold Lindsell noted in *Free Enterprise: A Judeo-Christian Defense*, that "people do not really need fifty kinds of perfume, thirty kinds of deodorant, a hundred different shoe styles, more than one style of automobile, not to mention the necessity for marbles, cards, curlers or the thousands of knickknacks sold in department stores." However, consistent with free enterprise, people who are free are also free to want what you and I might not particularly care for. And it is certainly the marketer's right to satisfy those wants in a society whose hallmark is freedom. Who are the elitists who should be privileged to dictate to us what we "need?"

A free market is itself a moral achievement.

The problem is not with our discipline but with the way in which it is practiced. Marketing, like medicine, law, and other professions, has its bad apples who misuse the tools of the trade. While unethical practices such as deception, high-pressure selling, shoddy and unsafe products, planned obsolescence, and unjustifiably high prices have occurred and will continue, marketing is still an essential ingredient in the free enterprise system. There is sometimes a temptation to behave in an unethical way since individuals can make decisions behind the corporate shield and thus can do things that they might not do in their private lives. Most experts believe that it is easier to be dishonest at work because ties are less personal there.

Fortunately, history teaches that the marketer who has his eye only on the bottom line will not last in the long run, although he might make a profit in the short run—and he certainly will tarnish our profession's image in the long run. After all, the firm's assets have little or no value without customer goodwill. The question is: What can be done to foster decisions that are in the consumer's and even in society's long-run interest in accordance with the societal marketing concept? Can we formulate some guiding principles for ethical responsibility in business and marketing?

To begin with, a businessperson can develop an awareness that every important decision of his life involves moral considerations. He can instill a sensitivity of this fact in his employees and co-workers through (1) example, (2) discussing with them the moral implications of company decisions and actions, and (3) continual reminders that he has values in life above profit or economic security.

Thus the American businessperson should literally place ethics on the agenda for himself at home and at work, for his company, and for his professional or trade association. He must devise an ethical foundation that can be defined in a goodwill policy statement defining the organization's mission as a whole. For example: "What is the good our organization is known for doing in today's society? How do we do it better than our competition?" His calendar should include periodic meetings of management to discuss the moral dimensions of his business. In order to curb corruption in the 1980's more and more businesses are adopting stringent codes of ethics. And in response to disclosures of wrong-doing, many people are reexamining their values and searching for guidance.

At the functional level of marketing there is needed some sort of broad policy to provide boundaries and guidelines for specific marketing operations. The policy should be enacted by the top operating official and should relate the general ethical philosophy to which the company's market-ing activities will adhere as well as specific rules or regulations.

The idea that businesspeople are unethical to pursue profits is fatally flawed.

The rub is this: How does one go about constructing an ethical philosophy? After all, marketing decision making is fraught with many grey areas where the rightness of one's actions is open to question. For instance, in doing business abroad, it is sometimes necessary to grease a few palms with gringo green before you will be considered as a supplier. Is it okay to do this since everyone else seems to be doing it? What if you pack a free dish towel in each box of your detergent and then include it in the net weight of the box—is that being deceptive? Suppose your assistant product manager is dating your competition's secretary and believes he could find out some proprietary information from her—would you encourage him to do it? What if your research showed that you could increase profits by adding a one dollar chrome strip to your appliance and charge an extra $20, calling it the "deluxe model"—would you try it? Is there anything wrong with taking an extra hour for lunch? What about padding expense accounts? The list goes on and on.

The answer in each case depends upon your ethical philosophy, which will help you to answer the all-important question: "Is it right?" There are two basic approaches to deciding the morality of a particular action: *relative standards* (also known as *situation ethics* and *speculative philosophy*) and *absolute standards* (also known as *moral idealism* and *moral revelation*). Traditionally, absolute standards seemed to be more popular, but in recent years the trend has been toward relativism, which appears to be the dominant approach to ethics today.

Relative Standards

Using relative standards, one denies that there are absolute answers which hold regardless of the situation; rather the correctness of a particular action depends on the specific circumstances involved. In other words, "The only thing that is absolute is that nothing is absolute." Ethics is subjective, situational, culturally determined, and autonomous. Moral values are derived from human experience, that is, the basis of ethical values lies in the minds of men. The rules are to be found inside a closed system; no appeal can be made to a principle or existence outside the system (as in an open system). The approval of others can be used to validate your decision according to this thinking; the "new morality" becomes acceptable. Unfortunately, human beings are fallible, even fallen according to Judeo-Christian teaching.

Businesspeople are entitled to a return for the risks they have taken.

Situation ethics comes in two basic forms — utilitarianism and intuitionism. *Utilitarianism* judges not the act itself but the consequences of the act. If the results mean a net increase in society's happiness or welfare, then the act is believed to be morally right. Here we strive to obtain the greatest good for the greatest number. This is nice since most people end up satisfied.

One problem with this approach, however, is that someone might get burned. For example, state lotteries are usually favored by taxpayers (the majority) since their taxes are consequently reduced. But there is a tradeoff in that the poor, who can least afford to squander their money gambling, are heavy users of state lotteries, and the lottery will help feed the gambling addict's habit. Or, for instance, we might decide to build a lower level of safety into an automobile since this will save each consumer $25. However, it will also result in the death or injury of one out of every 115,000 consumers. How can we balance lives against cost savings? As another example, some people might advocate "free sex" since it is physically gratifying, even though the consequent potential communicable diseases are making the headlines and people sometimes suffer guilt afterwards.

Marketing, by its nature, coordinates the variables of product, price, place, and promotion to most effectively and efficiently address need deficiencies.

Another problem with utilitarianism is that interpersonal comparisons are impossible — how can we measure the increase in welfare to the minority? Yet, utilitarianism puts the general welfare of society ahead of the individual's welfare; the real danger is that one group such as the disadvantaged consumer might be exploited for the betterment of the whole society.

In effect, utilitarianism is akin to saying that the ends justify the means. Karl Marx used this concept in proclaiming that anything that will bring about the defeat of the bourgeoisie and the victory of the proletariat is justified. To use

an extreme example of utilitarianism, we might be able to justify having prostitutes work out of church basements if all of the money is subsequently donated to the poor. Marketers could use utilitarian principles to justify lying to customers, cheating, stealing or just about anything they want to as long as the majority's utility is enhanced.

Intuitionism is appealing because it is flexible, lacks rigidity, draws upon the manager's experience, and hence is probably the most widely used philosophy by default. The decision is right if the individual's intuition or conscience tells him that it is right. If the person's sixth sense or gut feeling says that it is okay, that his motives are good, and that he doesn't intend to hurt anyone, then he can go ahead with it. For example, if a manager believes that making a minor cosmetic change in his product and calling it "new and improved" will bolster sales without hurting anyone, then all is well.

The only trouble here is that the manager could be well-meaning but misguided, sincere but sincerely wrong. Whenever I get an idea, my bias is toward thinking that I'm right. Intuitionism permits one's personal prejudices to become rule criteria. However, that old saying "The road to hell is paved with good intentions" appears to be true. A well-known proverb states that "There's a way that seems right to a man, but its end is the way of death." The question is: Whose intuition can we trust? Ours? (Certainly.) Our co-workers'? (Maybe.) Our boss's? (Possibly.) Are these people infallible? A political activist recently justified terrorism and violence in order to accomplish his political ends. I wouldn't trust his intuition, would you? Some people believe that "all is fair in love and war." We know that "business is war." So is all fair?

Using relative standards, one denies that there are absolute answers which hold regardless of the situation; rather the correctness of a particular action depends on the specific circumstances involved.

One problem that arises with relative standards is that there will seldom be agreement among all concerned parties that you have made a morally correct decision. Morality is then reduced to a nose-counting matter in which the majority or plurality decides what is right or wrong. Thus, if the latest Gallup poll shows that 52 percent of the public now believes that mercy killing is okay, then it automatically is okay. In managerial decision-making situations the nose-counting can be done either among consumers or simply among managers. Thus, if the consensus among managers is that it is all right to pollute the environment in order to produce the product, then so be it. Similarly, those in government positions of power might make a decision based on their consensus, for example, of what is a fair profit for the firm. Or, perhaps your boss is the one who holds the power and makes the decisions. Will you automatically abide by them without question?

Another trouble with relativism is that often the decision appears arbitrary. For example, college professors who grade on a curve are in effect applying situation ethics. The decision to give Yin an A and to flunk Yang depends on the situation — Yin might be the high scorer in the class with an 83 and Yang the low scorer with a 78.

Situation ethics also leads to uncertainty, since values in our society seem to be trendy and unstable over time; they are like shifting sands, turning tides, and blowing winds— here today and gone tomorrow. When morality becomes a moving target, we feel rather insecure about the correctness of our decisons since we have no anchor for those decisons. For example, recently the media have favorably played up stories about several well-known actresses who have had babies out of wedlock. It would appear that illegitimacy is "in" and therefore it is all right to accept this behavior.

Likewise, marketing violent war toys (also known euphemistically as "action figures") to children might be the latest phenomenon, but does that make it justifiable? The average American is now overweight according to medical doctors, so does that make it acceptable?

In short, situation ethics is the "Yeah, but" school of thought. "Doesn't that seem improper?" "Yeah, but this is 1987," or "Yeah, but everyone else is doing it," or "Yeah, but my situation is different." For instance, many people tend to justify dishonesty on the basis that it is okay to lie if there is a good reason to do so. These are just rationalizations. This is a bankrupt philosophy which has resulted in the amoralization of America.

Absolute Standards

A more defensible approach to ethical decision making can be found in the absolute universal standards of moral idealism. This philosophy supposes that there are permanent, rigid rules (moral ideals) to be followed regardless of the circumstances, that is, there are certain behaviors that are just plain wrong. The idea that there exist timeless truths which have worked in the past is unpopular and not very appealing to most humans because of its rigidity. At the same time there appears to be a growing need for stability in a society which continues to change at an accelerating pace.

Furthermore, the question naturally arises: Where do fixed standards of right and wrong come from? Some might turn to parental standards by which they were raised. In a work situation one could look to one's superiors or to ethical guidelines drawn up by the company. Again, however, we are talking about manmade rules here — where did your parents or superiors derive their standards? They could easily have come from the two philosophies examined above: utilitarianism and intuitionism.

The basis of ethical values lies in the minds of men.

Behind the notion of absolute, eternal, immutable moral ideals lies the concept of moral revelation. This approach postulates the universe to be an open system where morality is revealed from outside of the human mind and experience. Most religions claim to provide the absolute standards that provide the certainty for which the human heart longs.

In the United States the Judeo-Christian value system derived from the Bible provides fixed permanent guidelines which humans can choose to accept or reject. Granted, there sometimes needs to be interpretation in applying God's standards as stated in the scriptures. For instance, there is disagreement among Bible scholars as to whether drinking alcoholic beverages in moderation violates God's principles. Therefore it is not clear to some whether or not marketing beer, wine, and distilled spirits is morally wrong. However, there probably would be agreement among the faithful that most advertisements for alcohol should go no further than promoting moderation in drinking and that they should not glamorize it, especially among young people. As another example, the Bible commands "Thou shalt not kill." However, some have interpreted the scriptures to say that killing is justified in a "just war." However, it is unclear just what a "just war" is.

Traditionally in our culture it was believed by many that the Bible provides the answers to all of the tough issues encountered in the business world as well as in the rest of life. However, with the secularization of our society there was a turning away from this view. Now there is some evidence that with the return of a conservative mood in our country many people are getting back to the Bible. Religious leaders note that Christian fundamentalism (adhering to the fundamentals of the faith) has grown rapidly because it provides direct answers. Those outside of the Judeo-Christian tradition can turn to their religion's standards to provide definite guidelines. Nevertheless, the dominant religious culture in the United States provides for us a basis of consensus which is undisputable.

Fortunately, these moral ideals are not too burdensome. True, they are rigid and sometimes it takes great courage to stick up for what you believe in. However, Biblical standards basically boil down to the Golden Rule of Leviticus: "You shall love your neighbor as yourself," which is paraphrased in the Gospel of Matthew as: "All things whatsoever you would that men do to you, so do you even to them," which was stated by Confucius as: "We are not to do unto others what we would not want others to do to us." Most marketers claim to be "people people" and so would probably find it difficult to argue with this philosophy.

This Biblical mandate gives the free enterprise system, which has been so often castigated, a human face and helps dampen the innate selfishness of humans by requiring them to temper their business decisions with a measure of altruism. The faults with free enterprise noted above are not intrinsic to the system itself. Rather, they arise from the failure of businesspeople to practice what the Old and New Testaments teach.

Following moral ideals revealed by God in the scenarios above, one would rise above bribery, would not do something that might deceive others ("thou shalt not lie"), and would not take secrets from competitors ("thou shalt not steal"). The marketing concept puts people above profit, and marketers usually discover that if they serve others' interests they will, in the end, serve themselves and reap a financial reward. After all, another Biblical proposition warns, "Whatsoever you sow that shall you also reap." If one strives for unconditional love of others, both in business and in life, that person will most likely be happy, successful, and fulfilled. After all, God's guidelines are not for His pleasure: they always have our own best interests at heart. Keeping this in mind, absolute, fixed, permanent standards that are rooted and grounded in moral revelation provide the perfect answer to ethical business decision making. To base ethics on relative standards is to seek the impossible: morality without certainty; ethics without absolutes. All that remains is a moral vacuum.

Marketing and Its Discontents

Marketers say they give people what they want.
Critics say marketers get people to
want what they don't need and often
can't have. Something's wrong.

Steven H. Star

Steven H. Star is editor-in-chief of the Sloan Management
Review *and director of the Marketing Center at the MIT
Sloan School of Management.*

Business sometimes has a bad name, and marketing is particularly singled out, especially advertising. Even businesspeople often hold marketing in deep suspicion. It is widely suspected of trying, with all the intelligence, technology, and cunning it can command, to get people to want what they don't need, of overpromising and exaggerating what can be delivered, and, worst, of exploiting people's vulnerabilities to get them to value, want, and expect the unattainable and undesirable. This criticism amounts to an attack on the ethics of marketing and, by extension, on business itself.

What makes this situation remarkable is the fact that for 30 years the driving theme in the practice of modern marketing has been the marketing concept, whose central principle is that business succeeds best when it tries to serve customers by giving them what they truly want. Something seems not right, and it is useful to try to understand what is going on and going wrong.

Actually, marketing and its practices, especially advertising and selling, have always been subjects of criticism and controversy. Some of these complaints go back as far as the Bible, Confucius, and classical Greek literature. More recently, the introduction of "personal deodorants" in the 1960s was highly controversial—both the idea of the product itself and the way it was advertised. Ten years ago, there was bitter criticism of "war toys," advertising aimed at children, and the promotion of baby formula in Africa. Today it's junk mail, the glorification to the young of hedonic lifestyles, the sheer abundance and intrusiveness of commercial communications.

Criticism of marketing focuses largely on two areas: its "excesses" and its "expertness." "Excesses" are about purposefully shoddy and objectionable products, inadequate warranties, deceptive or objectionable advertising, misleading packaging, questionable selling practices, and emphasis on tawdry values. These are the basis of what's broadly referred to as the "consumer movement," or "consumerism."

"Expertness" refers to the special ways marketing thinks about and approaches consumers. Most people define consumer needs or wants in terms of products and their functional attributes—what a product does, how it performs, tastes, or looks. Marketers do the same, but lots more. They think also of how products perform in terms of consumers' psychological and psychosocial needs and wishes. These tend to be complex, subtle, and manipulatable. Individuals often don't perceive any need for particular products until they have been persuasively exposed to the possibility of having them—and it is marketing experts who expertly do the persuading. When an expert takes on an amateur, especially when money is involved, the general feeling is that it's unfair.

Remarkably, the debate about marketing has been silent about some of the mechanics of modern life that give rise to it, specifically, about the structure of modern media and audiences. Indeed, it can be argued that many of the social discontents, and even ethical issues, associated with marketing arise not from "excesses," "inappropriate" definitions of consumer wants and needs, or from greed or cunning but rather from functional limitations on the implementability of the marketing concept.

The true practitioner of the marketing concept is supposed to find out what consumers want or need and try to satisfy these needs—if that makes economic and strategic sense. Assuming for the moment that one wants to cater carefully to consumer wants and needs (and that's not always a justified assumption—there are charlatans and sharpshooters everywhere in all professions), if you think for a moment about the process of trying to practice the marketing concept carefully, you quickly see how things will necessarily go wrong.

First, the marketer identifies a market opportunity: an apparent consumer need—discovered by research, intuition, technological innovation, or some combination of these. Then the marketer determines its size, its intensity (how much the people who have the need would be willing to pay for its satisfaction), and whether the need could be satisfied at a profitable cost. In other words, would it be feasible and profitable for the marketer's company to seek to satisfy this particular consumer need?

Then there is target identification—the specific groups in the population that the necessary marketing effort (usually called "program") will go after—not just people with the indicated need but also with the wish, will, and money to try to satisfy it. Marketers identify potential consumers along demographic and, especially in consumer goods, psychosocial terms. If, for example, there are 500,000 potential consumers of the product, one wants to know specifically who they are—young or old, male or female, rich or poor, urban or rural, "with-it" or "square," active or passive, confident or concerned.

A basic thrust of behavioral research in marketing is to suggest that psychosocial factors are at least as important as demographic factors in defining a mar-

ket segment. In other words, consumers who share a common set of attitudinal, perceptual, and sociological characteristics are more likely to share a particular set of needs than, say, consumers in the same age or income group.

These findings are useful for developing communications themes and other marketing efforts aimed at the target audience. Unfortunately, the ef-

> Few media or distribution channels allow the marketer to hit only the target audience —and that spells trouble.

forts usually cannot be closely matched to the audiences. There are few media or channels of distribution that allow the marketer to direct a marketing program exclusively to an audience that has the highly specific behavioral or psychosocial characteristics of the targeted audience. No matter how specialized our media, how carefully computerized our audience data, how sophisticated the protocols of market analysis, there remain, as always, major misfits among products, audiences, messages, and media. As one marketing executive recently said, "This consumer and behavior research is interesting, but in the end we still tell our advertising agencies to cast a wide net, to go after middle-income housewives between 21 and 40."

In the end, the marketer develops a program to coincide, to the greatest extent possible, with the attributes of the consumer target group. Unfortunately, the "greatest extent possible" is always full of disjunctions and static. Given the target group, marketers must make trade-offs regarding specific product features, packaging, personal selling, copy strategy, distribution channels, attendant services, price, advertising media, and much more. And while marketers typically view the "audience" for the selected program as a function of a media plan, it also depends on the choice of channels of distribution. Also, depending on how much personal selling is used either directly or through the distribution channels, it is a function of the "call instructions" given to the sales force.

This brief look at what's involved in the development of a marketing program allows us to identify three groups of consumers who are affected by that process, and how it works. First, there is the *market segment*—people with the need in question. Second, there is the *program target*—people in the segment with the "best fit" characteristics for the product and program. (Lots of people may need trousers, but only a few qualify as likely buyers of Giorgio Armani.) Finally, there is the *program au-*

dience—all people who are actually exposed to the marketing program, without regard to whether they are in the segment of its best-fit component.

These three groups are rarely synonymous. The exception occurs occasionally in industrial products where customers for a particular product may be few and easily identifiable. Such customers, all sharing a particular need (a market segment), are likely to group themselves into a meaningful target (for example, all companies with a particular application of the product in question, such as high-speed filling of bottles at breweries). In such circumstances, direct selling is likely to be economically justified, and highly specialized trade media exist to help expose the members of the program target (and *only* the members of the program target) to the marketing program. Under these circumstances, the marketing segment, program target, and program audience often will be virtually identical.[1]

Most consumer goods markets are significantly different. Typically, there are many rather than few potential customers. Each represents a relatively small amount of potential sales. Rarely do members of a particular market segment group themselves neatly into a meaningful program target. There are substantial differences among households or individual consumers with similar demographic characteristics.[2] Even with all the past decade's advances in information technology, in microsegmentation of consumers, in communications, and in specialized media and distribution systems, the economic feasibility of direct selling of consumer goods is rare. Mass marketing remains the predominant mode.

The continued existence in consumer goods of significant differences between market segments and program targets and between program targets and program audiences is obvious enough. Assume that a market segment of one million household buyers has been determined to have a particular need—say for a heavy-duty laundry detergent. Seventy percent of these buyers share a particular set of demographic characteristics—they have small children who frequently play outdoors in muddy fields. The remaining 30% have demographic characteristics that are randomly distributed throughout the rest of the population—the households include adults who work as auto mechanics. Under these conditions, if the program target is democratically defined in terms of families with small children, it will include only 70% of the market segment.

Moreover, the set of demographic characteristics that provides a best-fit description of the market segment almost certainly also describes a group of consumers who are not members of the market segment (they do not have the need in question because, say, their children don't play in muddy fields). If, for example, the small-children households total 1,500,000, then mem-

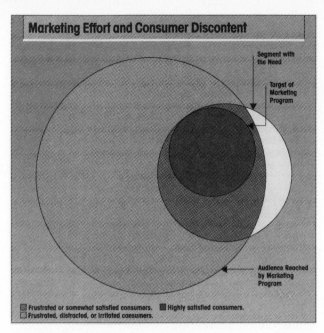

Marketing Effort and Consumer Discontent

Segment with the Need

Target of Marketing Program

Audience Reached by Marketing Program

☑ Frustrated or somewhat satisfied consumers.　■ Highly satisfied consumers.
☐ Frustrated, distracted, or irritated consumers.

bers of the muddy-fields market segment represent less than 50% of the members of the program target. The misfit is enormous.

Similar misfits accompany the translation of a program target into a program audience. The usual objective is to maximize advertising exposure of the program target for a particular budgetary expenditure. The most efficient media schedule will rarely reach all members of the program target. But it will almost certainly reach people who are not in the program target. The same kinds of misfits will almost certainly occur in distribution channels. From the marketer's perspective, these inefficiencies are unfortunate but totally unavoidable.

Thus marketing programs generate three partially overlapping groups of consumers—the market segment, the program target, and the program audience. Largely, these divide into six meaningful clusters:

1. Segment, target, and audience.
2. Segment and audience.
3. Target and audience.
4. Audience.
5. Segment and target.
6. Segment.[3]

The relative size of each of these clusters for a particular marketing program is a function of the level of congruence between the market segment, the program target, and the program audience (as shown in the illustration, "Marketing Effort and Consumer Discontent").

Cluster 1 (segment, target, *and* audience) represents the social value of the marketing concept. Consumers in this cluster have had their needs identified, have had a marketing program designed specifically around their characteristics, and have been exposed to the marketing program. The marketing program has satisfied the needs of these consumers.

Cluster 2 (segment *and* audience) consists of consumers whose needs have been identified, have had a product made available to them in the market, and have been exposed to the marketing program. But unfortunately, neither the product nor the program has been designed with their particular characteristics in mind. The product may be too expensive, sold through inconvenient channels (outlets that exist only in large urban centers), or the copy strategy may make them feel uncomfortable (a youth theme when they are of advanced years). Members of this cluster may be partially satisfied (if they purchase the product though it doesn't quite fill their needs) or frustrated (if, for example, they can't afford the product).

Consumers in Cluster 3 (target *and* audience) are exposed to the marketing program even though they have no interest in it (they don't feel the need to which it is addressed). The marketing program is likely to be distracting or even irritating, especially since it has been designed (copy, media, channels) to appeal to consumers with their particular characteristics.[4] Cluster 4 (audience *only*) is quite similar except that the marketing program is likely to be somewhat less distracting since it was not designed to appeal to members of this cluster (they are not members of the program target).

Clusters 5 (segment *and* target) and 6 (segment *only*) consist of consumers who have a need that a marketer has attempted to fill, but they are not aware of the product's availability because they are not members of the program audience. They've not heard or seen the message. They are the "dropped outs" of the marketing process. The marketing concept is not working for them. Behaviorally, these consumers are frustrated.[5]

It is obvious that the number of possible mismatches are from three to six times greater than possible close matches. (For a summary of the clusters, see the chart, "Marketing Clusters and Consumer Reactions.") The possibilities of disaffection are abundant, not because of carelessness, indifference, irresponsibility, ineptitude, or cupidity, but because the world is imperfect.

While a well-conceived marketing program certainly provides satisfaction to some consumers (Clusters 1 and some of Cluster 2), it most likely will also distract some consumers (Clusters 3 and 4) and frustrate others (Clusters 5 and 6 and some members of Cluster 2). And it is these consumers who almost surely give rise to much (though not all) of the criticism of marketing in our intensely commercial times.

It is quite possible that the effects of segment-target incongruence would be of little importance if they were randomly distributed through the population. A certain amount of dissatisfaction, distraction, and frustration seems inherent in the human condition, and—according to some psychologists—may even be a necessary condition of psychological health. Unfortunately, certain segments of society probably encounter disproportionately large amounts of distraction and frustration. In particular, people whose needs differ significantly from others who have their particular demographic characteristics are likely to experience an unusually large amount of distraction. They get exposed to a great deal of marketing effort (mostly via mass communications) that is not intended for them. And so they get mad.

This possibility was documented over 20 years ago in the Harvard Business School study, *Advertising in America.*[6] Users of products who encountered advertisements for those products had more favorable (or fewer unfavorable) attitudes toward those advertisements than nonusers. And users of particular brands of those articles had even better attitudes toward ads featuring those brands than users of other brands. Getting irritated or mad depends, as they say, on "where you're coming from."

The likelihood of getting mad is almost surely greater in the better educated sectors and among the professional commentators of our society. They fall disproportionately into Cluster 3 (target and audience, but not segment), where they probably share many of the demographic characteristics of the dominant middle class (age, income, location) but differ significantly in values and perceived needs. This subgroup may be exposed to a great many marketing programs in which it has little interest, or which it perceives as alien to its values. It probably also has disproportionately greater access to the institutions and instruments of public commentary (via lectures, news reports, columns, and articles) and is likely therefore to make a disproportionately large amount of critical noise about modern marketing.

Another group of consumers who are exposed to marketing programs that bother them are those who have the needs that the programs address but not the demographic characteristics of the best-fit program targets. They may have, for example, a strong desire for a high-performance sports car or expensive toys for their children (as advertised on Saturday morning TV) but not the resources to pay for them. Such consumers are likely to experience an unusual amount of frustration. The same is also true of variously disadvantaged members of society—falling disproportionately into Clusters 6 (segment only) and 2 (segment and audience).

Although their needs may be recognized and they may be exposed to relevant marketing communications, such consumers are rarely targets of the particular marketing programs. The marketing programs are rarely tailored specifically to their circumstances (low income, lack of "normal" credit, limited physical or psychological mobility), and so they are likely to be extremely frustrated. Presumably, this frustration would be higher for the segment-audience cluster (the urban disadvantaged) than for the segment-only cluster (the rural disadvantaged), but this is only conjecture. Nor is this to suggest that the frustrations of the disadvantaged are attributable to the marketing process. Clearly the causes are far more basic. But it does suggest some of the reasons why the practice of the marketing concept and the operations of the marketing process at least do not prevent, avoid, or minimize frustrations.

The marketing concept, like all good things that seem to make good sense, is burdened by process con-

Marketing Clusters and Consumer Reactions

Clusters	Reactions
1. Segment, target, and audience	Highly satisfied
2. Segment and audience	Somewhat satisfied or frustrated
3. Target and audience	Highly distracted or irritated
4. Audience	Somewhat distracted
5. Segment and target	Frustrated
6. Segment	Frustrated

straints that limit, in implementation, the achievement of its promises. In particular, the lack of congruence among segments, targets, and audiences seems a significant cause of consumer distraction and frustration. Marketing programs that produce social goods (consumer satisfaction) will almost surely also have dysfunctional social effects.

This line of reasoning takes us into the old, and not very reassuring, subject of welfare economics – a method of analysis that, like so much else in the rhetoric of the social sciences, suffers deeply from analysis paralysis. If a particular marketing program has both functional and dysfunctional effects, how does one make a trade-off between them? If a given program could be shown to have satisfied 1 million consumers, distracted 500,000, and increased the frustration of 300,000, would its net effect on society be negative or positive? While the relative intensity of these several social effects would certainly have to be an important part of the equation, even this information would leave the question unanswered, since reasonable people would surely continue to dispute the social importance of a unit of satisfaction as compared with a unit of frustration.

The social effects of the marketing process must,

If a marketing program satisfies a million people, distracts 500,000, and frustrates 300,000, what is the net effect?

like all social phenomena, be looked at in some sort of trade-off matrix. While there may never be agreement on the proper trade-offs among social effects, it would be useful to have a better picture of what these effects are. This would make it possible to determine the relative magnitudes of the effects occasioned by various marketing programs in each of the six clusters, to measure the intensity of the hypothesized behavioral effects of such clusterings, and to determine whether selected subgroups of society fall into particular clusters to a disproportionate degree. It should also be possible to identify specific points at which technical improvements in the marketing process would have significant social payoffs.

Of course, the analysis suggested here regarding marketing's sometimes bad reputation is independent of corrupt business practices, such as calculated duplicity, conscious misrepresentation, distortion, trickery, shoddiness, and the like – none of which is, in any case, unique to modern times. But at all times there will be misfits between products, segments, targets, and audiences. It is useful to understand their innocent origins and inevitability.

Still, any such understanding should not prevent asking what real problems are being missed because we argue about the wrong things. An explanation of a phenomenon is not its justification. Do we fail to exercise the self-restraint that civilized life requires? Do we get so intent in fighting our critics that we fail honestly to confront critical issues while avoiding the necessity to be honestly self-critical? Have we tried honestly to fix some of the misfits and alleviate some of the discontents?

References

1. The overwhelming success of IBM in the computer mainframe business, from roughly 1957 to 1980, was based largely on the congruence of its market segments, program targets, and audiences. It divided its data-processing business into 16 major segments, most of which were further divided into subsegments. In general, these segments were defined by applications commonality: the "distribution" segment, for example, included all companies for which inventory and physical distribution costs represented a major component of controllable expense. A separate program was developed for each segment (or subsegment), and individual salespeople and sales offices specialized in those segments. Every potential purchaser of data-processing equipment in the United States was assigned to an IBM salesperson who was expected to tailor marketing programs to the potential customer's specific needs. As a result, IBM achieved a high degree of congruence among segments, targets, and audiences, despite the fact that

its market was highly varied. See E. Raymond Corey and Steven H. Star, *Organization Strategy: A Marketing Approach* (Cambridge: Harvard University Press, 1971), pp. 108-155.

2. In theoretical terms, a consumer market segment consists of individuals who share psychological, sociological, and demographic characteristics, which – together – are likely to lead to a particular purchase act. In implementing a marketing program, however, it is frequently necessary to treat demographics as the sole variable of interest (except in copy formulation). Thus, while behavioral research in marketing helps explain the reasons for program-target incongruence, it has made remarkably little headway in helping marketers reduce the incongruence.

3. A separate "target" cluster is also possible but is not relevant for this present purpose.

4. Actually, a consumer who had the need but has satisfied it would also fall into this cluster. For example, a consumer who may have needed informa-

tion prior to purchasing a watch may find such information distracting after he has made the purchase, especially if it makes him question his purchase. Conversely, he may find advertising of the product he purchased useful in reducing postpurchase cognitive dissonance, as would seem to be the case with automobiles.

5. Of course, segment-audience incongruence is not the only (or even major) source of consumer frustration. In many cases, consumer needs will not be satisfied because of (1) technological constraints – it can't be done; (2) economic constraints – it isn't profitable; (3) strategic constraints – companies choose not to do it; or (4) information constraints – companies have simply not yet identified the need. In this context, we may view segment-audience incongruence as a *process constraint* on consumer satisfaction.

6. Raymond A. Bauer and Stephen A. Greyser, *Advertising in America: The Consumer View*, Division of Research, Graduate School of Business Administration, Harvard University, Boston, 1968.

Some food labels aren't on the level

The federal government is preparing to step in to help states force companies to support such claims as 'light' and 'fat-free.'

Denise L. Amos

Times Staff Writer

Krista Yurchak, a Lakeland mother of two, believes only half of what she reads on food labels and none of what she hears on TV.

"I don't buy food based on the front of the label," she said.

"I don't trust it. It could say 'low cholesterol' and still be high in saturated fats. . . . I don't like what those companies are doing: I think it's deceitful and misleading."

In the sometimes whimsical world of food marketing, a handful of Frosted Flakes seems healthier than an apple, a glass of V8 lets you off the hook for eating vegetables, and pork is a white meat that's good for your heart.

Companies making and selling these foods made those claims.

But consumer advocates and health organizations contended that many of these foods are healthier for companies' profits than for people.

As a result, regulators, legislators and even President Bush said they plan to toughen the Food and Drug Administration's rules on labeling next year. And some state attorneys general (including Florida's Bob Butterworth) call themselves the food police because they are penalizing national companies for ads the officials call misleading.

What this will mean to the consumer is unclear. Supporters of tougher food labeling rules expect that a federal crackdown will end liberal labeling.

But some advocates fear the food labeling crackdown won't go far enough and that pending legislation will actually weaken efforts by the food police. Company officials and industry analysts second that, saying they don't expect many changes in marketing strategies as a result of the crackdown.

"It's not going to have an impact on the way they market food," said Richard Elam, an investment analyst who follows the food industry for Blunt Ellis & Leowi in Chicago.

"(Nutritional advertising) has been an important part of their marketing strategy," he said. "They will still be able to do that; they will just have to document their claims."

Food companies have advertised health claims for decades, long before Wonder Bread asserted during the 1970s that its white bread "helps build strong bodies 12 ways."

In recent years the health pitch has broadened to include a host of goodies—cakes and cookies with fiber, fat-free ice creams and desserts, "light" potato chips and pretzels. Even cooking oils chimed in with the statement "made with 100 percent vegetable oil." (Some of the most commonly used vegetable oils are highest in saturated fats.)

Because many baby boomers are approaching middle age, they are taking to heart that they are what they eat. The $350-billion processed food industry has shifted its marketing to put its products in the healthiest of lights.

"Exploitation of the diet and health connection by food marketers runs the gamut all the way to positioning foods as medicine," said Nancy S. Wellman, president of the American Dietetic Association.

For instance, scientific studies that showed oat bran lowering cholesterol levels propelled sales of cereals, breads and dozens of other new products sprinkled with oats. Quaker Oats Co. sales of oat products jumped 33 percent between fall 1987 and December 1988. But just as quickly, sales fell after a later study discredited the findings; now oat bran sales are at 50 percent of last year's sales, said Ron Bottrell, a Quaker Oats spokesman.

"A lot of the people who were choking down oat bran now feel betrayed because Quaker went overboard," said Robert Parrish, a lawyer for the Center for Science in the Public Interest, a consumer group.

Bottrell said Quaker Oats' advertising did not go overboard because it said oats were only a part of a low-fat diet that can eventually reduce cholesterol.

In the absence of further scientific studies, many companies are developing their own "healthy" foods. For instance, Kraft General Foods last year introduced fat-free salad dressings, yogurts, pastries and ice cream.

"Ten years ago there weren't fat-free products; there were reduced-calorie products," said Kathy Knuth, a Kraft General Foods spokeswoman.

Many of the so-called "light" products are extensions of popular foods, such as "light" Ruffles potato chips and Doritos nacho chips, which Frito-Lay Inc. rolled out in April. Though the "light" chips boast a third less oil—therefore less fat and calories but with the same or more salt—they cost 20 cents more.

People who have added fish and white meat to their diets sometimes can't give up Doritos, said Polly Black, a senior product manager of Frito-Lay in Dallas.

"They're going to continue to eat the snacks they ate as children," she said. "This gives them permission to continue enjoying them."

Frito-Lay expects sales of the "light" versions to equal 15 percent of sales of its regular brands, she said.

Much of that could be added market share. With new versions of popular items, food processors are increasing their exposure on supermarket shelves, much like the cola companies, said Frederick Marx, a marketing consultant in Bloomfield Hills, Mich.

From *St. Petersburg Times*, August 19, 1990. Reprinted by permission.

"The parts are worth more than the whole," he said.

In some cases, food companies had not changed their products much; the merely emphasized the positive. Dozens of products that don't naturally contain dietary cholesterol, for instance, are advertised as "no cholesterol." The FDA is expected to propose banning that practice unless the products just as prominently display how much fat they contain.

In another case, Sara Lee Corp. last year was forced to withdraw its "light" snack cakes because they contained the same calories and fat as the originals; they were merely cut smaller and tasted lighter. Since then, Sara Lee has introduced Sara Lee Light Classics, containing fewer calories and less fat.

Through it all, the FDA allowed the liberal labeling, taking its lead from the Reagan Administration, which once asserted that ketchup fulfilled the vegetable requirement in school lunches.

The Bush Administration has pushed the FDA to devise new food labeling requirements, many of which are to be proposed this fall. And bills in both houses of Congress would put legal power behind the FDA's punch while giving it an 18-month deadline.

The proposals generally would require:

•that all packaged foods give nutritional information (currently only 60 percent do so, most voluntarily);

•That the nutrition information specify fat content—saturated and unsaturated—cholesterol, calories from fat and fiber information;

•that health claims be limited to certain areas and be FDA approved. Companies need to provide scientific proof.

Several companies including Frito-Lay, the Kellogg Co. and Quaker Oats, said they are confident they will be able to continue making health claims because they already have scientific documentation.

"The wording may change slightly," Quaker Oats' Bottrell said.

Nevertheless, food industry representatives say the industry wants to reform itself. Industry lobbies have publicly supported the FDA's move and the bills in Congress.

"We're prepared to change every label in the supermarket," said Jeffrey Nedelman, spokesman for the Grocery Manufacturers Association, a food processors' organization in Washington, D.C.

Nevertheless, food lobbyists have led a states-rights food fight in Congress and in the White House, endangering the food labeling bills.

Late last month, the House version of the bill passed, with the tougher bill still mired in the Senate. The sticking point is whether the new federal rules should preempt state's rules, which in a few cases are tougher.

Food processors don't want to deal with a patchwork of labeling laws, Nedelman said. The Grocery Manufacturers Association urged members to lobby legislators for preemption.

But states-rights advocates, many high in the Bush Administration, have been reluctant to give up states' ability to make tougher rules, especially in light of the FDA's previous inaction.

The food police already face threats to that power on another front. A number of attorneys general recently lost an appeal in a suit challenging national advertising involving airlines, a question that may go before the U.S. Supreme Court and affect their jurisdiction in other matters.

"We're concerned with having the ability to make the rules," said Mark Barnett, an assistant attorney general based in Miami. "We're concerned that federal standards will fall short of the protection consumers need. We want to be able to hold (food companies) to higher standards."

Children's Advertising Grows Up, But Not Everyone Approves

Jesus Sanchez

The ad campaign launched by the Seven-Up Co. 2½ years ago could have been called childish, and the soft-drink firm would have been the first to agree.

Children 6 to 12 were the target of a 7-Up television commercial that featured an animated character named Dot—modeled after the red circle found on the soda label—who played baseball with peas and carrot sticks inside a refrigerator.

"We've met with a lot of success," said marketing chief Russ Klein of the Dot campaign. Since its debut, kids are drinking 20% more 7-Up than before. "We felt that it was important to keep the brand present among that age group . . . it was important to address future consumers."

Madison Avenue is chasing television's Saturday morning crowd as growing numbers of companies—from hotels to makers of microwaveable meals—roll out new children's products and hope to win over future consumers. But many say the trend will only serve to further exploit and mislead children.

The overall thrust of most of the advertising to kids has not been informational," said Charlotte Baecher, editor of Penny Power, a consumer magazine for kids published by Consumers Union. "It has been emotional, and it has been unfair."

Despite the criticism, many companies have found the children's market has grown too large and too lucrative to resist.

Newcomers to children's advertising such as Tyson Foods, Reebok, Burger King and others have joined cereal and toy makers in pitching products to preteens. Ads have popped up in video games and in classrooms, courtesy of Whittle Communications' controversial Channel One. Television networks have sold a record $500 million worth of com-

---

BIG SPENDERS

Kid ages 4 to 12 spend about $6 billion a year from allowances and gifts . . .

Product/Service	Expenditures (in billions)
Snacks and candy	$2.077
Toys	1.879
Clothing	0.690
Movies and sports	0.606
Video arcades	0.486
Other (tapes, stereos, etc.)	0.264

. . . and influence at least another $50 billion a year in household purchases.

Product/Service	Expenditures (in billions)
Fast food	$19.0
Soft drinks	8.0–10.0
Clothing	8.0–9.0
Toys	6.0–8.0
Cereals	2.5
Cookies	2.0
Salty snacks	2.0

Source: James McNeal, Texas A&M University

---

mercial time on kids programs for the 1990–91 season, according to industry publication Advertising Age. Kids even get junk mail.

"There are more and more companies every day that are realizing the potential of the market," said Clifford M. Scott, vice president of Scott Lancaster Mills Atha, a Los Angeles agency that recently began to focus on children's advertising.

Companies are attracted by the size of the so-called baby boomlet of about 43 million children under age 12 who spend an estimated $6 billion a year from allowances and gifts.

More important, children raised by busy working parents influence at least $50 billion worth of household purchases, said James McNeal, a marketing professor at Texas A&M who studies the buying habits of children.

"It's not subtle influence," McNeal said. "This is 'I gotta have this or I will die' type of influence."

"The children are getting drawn more into the decision-making process," said Sam Ashenofsyk, co-founder of Network of Independent Broadcasters, which sells commercial ad time on after-school programs. "It would be a good idea if they are presented with what the product is all about."

Researchers have found that children as young as age 4 begin to develop brand awareness and influence what parents buy.

Young children "typically pay more attention to the commercials than the program," said USC marketing professor Henrianne Sanft, who studies the impact of advertising on children. "They think that ads are entertaining and entertainment."

The young readers of Sports Illustrated for Kids devote as much attention to ads—which kids refer to as "commercials"—as to stories, says publisher Ann S. Moore, who notes that ads give the magazine a grown-up look that appeals to kids. "The kids say, 'It's a real product just for me. It's not a textbook. It has commercials.'"

Creating ads for children has become more sophisticated. Firms such as Tyson Foods developed separate ad campaigns for kids and their parents to sell the same product, such as their microwaveable meals for children called "Looney Tunes." The television commercials emphasize the "fun" of Looney Tunes and were made primarily for children, while print ads aimed at parents stress nutritional aspects.

Many of today's ads borrow heavily from kids' popular culture such as music videos and video games. Cuteness, once the trademark of kids commercials, is now considered passe.

"It's not the warm and fuzzy teddy bear types of images," said Burke Cueny, director of national advertising for Domino's Pizza, whose recent first children's commercial was titled "Yo, Domino's." "What was making the greatest impact was the fast moving, quicker cut, and fairly stronger musical spots. That's the type of spot we put together."

Some companies have created tiers of products and ads aimed at creating lifelong customers from Day 1. Reebok, for example, makes a line of Weebok shoes for children up to age 5 and a line of sneakers—and ads—for kids up to age 10.

"We hope by the time he is 10," said senior marketing director Gordie Nye, "he is paying attention to the Reebok adult advertising."

Executives like Nye say their ads are not aimed at duping kids into buying their product. But advertising critics say kids age 8 and younger often confuse commercials with programs and do not realize that they are being persuaded to buy something.

"I think young kids can be deceived by thinking a product is something it is not," said Sanft. "Kids believe everything they see. Educating them is the key to keeping them from being deceived."

Advertising often pits children against parents in a battle to buy what has been promoted, says Baecher at Consumers Union, which will release a study next month on the impact of advertising on children.

"The marketers realize that if they get kids wanting something badly enough, the kids will wear down their parents enough until they get it," said Baecher.

Peggy Charren, president of Action for Children's Television, which is lobbying for a cap on commercials during children's programs, says she believes that parents have already been worn down. "I think we are able to accept more manipulation of kids than we did in the past."

But advertisers dismiss much of the criticism. "We know that parents are still the gatekeepers," said Klein at Seven-Up. "Our position has been all along to establish awareness among children."

"We have an obligation to make sure that the advertising is appropriate," said Moore at Sports Illustrated for Kids. The magazine requires ads, for example, to prominently display company symbols and will not place basketball shoe ads, for example, near stories about basketball.

It may be in the best interest for advertisers to keep on their toes because children become increasingly skeptical of ads as they grow older, said Sanft.

"They don't really trust commercials," she said. "They learned advertisers were trying to sell them something."

Research, Markets, and Consumer Behavior

- Market Research (Articles 19-23)
- Markets and Demographics (Articles 24-29)
- Consumer Behavior (Articles 30-32)

If marketing activities were all we knew about an individual, we would know a great deal. By tracing these daily activities over only a short period of time, we could probably guess rather accurately that person's tastes, understand much of his or her system of personal values, and learn quite a bit about how the individual deals with the world.

In a sense, this is a key to successful marketing management: tracing a market's activities and understanding its behavior. However, in spite of the increasing sophistication of market research techniques, this task is not easy. Today a new society is evolving out of the changing life-styles of Americans, and these divergent life-styles have put great pressure on the marketer who hopes to identify and profitably reach a target market. At the same time, however, each change in consumer behavior leads to new marketing opportunities.

The articles presented in this unit were selected to provide information and insight into the effect that life-style changes and demographic trends are having on American industry.

"How to Hunt for the Best Source," begins the first subsection by guiding the reader to some invaluable sources of research data. The next article provides some helpful insight into global market research. The following two articles delineate how psychographical data and psychological research can be used to better understand consumers' values and attitudes underlying their selection of particular products and services. The final article discuss the importance and proper implementation of focus groups as an effective tool of marketing research.

The next six articles examine the importance of demographic data, geographic settings, economic forces, and age considerations in making marketing decisions. The lead article in this subsection, "A Symphony of Demographic Change," gives a thought-provoking look at some possible areas of future demographic change. The next article describes the importance of finding the appropriate promotional vehicle to target the low-income consumer. The author of "Different Folks, Different Strokes" explains how targeted advertising gears its products toward local tastes, problems, and events. " 'Real' Consumers Just Aren't Normal" articulates the importance of formulating marketing strategies for the large segment of the population with disabilities. The following article describes social, economic, and demographic characteristics of the average American—Jane Doe. The last article scrutinizes important characteristics of the life-styles and the consumer purchasing power of the 50-plus-year-old consumers and suggests some marketing strategies being employed to sell to this sector of the market.

The remaining articles in the final subsection look at how consumer behavior, social attitudes, cues, and quality considerations impact the evaluation and purchase of various products and services for different consumers (children and shoppers).

Looking Ahead: Challenge Questions

As marketing research techniques become more and more advanced through the use of automation and the computer, and as psychographic analysis leads to more and more sophisticated models of consumer behavior, do you believe marketing will become more capable of predicting consumer behavior? If so, what ethical considerations must confront the marketing profession?

Where the population lives, its age, and its ethnicity are demographic factors of importance to marketers. What other demographic factors must be taken into account in long-range market planning? What industries do you think are most concerned with these factors?

What are some marketing situations where focus groups would be a viable and worthwhile marketing research tool to use? Why?

Psychographic segmentation is the process whereby consumers markets are divided into segments based upon similarities in life-styles, attitudes, personality type, social class, and buying behavior. In what specific ways do you envision psychographic research and findings helping marketing planning and strategy in the next decade?

Unit 2

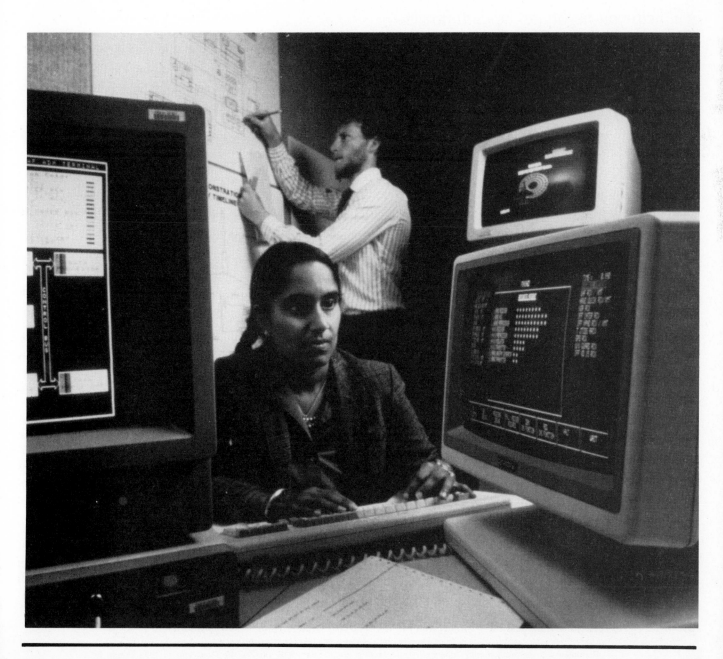

HOW TO HUNT FOR THE BEST SOURCE

This hunter's guide to consumer information will help you negotiate the data jungle.

Diane Crispell

Diane Crispell is associate national editor of American Demographics.

Once upon a time, demographic data were as scarce as polar bears in Miami. But times have changed—there are more data today than locusts in a plague. So how do you track down the information you need? As with any quarry, knowing what you're after provides clues to its whereabouts. The following guidelines will help you in your hunt.

■ **Identify the Species** Consumer information ranges from simple population numbers to socioeconomic characteristics, media and purchasing behavior, and attitudinal and lifestyle classifications. Pinpoint the type of data you need, and the source becomes apparent.

The government specializes in socioeconomic characteristics of the population—including age, race, sex, educational attainment, labor-force status, household composition, marital status, occupation, income, immigrant status, and more. The agencies that compile these data are often obvious. The Department of Education surveys students, teachers, and schools. The Department of Health and Human Services studies health knowledge and practices, illnesses and injuries, and the use of health-care providers and facilities. The Bureau of Justice Statistics compiles data on criminals and the victims of crime. The Bureau of Labor Statistics follows employment trends. The Census Bureau tracks just about all socioeconomic characteristics.

If you don't know which government agency does what, get a copy of the latest *Statistical Abstract of the United States*. This annual tome justifiably bills itself as the "national data book and guide to sources." It is published by the Department of Commerce and is available from the U.S. Government Printing Office in Washington, D.C.; telephone (202) 783-3238.

There are many nonprofit organizations that produce consumer information. Trade associations, for example, are excellent sources of information on their particular industries. It's a good bet that the National Association of Realtors is interested in homebuying trends, and indeed, it publishes regular studies of homebuyers. The annual *Encyclopedia of Associations,* produced by Gale Publications of Detroit, will tell you where to find the organization you need.

An information industry has grown up around the need for consumer data. Hundreds of companies specialize in collecting and selling data in the form of syndicated surveys, media-measurement research, market studies, lifestyle analyses, and so on. An increasing number of firms link demographics, psychographics, media use, and purchasing behavior to offer a complete market research system.

Listings and descriptions of government agencies, consumer information companies, and other sources of consumer data are available in *The Insider's Guide to Demographic Know-How*, published by American Demographics Press of Ithaca, New York. The FINDEX *Directory of Market Research Reports, Studies, and Surveys* contains a comprehensive listing and description of market studies produced in the private sector; it is published annually by Cambridge Information Group Directories in Bethesda, Maryland.

■ **Mark Off the Territory** Do you want data for the U.S. as a whole or for smaller areas like states, cities, or zip codes? Do you want standard census geography—counties, Metropolitan Statistical Areas, places, minor civil divisions, blocks, and census tracts? Or do you need other kinds of standard areas, like telephone area codes, ADIs (Areas of Dominant Influence), or DMAs (Designated Marketing Areas)? Do you need customized geography like sales territories or a radius around a store?

Before you hunt for data, know the level of geography you need. That will guide you to the right source. Except for the decennial census, most government data are limited to the national, regional, and sometimes state level. So are much of the data available from nonprofit organizations and private data companies. But a number of data companies produce population estimates and projections for any geographic area, including sales territories and trading areas.

■ **Select the Season** Do you need 1989 data? Can you live with 1987 numbers, or even 1980 census data? Trend data can be hard to find, and projections are especially scarce.

Government surveys are an invaluable resource for tracking trends over time, because they are conducted in a consistent way year after year. A few private companies conduct ongoing surveys, especially the public opinion pollsters. The Gallup Organization has been studying Americans' religious beliefs for over 50 years, for example.

Simple population projections—by age, race, and sex—are easy to find, in both the public and private sectors. Socioeconomic projections are rare beasts, limited in most cases to private-sector forecasts of household income.

You may have to make a trade-off between length of forecast and level of geographic detail. Most demographic data companies project basic population and a few socioeconomic characteristics only five years ahead, but for all geographic areas. Econometric forecasting firms have a longer view, often going 20 years into the future, but their geography is limited to counties, metropolitan areas, and states. The Census Bureau projects population by age, sex, and race to 2080, but only for the entire U.S. State projections are available to the year 2010.

If it's vital that the data be fresh, go to the private sector. Private companies offer up-to-date numbers and quick service. Government agencies sometimes accept requests for custom tabulations of data, but their turnaround time is slow. Government reports are notorious for being out of date—analysis and publication can take years.

■ **Choose Wild or Domestic Quarry** People tend to think of government data as unfriendly, arriving as masses of printed tables or hefty computer tapes. The government produces no-frills data to avoid competing with the private sector. This makes the government data relatively inexpensive. Some government publications are relatively easy reads, however, especially those from the Census Bureau's *Current Population Reports* series and the Bureau of Labor Statistics' *Monthly Labor Review*.

If you want CD-ROMs with crackerjack software, go to the private sector. But be aware that some of the data you get from private suppliers can be as unwieldy and unusable as any government report. Find out ahead of time what kind of analytic support you can expect from a vendor.

■ **Consider Cost** Will you spring for a luxury two-week safari, or are you limited to the local fishing hole? If you're a do-it-yourselfer, you can buy data inexpensively from the government and manipulate it yourself. But if you need a powerhouse computer system loaded with current data for every place in the country—yet simple enough for the beginner to use—expect to pay more in the private sector.

Today the challenge is to find the best data for your needs among many bewildering choices. If you keep your goal in mind, the odds are that you'll bag your data in the end.

Market Research the Japanese Way

Johny K. Johansson and Ikujiro Nonaka

A professor at the University of Washington's Graduate School of Business Administration, Johny K. Johansson has done research in marketing strategy, advertising management, international marketing, and Japanese business. Ikujiro Nonaka is a professor at the Institute for Business Research at Hitotsubashi University in Tokyo. He has published six books on management and organization and with Hirotaka Takeuchi wrote "The New New Product Development Game" (HBR January-February 1986).

When Sony researched the market for a lightweight portable cassette player, results showed that consumers wouldn't buy a tape recorder that didn't record. Company chairman Akio Morita decided to introduce the Walkman anyway, and the rest is history. Today it's one of Sony's most successful products.

Japanese companies *do* use surveys— but they trust their instincts first.

Morita's disdain for large-scale consumer surveys and other scientific research tools isn't unique in Japan. Matsushita, Toyota, and other well-known Japanese consumer goods companies are just as skeptical about the Western style of market research. Occasionally, the Japanese do conduct consumer attitude surveys, but most executives don't base their marketing decisions on them or on other popular techniques. As the head of Matsushita's videocassette recorder division once said, "Why do Americans do so much marketing research? You can find out what you need by traveling around and visiting the retailers who carry your product."

Hands-on research

Of course, Japanese corporations want accurate and useful information about their markets as much as U.S. and European companies do. They just go about it differently. Japanese executives put much more faith in information they get directly from wholesalers and retailers in the distribution channels. Moreover, they track what's happening among channel members on a monthly, weekly, and sometimes even daily basis.

Japanese-style market research relies heavily on two kinds of information: "soft data" obtained from visits to dealers and other channel members, and "hard data" about shipments, inventory levels, and retail sales. Japanese managers believe that these data better reflect the behavior and intentions of flesh-and-blood consumers. Japanese companies want information that is context specific rather than context free—that is, data directly relevant to consumer attitudes about the product, or to the way buyers have used or will use specific products, rather than research results that are too remote from actual consumer behavior to be useful. When Japanese companies do conduct surveys, they interview consumers who have actually bought or used a product. They do not scrutinize an undifferentiated mass public to learn about general attitudes and values. When Toyota wanted to learn what Americans preferred in small, imported cars, for example, the company asked owners and others who had driven the car what they liked or disliked about the Volkswagen Beetle.

Soft-data gathering. Senior as well as middle-level Japanese managers get involved in gathering soft data because they see the information as critical both for market entry and for maintaining good relationships later. Though impressionistic, such hands-on data give the managers a distinctive feel for the market—something they believe surveys or quantitative research methods can't supply. Talks with dealers yield realistic, context-specific information about competitors' as well as their own market performance.

A good example is Canon's decision on a new U.S. distribution strategy. In the early 1970s, the company's senior management became concerned about U.S. camera sales. Other product lines were doing well, but camera sales had lost ground to the chief competitor, Minolta. Canon finally de-

cided it needed its own sales subsidiary because its distributor, Bell & Howell, wouldn't give additional support for the Canon line. Senior managers didn't use a broad survey of consumers or retailers to make this decision. They sent three managers to the United States to look into the problem and changed strategies based on their observations.

To learn the market, track the channels.

Canon's head of the U.S. team himself spent almost six weeks in 1972 visiting camera stores and other retail outlets across the United States. From talks with store owners, Tatehiro Tsuruta learned that U.S. dealers weren't giving Canon much support because their sales forces were too small. He also found out what kinds of cameras and promotional support would get them excited about the company's line.

This soft-data approach appears to lack the methodological rigor of scientific market research, but it's by no means haphazard or careless. In fact, Tsuruta's results were more meaningful because he actually observed how consumers behaved in the stores and how salespeople responded. On entering a store, Tsuruta would act as if he were just a customer browsing around. He would note how the cameras were displayed and how the store clerks served customers. Then by simply asking "What cameras do you stock?" he could assess whether the dealer was enthusiastic or indifferent about the Canon line. He could also determine

how knowledgeable people were about camera features.

Tsuruta would then identify himself and invite the store manager to lunch to discuss cameras and whatever else happened to be on the dealer's mind. The payoff was more than just market research. He was building lasting relationships with the dealers—an important competitive advantage.

When Tsuruta visited drugstores and other discount outlets that Minolta favored, he could see that these markets wouldn't work for Canon. Customers got poor service—in part because salespeople knew little about the products they were selling. The mass merchandisers' heavy price competition also made it difficult to project a quality image.

Tsuruta's research decided Canon's distribution strategy: sell exclusively through specialty dealers serving an upscale, high-quality niche just below Nikon's targeted segment. The successful introduction of Canon's AE-1 camera in 1976 proved the strategy right.

Canon is by no means unique among Japanese companies in the sales and distribution problems it experienced in the United States or in the means it used to remedy them. A group of managers Honda sent to the United States in 1965 learned to their surprise that few dealers there stocked and serviced motorcycles exclusively. Company executives realized they would have to develop their own dealer network. Sony entered the U.S. radio and TV market in the late 1950s and almost immediately decided to establish its own U.S. distributor so it could be sure to get adequate sales support.

This soft-data approach is popular even after a Japanese company has penetrated the market. Frequent visits to people on the distribution channel help manufacturers resolve problems before they escalate and damage sales or relationships. Isao Makino, president of Toyota's U.S. sales subsidiary from 1975 to 1983—a period of great gains in market share—used to visit every Toyota dealer in the United States at least once a year. "I found," he said, "that out of the ten complaints from each dealer, you could attribute about five or six to simple misunderstandings, another two or three could be solved on the spot, and only one or two needed further work."

Hard-data gathering. When Japanese managers want hard data to compare their products to competitors', they look at inventory, sales, and other information that show the items' actual movement through the channels. Then they visit channel members at both the retail and wholesale levels to analyze sales and distribution coverage reports, monthly product movement records (weekly for some key stores), plant-to-wholesaler shipment figures, and syndicated turnover and shipment statistics on competitors.

Japanese managers routinely monitor their markets at home and abroad this way. Consider how Matsushita dealt with the weak performance of its Panasonic line distributor in South Africa. The sales figures he reported were reasonable, but he couldn't produce reliable data on sales and shares for the various types of stores or on inventory levels in the distribution chain.

In early 1982, three managers from the company's household electronics division paid a call on the South African distributor. Then they dropped in on the distributor's retail stores and wholesale facilities. Customarily, after exchanging greetings and presenting a token gift from headquarters, they got

right down to business. They asked to see inventory, shipment, and sales records as part of a complete store audit covering Matsushita and competitive products. Six weeks later, after analyzing all the data, they gave the incredulous distributor a complete picture of Panasonic's product movement and market share through the entire South African channel. They also told the distributor what figures he should collect and report to the home office in the future.

2. RESEARCH, MARKETS, AND CONSUMER BEHAVIOR

Monitoring the channels

Japanese managers try to track changing customer tastes closely and quickly. Their "one step at a time" management style for decision making also applies to how they approach marketing. After analyzing both hard and soft data on their channels, they make small, incremental changes in product features, packaging, and promotional efforts. Awareness of what's happening in the channels on a weekly or even daily basis gives them a deep and focused understanding of the marketplace and enables them to fine-tune their marketing rapidly – thereby protecting their competitive edge. This skill is especially important in the highly competitive packaged goods and consumer durable goods markets.

Kao Corporation, which dominates the detergent and soap market in Japan, illustrates this tight channel monitoring and incremental changes in marketing strategies. Kao executives analyze point-of-sales data weekly and wholesale inventory and sales statistics monthly.

The company occasionally uses consumer surveys and other quantitative research tools, but executives never base marketing decisions primarily on the information from them. These findings merely trigger more thorough audits of the channels using both soft- and hard-data gathering. If a survey or household panel study, for example, shows a sudden change in brand preferences or in family purchase patterns, Kao will send a high-level management team out to the stores. The group will spend one day at each store just observing customer behavior. The next day the team will talk to the store owner or manager to learn what kinds of support will move the products better. They'll also ask if the dealer needs help stocking shelves or if special promotions would help.

Such tight channel monitoring has paid off handsomely for Kao, among others. When Procter & Gamble introduced disposable diapers in Japan in the mid-1970s, it immediately took 90% of this new and growing market. Lured by the big sales and earnings potential, Uni Charm, Kao, and other Japanese manufacturers created their own lines. With tight channel monitoring, the Japanese could quickly change product features to better suit consumer

tastes, and by 1984 P&G's market share had plummeted to an anemic 8%.

One factor that frustrates U.S. and other Western corporations' efforts to enter Japanese distribution channels is their lack of knowledge about distributor expectations, which limits their ability to respond to con-

---

> You can't teach marketing in school— you learn it in the field.

---

sumer tastes. The handicapped Westerners can't refine their marketing quickly enough in Japan to parry competitors' moves.

Tight channel monitoring also improves operations and cost control. Kao and other Japanese companies would never be caught with the kind of inventory pileups that Warner Communications' Atari subsidiary found itself saddled with in 1983. A six-month lag in reports from retailers led to disastrous inventory levels of TV game cassettes.

Strong vertical integration.
Japanese companies exert considerably more control over their distribution channels than do most U.S. and European corporations. Toyota has been more successful than Nissan in the Japanese market because of its stronger distribution network. In many cases, this control is nearly absolute because the manufacturer actually owns the distributors or has sufficient market power to dominate the channel. Shiseido, for example, a cosmetics manu-

facturer, has a strong market presence in Japan. It sells through a network of independent stores that use company-trained salespeople and reserve exclusive shelf space for the company's brands. In Japan, a consumer's choice of store often dictates what brand he or she will buy.

Such strong vertical integration affects the kind and quality of market research information Japanese managers can gather. They can shift some research tasks to the dealers, for example. It's not unusual for store employees to survey Japanese households by mail or phone, interview people when they come into a store, or even visit customers' homes for a talk.

Japanese salespeople change jobs less often than U.S. and European retail employees, so they are in a better position to develop expertise about customers and competitors. Moreover, stores tend to remain in the same locations. When Matsushita wants information on its Japanese customers, it goes to its 4,000 retail stores to find out.

Generalist managers. Few Japanese managers at all corporate levels have received a formal business education; it is still something of a novelty in Japan. Other than Keio Business School, only a few business institutes exist there, and those offer continuing education programs more often than degree options.

That's one reason why marketing isn't yet a specialized business profession in Japan – and hence one of several reasons why Japanese companies haven't adopted Western-style market research. But even if formal training in marketing did exist, Japanese executives would probably consider the marketing function too important to leave to mid-level specialists.

Honda is a case in point. When it picked Kihachiro Kawashima to head its U.S. sales organization, the company chose a domestic sales expert who knew very little about the United States. Kawashima ascribes his ultimate success in America to three principles: "Be real, be close to the action, and be localized." What made the difference for Honda in the United States was the senior managers' decision to spend up to 50% of their time visiting and talking with distributors and dealers – the people who knew what U.S. customers really wanted. The ultimate goal of this hands-on, close-to-the-customer approach is to generate a better understanding of customer desires and behavior. The Japanese don't see marketing as something like engineering or finance that can be taught in school. Sensitivity to customers' desires is learned through hard work and experience.

Consensus decision making.

In contrast to Western practice, Japanese executives don't give managers sole responsibility for a research area. They conduct research and make decisions by consensus, and they lean toward their intuitive judgment. Rarely do Japanese executives call in an outside professional, and when they do, they often disregard the consultant's report if it goes against their instincts about the best course of action. When Kozo Ohsone, the executive in charge of developing Sony's portable, compact Discman, heard that the company's marketing people were thinking about commissioning a research study, he told them not to waste their money.

Lack of diversification.
Tight channel monitoring is also closely associated with the more specialized nature of Japanese industry. Most Japanese corporations have only one or a few related product lines, so managers and employees at all levels can learn more easily what's needed to succeed in the business. This specialization fosters an inductive, bottom-up approach to business planning and problem solving, whereas U.S. and European managements favor more deductive, top-down planning methods. Many large, diversified American corporations have to depend on Western-style market research because they lack the experience and knowledge to sell effectively in multiple industries. But outside marketing consultants and the battery of survey and other research tools they offer cannot fully substitute for intimate knowledge of distribution channels and customer tastes.

But will it be enough?

General Electric's chief, John F. Welch, put it this way, "The Japanese have got the American consumer's number." Hands-on market research has given Japanese companies solid beachheads in the United States and other countries. Especially in mature industries like consumer goods, where customer preferences are so well understood, incremental adjustments in product features or promotional tactics may be all that is needed to have a competitive product.

Japanese-style research is starting to catch on in the United States and in other Western countries. Western executives are trying to get close to the customer and fine-tune product lines and marketing practices after listening carefully to what customers and distributors tell them. But this practice is still the exception in the West.

Ironically, just as some American and European executives are adopt-

ing a hands-on approach, a few Japanese companies are asking if their market research style can sustain their competitive edge over the long run—especially in the global marketplace. Some Canon executives, for example, are coming around to the view that surveys and other more scientific methods may be necessary as the company begins to look for ways to diversify.

Why are both sides changing like this? Increasing internationalization of both industries and business

practices is doubtless one important reason. Global marketing is leading to a blending of managerial cultures and practices for all countries. Japanese executives are now thinking they may need some Western practices to keep their overseas footholds.

Consider, for example, the problem that Shiseido experienced in the U.S. market. Because it followed the Japanese tradition of sending in executives and managers from the home country, rather than hiring foreign nationals to fill top overseas posts, the company made no headway in the United States for ten years. No one at Shiseido headquarters understood that its cosmetics had to be introduced first into the high-status New York City stores before they could be sold successfully elsewhere. Only after hiring an experienced American cosmetics executive did Shiseido finally get its U.S. marketing effort on the right track.

Japanese corporations' reluctance to hire non-Japanese executives reflects a kind of provincialism that now poses hazards in an era of global markets. Their approach to market research could reinforce this parochialism because it focuses management attention on products and markets that the company already knows well—rather than on potential markets and industries. In their intensive channel monitoring, Japanese business leaders may see only narrow paths and miss the big picture.

Japanese executives today may need a broader perspective than they have taken in the past. Concentration on step-by-step marketing changes may keep them from spotting the social and economic trends that can throw seemingly unshakable industries into upheaval—precisely the changes that large-scale surveys and other Western-style methods uncover very effectively. As bulging surplus cash reserves and global marketing pressures push big Japanese corporations to diversify, more Japanese managers may begin to consider the potential advantages of Western-style market research.

THE SELLING *Of* LIFE-STYLES

Are you what you buy? Madison Avenue wants to know.

BERKELEY RICE

Berkeley Rice is a contributing editor at Psychology Today.

You may not care about psychographics, but psychographics cares about you. It cares about what you think, what you feel, what you believe, the way you live and, most of all, the products and services that you use.

Ever since the snake convinced Eve to sample an apple in the Garden of Eden, advertisers and marketers have been trying to discover why consumers buy what they do. A few years ago, marketers thought the reason was demographics, and that buying was governed by consumers' age, sex, income, education, occupation and other characteristics. They also tried to divide the purchasing world up according to social class.

These mass-marketing strategies, however, are now considered crude and overly general. Marketing researchers today want to get into the individual consumer's head, so that companies can aim their products at more specific segments of the population. Some think that psychographics is their ticket inside.

Psychographic analyses for Schlitz beer, for example, revealed that heavy beer drinkers were real macho men who feel that pleasures in their lives are few and far between, and they want something more, according to Joseph Plummer, the researcher who conducted the study. This insight led to Schlitz commercials that told people "You only go around once," so you might as well "reach for all the gusto you can."

When the current walking-shoe boom began, the athletic-shoe industry assumed that most walkers were simply burned-out joggers. Psychographic research, however, has shown that there are really several different groups of walkers: Some walk for fun, some walk with religious dedication, others walk to work and still others walk the dog. Some really want to exercise, and some want the illusion of exercise. As a result, there are now walking shoes aimed at several groups, ranging from Nike Healthwalkers to Footjoy Joy-Walkers.

When Merrill Lynch learned through psychographics that the bulk of its clients saw themselves as independent-minded, upwardly mobile achievers, the investment firm changed the image in its commercials. Instead of the familiar thundering herd of bulls from the 1970s, Merrill Lynch ads portrayed scenes of a solitary bull: "a breed apart."

The term psychographics first began to pop up in the business community during the late 1960s, referring to attempts to classify consumers by their beliefs, motivations and attitudes. In 1970, psychologist Daniel Yankelovich, who headed his own social-research firm, launched an annual survey of changing values and attitudes called the Yankelovich Monitor. It tracks more than 50 trends in people's attitudes toward time, money, the future, family, self, institutions and many other aspects of their life-style. By measuring these shifts in attitudes, Monitor researchers claim to have spotted or predicted trends such as the shift to white wine and light alcoholic beverages, and the rising sales of supermarket-chain brands and generic drugs. About 100 companies now pay $28,500 a year to subscribe to the Monitor survey.

By the mid 1970s, "life-style" had become a popular buzzword in advertising and marketing circles. Many advertising agencies began to do their own psychographic research: Needham, Harper and Steers (now DDB Needham), for example, divided consumers into 10 life-style categories typified by characters such as Thelma, the old-fashioned traditionalist; Candice, the chic suburbanite; and Fred, the frustrated factory worker. A flurry of ads tried—often blatantly—to pitch products by appealing to the life-style of people commonly referred to as the "upscale market." An ad for Chrysler's 1979 LeBaron, for example, featured an attractive young couple engaged in typically active, upscale pursuits such as tennis and sailing. The ad copy gushed: "It's got style. It's got life. Put some life in your style."

While all of this was going on, a researcher named Arnold Mitchell wrote a series of reports analyzing the way people's basic needs and values influenced their attitudes and behavior, particularly as consumers. Working at what is now SRI International in Menlo Park, California, he had administered a lengthy questionnaire to nearly 2,000 people. Using the results, Mitchell divided consumers into categories based in part on the theories of the late psychologist Abraham Maslow and his hierarchy of "needs growth."

Maslow believed that most human behavior is based on certain internal drives or needs, and that personal development consists of stages of maturity marked by fulfillment of these needs. Until the needs of one stage are satisfied, an individual cannot progress to the next level of maturity. At the lowest level are basic bodily needs such as hunger and sleep,

Psychographic ideas about consumers are engaging but fruitless, some say. But bear fruit VALS has.

followed by needs for safety, shelter and comfort. The next levels consist of psychological needs: to belong, to have self-esteem and to be respected by others. Near the top comes the need for self-actualization: fully developing one's potential. People who reach this level are likely to be more creative, successful and influential than people who haven't attained it. Finally, Maslow said, the needs for spirituality and sensitivity lead to the highest level of consciousness.

Mitchell also claimed that each stage of an individual's development is marked by a "particular pattern of priorities... a unique set of dominating values and needs." He used his survey findings to create nine psychologically graphic portraits of consumers, one for each pattern he identified. By 1983, when Mitchell published a book called *The Nine American Lifestyles*, his work had attracted considerable interest from marketers and advertisers. Based on his work, SRI had formed a commercial marketing-research program called VALS, an acronym for Values and Life-styles. Before he died in 1985, Mitchell saw VALS become the country's most widely used system of psychographic research.

The VALS typology begins with two life-styles, the Survivors and the Sustainers, both small groups with limited financial resources. Survivors are typically elderly and poor: Most feel trapped in their poverty, with no hope of escape. Sustainers, only slightly better off, are struggling at the edge of poverty. Although they often bitterly blame "the system" for their troubles, Sustainers have not quite given up.

VALS then divides into two pathways, Inner-Directed and Outer-Directed, terms drawn from the work of sociologist David Riesman. There are three Outer-Directed types: Belongers, Emulators and Achievers. Belongers are the largest VALS group of all, making up 38 percent of the country's population. These stable, hard-working blue-collar or service-industry workers are conservative and conforming; they know what's right and what's wrong, and they stick to the rules because they want to fit in.

Emulators are more ambitious, more competitive and more status conscious than Belongers. They also make more money, but they envy the life-style of the Achievers, one level above them. Emulators would like to feel they're "on the way up," but most will never make it. They wonder if they're getting a fair shake from the system.

Achievers, who make up 20 percent of the population, are the successful business managers and professional people. Competent and self-reliant, "they know what they want and they make it happen." They want the trappings of success—expensive homes, cars and vacations—and most expect to get them. Having achieved the American Dream, they are generally staunch defenders of the society that rewarded them.

Parallel to but quite different from the Outer-Directed types are the three Inner-Directed VALS categories. The first, the I-Am-Me's, is a tiny group: generally young, highly individualistic, very egocentric and often confused about their goals in life. As their outlook broadens and they become more sure of themselves, they tend to mature into Experientials. If they then extend their view to include society as a whole, they become the Societally Conscious. This is the largest of the Inner-Directed groups; its members tend to be knowledgeable and concerned about social causes such as conservation. Many earn a good deal of money, but their life-styles emphasize simplicity and involvement.

At the pinnacle of VALS is the tiny group of psychologically mature Integrateds, the lucky few who have put it all together. They combine the best of Inner and Outer Direction: the power and drive of the Achievers and the sensitivity of the Societally Conscious. They have a sense of balance in their lives and confidence in their place in the world.

SRI has produced a half-hour video that provides brief looks at people in different VALS categories. Estelle, an elderly Survivor in the film, lives alone, scraping by on a tight budget. Moe is a Hispanic Sustainer who spends his afternoons at the racetrack **hoping for a big win. Dave and Donna, a young Belonger couple who believe in God, family and country, live in a small house in a development of similar homes. Art, the Emulator, is a door-to-door salesman who drives through a fancy neighborhood and wonders, "What did they do right?" Steve, a lawyer-entrepreneur Achiever who's pictured soaking in his hot tub with his attractive wife, insists that money's "just a way of keeping score."**

Mitchell's idea that basic psychological needs or drives affect consumer behavior makes a good deal of sense, and few researchers would quarrel with it. It's less clear, however, that VALS survey methods really tap into the things that Maslow was talking about. VALS "does not measure basic psychological characteristics, but social values which are purported reflections of those characteristics," says psychologist Joseph Smith, president of the market-research firm Oxtoby–Smith. Those values, Smith contends, don't predict consumer behavior very well: "Maslow was working in the world of clinical and developmental psychology. To try to adapt his theories and language from that world, as VALS has done, is an engaging idea but bound to be fruitless."

But bear fruit VALS has. Since SRI began marketing psychographic research, 250 corporate clients or "members," as SRI calls them, have used VALS data. Most VALS clients sell consumer products and services: packaged goods, automobiles, insurance, television, publishing and advertising. Depending on how much customized service they want, 150 current VALS members pay from $20,000 to more than $150,000 per year, producing reported annual revenues of more than $2 million for Mitchell's brainchild.

Member companies can combine VALS profiles with much larger marketing systems that provide information on specific product brands and media use. Or they can link VALS to several "geodemographic"

marketing services that group people by ZIP codes or neighborhood, according to the demographic features of typical households.

Advertising agencies such as Young & Rubicam, Ogilvy and Mather and J. Walter Thompson have used VALS information to place ads on TV shows and in magazines that draw the right psychographic segments for their clients' products or to design commercials and print ads that target specific consumer groups. They have learned, for example, that TV's daytime soap operas draw heavily among Survivors, Sustainers and Belongers, because they're often home alone. Achievers watch a lot of sports and news shows, while the Societally Conscious prefer dramas and documentaries.

Magazines such as *Time* and *The New Yorker* have a lot of Achiever readers, while *Reader's Digest* has more Belongers (*Psychology Today*, which uses a different psychographic system, has readers who are broad-minded, style conscious and experimenters—probably more Inner- than Outer-Directed).

VALS has attracted many clients from the auto industry, including GM, Ford, Nissan, Honda and Mercedes-Benz. VALS studies show what you might expect: that Belongers tend to buy family-sized domestic cars, while Emulators and I-Am-Me's prefer "muscle" cars like the Chevy Camaro. Achievers usually buy luxury cars, often foreign models like Mercedes or BMW, not so much because of their superior quality but because they represent achievement and status. Societally Conscious types might also buy a Mercedes, but more for its technical excellence than what it "says" about them.

To complicate matters for advertisers, nearly half of all couples are "mixed" marriages of two different VALS types. Ads for mini-vans, therefore, may need to carry a double message: one to appeal to an Achiever husband who might use it for golfing or fishing expeditions with his buddies and another to appeal to his Belonger wife, who sees it primarily as a vehicle for ferrying the children.

Corporate clients can use a 30-item VALS questionnaire to survey their own markets and have SRI classify the results into VALS types. The questionnaire asks people to indicate their agreement or disagreement with statements such as "What I do at work is more important to me than the money I earn" or "I would rather spend a quiet evening at home than go out to a party" or "I like to be outrageous."

By using such research methods, client companies can construct VALS profiles for their own markets or those of their competitors; position products or design packaging to appeal to particular groups; or spot trends in product use and consumer needs.

Ray Ellison Homes, a big real estate developer and builder in San Antonio, Texas, took advantage of this type of VALS research. The company began by mailing a VALS questionnaire to 5,000 home buyers in the area and also asked them how much they valued items such as wallpaper or landscaping. "We needed to find out their values," says Jim Tilton, vice presi-

Sustainers watch TV soap operas, Achievers watch sports, and the Societally Conscious prefer dramas.

dent of merchandising and advertising, "so we could really build to their needs and desires."

The company then conducted in-depth group interviews with the three VALS types most likely to buy its homes—Belongers, Achievers and Societally Conscious—to probe for further insights. When a group of Achiever women saw pictures of a big country kitchen, one of them exclaimed, "There's no way I'd clean all that tile!" A similar display of tile in the luxurious master bathroom, however, did not put her off. Apparently, the kitchen made her think of work, but she viewed the bathroom as a place of relaxation.

On the basis of these interviews and the survey results, Tilton says, "we took our standard houses apart and started from scratch, putting them back together piece by piece." To attract Achievers, for instance, the company added impressive facades, luxury carpeting and elaborate security systems. For the Societally Conscious, they designed energy-efficient homes. "What we've done," executive vice president Jack Robinson explains, "is really get inside the consumer's head, into what his perceived values are, and give them back to him—in land, in financing and in the features of a home."

While VALS is the best-known and most successful psychographic research program around, it is hardly the only one doing this kind of work. Yankelovich's Monitor is still going strong, and many smaller firms do custom-tailored research for individual clients or specific markets. Some large consumer-goods companies and TV networks now do their own psychographic studies.

Despite this popularity, psychographics has plenty of doubters. Some critics, like Smith, question its utility: "We can't really measure the important personal attributes based on surveys," he says. "Psychographic research gives you a lot of superficial, inconsequential and titillating material but very little of pointed use to the guy who is designing products or trying to advertise and sell them." Because psychographic research firms guard their methods very carefully, as trade secrets, outsiders have been unable to test the data's validity and reliability (most firms claim they do their own validity testing).

Russell Haley, a professor of marketing at the University of New Hampshire, who heads a market-research firm, points out that decisions to buy some products are simply not closely related to personal values. "If you're dealing with paper towels," he says, "personal values are not likely to be that relevant. On the other hand, if you're selling cosmetics or insurance, VALS may be quite useful because peo-

ple's attitudes toward beauty or money are very relevant." He concludes: "I have some clients who like it, and some who don't."

Some companies that have used VALS and other psychographic research in the past no longer do so, having decided it's not worth the extra cost. Some claim that psychographics merely reveals the obvious or that it duplicates what demographic data show more clearly. In demographic language, Belongers are 57 years old on average, and the majority earn less than $20,000 per year; 72 percent of them are married, and only 3 percent have graduated from college. Experientials are 28 years old and earn $32,000 per year, on average; only 31 percent of them are married, and 40 percent attended college.

"When VALS first came out," says Bob Hoffman, president of Mojo MDA, a San Francisco advertising agency, "it enlightened us and described behavior in certain ways that some people hadn't thought of before. But now it makes people think in boxes." Hoffman and others argue that psychographics tries too hard to categorize everyone into discrete types, ignoring the fact that most people have traits and behavior common to several types. People also don't always think and behave consistently in every context. Some individuals may vote as Belongers but think like Achievers when they walk into the automobile showroom. Some Achievers may act like Belongers when pushing a baby's stroller through a supermarket.

In response to such critics, VALS marketing director Jack Tyler insists that "We've never claimed that all individuals fit neatly into one category, like cookie-cutter types, or that they have a stereotypical response to every situation. We provide our clients with secondary VALS scores that indicate these other characteristics." VALS simply claims that people's general behavior fits the profile of a given category, Tyler says, and that these categories offer valuable insights into the consumer.

What VALS and other life-style studies have done is provide vivid portraits of American consumers; while the accuracy of the pictures is debatable, psychographics still has many believers. Says Jerry Hamilton of Ketchum Advertising in San Francisco, "VALS makes it possible to personalize marketing and to understand the target we're trying to reach better than any other piece of research. Sure, it may oversimplify. No matter what classification system you use you're distorting everybody's individuality. But the alternative is to tailor advertising to 80 million individual households."

> We got insight into consumers' values, says a VALS user, and gave those values back to them.

New Species for Study: Consumers in Action

Kim Foltz

Even as car shoppers look over new models in dealer showrooms, some of them are being sized up themselves.

In Cadillac, Mercedes and BMW showrooms around the nation recently, researchers hired by the Toyota Motor Corporation discreetly watched prospective car buyers inspect the cars. The researchers noted not only whether the customers kicked the tires but also how they dressed, what questions they asked and whether they appeared timid or confident.

"Just asking people questions isn't going to reveal everything about them," said Bobby Calder, the Montgomery Ward professor of marketing and psychology at Northwestern University. "The best way to get an in-depth understanding of consumer values is to watch people buying and using products."

Such people-watching is the newest trend in consumer research, marketing experts say. A rather daring technique five years ago, the hiring of cultural anthropologists to observe and often videotape consumers in stores, shopping malls and even their own homes has become a standard practice for many large corporations and some of the nation's leading advertising agencies.

Observational research, for example, has shown marketers that consumers prefer to take several cold remedies, not just one. By watching people eat breakfast, researchers concluded that enjoyment is a leading factor in selecting what to eat. While most Americans say they want a nutritious morning meal, they especially want it to taste good.

During some projects, said Margaret Mark, director of research at Young & Rubicam, people allowed researchers to watch them while they talked to friends and family members, even about disturbing subjects like sex and death.

There is an incentive. Families that allow researchers into their homes are paid $40 for several hours to $300 for a week or more.

Companies with radically different approaches to marketing—from Toyota, known for its adventuresome style, to the far more conservative Procter & Gamble—have come to rely on what is known in the industry as observational research. Such research studies consumer attitudes toward a wide range of products and services, including fast food, over-the-counter medicine, household products, travel and personal care items.

"We use observational research for every one of our major clients," said Penelope Queen, director of research for Saatchi & Saatchi Advertising, a large agency that pioneered this type of monitoring. "By observing, we can get underneath the surface and interpret consumer behavior."

A couple in California are accusing Nissan of spying on them.

What companies spend on such research is usually a closely held secret. Most marketers refuse to discuss details of people-watching projects and the way the information is being used. But industry analysts estimate that companies spend millions of dollars watching Americans to discover the often-hidden impulses that prompt them to buy an expensive car, eat gourmet ice cream and wash their clothes with a particular detergent.

The growth of observational research has also raised troubling legal questions about privacy, particularly when the research is conducted in public places where people shop and do business.

'We Are Deeply Concerned'

"We are deeply concerned that there is any kind of secret filming going on," said Janlori Goldman, a staff lawyer on the American Civil Liberties Union's privacy project. "People should never be recorded or watched without their knowledge. We are very worried about how this information will be used."

Most Americans do not seem to resent what many civil libertarians regard as unnecessary prying into their private lives. "People are usually flattered by the attention," Ms. Mark of Young & Rubicam said. "They are quite willing to be open about their lives and emotions."

Not everybody agrees. Stephen and Maritza French of Costa Mesa, Calif., filed a suit two weeks ago against the Nissan Motor Company, accusing the auto maker of invasion of privacy. The couple assert that a researcher working for Nissan whom they agreed to let live in their home for six weeks spied on them to gain insight into how American families live.

Nissan denies the charge. "The researcher was compiling a study on how Americans feel about cars, but it did not include the French family," said Don Spetner, a Nissan spokesman.

Legal problems like the one facing Nissan are rare. Most researchers require people to sign a consent form if they are going to be observed or filmed in their homes.

Some industry analysts say invasion-of-privacy problems will increase as the use of observational research grows. "I worry that a lot of awful stuff could be done that is intrusive," said Langburne Rust, an independent researcher specializing in television viewing habits. "Some people are going to get burned."

Products as Symbols

In the more primitive days of consumer research, most companies tried to study the consumer's psyche simply by asking people what they thought about products and how they used them. Now, many research experts believe that questionnaires and surveys alone do not dig deeply enough.

"People are often not aware of what they are actually doing and why," said Steve Barnett, a cultural anthropologist who taught at Princeton University and the Massachusetts Institute of Technology and is now the director of product strategy for Nissan. "The way consumers use products symbolizes how they view themselves."

By watching people, observational researchers think they may also better understand the bond between people and products that is the essence of brand loyalty.

In watching car buyers last year, for example, Toyota concluded that some people think of their cars as art objects that are on display whenever they drive them. The auto maker worked that theme into a print advertisement for its new luxury car, the Lexus, which discusses the creation of the car as if it were a Henry Moore sculpture.

Observational researchers also hope to unravel the mystery of what a product symbolizes to a consumer. Take the case of gourmet ice cream eaters. For one client, which it would not identify, Young & Rubicam wanted to find out what goes on between an ice cream lover and his bowl of macadamia nut fudge swirl. After several weeks of observation in consumers' homes—and gallons of ice cream—researchers discovered that ice cream eating is often a highly ritualized activity.

'The Ultimate Indulgence'

"Ice cream lovers have a special spoon, a special bowl and a favorite chair," Ms. Mark of Young & Rubicam said. "They like to get comfortable and let their hair down. For them, it symbolizes the ultimate indulgence."

So when advertising for the product was developed, the agency knew it would be a mistake to show people eating ice cream in any formal setting. Instead, the ads have focused on the personal joy of eating what is for many dieters a forbidden food.

To get a better fix on consumers' lives, anthropologists hired by Ms. Mark are given permission to snoop around people's homes. "We look in the refrigerator, the kitchen cabinets and the closets," she said. "We ask people to show us their favorite things. We learn a lot more by looking around than we'd ever find out just asking people about their homes. Nothing is hidden from us."

Friendly Mail Carriers

Observing consumers often provides valuable insights that can be used to custom-tailor advertising. Young & Rubicam, for example, hired anthropologists to tag along with mail carriers on their delivery routes to find out for its client, the United States Postal Service, what the public thought of letter carriers. As their research showed, most people think of their mail carriers as friends; many even know their first names. As a result, the

Postal Service began prominently featuring mail carriers in its ads.

Researchers often discover behavior patterns that surprise the people being observed. Saatchi & Saatchi, for example, videotaped women washing clothes in their homes for its client, Procter & Gamble, which produces Tide. When the tapes were shown to the women, some said they were astonished to see the amount of time and care they put into this task.

As competitive pressures increase, researchers have been monitoring some unusual targets to detect changing social trends. For example, when Unilever N.V. wanted to find out what Americans now consider to be glamorous, a behavioral research firm, Holen North America, studied transvestites working in New York nightclubs. "When these men dress as women, they have to think more carefully about what is glamorous because they have to construct it from the ground up," said Dr. Barnett, who headed Holen before joining Nissan.

The growing emphasis on people-monitoring is also a function of cost. "Depending on the scope of the study, it can be less costly than traditional research," Ms. Mark said.

That does not mean that questionnaires and surveys and other forms of customary market research have disappeared. Companies and advertising agencies use other techniques as well as observational research.

"Like everyone else, we still do surveys," Ms. Queen said. "But we use observational research to help explain the results and find out the why's behind behavior."

Focus Groups Emerging as Important Business-to-Business Market Research Tool

Alan Zimmerman

In the early 1980s a PC memory board manufacturer (call it Acme) began to see slowing growth. The firm had taken advantage of the "go-go" years of the personal computer revolution and had positioned itself to supply the seemingly endless number of personal computer outlets, both chains and independents, springing up around the country. Now sales were topping out.

Company data didn't show it, but marketing management suspected that the firm was not getting its fair share of major purchases from corporate buyers. The marketers wanted to know how these major corporations went about making purchase decisions on memory boards.

Acme called in a research firm concentrating in business-to-business focus groups, at that time an emerging tool for business-to-business marketers. Groups were arranged with data processing professionals in New York, Denver, and Los Angeles. The focus groups revealed that Acme's competitors had quietly established direct national account sales forces to call on corporate customers. Additionally, the focus groups discovered that buyers preferred to deal directly with manufacturers rather than small, local PC retail outlets. Large orders were being placed that Acme knew nothing about.

Acme gained other quantitative information that it used to formulate a new strategy. For example, it learned which magazines corporate buyers relied on for PC information and what kinds of advertising messages they believed.

Growing Popularity

The story of the PC enhancement firm is just one example of the growing use of focus groups by business-to-business marketers. Using focus groups as a market research tool goes back to the early 1950s when some psychiatrists and sociologists working with advertising agencies began using the technique to probe the feelings of more than one respondent in a single setting. This technique turned out to be as effective as an individual depth interview for most purposes and far more cost effective. It wasn't until the mid-1960s that many specialized focus group facilities began springing up around the country.

A focus group facility is a specially designed room, usually wired for audio taping (and sometimes video taping) which features a one-way mirror at one end of the room. This allows the sponsoring clients to observe their customers as they talk about prearranged subjects.

While no studies have been completed to determine how many business-to-business focus groups are being held, a reliable estimate can be developed. One writer has recently estimated that nearly 140,000 focus groups are held per year. Of these, projections of the number of business-to-business groups range up to 40 percent. This would mean that companies are sponsoring about 56,000 focus groups per year on business-to-business subjects. The leaders by far in the business-to-business category have been financial services firms, especially the big banks and brokerage companies. Only recently have old-line industrial firms looked carefully at focus groups as a key marketing research tool.

Best Uses

As with any popular technique, focus groups are sometimes misused. First, some firms think groups are just informal meetings with company personnel. The problem is that informal meetings do not yield the same results as carefully designed focus groups where the sponsoring client remains anonymous. It's only human nature for customers to pull their punches (or, on the other hand, be slightly overcritical to prove their independence) in the presence of host personnel. The anonymity allows respondents to say what's really on their minds, affected only by group pressures, which many scientists believe impact buyers in their real business decision making.

Another problem is substituting focus groups where quantitative studies are required. Focus groups should not be used as substitutes for massive quantitative studies. There are times when it is necessary to talk to many people in order to develop statistically projectable information for making decisions.

But there are times when focus groups are the only method that can be used by business marketers. First, most business-to-business markets operate on the 80/20 rule, that is the largest percentage of purchases are made by a small percentage of all buyers. Statistics are not as valuable in these situations as talking to a good selection of key buyers. Frequently, Radley Resources conducts eight focus groups of eight to nine people each for a single product. These individuals may represent a large percentage or even a majority of all buyers interested in a particular product and, in many cases, the overwhelming majority of the dollars committed for that product.

Focus groups are also the recommended method for research when:

- A firm needs to learn about a new field.
- Buyers need to see a demonstration of the product in order to react to it.
- Very large products (yet small enough to fit in a conference room) must be shown to buyers.
- A manufacturer wants its customers to have hands-on experience with a product.
- Confidentiality is critical, such as for a new advertising campaign or a new product prototype.

In these cases, many clients decide to use focus groups to get a good reading on a particular problem.

We believe the best purposes for business focus groups include:

- To study the purchase decision process.
- To review new products or services.
- To review advertising concepts.
- To discern perceptions of company image.
- To attempt to unearth customer problems.
- To identify industry trends.
- To brainstorm for new product/ service ideas.

We generally recommend using focus groups with professionals who do not see themselves as competitors. Telecommunications managers, MIS managers, lighting engineers, architects, and facilities managers are good examples. We don't believe focus groups are particularly useful for company employees or local dealers or wholesalers who compete with each other.

Recent Projects

Here are some examples of how businesses have used focus groups recently:

- One firm was contemplating the introduction of a new and very different office furniture system.

We held focus groups in New York, Chicago, and Los Angeles with independent interior designers and facility managers of large corporations. In order to do this, a large prototype of the system was developed and shipped from facility to facility. In addition, a video tape and small scale mock-up were developed. The moderator gave a forty-five minute presentation so that the respondents would fully understand the new concept. While the product was generally well received, there were some aspects that required redesign and the firm proceeded to do that, thereby postponing a multimillion dollar investment in its plant.

- Another firm was planning to introduce a new landscape lighting product line. Focus groups held in Atlanta and Northern New Jersey with electrical contractors, lighting consultants, landscape architects as well as homeowners gave this firm invaluable information for designing advertising, promotion and distribution. First-year sales were well above expectations as a result of the information developed.

- A large telephone company was interested in determining customer perceptions of a new service to be provided on corporate premises. Four focus groups were held in New York and Chicago with telecommunications managers representing major corporations. The sponsoring firm found out that the need for this service was limited to a very small number of heavy users. This segment was easily identified from only four focus groups and the client developed a targeted marketing program to reach this small number of important customers.

Another client was marketing a computer-based, electronic presentation system. The client had to decide whether to proceed full speed with this product or deemphasize it. Focus groups were held with people responsible for the selection and purchase of this equipment. One of the most important findings from this research was that the respondents were not the current customers of the research sponsor. In addition, the product was perceived to perform significantly worse than its major competitor. These facts convinced the client to reevaluate any further investment in the product line.

Numbers and Costs

We recommend four focus groups with any one target segment in order to get a good understanding of the participants' feelings. In almost every case, at the end of the four groups we have heard the same comments so many times that we're sure we have the right answers. A four-group project conducted in two geographical locations usually falls in the $22,000 range, including all expenses except video taping. An eight-group project addressing two different but related segments will probably cost about $38,000. Our clients claim focus groups have saved them from $300,000 to several millions of dollars by helping them avoid failure, improve offerings, or hone marketing programs. Many business marketers seem to agree.

Radley Resources is a business-to-business marketing research and consulting firm. The company was founded in 1982 by Alan Zimmerman after a 20-year career in marketing with the Westinghouse Electric Corporation and The EF Hauserman Company.

As American society ages, growth slows and segments become harder to pinpoint, marketers making their decisions on how best to reach their targets will put a greater burden on research experts.

A SYMPHONY OF DEMOGRAPHIC CHANGE

Peter Francese

Demographic, social and economic change has transformed America's consumer markets from being relatively easy pickings to elusive targets. Today's intensely segmented consumer markets are more difficult to predict, harder to reach and tougher to sell than ever before.

In such an environment it should surprise no one that advertisers are searching for greater efficiencies in their marketing and advertising efforts. For many years management's focus has been on achieving greater efficiency in operations such as manufacturing and distribution. But with the shift to smaller production runs of more highly differentiated products, the focus has switched to selling more products with the same or fewer advertising and promotion dollars.

An essential element for more efficient marketing is a deeper understanding of the consumers. Such understanding is rarely achieved but is, in fact, an ongoing process as consumer trends unfold and the American family changes in size and character.

As we prepare to move into the last decade of the 20th century there are many population and household trends developing simultaneously. Some, like the shortage of teen-agers, are in evidence now, while others will appear throughout the decade.

There are three major themes in a symphony of demographic change with numerous melodies: slowing population and household growth; an aging society; and an increasing fragmentation of consumer markets.

Each of these trends and its components has implications for the way we communicate with consumers, the types of messages that will influence

their behavior and the kinds of products and services they will buy.

. . .

The U.S. population is growing at just under 1% per year, and each year the rate of growth diminishes slightly. The major component of growth is births, which at 3.8 million have hit a post-baby boom record low. No one expects total births to keep rising. In fact, they will probably start declining sometime in the early 1990s.

The other component, immigration, was growing rapidly and adding between 500,000 and a million-plus people a year (including an estimate of illegal aliens) until Congress passed a law prohibiting the employment of undocumented workers. That may have serious long-term consequences for U.S. growth because as the population ages, deaths will rise to completely offset births. Thus, within the next generation, immi-

From *Advertising Age*, November 9, 1988, pp. 130, 132. Reprinted by permission of the author.

gration will be our major, and perhaps only, source of growth.

Households grew more than twice as rapidly as the population during the 1970s, fueling the demand for all kinds of home-related products. But now households are increasing only 1.5 times as fast, and during the 1990s the growth rates will probably converge.

The major consequence of such low overall growth is to intensify the search for the more rapidly growing consumer market segments. Almost no one will be satisfied with sales or profit growth of less than 1% per year. The trick is to find a faster-growing segment before everyone else does or build market share faster than anyone else. Some of the faster-growing segments are demographic (i.e., working women with

very young children), but some are geographic (i.e., Florida). A sharper focus on demographic segments means advertisers will want more tightly targeted marketing campaigns. A heightened awareness of geographic segments means more regional and local marketing.

The U.S. population is aging because while the number of young adults is falling, the number of mid-age and very old people is rising rapidly.

The number of young adults 18 to 24 peaked in the early 1980s and is projected to decline by 12% over the next decade. This means 3 million fewer young people to buy beer, motorcycles, college educations, cosmetics or any of the other products and services designed for young consumers.

There is some evidence that this decline may be at least partly offset by rising purchasing power due to higher wages and lower unemployment rates. But while cash-register receipts may not be deeply affected, there will be fewer people to run those cash registers or to provide service in what is supposed to be a service-based economy. This suggests the telephone and the modem-equipped personal computer as major shopping methods of the future. Catalogs now in print form will more and more appear in video form and the sales clerk will more often appear as the UPS or U.S. Postal Service delivery person.

Contrary to the decline in young adults is the growing children-and-young-teen market. By 1998, 5-to-12-year-olds will be up 10%, and they are becoming more sophisticated consumers every year. This should mean growth for videogames, pre-teen cosmetics and microwavable foods.

The majority of young children today who live with both parents see them go to work every weekday. So they are taking on more household responsibilities and making more and bigger purchasing decisions for themselves.

The difference between men's and women's patterns of lifetime employment becomes smaller every year. Even a majority of mothers with children under age 1 are in the labor force. This tends to fragment purchasing behavior within the household, change how people spend their time and reduce the opportunities for reaching an entire household with one advertising message.

The second reason why this country is getting older is the middle-aging of the baby boom. During the next decade the market segment called the baby boom will move into middle age and in the process move into its peak earning and spending years. In 1990 the baby boom will be about 25 to 44 years old. In 2000, therefore, they will be about 35 to 54. During the next decade the 35-to-44 age segment will grow 23% and the 45-to-54 age segment will jump 45% *(see chart)*. Only one other age segment will grow faster: those 85 and older. But no other group earns or spends more than the 45-to-54s.

According to the latest Consumer Expenditure Survey consumers 45 to 54 spend the most on food (30% above average), apparel (38% above average) and retirement programs (54% above

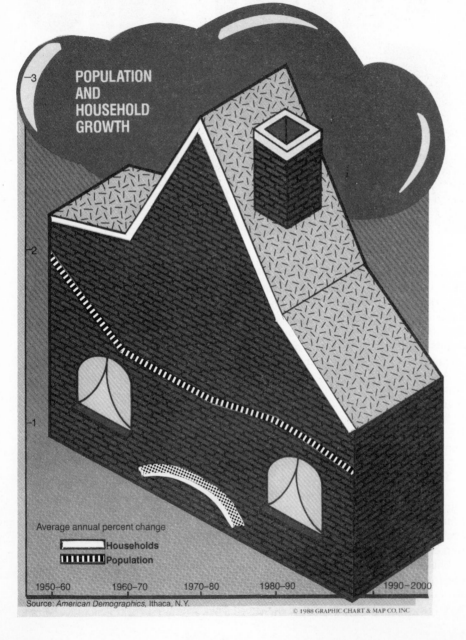

POPULATION AND HOUSEHOLD GROWTH

Average annual percent change

☐ Households
|||||| Population

1950–60 1960–70 1970–80 1980–90 1990–2000

Source: *American Demographics*, Ithaca, N.Y.

© 1988 GRAPHIC CHART & MAP CO. INC

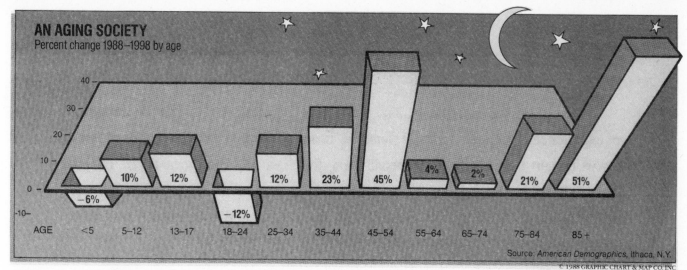

AN AGING SOCIETY
Percent change 1988–1998 by age

AGE	<5	5–12	13–17	18–24	25–34	35–44	45–54	55–64	65–74	75–84	85+
	−6%	10%	12%	−12%	12%	23%	45%	4%	2%	21%	51%

Source: *American Demographics*, Ithaca, N.Y.

average). The 35-to-44 age group spends the most on housing, motor vehicles and entertainment. At current spending levels a 1% increase in householders 35 to 54 means an additional $8.9 billion in consumer expenditures.

As they get older, baby boomers are also settling down in a big way. Interstate mobility declines sharply with age and people in their 30s and 40s take a greater interest in their home and in their community. As baby boomers put down roots, literally and figuratively, the lawn and landscape business should do well. But there will also be a greater interest in locally produced products. This suggests greater regional as well as market-by-market diversity and a rising demand for advertising with a local flavor and content.

Time management is a big deal with baby boomers. Thus, retailers that find ways to reduce the time and hassle of shopping will get a competitive edge. This may mean an increase in the information content (i.e., size, location, colors available, price, etc.) of print advertising to make shopping easier.

One market segment for which time does not seem a problem is the mature market. No consumer group has been more misunderstood than older Americans. The 55-plus market has had a reputation for high growth but low income. For part of this market that is the

case, but for the majority the exact opposite is true.

Almost half the nation's discretionary income accrues to people 55 or older. The word growth hardly describes most of this population. Three quarters of the mature market is between 55 and 75; the Census Bureau projects that age group to grow a mere 3% in the next 10 years. But the population 75 to 84 is expected to grow rapidly (up to 21%) and the oldest old, those 85-plus, will increase 51% by 1998. More than one in five people in this oldest age group are in a nursing home or hospital and many live at or near poverty.

The rapid increase in the very old will create enormous demand for long-term health-care facilities along with the staff and equipment to maintain them. Assuming present levels of institutionalization, there will be a demand for about one new 100-bed nursing home every single day for the next 10 years. The sharp contrasts in the mature market—from bedridden patients in a nursing home to big spenders on a cruise—makes this consumer group difficult to understand and hard to communicate with.

More than the usual amount of consumer research is required before developing an advertising campaign targeted to this group.

The fragmentation of consumer markets combined with increasingly diverse

media means more research information about consumers must be processed and understood before making marketing and advertising decisions.

If advertisers, responding to demographic change, want more highly targeted messages and more efficiency in their advertising efforts, perhaps they also will obtain research to measure marketing performance.

Maybe a new breed of efficiency expert will move from the assembly line to the advertising agency.

More complicated consumer markets require more sophisticated consumer research and the integration of consumer information into media buying and marketing decisions. This is what is often called data base marketing and never have we had more data with which to do such marketing.

In a few years billions of figures from the 1990 census will be available to add to the already substantial output from scanner cash registers, people meters, panel diaries, syndicated studies and market-research reports. The marketing or advertising director in the 1990s will have to be extraordinarily skilled at processing vast amounts of data and making sense of it.

Out of those oceans of numbers must come not only a better understanding of consumer markets but also more precise measurements of marketing efficiency.

Downscale Consumers, Long Neglected, Start to Get Some Respect From Marketers

Kathleen Deveny

Staff Reporter of The Wall Street Journal

Homer Simpson, the decidedly downscale patriarch of Fox Broadcasting's "The Simpsons," has become a pop icon. So has Roseanne Barr, the proletarian star of ABC's hit series "Roseanne."

Regular folks are back in fashion, a fact that hasn't escaped the attention of some of the nation's most powerful marketers. Blue-collar and other nonprofessional people have always represented a vast and loyal group of consumers. But now, with growth in most upscale markets slowing to a crawl, more companies than ever are viewing them with renewed respect.

Consider: McDonald's Corp. features working stiffs in new TV commercials. Burger King Corp. plans to use cartoon characters from "The Simpsons" in promotions. A Southern cable operator has revamped its marketing to lure low-income viewers. Clothing maker Gitano Group Inc. cultivates a trendy image, but focuses its products and prices on middle America. Procter & Gamble Co. advertises some of its top brands in the National Enquirer.

Of course, it wouldn't make sense to peddle luxury items to consumers who can't afford them. But for most of the past decade, Madison Avenue has been loath to target downscale markets for even mundane products. In part, that's because advertisers like to show their products as part of an affluent life style.

Some critics also attribute the lack of interest to a cultural bias on the part of image makers, who often create marketing campaigns that tend to reflect their own life styles more than the lives of average consumers. "Nobody wants to work on a downscale product," says a New York ad executive. "We're all pretty upscale people, and we all wear the prestige products we've worked on on our sleeves."

It's hard to dispute the demographic appeal of Middle America. The average household earns about $34,000 a year, according to the most recent Census Bureau figures. That may not be in a league with gilded yuppiedom, but because of their numbers, households that live on that figure or less control more than 30% of total income in the U.S.

Moreover, middle-class consumers may respond to down-to-earth pitches in growing numbers because more are feeling squeezed. Since the early 1970s, family incomes have hardly managed to stay ahead of inflation. For baby boomers starting out, that makes upward mobility more difficult. Allow for climbing health-care costs, property taxes and tuition bills rising much faster than inflation, and the ranks of penny pinchers swell.

"It's the phenomenon of the fading fortunate," says Carol Colman, a partner in the New York consulting firm Inferential Focus. "Marketers may have made the mistake of thinking average Americans made $75,000, and now even that aspirational group is feeling squeezed."

The appeal of the blue-collar market goes beyond the numbers. Despite their image as traitorous coupon clippers, lower-income consumers may actually be more brand-loyal than their wealthier counterparts. Because they can less afford to make mistakes, experts say they're more likely to stick with a brand that pleases them. "A brand is a safety net for these groups," says Stewart Owen, director of research at Landor Associates, a San Francisco image consulting firm.

Marketers are trying a range of techniques to woo the diverse downscale market. McDonald's, for example exalts the average guy in several new TV commercials created by Leo Burnett Co. Though the nation's largest purveyor of meals for the masses has never courted the silk-stocking set, several ads rolled out in early May more pointedly reflect the modest life styles of some of its customers.

In one spot, a nervous suitor launches into a monologue on his prospective date's doorstep. He's not a doctor or a lawyer, he proclaims, but a record-store salesperson. The awkward Romeo is eager to set the record straight on a few other points: He doesn't wear designer clothes or go to restaurants that refer to themselves as "bistro." The woman is enchanted, of course, and happily follows him to the curb—where his 1980 Chevrolet Citation awaits.

In another ad, a little girl waits for her mother to return from work on a rainy night. When the woman—apparently a single mom—finally arrives looking exhausted, the child reminds her of a promised meal at McDonald's. On the way to the restaurant, the daughter listens to the account of her mother's trying day at work. "We're saying it's OK to be regular," says a McDonald's spokesman.

Meanwhile, rival Burger King, a unit of Grand Metropolitan PLC, seems to be sending the message that it's all right to be a little weird. The fast-food chain plans a series of promotions starting this summer based on "The Simpsons." A spokesman for Fox confirms that Burger King has licensed the characters Homer Simpson, a safety inspector at his town's nuclear power plant, and his puckish son, Bart, to push burgers.

Other marketers are going much further. Birmingham Cable, which operates cable-TV systems in Birmingham,

Ala., and nearby Bessemer, has repositioned its service to draw working-class customers. Though the company was doing well among upscale residents, lower-income people weren't hooking up in large numbers—bad news since such customers account for about two-thirds of the population in the systems' territories.

Through a research firm that develops neighborhood profiles, the cable operator found its territory includes a cluster of neighborhoods occupied mainly by single adults and one-parent families who earn an average of $15,000 a year. Market research also showed that such consumers are put off by complicated pitches.

So, Birmingham Cable changed its approach. The company ditched a glossy brochure, which had included a letter and a response form, in favor of a brief appeal, and it began to push the service as cheap family entertainment rather than as a luxury. Response to the modified mailer more than doubled.

The cable operator also started advertising its monthly charges, rather than breaking the cost of the service down to 40 cents a day, a tactic customers found suspicious. "The people

in these market segments are very good money managers," says Rod Clark, vice president of marketing at Birmingham Cable. "They're worried about hidden costs."

For many marketers, targeting the blue-collar brigades is a matter of finding the right vehicle. Procter & Gamble places ads in some unexpected publications. For several years, P&G has been advertising some of its best-known brands in the nosy pages of the National Enquirer. Tucked near the tale of a woman who was run over by her own "van from hell" in a recent issue was this unfanciful claim: "If it's got to be clean, it's got to be Tide."

Other marketers court downscale consumers by presenting a middle-class or affluent image to which they can aspire. Gitano Group spends some $15 million a year to promote its women's clothing with slick ads in swanky publications such as Vogue and Mademoiselle.

But in fact, Gitano clothing is aimed squarely at the discount crowd. The primary outlets for the company's wares—mostly women's tops and bottoms that sell for around $20—are mass merchandisers such as K-mart Corp.

and Wal-Mart Stores Inc. And despite Gitano's trendy, youthful ads, most of the clothes are cut to fit more mature bodies. Some of the brand's big sellers are maternity clothes and jeans for larger-sized women.

General Mills Inc.'s Hamburger Helper brand of dinner mixes uses a similar marketing illusion to create a comfortable, middle-class image. The product, whose sales are booming, was created in the mid-1970s, when meat prices soared, as a way to stretch ground beef. But ads for the boxed dinners stress convenience and taste over economy, and often feature an affluent-looking suburban family.

Despite the size—and spending power—of working-class America, most marketers don't want their products associated with the masses. "The marketing community has no aspirations to address the needs of a demographic group of which it is not a member," says John Quelch, a professor at Harvard Business School who specializes in consumer marketing. Indeed, most brand managers and ad executives have far more in common with Mr. Quelch's students than with Roseanne or Homer.

DIFFERENT FOLKS, DIFFERENT STROKES

With the help of sophisticated new technology, national marketers are learning what traveling salesmen always knew—where people live is one of the best clues to what they want to buy. Southwesterners love pickup trucks; folks in the Northeast want vans.

Thomas Moore

THE MAN IN THE STREET may believe that national media and fast-food chains are homogenizing the U.S. into one bland culture, but smart marketers are rediscovering the importance of regional differences. For products from soups to cars, the shotgun approach of a single national advertising campaign is giving way to precisely targeted regional strategies. The new marketing conjures up local color, caters to regional tastes, problems, and styles, taps local celebrities for testimonials, ties in with local events, and occasionally features a regional version of a product.

Regional marketing is as old as the traveling salesman, but it has been elevated to a new art by sophisticated sales technology. With computers and laser scanners, companies can now figure out how buying habits change from store to store and thus pinpoint problems and opportunities across the country. By focusing on the unique characteristics of local markets, big companies with mature products have gained market share, often at the expense of local competitors.

Companies pitching national brands are spending more on regional television, radio, and newspaper promotion and less, proportionately, on national media. According to the Television Bureau of Advertising, the national networks' share of total spending on television advertising has declined from 45% in 1980 to an estimated 40% this year. Some consumer product companies are beefing up the powers and budgets of regional managers and even restructuring manufacturing operations to make products in the areas where they sell best. In August, Campbell Soup created a "czar for sales" for each of four U.S. sales regions. "The next step will be to put plants in each of our regions to make the products that sell best there," says Herbert Baum, Campbell's marketing vice president. "And the third step might be to

RESEARCH ASSOCIATE *Kim Bendheim*

No. 1 Markets for Selected Products

ATLANTA	**Antacids & aspirin**
DALLAS/FORT WORTH	**Popcorn**
DENVER	**Vitamins**
GRAND RAPIDS	**Rat poison**
INDIANAPOLIS	**Shoe polish**
MIAMI	**Prune juice**
NEW YORK	**Laundry soaps**
NEW ORLEANS	**Ketchup**
OKLAHOMA	**Motor oil additives**
PHILADELPHIA	**Iced tea**
PITTSBURGH	**Coffee**
PORTLAND (Oregon)	**Dry cat food**
SALT LAKE CITY	**Candy bars & marshmallows**
SAVANNAH	**MSG & meat tenderizers**
SEATTLE	**Toothbrushes**

It is hard to guess *why residents of Seattle buy more toothbrushes per capita than, say, candy-bar-eating Salt Lakers. Selling Areas-Marketing Inc., a subsidiary of Time Inc.,* FORTUNE*'s publisher, collects sales data from over 100,000 food outlets around the U.S. but does not try to explain the information. That's the job of marketers, who buy the data and mix them with demographic profiles and market-share percentages to shape regional selling pitches.*

replace national brand managers for each product with regional brand managers, who might handle several products in their area."

S.C. Johnson & Son, maker of the Raid arsenal of bug killers, is a born-again advocate of regional marketing. Concerned that its dominant share of the household insecticide market had plateaued just above 40%, Johnson figured out where and when different bugs were about to start biting, stinging, and otherwise making people's lives miserable. The company promoted cockroach zappers in roach capitals such as Houston and New York and flea sprays in flea-bitten cities like Tampa and Birmingham. Since the program began last year, Raid has increased its market share in 16 of 18 regions and its overall piece of the $450-million-a-year U.S. insecticide market by five percentage points. "Before, we used to get a lot of salespeople in a big room and they would say, yes, it *feels* right to start advertising flea sprays at a particular point in time," says John Bleharski, Raid's category manager. "Now, because of new computer software systems that can cut up our data quickly, we can do the same thing precisely."

LIKE BUGS, people are different in different parts of the country. For example, Northeasterners and Midwesterners prefer chicken noodle and tomato soups, but in California cream of mushroom is No. 1. Pepperpot soup sells primarily in the Philadelphia area, and cream of vegetable on the West Coast. People in the Southwest drive more pickup trucks, people in the Northeast more vans, and Californians like high-priced imported cars such as BMWs and Mercedes-Benzes. Texans drive big cars, New Yorkers like smaller ones. New Hampshirites drink more beer per capita than other Americans. The anxious denizens of Atlanta consume more aspirin and antacids a head, and sweet-toothed Mormons of Salt Lake City eat more candy bars and marshmallows (see chart).

Campbell Soup has cooked up several new products that cater to local tastes. When its pork and beans did not sell well in the Southwest vs. a local competitor's Mexican-style pinto beans, the company cut out the pork, added some chili pepper and, *caramba*: Ranchero beans. The change increased Campbell's sales of pinto beans in the Southwest

from virtually nothing to 75,000 cases in 1984. Similarly, Campbell Soup's Vlasic pickle subsidiary created Zesty Pickles primarily for Northwesterners, who like sourer pickles than most Americans.

In 1978 Anheuser-Busch, the No. 1 U.S. brewer, trailed Schlitz and Coors in Texas. Using a "target market concept," the company divided the state into three zones. "Texas is so big, you can't look at it as one state," says Joseph Martino, vice president of sales. Working closely with local wholesalers, the company sponsored rodeo events in the north (traditional cowboy country) and Hispanic band tours in the south (where a large number of Mexican-Americans live). Since then Anheuser-Busch has chugged into the lead in the state. The program was so successful the beermaker created similar campaigns for other states where it wanted to either capture or defend the top position. Anheuser-Busch has increased its share of the national market from 22.6% in 1977 to 36.7% in June.

While companies have long analyzed consumer markets according to demographic characteristics, such as age, income, and education, marketers have only recently started to focus on the unique characteristics of local markets. The trend was reinforced in 1981 by *The Nine Nations of America*, a book by Joel Garreau, an editor at the *Washington Post*. Garreau argues that North America is divided into nine "nations," regions populated by people sharing distinct values, attitudes, and styles. The book is required reading at some consumer product companies.

Ogilvy & Mather, a New York advertising agency, using data from several market research firms, created consumer profiles for eight of Garreau's nine nations to help clients identify regional opportunities for established brands, new ventures, advertising strategies, and tactical marketing programs. "A lot of marketers are shocked to realize that the traditional American family [father, nonworking mother, and two children] is less than 10% of the American public," says Ogilvy & Mather research development director Jane Fitzgibbon. "They are much more comfortable marketing to Norman Rockwell's vision."

Some research firms use census data to segment the country into even finer "geo-demographic" blocks averaging 340 households each. Starting from the premise that

people with similar cultural backgrounds, circumstances, and perspectives cluster together, Claritas, an Alexandria, Virginia, market research firm, classifies U.S. neighborhoods into 40 groups. According to its Prizm marketing model, Chappaqua, New York, and Winnetka, Illinois, count as "Blue-Blood Estates" ("America's wealthiest socioeconomic neighborhoods, populated by super-upper established managers, professionals, and heirs to old money, accustomed to privilege"). Weatherford, Texas, and Waverly, Ohio, come under the classification "Shotguns and Pickups" ("hundreds of small, outlying townships and crossroads villages that serve the nation's breadbasket and other rural areas"). A Prizm client might be a bank that wants to find out what kinds of people are buying Individual Retirement Accounts, where its best potential IRA customers live, and how its customers compare with national profiles of people buying IRAs.

Regional marketing won't work magic for every product. For instance, David Gustin, marketing manager for breakfast foods at General Foods, found regional marketing effective when he was in charge of General Foods' Maxwell House coffee, a product that faces radically different competition from city to city. But regional variations matter less for cereal, which faces roughly the same competition around the U.S. and appeals mainly to two broad demographic segments: old people and families with children. McDonald's, the hamburger king, tests new promotions and locations regionally, but insists on offering the same fast-food menu nationwide so that customers anywhere know what to expect.

Though it is expensive to compile large databases and hire marketing staffs to analyze them, many consumer product companies believe they must have a regional strategy because everyone else does. "A lot of companies feel geo-demographic marketing gives them a competitive edge, which is true in the short run," says John M. McCann, a marketing professor at Duke University's Fuqua School of Business. "But in the long run everyone will do it." When that happens, the competitive edge of regional marketing will be dulled. Then marketers will doubtless come up with some other new technique—even if it's an old one.

"REAL" CONSUMERS JUST AREN'T NORMAL

James L. Mueller

James L. Mueller has been president of his own consulting firm since 1981. He has worked in the field of rehabilitation technology since 1974, when he joined The Job Development Laboratory at The George Washington University Medical Center. Prior to this, he held staff design positions at two private industrial design consulting firms. He holds design degrees from both Syracuse University and George Washington University.

Signs of The Times?

It looked just like many other TV commercials for Levi's 501 jeans: good-looking people looking good in Levi's jeans, except...one was doing wheelies—in a wheelchair!

It was obviously a McDonald's commercial, with all the hamburgers, fries, and arches, but...no sound. Two people were obviously enjoying lunch and a lively conversation, but neither was saying anything—they were using sign language! (Captions were thoughtfully provided for those viewers who are not "handicapped.")

Signs of the times? These commercials seem to beg the question, "What's wrong with this picture?" But the fact is, these commercials couldn't be more right.

36 Million People

American businesses are just discovering vast new market opportunities among people with disabilities. Historically referred to as "cripples," "invalids," and, more recently, "the handicapped," they are now claiming their identity first as *people*. Disability is secondary. They no longer fit the stereotypes characterizing them as feeble, passive, and dependent.

There are roughly 36 million people in the United States with chronic disabilities. This sizable group has been summarily dismissed as insignificant or unreachable (or both) by American consumer businesses—until recently. Levi Strauss and McDonald's are among the first companies to develop marketing strategies that include consumers with disabilities.

Those of us who have no experience with disability, either personally or through a friend or relative, can probably identify with the attitudes that have prejudiced businesses away from people with disabilities. The word "disability" itself is negative, although not as blatantly so as other terms mentioned above. Being disabled is certainly not something we would aspire to if we seek respect, opportunity, and love.

However, wheelchair athletes, actors and actresses with disabilities (e.g., Marlee Matlin, *Children of a Lesser God*), and political figures such as Senator Robert Dole are among contemporary illustrations that a disability need not prevent a person from greatness. But most people with disabilities are not great. Most of them are just like us.

Medical Progress

Not only is 36 million people a large potential market, it is a fast-growing market. Medical technology is allowing people to live longer and more independently than ever before, despite chronic limitations. In 1900 a person suffering a spinal cord injury had a 10 percent chance of survival. By 1980 the survival rate had reached 80 percent. Other serious conditions such as kidney disease and cerebrovascular disease are no longer certain killers. The mortality rates for kidney failure, diabetes, heart disease, and hypertension have decreased by as much as 50 percent over the past 20 years.

Disability and Aging Consumers

Some of the disproportionate growth of the disabled population can be attributed to an

From *The Journal of Consumer Marketing*, Vol. 7, No. 1, Winter 1990. Copyright © 1990 by The Journal of Consumer Marketing, published by Grayson Associates.

aging population. All of us, including the "baby boom generation," are aging. Functional limitations due to arthritis, heart disease, cerebrovascular disease, and eye disorders are among the most common problems in people 45 to 84 years of age. By the year 2000, one-third of the U.S. population will be physically disabled, chronically ill, or over 65 years of age. This is not tragedy, this is life. The tragedy would be to assume that life ends at a certain age, or with a disability. The stereotypical "granny" or "cripple" simply doesn't exist.

Inclusivity, Not Exclusivity

Though a large segment of the population have disabilities, they are far from a homogeneous group. This is equally true of aging consumers. Marketing strategies such as those of McDonald's and Levi Strauss focus on people with disabilities as a part of the "mainstream." The characteristics that make them similar to nondisabled people are far more important than those that set them apart. These successful strategies are *inclusive of* rather than *exclusively for* people with disabilities.

This is a very important concept in planning product design and marketing strategies. A common misconception is that what is good for disabled people is, by nature, not good for "normal" people. Just who is "normal," anyway? How many of us would prefer a doorknob to a lever when carrying two bags of groceries into our house? Are we "disabled" because we find a device installed for disabled people useful? Are we offended that Whirlpool home appliances have simple, large, high-contrast lettering for users with visual limitations? Conversely, do we suppose that people who have difficulty dialing telephone numbers avoid memory-dial phones because they are not exclusively for "them"? In similar ways, packaging and advertising design affect disabled consumers. If a magazine ad's copy is difficult to read, or a package is difficult to open, consumers are likely to seek alternative products.

Nearly everyone experiences some functional limitation during his or her lifetime. Broken arms, low back pain, flu—each causes at least minor, temporary limitations that make even simple tasks difficult or impossible. Products that are designed to accommodate consumers who have chronic limitations due to disabilities will be more useful for everyone. This is the basis for a product design trend called "universal" or "transgenerational" design which is enabling consumer product manufacturers to broaden their market share by redefining the "normal" consumer.

Universal Design At National Rehabilitation Hospital

The Rehabilitation Engineering Center at the National Rehabilitation Hospital in Washington, D.C., is currently developing market data and product design guidelines to help consumer product businesses include the disabled consumer market. The reason for their interest in this project is the overall improvement in rehabilitation outcome for people who become disabled. Usable products, just like accessible buildings, increase the ability of people with disabilities to live independently outside the sheltered environment of the rehabilitation hospital. As the cost of providing this sheltered environment rises, the benefits of independence in the community also rise. These financial benefits are felt by those of us who pay taxes and insurance premiums, as well as by the disabled person and his or her family.

Reports Available

Door levers, appliances with readable markings, and memory-dial telephones are only a few of the products that can reach a more "universal" market. The National Rehabilitation Hospital is currently evaluating a number of products that are integral to the independence of people with disabilities. The results of these evaluations will yield practical information concerning how specific products perform for users with disabilities and how this performance might be enhanced through a more "universal" approach to product design. Demographic and ergonomic information about consumers with disabilities, developed through the project, will enable product and marketing planners to make decisions based on real market data.

The first of these reports is now available from the Rehabilitation Engineering Center at the National Rehabilitation Hospital. Single copies are available free from: Rehabilitation Engineering Center, National Rehabilitation Hospital, 102 Irving Street, NW, Washington, D.C. 20010-2949.

MEET JANE DOE

Blayne Cutler

Blayne Cutler is an associate editor of American Demographics.

Jane Doe is in a rut. She's better educated than ever before. She's going to live longer, too. But Jane's sitting in the suburbs watching thirtysomething close in on fortysomething. She can't help but notice she's shorter (5'4"), fatter (143 pounds), and older (32) than most of the people she sees on TV. Jane's got ten credit cards but little to spend on anything but food and shelter.

At about 6:30 every morning, Jane gets in her eight-year-old car, as she will do over 1,500 times a year. She has made

sure her two television sets, six radios, VCR, stereo, and kitchen appliances are all turned off. She tucks $104 securely in her wallet and drives about ten miles to the office.

When she comes home to her husband and one or two children, Jane will face another three and a half hours of housework and child care. Little does she know it, but she is sure to be a victim of crime—not once, but three times in her life. Poor Jane. It wasn't always this way.

Fifty years ago, the average American—a 29-year-old man—could find a blue-collar job in the country's growing cities with no more than a ninth-grade education. One hundred years ago, single

and 22 years old, he was America's farmhand.

No one really lives the average American life. But a look at the average American's characteristics reveals the most important trends in how people live. Marketers spend millions trying to determine the direction of American lifestyles, but all it really takes is a little perspective.

NO PLACE LIKE HOME

The home of the average American today is often temporary and costly. She lives in a 1,700-square-foot dwelling that's more than 25 years old, and she spends more than one-third of her income on housing.

Although the average American still lives in the state of her birth (as 61 percent of all Americans do), she has a one-in-five chance of picking up and moving in a year. She moves at least 11 times in her life. Although her home is worth about $60,000, the average American could sell her house for more than $84,000 if she leaves it on the market for the usual 86 days.

The odds of owning a home are no better today than they were in 1890, when the share of owner-occupied households was 66 percent. Home ownership fell to 41 percent in 1940, then rose to 65 percent by 1986. As a home-owner, the average American has a median net worth of $75,000. Her friends who rent have a median net worth of just $5,000, according to the Federal Reserve Board.

Marriage is still the lifestyle of choice for the average American, who considers herself romantic, traces her first "crush" back to age 13, and is bound to fall in love at least six times in her life, according to the book *Lover's Quotient* by Nancy Biracree. She waited until age 24 before tying the knot, but the more educated she is, the longer she waited to marry. At age 32, she has more than a 50 percent chance of becoming single again through divorce. The odds are nine out of ten that she will be widowed at some point in her life.

But single life is not new to Americans. It was more common before World War II, in fact. Thirty percent of men and 23 percent of women have never married today. But 44 percent of men and 34 percent of women had never married in 1890. In 1940, 35 percent of men and 28 percent of women had not married.

Average Americans in 1890 and 1990 both experience many years of single life, but the woman in 1990 may be lonelier than her great-grandmother was. That's because today's average American lives with fewer people. Average household size has shrunk from nearly five people in 1890 to fewer than three today. Americans have fewer children, and they rarely live with grandparents, aunts, uncles, or cousins as they more often did in the past.

Although the average American still lives in a family household, many Americans do not. Just 72 percent of households are families today, compared with 92 percent in 1940. Married couples were 71 percent of households in 1940, and just 58 percent today.

MATERIAL GIRLS

Today, Americans own 150 million televisions, 495 million radios, 182 million telephones, 137 million cars and light trucks, 111 million bicycles and tricycles, 14 million pleasure boats, and almost 6 million motorcycles.

Homes are no longer a quiet refuge. Televisions or radios are on for 11 hours a day in the average American home—most of the time people are awake. With cable, the average household can browse among nine channels.

Thirty-seven percent of what's in the mailbox is an unsolicited sales pitch (18 pieces of direct mail per month). Moreover, the average American will make six telephone calls a day. In the future, as cordless telephones, answering machines, computers, camcorders, satellite dishes, and hand-held TV screens become part of the life of the average American, white noise will come of age.

Consumer spending began on a massive scale when John Doe first moved to the city in 1920. In that year, the census

ARE *You* THE
Average
AMERICAN?

The average American is a 32-year-old woman.

The average American woman can't see over a crowd in a parade: she is only 5'4", has brown hair (69% of all Americans do). She weighs 143 pounds, and is trying to lose weight. Still, she thinks she looks younger than she is (57% of all Americans think so).

The average American wears glasses or contact lenses.

Although she hasn't been to church in the past week, the average American was born Protestant (65% of all Americans). She believes in God (94% of all Americans) and life after death (69%).

The average American owns an 8-year-old blue sedan that gets 18 miles to the gallon and costs about $3,000 a year to own and operate. The average American will drive this car almost 9,000 miles a year. Two more people will buy it before it goes to the junkyard.

By age 32, the average American is married and has a child. It will cost her more than $140,000 to raise her child to the age of 18. If it's a boy, the average American's child is named Michael. If it's a girl, Jennifer.

The average American woman wears a size 7-1/2 B shoe. Although she reports foot pain and related problems (as do 62% of all women), the average American woman wears high heels regularly (59% of all women).

The average American has lost two teeth by the age of 30. She'll lose ten by the time she's 70.

The average American woman wears a size 10 or 12 dress. In 1986, she spent $339 on clothes. She spent almost one-third of the money on blouses and sweaters, followed by dresses (16%), skirts/suits (14%), lingerie/hosiery (12%), and pants (11%). In 1985, working women with children bought an average of 37 items of clothing a year. Working women without children bought an average of 55 items.

70% of women say they wear jewelry every day, and they buy most of it themselves. The average American woman wears a size 6 ring. The median price of her engagement ring is $800.

She may not be rich, but the average American carries $104 in her purse. Also in her purse: keys (97% of all women report them in their purse), a wallet (94%), a comb (80%), checks (76%), makeup (69%), and an address book (69%).

The average American works in a technical, sales, or administrative job. She makes less than $20,000 a year. Her earnings account for only 78% of her total annual income. The rest comes from investments, government benefit programs, and self-employment.

The average American household writes 16 checks a month. As fast as the average American makes money, she spends it. She charges about $2,000 worth of goods on her ten plastic credit cards each year.

Source: From the Almanac of the American People, *by Tom and Nancy Biracree, © 1988 by Tom and Nancy Biracree. Reprinted by permission of Facts on File, Inc., New York.*

found more urban residents (51 percent) than rural for the first time. The number of cities with 100,000 or more residents has grown from 28 in 1890 to 93 in 1940 and 182 today.

Unlike the average American 50 years ago, whose factory job often was located downtown, today's average American has a white-collar job somewhere on the "urban fringe" and will spend about 20 minutes commuting the ten miles to work. Commuting alone costs over $1,300 a year.

But the sprawl of urban life also means a smaller share of Americans live in the largest cities. In 1940, 12 percent of the population lived in central cities with a population of 1 million or more, compared with only 8 percent today.

By 1980, the suburbs overshadowed Main Street. In that year, the census found more people living in the suburbs of metropolitan areas than in the cities. If current trends continue, Main Street will continue to lose customers: the suburban population is projected to reach 62 percent of the total metropolitan population by 2000.

Regionally, the average American is moving southwest. Florida, Texas, California, and other states in the South and West account for more than half the population today, up from 37 percent in 1890 and 42 percent in 1940.

More than half of all Americans live within 50 miles of a coastline. It is only a matter of time before the West Coast outgrows the East. The West has been the fastest-growing region in the country for more than a century. In 1940, 1 in 10 Americans lived in New York State. Today, 1 in 10 Americans lives in California—up from 1 in 50 a century ago.

The center of the American population—the place where an equal number of Americans live in all directions—was somewhere east of Baltimore in 1790. The population center was near Cincinnati by 1880. In 1940, it had reached the Indiana-Illinois border and was veering to the southwest. Today it is in Jefferson County, Missouri, just south of St. Louis.

"The geographic center of the U.S. is in Kansas," says Joel Miller at the Census Bureau. "The population center is to the east, but it has been

dragged west and south every decade since 1920."

WHITE-COLLAR BLUES

Marketers who think they're targeting the "new" American working woman are short sighted. "In the 1890s, when the population was employed in agriculture, the two-earner household was normal," says Tom Merrick, president of the Population Reference Bureau.

Industrial life forced spouses into the roles of breadwinner and bread baker. But postindustrial society is blurring the mix of home and market economies, says Merrick. The share of households in which men are the sole earners "peaked around 1940. Now it's swinging back the other way."

In large part, the return to dual-earner marriages comes from the changing job structure. In the mid-1970s, the American labor force became more white-collar than blue-collar. In 1940, the average American was a manual laborer or service worker. In 1890, nearly half of workers were farmers.

In 1970 the average American was a high school graduate. Today, she has nearly one year of college, according to the National Center for Education Statistics. In 1940, the average American had only 8.6 years of schooling under his belt. In 1890, he barely had a grammar school education.

After taxes, the average American now has $10,964 (1982 dollars) in disposable income. That's nearly three times the amount he had in 1940 ($3,700 in 1982 dollars), according to the Department of Commerce.

Food and shelter have always absorbed most of the average American's disposable income. But in recent decades, housing costs have replaced food costs as the number-one financial drain. Food cost the average household nearly half of its spending money a century ago,

compared with 28 percent in 1940, and just 15 percent today. But housing costs now account for more than 30 percent of the total budget—up from 28 percent in 1940 and 15 percent in 1890.

Transportation spending as a share of the household budget has doubled since 1940. Households spent 10 percent of their income on transportation then, versus 21 percent today. Clothing expenses have fallen from 12 percent in 1940 to 5 percent today. And despite the alarm about rising medical costs, health care takes only about five cents of every household dollar now, up from four cents in 1940.

UNMELTING POT

Today, racial diversity is becoming the norm. Non-Hispanic whites are 78 percent of the population, but they will make up only 74 percent by 2000.

"In 1890 we had lots of immigrants, and in the 1980s we have lots of immigrants," explains Tom Merrick. "The country moved from great diversity to homogeneity in 1940. Now it has gotten more diverse again."

Rather than meeting German, Polish, or Italian coworkers as he did in the last century, the average American now works with Hispanics and Asians. But the challenges are the same. The important issues today, such as whether English should be the official language, and whether immigrants take jobs from native-born Americans, were also important issues a century ago, says Merrick.

The nation's racial and ethnic diversity directly affects the kinds of goods and services the average American buys. "The more homogeneous the society, the more there is a mass market," says Merrick. That's why General Motors and General Electric succeeded when they did. And it's also the reason they could fail today.

"If you look at the typical market basket in the 1890s, it was limited—a dozen items or so. With the growth of manufacturing and the mass market, consumption increased, but there was still a narrow range of choice. Segmentation is really something that has happened since 1960," says Merrick.

While the population becomes increasingly diverse, national attitudes are converging, thanks to telecommunications. "The information explosion is exposing people to ideas they couldn't get before," explains Tom Biracree, author of *The Almanac of the American People*. "From a marketer's standpoint, that means you can reach more people. But if you fail, you fail with everyone. If Ralph Nader complains about something in Washington, the news gets out faster than ever."

The average American is fictitious, but her importance is not. Using short-sighted comparisons is a common and costly business practice. "We hear people in campaigns talk about who the American people are and what they want," says Biracree. But the numbers show that some national leaders need to brush up on the average American's history.

What does a poor Hispanic woman in Queens have in common with a middle-aged Mormon in Walla Walla, anyway? "A woman from the inner city and a woman from Washington State have the same hopes and dreams for their kids, the same concerns about crime, the desire to have a home and to balance careers with raising a family," says Biracree. "There are certain areas of life in which people have almost universally average interests."

U.S. COMPANIES GO FOR THE GRAY

They're planning a major marketing shift as baby boomers age

American Telephone & Telegraph Co. is learning how to reach out and touch some older customers. The company hires retirees, briefs them on AT&T products, teaches them how to give presentations, and sends them on the road to win over other consumers their age. The result? AT&T credits the salespeople with helping it keep older customers from switching to competitive long-distance services. And managers are learning a few things about the elusive 50-plus market. "They want plenty of information about products," says Sheila Spencer, national manager for the mature market. "And they don't want you to beat around the bush."

AT&T is confronting one of the biggest challenges in marketing since the end of World War II: the aging of America. The full impact won't be felt for several years, when the first baby boomers start hitting 50, but smart companies are changing the way they do business now. That's because people over 50 already control 75% of the nation's wealth and half the discretionary income. In ways both subtle and obvious, this age wave is rapidly transforming everything from product development and design to marketing and advertising.

Today's 50-plus consumers aren't behaving like their parents and grandparents. They're wealthier, healthier, and better educated. This presents lavish opportunities for marketers. But inadequate planning can also create major risks: Executives are often amazed to find out how fast their mainstream customers are aging, and some companies first encounter the senior market when they begin receiving complaints from older customers.

Even companies that have long catered to an older clientele have to work hard to keep their franchises. On the cruise ship Crown Odyssey, for example, passengers take water-aerobics classes, order broiled fish with lemon, and attend seminars on stress reduction. Sounds like a shipful of health-conscious yup-

pies, right? Wrong. Royal Cruise Line, the San Francisco-based operator of the Crown Odyssey, is simply trying to please its customers, most of whom are 55 and older. "Passengers are probably more active mentally and physically at 60 than even they thought they would be," says Executive Vice-President Duncan Beardsley.

As Royal's efforts show, these people don't fit the stereotype of sickly, set-in-their-ways, tight-fisted old folks that has dominated marketing images in the past. And companies that have learned to sell to this generation of 50-plus consumers will have a big headstart when the first baby boomer turns 50 a scant eight years from now. For decades, the baby boom's demography has been destiny for much of American society and business. As this population bulge moved through its teens, twenties, and thirties, it influenced politics, shaped media, and determined the rise and fall of whole industries. Now these affluent boomers are growing older—and the U. S. will increasingly become a senior society.

NEW PITCHES. That means almost all marketers will have to reject their conventional wisdom of targeting 18-to-49-year-olds and find new ways to appeal to the aging consumers who will make up the bulk of U. S. buying power. "There is no reason to believe the entire baby-boom generation will stop consuming once they turn 50," says Penelope Queen, planning and marketing director at Saatchi & Saatchi Advertising.

General Motors Corp.'s Cadillac Motor Car Div. is struggling to prepare for that day. Cadillac's average buyer is 57, and the company has long been considered a veteran at attracting older drivers. But it is already having trouble keeping customers: Cadillac's market share has dropped significantly since 1983, and its appeal could shrivel even more among aging baby boomers, who grew up buying imports. To lure them, Cadillac has introduced European styling in a limited edition of its Seville

model, which features leather seats, firm suspension, and a clean, no-chrome look. Foreign competitors as well are trying to keep their aging car buyers. Honda Motor Corp., for example, used an over-50 couple in one of its ads for the first time this year. Instead of the usual pitches for speed and performance, the commercial stressed room and comfort.

A broad range of products and industries stands to gain as America ages. Take health care. The medical rehabilitation market alone, now an estimated $11 billion business, is expected to exceed $15 billion in three years. People over 50 already account for more than 80% of all leisure travel, according to the American Association of Retired Persons (AARP). That number will only increase as more people retire. Financial services companies such as Travelers Corp. and American Express Co. are offering special financial-planning services for retirees. Home exercise equipment, retirement housing, and cosmetic industries will all get a boost from the 50-plus explosion.

But buying patterns are also shifting in unpredictable ways. When Sharp Electronics Corp. introduced its Half-Pint microwave oven, for example, it figured the product would appeal to young singles too busy to cook. Actually, more than a third of all Half-Pint buyers are people over 65 who no longer cook big family meals, says Anne Howard, Sharp's national marketing manager for appliances. Makers of musical instruments have found a growing audience in retirees who may have studied music as children but only now have the time to take it up again. A particular favorite: the electronic keyboard, which can be played using earphones so no one else can hear.

ENGINEERING EDGE. Increasingly, companies realize that new products and services need to be developed with the aging consumer in mind. Beecham Products USA, maker of Geritol, is developing new skin-care products for its Calgon line of bath products to help pamper older skin. AT&T's phone-receiver amplifiers, automatic emergency dialing attachments, and daytime long-distance discounts cater to retired customers.

Similarly, plumbing and fixture maker Kohler Co. makes shower stalls with grab bars, wheelchair-friendly sinks, and higher toilets that don't look institutional. Such catalogs as *Comfortably Yours* offer nonslip bathmats and dishes that can be filled with hot water to keep food warm longer. General Motors engineers are experimenting with bigger buttons, simpler operating instructions, and larger doors on cars such as Oldsmobiles.

Retailers, too, are looking at improving their store design and merchandising mix to attract older consumers. Several supermarket chains have installed benches and restrooms in some of their stores. Recognizing that body shapes change as people grow older, The Limited Inc. is expanding its Lane Bryant large-size women's apparel chain. Dress Barn Inc. in Stamford, Conn., has started a new store carrying large sizes. Even Perry Ellis and Ralph Lauren are producing larger designs.

The aging of American consumers is changing not just the products and services aimed specifically at seniors but many mass-market products as well. Sharp discovered that older buyers found touch-control microwaves unnecessarily complicated. So the company came up with preprogrammed keys for the most common dishes, such as baked potatoes or frozen meals. Beecham has begun using easier-to-read type on its labels and instruction pamphlets. And Whirlpool Corp. replaced the hard-to-read operating instructions on washing-machine lids with high-contrast, oversize graphics. The company also added bigger, softer knobs.

To reach older consumers, many mass-market companies are sponsoring special events and promotions. General Foods, Digital Equipment, Holiday Inns, and Trans World Airlines all back the U.S. National Senior Olympics, for example.

TUNNEL VISION. Such innovation and flexibility is still more the exception than the rule, however. So far, most companies are doing little to prepare for the demographic switch. More than 40% of the nation's leading advertisers said the 50-plus market has little impact on their current marketing strategies, according to a survey by Vitt Media International Inc. "Almost every study we do deals with consumers 18 to 49," adds Judith Langer, head of Langer Associates Inc., a New York-based market

research firm. "I want to ask, 'What about older people?' But I know it's a lost cause."

If marketers are slow to understand the mature consumer, blame it on years of practice. "In our culture, we value young people and think of them as the future. That automatically denigrates older people," says Ken Dychtwald, head of Age Wave Inc., a research company in Emeryville, Calif. Seniors have long been considered an undesirable consumer market. And not too long ago there was some basis to that belief. As recently as the late 1950s, one-third of the nation's elderly were impoverished. Even those who had money were slow to spend because their attitudes were shaped by the Great Depression.

But yesterday's wisdom doesn't apply to the growing 50-plus population. By the year 2000, 21% of seniors will have household incomes in constant dollars of more than $50,000, up from 12% in 1985. By 2005, 40% of people older than 50 will have a college degree, up from less than 25% now. Thanks to medical advances and healthier lifestyles, older consumers will be more active than ever before. And studies show that they will try new products and change brands often, if manufacturers give them a reason to switch.

'FOR OLD HAIR.' But there are pitfalls in courting this growing market. Companies must be careful that they don't just slap a new label on an existing product and figure they've got the 50-plus crowd snagged. When Gerber Products Co. introduced Singles, a line of pureed foods for adults, it seemed like a natural for denture wearers. But the product never took off, partly because older consumers were embarrassed to buy meals that came in baby food jars.

Johnson & Johnson Inc. made a similar mistake. The company first marketed its Affinity shampoo as the shampoo for old hair—and who wants old hair? When sales went nowhere, J&J repositioned the product for a more general audience. Kellogg Co. may be falling into the same trap with its 40-Plus Bran Flakes. It put the new name on an existing cereal when it discovered that more than 60% of bran-flake buyers were over 45. "You can't target age so blatantly," says Langer. "I doubt people over 40 need a special cereal."

Mistakes in the mature market can be costly. This new breed of consumers will not be pushed around. One-third of older Americans have boycotted products and services because of inappropriate age stereotyping, according to a Georgia

State University study. "Many marketers seem to be replacing tired old misconceptions with bright new distortions," says James M. Thompson, AARP's manager of consumer affairs.

AARP, with 30 million members, has become one of the most powerful lobbying groups in the country. It is also a strong marketing force. Members can buy health, auto, and homeowner's insurance and get discounts on air travel, motels, rental cars, prescription drugs, and health aids. AARP's 19.4-million circulation *Modern Maturity* magazine, reflecting readers' wishes, won't take advertising that puts older people in a negative light or focuses on pain and suffering.

BRIGHTER IMAGE. While plenty of companies have offended the 50-plus market, advertisers more often simply ignore it. "You only see 35-year-olds and 75-year-olds on TV," says Barbara S. Feigin, executive vice-president of strategic services at Grey Advertising Inc. "It's as if people in their fifties are a lost generation."

And a lost opportunity. People in this market respond well to advertisers who show older people in happy, productive, and fun settings. Sales of General Foods Corp.'s Post Natural Bran flakes have gone up 10% since GF began using ads with Lena Horne, Rue McClanahan of *Golden Girls*, and Steve Allen. Research also shows that older viewers like Coke Classic ads featuring Art Carney with a young boy who plays his grandson.

Discounts and promotions that play down age but play up value are also effective. About 60% of 50-plus consumers use senior-citizen discounts at least occasionally, according to market research firm Yankelovich Clancy Shulman. Waldenbooks Inc. and Sears, Roebuck & Co. have been successful with special deals for people over 50. Some 300 skiers joined the "Over the Hill Gang" this winter at Copper Mountain, a Colorado ski area that offers discounts and activities for skiers over 50.

"Discounts are nice, but they don't go the distance," warns Dychtwald. "Companies need to sit down and determine exactly what strategies they are going to use to capture this consumer." Marketers that don't heed that advice may be overlooking America's most influential group of spenders.

By Walecia Konrad in New York and Gail DeGeorge in Miami, with bureau reports

BEYOND CONSUMER DECISION MAKING

John C. Mowen

John C. Mowen is the Grayce B. Kerr Centennial Professor of Business Administration at Oklahoma State University, as well as the coordinator of the doctoral program in Marketing.

Dr. Mowen has been published in numerous journals, such as the Journal of Marketing Research, Decision Sciences, Journal of Public Policy and Marketing, *and the* Journal of Personal Selling and Sales Management.

Dr. Mowen's current research interests focus on consumer judgment and choice and on source and message effects in marketing communications.

This article proposes that consumer purchase behavior may be viewed from three perspectives —the decision making, the experiential, and the behavioral influence. The decision-making perspective holds that buying behavior results from consumers' engaging in a problem-solving task in which they move through a series of stages. The experiential perspective argues that in certain instances consumers make purchases in order to create feelings, experiences, and emotions rather than to solve problems. The behavioral influence approach proposes that in other instances consumers act in response to environmental pressures. Each approach can be linked to the predominant effect of one of the three components of the classic hierarchy of effects. Managerial implications of the three perspectives on consumer buying behavior are discussed.

Introduction

In 1985 Coca-Cola changed the taste of Coke.

Responding to a long, slow decline in market share and to the Pepsi challenge, corporate officers announced with much fanfare that a new and better soft drink was developed. Public response was swift. Within a few days a mass revolt was underway. Lawsuits were filed. Over 40,000 letters poured in. One letter said, "I don't think I would be more upset if you were to burn the flag in the front yard."[12]

Of course, Coca-Cola finally capitulated and brought back the old flavor in the form of Coke Classic. What had happened? After all, taste tests had demonstrated that people liked the "new" Coke better than the old. The answer lies in part in the failure of management and marketing researchers to consider emotion. Managers approached their declining market share problem from a cognitively oriented, decision-making perspective. They identified taste as the problem and believed that merely changing the taste would change consumer beliefs, affect, and behavior.

Why did consumers react as they did? A likely explanation is psychological reactance, an emotional state that occurs when consumers perceive that their freedom of choice has been violated. When psychological reactance occurs, people take steps to restore their behavioral freedom, and Coke drinkers did so with a vengeance. Indeed, as one Coke executive stated, "It didn't matter how 'New Coke' tasted: what these people resented was the audacity of Coca-Cola in changing the old taste."[12]

The Coca-Cola case illustrates what can happen if consumer behavior is viewed from a one-sided, decision making perspective. In this article we will first briefly discuss two additional perspectives of consumer behavior—the experiential and the behavioral influence approaches. Then we will see that the three perspectives are related to how beliefs, feelings, and behavior are formed into hierarchies of effects. Finally, we will discuss the managerial implications of the perspectives.

The Decision-Making Perspective

During the 1970s and early 1980s much of consumer behavior research focused on the consumer decision-making process. From the decision-making perspective, purchasing is viewed as a problem-solving activity in which consumers move through a series of stages in order to solve a problem. The stages include problem recognition, information search, alternative evaluation, choice, and postpurchase evaluation.[7] The vast amount of research performed on consumer search, attitude models, consumer choice, and high and low involvement information processing illustrates the decision-making perspective's domain. Table 1 briefly describes various aspects of the decision-making perspective.

When psychological reactance occurs, people take steps to restore their behavioral freedom.

Print advertising by Mercedes-Benz illustrates a promotional campaign built around the decision making approach. The ads are lengthy and contain a great deal of technical information about the cars. The use of such ads makes sense because of the high involvement processing that many consumers perform prior to buying a car in that price range and because of the general characteristics of the Mercedes target market.

An emphasis on consumer decision making, however, may result in managers focusing on a narrow set of factors influencing consumer purchases, such as the tangible benefits and the objective features of products.[8] The narrow emphasis may result in the inadvertent neglect of other important aspects of buying behavior, such as affect and the impact of the environment on purchasing. For this reason and others, two additional perspectives on consumer purchase behavior are proposed—the experiential and the behavioral influence.

The Experiential Perspective

In the late 1970s and early 1980s the decision-making approach began to be challenged directly by consumer researchers. For example, some authors noted that in many instances consumers may simply not engage in decision making prior to making a purchase.[13] Another critic noted that the focus on the decision-making perspective resulted in the neglect of important consumption phenomena, such as playful leisure activities and actions taken for emotional reasons.[8] This emphasis on feelings and emotions has been labeled the "experiential perspective." Thus, while the decision-making approach stressed the study of goods, the experiential perspective focused on investigating entertainment and leisure activities, as well as the arts.

A variety of purchase phenomena are categorized within the experiential perspective, including reactance, impulse buying, and variety seeking behavior. As was noted earlier, reactance is a motivational state that occurs when consumers perceive their behavioral freedom to be threatened. An impulse purchase is a "buying action undertaken without a problem previously having been consciously recognized or a buying intention formed prior to entering the store."[4] Estimates are that as many as 39 percent of department store purchases and 67 percent of grocery store purchases may be unplanned.[1]

Another type of purchase behavior categorized in the experiential domain is variety seeking. Variety seeking refers to the tendency of consumers to spontaneously buy a new brand of a product even though they continue to express satisfaction with the previously purchased brand. One explanation of variety seeking is that consumers are attempting to reduce boredom by purchasing a new brand.[17] In sum, the experiential perspective moves the focus of consumer researchers to a new set of problems and

---

Table 1

The Three Perspectives on Consumer Bahavior

Perspective	Environmental Inputs	Intervening Response System	Behavior
Decision Making	Information inputs to decision Verbal and written information Tangible benefits Economic benefits	Cognitive Focus Belief formation Memory processes Cognitive responses Information processing High/low involvement processes	Purchase of utilitarian products/services
Experiential	Emotional Inputs Symbols Visual information Affective themes, e.g., fear, sexual, patriotic Music, textures odors	Affective Focus Affect formation Emotional responses Imagery/exploratory processes Need for optimal stimulation Opponent-processes Reactance	Purchase of affective/experiential products/services Impulse purchases Variety seeking
Behavioral	Reinforcement structure of environment Physical layout of environment Unconditioned stimuli, e.g., music, money Cultural values and norms Situational factors	Disavows need to discuss an intervening response system Will admit that different consumers may respond divergently to reinforcers	Argues that many purchases occur without strong beliefs or feelings Movement of consumers through environment Primitive consumption behaviors

---

theories. Table 1 also summarizes the experiential focus.

Once a belief is formed feelings and behaviors tend to develop.

The importance of appealing to consumer emotions has not been lost on advertisers.[9] In the automotive arena Chevrolet has made extensive use of affective advertising. For example, in early 1987 Chevrolet began using the theme, "Heartbeat of America," to create emotional feelings about its cars. Similarly, Chevrolet launched its new model, the Berretta, with ads featuring glimpses of a swimming shark that emerges from the water as a Berretta. The ads provide no product information but feature arousing musical scores and outstanding photography to turnon the audience.

The Behavioral Influence Perspective

Another challenge to the decision-making approach emerged from the research emphasizing the effects of environmental stimuli on purchase behavior. Such environmental stimuli include various situational factors, the effects of societal and group norms, and the contingencies of the environment. From the behavioral influence perspective, one does not have to appeal to internal processes to explain certain types of consumer actions. Thus, rather than focusing on decision making or on feelings and experiences, the behavioral influence perspective emphasizes the direct influence of behavior via environmental forces.

Behavioral influence may result from a number of sources. For example, it could occur because of the design of a building that channels consumers in certain directions so that they confront specific products. Similarly, the arrangement of seating and the type of lighting found in restaurants will influence the actions of patrons. Another example is the effect of music on consumers. One study found that the tempo of music played in a retail store influenced not only the pace at which people moved but also the amount they purchased.[8]

Operant conditioning also fits within the behavioral influence perspective. Operant conditioning principles are useful for predicting how consumers will react to various reinforcers in the environment, such as sales promotions like automobile rebates.[11,15]

Classical conditioning represents another behavioral influence technique. Classical conditioning processes have been used frequently by researchers to explain the effects of advertising. They also explain the findings of one recent study in which the mere presence of credit card stimuli influenced the amount that stimulated consumers were willing to pay for a variety of products, as well as how much they actually contributed to a charity.[5] Thus, just having the symbol of a credit card in sight seemed to predispose consumers to spend more.

Table 1 summarizes the major features of the behavioral influence perspective.

Making Sense of the Hierarchies of Effects

The idea that a hierarchy of effects exists — in which beliefs about an object occur first, followed by the formation of feelings toward the object, and finally by the appearance of behaviors — was first proposed 25 years ago. Since the initial proposal, the concept has been expanded to include a variety of hierarchies. For example, in the dissonance-attribution hierarchy, behavior occurs first, followed by affect, followed by belief formation.[14]

The hierarchy of effects concept meshes well with the three perspectives of consumer behavior. What the perspectives suggest is that beliefs, attitudes, and behaviors may be formed directly and independently of each other. That is, in some instances beliefs are formed prior to the creation of feelings or the implementation of behavior; in other instances feelings/affect may occur prior to the formation of beliefs or the implementation of behavior; finally, in other circumstances behaviors may occur first. Once a belief, feeling, or behavior occurs, however, the remaining components tend to change in order to create a set of consistent cognitions and actions. Thus, once a belief is formed feelings and behaviors tend to develop. Similarly, if a strong feeling occurs, behaviors and beliefs consistent with the feeling will form. Finally, if a behavior occurs, beliefs and feelings may form that support and justify the behavior.

From this multi-perspective view of consumer behavior, one can identify four basic hierarchies of effects. In the decision making perspective two hierarchies are proposed to exist. One is the standard high involvement hierarchy of beliefs → affect → behavior. The second is the low involvement hierarchy of beliefs → behavior → affect. In addition, it is proposed that experiential and behavioral influence hierarchies also exist. The experiential hierarchy begins with strong feelings of affect leading to behavior; belief formation then follows the behavior in a self-justification manner. The behavioral influence hierarchy begins with behavior being elicited by the environment; the behavior is then followed by belief formation and affect.

When should marketers focus on attempting to create affect or behavior without first creating beliefs about the product? One situation is certainly when little product differentiation exists. Particularly in highly competitive, mature industries few product differences may exist. As a result, companies may attempt to position a brand on the basis of affect. The cosmetics industry exemplifies this emphasis.

The behavioral influence perspective emphasizes the direct influence of behavior via environmental forces.

In addition to positioning based upon affect, a manager may use a behavioral influence strategy of employing sales promotion tactics to induce consumers to purchase a particular brand. The multi-billion dollar sales promotion industry has developed a myriad number of reinforcers to activate buying.

Managers should be aware, however, that sales promotion devices are narcotics. They are so potent as reinforcers that consumers become dependent upon them. As the auto makers have learned, once a pattern of sales incentives is begun, it is extremely difficult to turnoff. Consumers simply stop buying when the incentives are removed. Furthermore, sales promotion devices can act as a large drain on profits. The extremely poor financial performance of General Motors during the fall of 1986, when the company employed a massive sales promotion campaign, illustrates this point.

Managerial Implications

The concept that three perspectives on consumer purchase behavior exist have important managerial applications. Table 2 cross-tabulates the three perspectives with the major managerial application areas of consumer behavior theory and research — environmental analysis, segmentation, positioning and brand differentiation, market research, and developing the marketing mix.[10]

Applications to Environmental Analysis

Each of the three perspectives makes divergent statements about how managers should approach environmental analysis. The relationship between the decision-making perspective and environmental analysis is illustrated by the effects of time on the consumer decision process. Thus, one can predict that time shortages should dramatically shorten the information search process. Indeed, as was noted in a recent *Business Week* article, the convenience industry has expanded dramatically during the 1980s because of the shortage of time in households.[2] The result is consumers who lack the time and interest to search for products and will let others do so for them.

From the experiential perspective managers should investigate how features of the environment, such as music, textures, and odors, influence moods, feelings, and emotions. For example, one study found that nice weather correlated positively with mood and with tips left in restaurants.[3] These results suggest the possibility that retailers may be able to increase consumer buying by doing things to improve the mood of their customers, such as providing

Managerial Application Area	Decision-Making Perspective	Experiential Perspective	Behavioral Influence Perspective
Environmental Analysis	Analyze how environment influences decision making — e.g., effects of time on decisions.	Analyze how environment affects emotions/feelings — e.g., how does atmosphere influence mood?	Analyze how environmental forces influence behavior — e.g., study of cultural norms and design of buildings.
Segmentation	Do segments differ in their decision process regarding a brand or product class? E.g., do some segments undertake more search than others?	Do individuals differ in their feelings/emotions that are aroused by a product class? E.g., are some people aroused by a patriotic theme and others unaroused?	Do similar environmental stimuli cause different people to react in different ways? E.g., do some car buyers respond favorably to the reinforcer of low finance rates while others respond to lower prices?
Positioning/ Differentiation	Analyze the extent that brands can be positioned on the basis of their attributes, such as low price.	Analyze the extent that brands can be positioned on the basis of the emotions they elicit — e.g., position brand on sexual theme versus a patriotic theme.	Not relevant.

Table 2
Managerial Implications

Table 2
(continued)

Managerial Implications

Managerial Application Area	Decision-Making Perspective	Experiential Perspective	Behavioral Influence Perspective
Marketing Research	Measure steps in the decision process through which target market moves. In particular, assess search process, belief formation, and choice criteria.	Measure affective responses to brand. Use procedures that assess affective states such as arousal levels or moods.	Measure the characteristics of the environment that may influence target market. Assess the norms that may operate. Develop measures to assess the characteristics of situations and the effects of the physical environment.
Designing the Marketing Mix			
A. Product	Develop products that emphasize specific attributes influencing choice.	Develop products that elicit the desired feelings/emotions.	Consider physical environment as part of product, such as building interiors by retailers.
B. Price	Identify the beliefs and associations that various price levels elicit. Identify importance of price in choice process.	Identify whether price has symbolic meaning for product category. Do certain price levels elicit feelings/emotions?	To what extent are various price levels consistent with norms?
C. Promotion	Identify how brands should be promoted according to type of decison process. Consider involvement levels particularly.	Identify to what extent brand can be promoted on the basis of the feelings/emotions it elicits. Identify and use promotional stimuli that create appropriate emotions.	How can sales promotions or sales personnel utilize reinforcers to shape customers?
D. Distribution	Is distribution consistent with the decision process of the target market? In particular, does it match the search process?	Attempt to match the emotions/feelings elicited by brand to those elicited by distribution channel. E.g., if brand elicits sensual feelings, so should distribution outlet.	Is brand placed at locations along routes that consumers travel? Create environments that move consumers in desired directions.

outstanding service and improving the general decor of the store environment.

Of course, the behavioral influence perspective focuses on how the environment influences consumers. Of particular importance to managers is the evaluation of the contingencies of the environment. That is, managers should examine carefully the reinforcing properties of the environment and whether the reinforcers encourage or discourage consumers from buying. The entire marketing mix should be carefully examined for hidden punishers that may discourage buying. Such hidden punishers include employees who are discourteous, procedures that make it hard to order merchandise (such as a lack of toll free numbers), and store locations that are difficult to find.

The contingencies of the environment are also influenced by changing societal norms. Thus, recently societal norms regarding acceptable sexual activities have undergone rapid change due to an environmental variable—the effects of AIDS. These changing norms have influenced the purchase of products (e.g., condoms), the use of certain services (e.g., prostitutes), and the portrayal of couples in advertising (i.e., more frequently portrayed as married).

Applications to Segmentation

The three perspectives make divergent statements about how the market should be segmented. For example, from the decision-making perspective managers could segment on the extent that different consumers search for information. Similarly, from the experiential perspective segments could be based upon groupings of people who are more or less emotional in their purchase patterns. The behavioral influence perspective suggests that managers should investigate how various groups of consumers differentially respond to various reinforcers, such as the use of coupons or rebates.

Applications to Positioning

From the decision-making perspective managers should ask how brands may be positioned on the basis of their attributes, such as price. In contrast, the experiential perspective focuses on how one can position brands on the basis of the feelings and emotions they produce. (The behavioral influence perspective is irrelevant to positioning, because to position something requires an internal representation of it.)

A nice illustration of positioning that uses concepts from both the decision-making and experiential perspectives comes from General Motors. GM's marketers have identified two dimensions on which to position their cars—price and expressiveness.[16] Figure 1 diagrams the positions of the various GM divisions as of late 1986, and Figure 2 shows GM's goal for 1988-1989. Positioning autos on price nicely fits a decision-making approach. However, positioning on the expressiveness of an auto matches the experiential approach, because it recognizes the more emotional symbolic/personal value of automobiles.

Applications to Marketing Research

The Coca-Cola case, which began this article, illustrates the importance of a multi-perspective view of consumer behavior. By approaching the change in the taste of Coca-Cola via the lens of the decision-making perspective, it was extremely difficult for the corporation's management to predict consumer reactions through traditional market research studies. Consumer feelings of reactance caused by the loss of choice would directly influence affect, and the experiential hierarchy of effects would occur. Thus, ratings of the beliefs about the taste of the product would not be relevant to the problem, if such beliefs were measured prior to consumers' learning that "old Coke" would be withdrawn from the marketplace. (Coca-Cola in its taste tests did not inform consumers that it was planning to withdraw the brand.[12]) In sum, marketing researchers must match their data-gathering techniques to the operative hierarchy of effects.

Applications to Marketing Mix Development

Table 2 also describes a variety of applications of the three perspectives to the development of product, price, promotion, and distribution strategies. One major point is that the marketing mix should be consistent with regard to the dominant perspective of the target market. If an emotional theme is chosen, the product, its packaging, its advertising, and its distribution should be consistent with this theme. This was a major problem for Chevrolet in its 1987 "Heartbeat campaign." The ads were beautifully photographed and the sound effects of a beating heart were terrific. The ad campaign won an award from *Advertising Age* for best advertising. However terrific the ads were, though, they did not stem the loss of market share of the division. The reason is that though the ads were arousing, the autos were not. Similarly, the showrooms and sales personnel lacked the pizazz one would expect from an emotion-arousing product. In sum, a coordinated marketing effort must be maintained in order to effectively use either an expressive or a decision-oriented approach to influence the consumer.

Conclusions

We have outlined the proposal that consumer actions can be viewed from within three general perspectives — the decision making, the experiential, and the behavioral influence. The perspectives provide complementary rather than competitive views of the factors that influence consumers. That is, each tends to focus on divergent aspects of the buying and consumption process.

Also two or more of the processes may occur simultaneously. For example, when purchasing an automobile, buyers may attempt to follow a logical, decision-making approach to the purchase. At the same time, however, they may also base their decisions on feelings totally outside of their ability to articulate them. Saab recognizes the dual importance of decision making and emotion in motivating car buyers in recent two-

page advertisements. The first page is headlined, "21 Logical Reasons to Buy a SAAB" and then the second page is headlined, "One Emotional Reason." The first page illustrates the decision-making perspective with detailed information on the attributes of the Saab. The second page, however, depicts the experiential perspective with a page-filling dynamic photograph of the Saab powering through a rain-slick road. (The possibility that decision-making and affective processes may occur separately and simultaneously should not be surprising given the mounting evidence that divergent cognitive and affective physiological systems may exist.[18]) Finally, skillful salespeople may utilize behavioral influence by selectively applying reinforcers to shape customer behavior in desired ways.

It is hoped that the articulation of the three perspectives of consumer behavior will continue the trend away from the dominance of the decision-making approach on the thinking of consumer researchers. As the Coca-Cola vignette that began this article suggests, a failure to attend to how people react emotionally can lead to devastating results. Fortunately for the com-

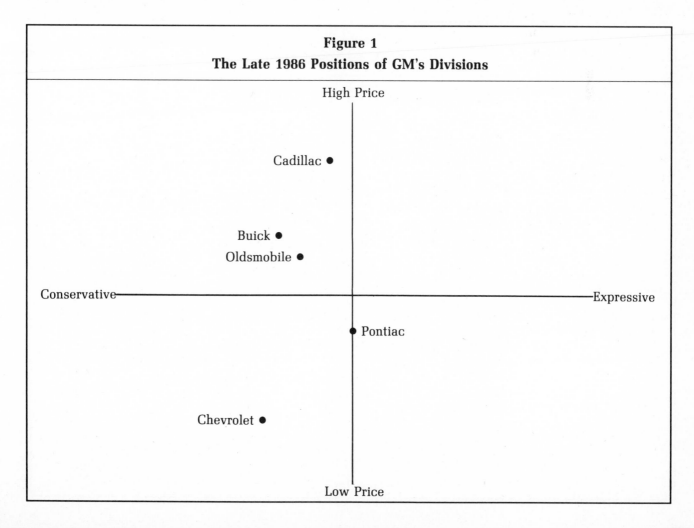

Figure 1
The Late 1986 Positions of GM's Divisions

pany, executives reacted in time, and Coke drinkers breathed a collective sigh of relief when the decision was made to bring back Classic. On the day of the announcement the consumer affairs department received 18,000 calls of thanks.[12] With their behavioral freedom restored, consumers felt as though the public had beaten the corporation. Even the company's image improved, and at the end of 1985 image ratings were substantially higher than Pepsi's. (At the beginning of the year they had been considerably lower.) By bringing back Classic and admitting its mistake, the company took responsibility for its actions. The net effect of the pratfall was to elicit an outpouring of positive emotions that could not have been predicted from a decision-making approach to understanding consumer behavior.

END NOTES

1. *Beverage Industry*, "Industrial Retail Selling Strategies Designed to Induce Impulse Sales," June 3, 1977, pp. 6ff.

2. *Business Week*, (1987), "PRESTO! "The Convenience Industry: Making Life a Little Simpler," April 27, 1987, pp. 86–94.

3. Cunningham, Michael, "Weather, Mood, and Helping Behavior: Quasi Experiments with the Sunshine Samaritan," *Journal of Personality and Social Psychology*, 37, no. 11 (1979).

4. Engel, James F., and Roger D. Blackwell, *Consumer Behavior*, New York: Holt, Rinehart and Winston, 1982.

5. Feinberg, Richard A., "Credit Cards as Spending Facilitating Stimuli: A Conditioning Interpretation," *Journal of Consumer Research*, 13 (December 1986), 348–356.

6. Holbrook, Morris B., and Elizabeth C. Hirschman, "The Experiential Aspects of Consumption: Consumer Fantasies, Feelings, and Fun," *Journal of Consumer Research*, 9 (1982), 132–140.

7. Howard, John A., and Jagdish N. Sheth, *The Theory of Buyer Behavior*, New York: John Wiley, 1969.

8. Milliman, Robert E., "Using Background Music to Affect the Behavior of Supermarket Shoppers," *Journal of Marketing*, 46 (1982), 86–91.

9. Mowen, John C., *Consumer Behavior*, New York, N.Y.: Macmillan Publishing Company, 1987.

10. Mizerski, Richard W., and J. Dennis White, "Understanding and Using Emotions in Advertising," *Journal of Consumer Marketing*, 3 (Fall 1986), 57–69.

11. Nord, Walter, and J. Paul Peter, "A Behavior Modifica-

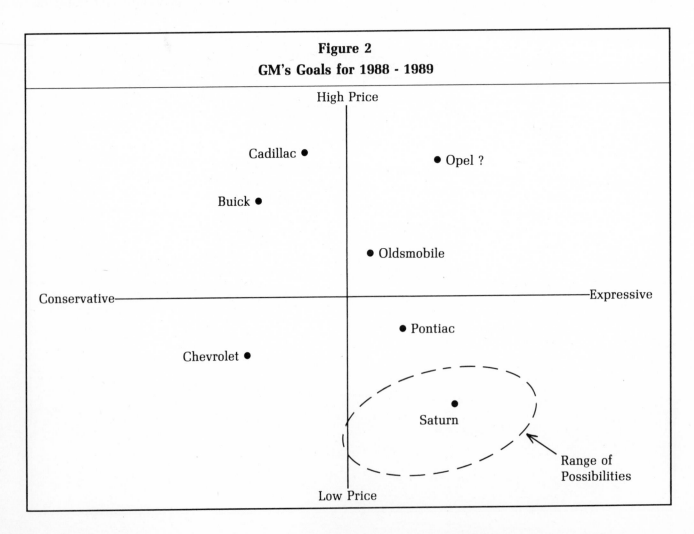

Figure 2
GM's Goals for 1988 - 1989

tion Perspective on Marketing," *Journal of Marketing*, 44 (1980), 36–47.

12. Oliver, Thomas, *The Real Coke, The Real Story*, New York: Random House, 1986.

13. Olshavgsky, Richard W., and Donald H. Granbois, "Consumer Decision Making—Fact or Fiction," *Journal of Consumer Research*, 6 (1979), 93–100.

14. Ray, Michael, "Marketing Communications and the Hierarchy of Effects." In M. P. Clarke (Ed.), *New Models for Mass Communication Research*, M. P. Clarke, Beverly Hills, Cal.: Sage Publications, 1973.

15. Rothchild, M. L., and W. C. Gaidis, "Behavioral Learning Theory: Its Relevance to Marketing and Promotions," *Journal of Marketing* (1981), pp. 70–78.

16. Snyder, Jesse, "4 GM Car Divisions Are Repositioned in Effort to Help Sales," *Automotive News*, September 15, 1986, 1, 49.

17. Venkatesan, M., "Cognitive Consistency and Novelty Seeking." In Scott Ward and Thomas Robertson (Eds.), *Consumer Behavior: Theoretical Sources*, Englewood Cliffs, N.J.: Prentice-Hall, 1973, pp. 354–384.

18. Zajonc, R. B., and Hazel Markus, "Must All Affect Be Mediated by Cognition?" *Journal of Consumer Research*, 12 (1985), 363–364.

CUEING THE CONSUMER: THE ROLE OF SALIENT CUES IN CONSUMER PERCEPTION

Gail Tom
Teresa Barnett
William Lew
Jodean Selmants

Gail Tom is professor of marketing, Department of Management, in the School of Business and Public Administration at California State University, Sacramento. She holds a B.A., an M.S., and a Ph.D. from the University of California, Davis; and an M.B.A. from the University of California, Riverside; and an M.S. from California State University, Sacramento.

Dr. Tom's research has appeared in *Human Factors, Interface, International Journal of Obesity, Sociology and Social Research, Behavioral Science, Journal of Marketing Educators, Journal of Personality and Social Psychology, Current Issues,* and *Research in Advertising.* She is the author of the textbook, *Applications of Consumer Behavior.*

Teresa Barnett is a graduate student at California State University of Sacramento and is graduate intern with the Marketing and Communications Unit of the State of California Department of Commerce. She holds a B.S. in Business Administration with an emphasis in marketing from California State University, Sacramento.

William Lew is a graduate of California State University, Sacramento, with a B.S. degree in Business Administration, with a marketing concentration. He is currently in management with Macy's of California.

Jodean Selmants is currently completing her M.B.A. at California State University, Sacramento, and holds a B.S. degree in Finance Management from the same institution. She also has an A.A. degree in Nursing.

Consumers buy what they perceive, and what they perceive is heavily influenced by the cues — brand name, packaging, color — that marketers send to them. This article reports on an empirical study that demonstrates the influence of color in cueing consumers to the taste of pudding. Vanilla pudding, colored to look like chocolate pudding, was perceived by consumers as tasting like chocolate pudding. The results indicate that color is a more influential cue than taste in the consumers' perception of the flavor of the pudding.

It is hard to believe that within a two-week period, 33 adults and 45 children mistakenly drank dishwashing liquid, thinking it was lemon juice. The confusion arose in 1982 when, as a part of a promotional campaign, Lever Brothers Co. mailed samples of its new product Sunlight, a dishwashing liquid containing real lemon juice for extra cleaning, to households in Maryland. The package label clearly stated that Sunlight is a dishwashing liquid. Apparently, however, people saw the word Sunlight, the large picture of lemons, and the phrase with "real lemon juice" and thought it was lemon juice. When consumers opened the package, it smelled like lemon juice, so their conclusion that it was lemon juice was further reinforced and they used the liquid in their ice tea.[3]

Consumers use cues to identify and give meaning to products and brands.

What happened in the Sunlight promotional campaign illustrates the critical role of cues in the consumers' perceptual process. Consumers use cues to identify and give meaning to products and brands. It has been suggested that the process by which consumers do this in response to stimuli occurs in the following steps:

1. *Primitive categorization.* The basic char-

From *The Journal of Consumer Marketing*, Vol. 4, No. 2, Spring 1987, pp. 23-27. Copyright © 1987 The Journal of Consumer Marketing, a quarterly Journal for professional marketers. All rights reserved. Published by Grayson Associates.

acteristics of the stimulus or event are isolated. In the case of Sunlight Detergent, consumers isolated the sample package of Sunlight Detergent from the rest of the materials that came in the mail.

2. *Cue check.* The characteristics of the stimulus or event are analyzed in preparation for the selection of the schema or operational plan to identify, categorize, and interpret the stimulus or event. Consumers attended to (or their attention was captured by) the "pertinent" cues of the Sunlight Detergent sample: the picture of the lemon, the phrase "real lemon juice," and the word "Sunlight."

3. *Confirmation check.* A schema is selected. On the basis of past experiences, consumers have developed preexisting categories and classification procedures in their memory to identify, classify, and give meaning to the objects, persons, and events. Consumers followed a preestablished classification procedure and classified the sample of Sunlight Detergent into a preexisting category.

4. *Confirmation completion.* A decision is made as to what it is.[1] Finally, consumers decided that the sample of Sunlight Detergent was a lemon juice and accordingly used it in their ice tea.

Usually this perceptual categorization process occurs instantaneously and unconsciously. It is precisely because the process is instantaneous and unconscious that it deserves the marketer's explicit attention. Consumers are bombarded with constant marketing stimuli. Marketers have only a few precious seconds to cue the consumer to the proper identity and meaning of their products and brands.

Consumers use the cues that marketers send them to identify and give meaning to brands and products. For example, consider how the animal names of cars cue consumers both to the car's identity and to its qualities: the Jaguar — sleek, fast, exotic; the Mustang — youthful, playful; the Ram Pick-up — tough, strong. It is not surprising that there are no cars on the market bearing names of animals such as chicken or snake or skunk. Think how the following product names immediately identify and impart meaning to consumers: Close-Up toothpaste, Frigidaire refrigerators, Best Food mayonnaise, Die Hard batteries.

Like the selection of brand names, the mar-

keter's choice of packaging sends powerful cues to consumers. Shiny labels on wine bottles are a cue to consumers that the wine is a less expensive one, while dull labels are a cue that the wine is more expensive. Similarly, consumers will willingly pay more for expensive-looking, foil-packaged chocolate candy, especially a package with a designer label (e.g., Bill Blass), than for chocolate candy with less fancy packaging.

Marketers must first identify the important attributes that consumers desire in a product or service and then design the critical cue(s) to communicate these desired characteristics to the consumers.

Children also use packaging cues. Given a choice between Bugs Bunny children's vitamins or Tivisol children's vitamins, they will invariably choose the Bugs Bunny brand. To them, Bugs Bunny vitamins must be better because Bugs Bunny is on the package. Although Silly Putty and Superman Silly Putty are identical, children will demand Superman Silly Putty. How could Superman Silly Putty not be better with Superman as a cue? As anyone with children will attest, no amount of logical argumentation will convince them that Silly Putty and Superman Silly Putty are identical products.

Cueing the Consumer with Color

Color plays a key role in the consumer's perception of products and brands in a variety of ways.

Consumers use color as a cue to identify brands. For example, color is used to identify brands of soft drinks — 7-UP is green, Coke is red, and Pepsi is blue — and to identify brands of car rental — Hertz is yellow, Avis is red, National is green. Consumers also infer the weight of products by its colors. They perceive light-colored objects as weighing less than identical darker-colored objects. Pastel-colored appliances such as vacuum cleaners and irons are perceived as weighing less than identical products of darker colors.

Color plays a key role in the consumer's perception of products and brands in a variety of ways.

Color cues are also used by consumers as indicators of temperature. Reds, oranges, and yellows indicate warmth while blues, greens, and white indicate coolness. It is not surprising that advertisements for menthol cigarettes are awash in greens, blues, and whites to communicate to consumers the refreshing and soothing nature of the products. Vitamin pills are colored red, yellow, or orange to cue consumers to their health-maintenance qualities.

Even though we are living in the post-peacock revolution, consumers infer the proper gender for a product by its color. Girl babies have pink and boy babies have blue.

Tasting With Our Eyes

The extent to which color's key role can influence the consumers's taste of a food was investigated empirically. The product chosen for the study was chocolate pudding. Intuitively, it was believed that color is an important cue in the consumer's identification of the flavor of pudding, and it was believed that consumers use the color of the chocolate pudding to infer other attributes of the product.

To create the chocolate pudding used in the study, food coloring was added to vanilla pudding. Three "flavors" of pudding were created: dark brown, medium brown, and light brown. Eighty college students were asked to taste the chocolate pudding and to answer a short questionnaire. The participants were informed that the study was being conducted to determine consumer preference for a new variation of chocolate pudding. Although all the participants were actually tasting vanilla pudding, none of the participants indicated that they were tasting a flavor of pudding other than chocolate. Some participants even spontaneously stated that the chocolate pudding was delicious.

The majority of participants perceived the darkest brown pudding as having the best chocolate flavor (62%) and as being the thickest (61%). Participants perceived the lighter chocolate puddings as being creamiest (37% for the medium chocolate pudding and 36% for the light chocolate pudding). Clearly, color was an important cue in the identification of the product: the pudding looked like chocolate pudding and it therefore tasted like chocolate pudding. Color was also used by consumers to make inferences about the product. The darkest pudding was perceived to have the most chocolate flavor and to be the thickest; the lighter chocolate puddings were perceived to be the creamiest, probably because

cream is white colored. These results applied to both men and women.

Color proved to be a critical cue for chocolate pudding. In fact, we might correctly conclude that the color of the pudding was more important than its taste in the consumer's identification and evaluation of the product. These results would suggest that the positioning of this product should focus upon the important attribute of the pudding's color.

Other research has demonstrated the extensive effect that color can have on a consumer's perception of food. Eating food that is the "wrong color" can make people physically ill. A "group of young children taking part in a test with dyed vegetables became decidedly ill after eating harmless, blue-colored potatoes."[9]

Studies have shown that even "experts" taste as much with their eyes as with their mouths. Experienced pharmacy students had difficulty identifying the flavors of colorless jellies and syrups by taste and had even more difficulty identifying the jellies and syrups when they had been inappropriately colored.[4] Expert wine tasters rated rose-colored wines as sweeter than uncolored wines, when in reality both wines were identical. These expert wine tasters' evaluations may have been influenced by their knowledge that rose wines contain more sugar and are, therefore, sweeter than white wines.[7]

Most important, from a marketing point of view, the wrong color can drastically affect sales. In 1969 the managing director of the major American market research firm, Ernest Dichter International, recounted the following tale: "there was a celebrated case in Switzerland, where a famous designer completely reorganized the visual side of an instant coffee. It was beautifully integrated with display material, packaging, everything, in diagonal stripes of mauve. It won a prize for design, but the sales dropped off alarmingly." The problem was simply that mauve was absolutely wrong for coffee.[8]

Marketing Potentials

Marketers must recognize the importance of cues in the consumer's identification, categorization, and perception of the product. Marketers must first identify the important attributes that consumers desire in a product or service and then design the critical cue(s) to communicate these desired characteristics to the consumers. For example, ceiling tiles are perforated with holes because consumers want sound-absorbent tiles, and they perceive perforated tiles as possessing greater sound absorbency. Blenders are noisier than they need to be because consumers want powerful blenders and perceive noisy blenders as being powerful.

It's the consumer's subjective perception of the product that counts, not the product's objective reality.

Marketers must keep in mind that consumers do not always consider cues in isolation or in sequence. Rather, they consider the cues holistically and interactively. The different cues that marketers send to consumers should all be reinforcing and congruent. The consumer should perceive all the cues as pointing to the same product position. For example, Procter & Gamble's Cheer laundry detergent has blue crystals to cue consumers to the blueing (whitening) power of the product, and the bold primary colors of the package further cue the consumer to its cleaning power.[5]

It is also important for marketers to identify contradictory cues and eliminate or modify them or explain them away. Contradictory cues can lead to disastrous consequences. Brown-Forman Distillers' experience with Frost 8/80 exemplifies this unfortunate outcome. 8/80 was a dry-white whiskey that tasted like whiskey but looked like vodka. After less than two years on the market, 8/80 was withdrawn at a loss of $2 million and costs of $6.5 million.[2]*

On the other hand, Toro Corporation's experience with its snow thrower illustrates the successful handling of a contradictory cue. Toro Corporation developed a lightweight, efficient snow thrower and named it Snow Pup. When sales fell below projection, research revealed that the name Snow Pup was at fault. The name Snow Pup erroneously cued consumers to believe that the snow thrower lacked power. Toro

---

*Brown-Forman noted a consumer trend towards lighter whiskies and was attempting to develop a completely new light whiskey market when it unveiled its Frost 8/80 in 1971. The approximately $500,000 spent on eight outside research and packaging companies revealed that consumers rated Frost 8/80 very high on "uniqueness." Brown-Forman interpreted the meaning of "uniqueness" to mean that consumers would be anxious to adopt Frost 8/80. Unfortunately, "uniqueness" turned out to be its biggest problem.

subsequently renamed the product to Snow Master and sales have increased significantly.[6] In this case, the product's name proved to be an important cue to the consumer's perception of it.

Do you know what Thixo-Tex is? Neither did consumers. The name Thixo-Tex was not an identifying cue. Matex Corporation had developed a superior rust-proofing compound, but the name it chose for its product, Thixo-Tex, did nothing for the product. A name change to Rusty Jones, along with the creation of a trade character, increased sales from $2 million to $100 million in four years.[10]

The consumer's perception of the product is the starting point for the marketer's strategy formulation. In the final analysis, it's the consumer's subjective perception of the product that counts, not the product's objective reality. A noisy blender may not be more powerful than a quieter blender, but if consumers perceive a noisier blender as being more powerful, then it *is* more powerful. A dark brown colored pudding may have no chocolate in it, but if consumers taste chocolate pudding, then it *is* chocolate pudding. Consumers buy what they perceive.

END NOTES

1. Bruner, J.S., "On Perceptual Readiness," *Psychological Review*, 64 (March 1957), 123-152.

2. Copulsky, W. and K. Marton, "Sensory Cues: You've Got to Put Them Together," *Product Marketing Cosmetic and Fragrance Retailing*, January 1977, pp. 31-34.

3. "Don't Use This Lemon for Lemonade," *Sacramento Bee*, July 15, 1982.

4. Kanig, J.L., "Mental Impact of Colors in Foods Studied," *Food Field Reporter*, 23 (1955), 57.

5. Martineau, P., *Motivation in Advertising*. New York: McGraw-Hill, 1957, p. 114.

6. Nether, J., "Toro Cutting a Wider Swath in Outdoor Appliance Market," *Advertising Age*, February 25, 1978, p. 21.

7. Pangborn, R.M., H.W. Berg, and B. Hansen, "The Influence of Color on Discrimination of Sweetness in Dry Table Wine," *American Journal of Psychology*, 76 (1963), pp. 492-495.

8. Op. cit., Tysoe.

9. Tysoe, M., "What's Wrong with Blue Potatoes?" *Psychology Today*, 19:12 (December 1985), pp. 6, 8.

10. White, H., "Name Change to Rusty Jones Helps Polish Product's Identity," *Advertising Age*, February 18, 1980, pp. 47-50.

Shoppers' Blues: The Thrill Is Gone

Dropouts Cite Poor Service, Tight Schedules

Francine Schwadel
Staff Reporter of The Wall Street Journal

Marlene Dash would appear to be a marketer's dream come true. The corporate manager likes to dress smartly, both on and off the job. She owns a condominium in Chicago and takes pride in furnishing it well.

Yet Ms. Dash, in her mid-30s, loathes shopping. Lousy service and poor selections at many stores have turned a once-favorite pastime into what she calls a "frustrating" experience. These days, she would rather exercise, visit friends or read. "If you don't make it reasonably easy for me," she says of shopping, "I'm not going to waste my time."

Ms. Dash is far from alone. Shopping has become such a chore that more people hate browsing in stores than hate doing household work, according to The Wall Street Journal's "American Way of Buying" survey. Nearly a third of the 2,064 people interviewed by the pollster Peter D. Hart Research Associates said they "do not enjoy at all" window-shopping or browsing.

That feeling is amply confirmed by the spectacular growth of catalog companies that have stolen sales from retail stores for much of this decade. Yankelovich, Clancy, Shulman, a market research firm in Westport, Conn., warns clients that Americans' love affair with shopping is on the rocks: More than half the women it has surveyed in recent years, and an even larger percentage of men, say shopping for clothes is a hassle.

Stressed-out consumers—juggling jobs, families and leisure activities—feel they have less time to shop. They also complain about obnoxious and poorly trained salespeople, lower quality merchandise and exorbitant prices.

But underlying these complaints is a more far-reaching change: For many shoppers, the thrill is gone.

Back in the 1970s, when malls were sprouting across the country, consumers were content to browse away an afternoon and buy whatever struck their fancy. Then in the early 1980s, Americans viewed shopping as a quest for the trendiest merchandise or the best bargains they could brag about to their friends.

Now, on the eve of the 1990s, consumer researchers say that for most people, shopping is simply less fun. Retailers hawk look-alike merchandise in stores that are numbingly similar in appearance.

Shopping has become "just one of the activities that we have to do," says Susan Hayward of Yankelovich. "It's not an end in itself anymore."

In the Journal poll, more than a third of the people interviewed said they probably wouldn't spend a free hour poking around in stores, even if a prime shopping district were nearby.

That isn't to say consumers don't like new things. But when they go to a store today, they're more likely to think of the trip as a mission rather than an adventure. "They're buyers as opposed to shoppers," says Thomas Rauh, a retail consultant at the accounting firm of Ernst & Young.

Surveys and focus-group research show that most people are indeed shopping more purposefully. Consumers visit fewer stores per trip (an average of three last year, down from 3.6 in 1982, according to consultant Stillerman Jones & Co.) and spend less time in malls (an average of 68 minutes per trip last year, down from 90 minutes in 1982). "I leave rather than hunt for something," snaps Lisa Max, a 46-year-old real estate broker in New York.

Despite such negative attitudes, retailers generally say consumers aren't cutting back on what they buy. "If it is dropping off, it would be more likely that they're shopping less often and buying more when they do shop," says Michael Wellman, vice president of marketing at K mart Corp.

"There's no question our customers' time has become more valuable than ever," says Stephen Watson, chairman and chief executive officer of Dayton Hudson Corp.'s department store unit. But he contends the company's record sales and profits indicate it is making the shopping experience easier. For example, the company is hiring more sales people than in the past and paying them more. It also is laying out remodeled and new stores with a center-aisle design and installing escalators and elevators in more convenient central locations.

A Passion With Pitfalls

Of course, there are still people for whom shopping is a joy, even a passion. But some of those people have complaints, too. Take Cyd Hinman, a mother of two from Norwood, Mass. She often enjoys shopping, but is so fed up with the clerks at a nearby Filene's department store that she refers to them as "idiots."

Twice, Mrs. Hinman picked merchandise off Filene's racks labeled with "sale" signs, only to be told when she got to the cash register that the goods weren't on special. The second time, she demanded that she receive the discount anyway, and the clerk gave in. "I'm willing to spend a lot of money," she says, "but not if I feel like I'm getting jerked around."

Complaints about service are so widespread that six of 10 people in the Journal survey said they have boycotted stores because of the way they were treated. The percentage was even higher—roughly three-quarters—among professionals and those earning more than $50,000 a year.

Service has declined just at a time when consumers are more impatient than ever. "The whole tone of voice is different now in terms of what people expect from a store," says William Ress, whose Columbus, Ohio, management consulting firm has surveyed consumers for more than 20 years.

Despite the rising resentment, few stores are making shopping more appealing. Sales people spraying perfume still assault shoppers at many department stores, even though some consumers complain that the spritzers could provide a far more useful service if they were trained to operate a cash register.

Consumers want selection to be easy and efficient, but that's not what most merchandisers want. Retailers generally go to lengths to keep shoppers in their stores as long as possible. Many stores, for example, require customers to walk through a maze of boutiques designed to show off their wares just to find, say, a simple white blouse. But rather than tempt people to buy more, consumer researchers say, this tactic just irritates many shoppers. Over half the respondents in the Journal survey said they rarely buy on impulse anyway.

So what should a retailer do? "Those that do the best job of making the shopping experience enjoyable and making the customer feel like a human being are very

well rewarded," says Leo J. Shapiro, a market researcher in Chicago.

He cites Nordstrom Inc., the Seattle-based department store. The chain's strategy: pay sales people an incentive to provide good service and keep more merchandise in stock than competitors.

Realistic Regular Prices

Other retailers are trying to mollify miffed shoppers by doing away with their decades-old practice of setting high "regular" prices that can later be cut to "sale" levels. Under a new approach being hyped as "everyday low pricing," retailers such as Sears, Roebuck & Co. now run fewer sales. Instead, they set prices between their old "sale" and "regular" prices.

Last month, R.H. Macy & Co. started promising in ads that shoppers in search of women's coats could "cut through all the confusing sales, special buys and clearances out there" and pay what Macy's says is the "lowest prices . . . every day."

Sears started its "everyday pricing" approach in March, but so far sales results don't reflect strong consumer response.

Still, such a pricing strategy just might appeal to people like Connie Bates, a respondent in the Journal survey. She recently walked out of a furniture store because the salesman offered to cut the price of a sectional couch three times. When a store keeps dropping prices, the Farmington, Mich., resident says, "I get suspicious that they're trying to get the most they can out of you."

Developing and Implementing Marketing Strategies

- **Product (Articles 34-38)**
- **Pricing (Articles 39-42)**
- **Distribution (Articles 43-48)**
- **Promotion (Articles 49-51)**

Marketing management objectives, the late Wroe Alderson once wrote, "are very simple in essence. The firm wants to expand its volume of sales, or it wants to handle the volume it has more efficiently." Although the essential objectives of marketing might be stated this simply, the development and implementation of strategies to accomplish them is considerably more complex. Many of these complexities are due to changes in the environment within which managers must operate. Strategies that fail to heed the social, political, and economic forces of society have little chance of success over the long run. The lead article in this section provides helpful insight on some key ways to "Seize Tomorrow's Markets."

The selections in this section provide a wide-ranging discussion of how marketing professionals and American companies interpret and employ various marketing strategies today. The readings also include specific examples from industry to illustrate their points. The articles are grouped into four sections, each dealing with one of the main strategy areas: product, price, distribution (place), and promotion. Since each selection discusses more than one of these areas, it is important that you read them broadly. For example, many of the articles covered in the distribution section discuss important aspects of personal selling and advertising.

Product Strategy. The essence of the marketing concept is to begin with what consumers want and need. After determining a need, an enterprise must respond by providing the product or service demanded. Successful marketing managers recognize the need for continuous product improvement and/or new product introduction.

The articles in this subsection focus on various facets of product strategy. "Enduring Brands Hold Their Allure By Sticking Close to Their Roots" provides proof that some brands like Coca-Cola, Levi's, and Hershey seem to grow stronger over time. The next article addresses the ways of strengthening brands and using brand extensions. "Masters of Innovation" exemplifies how 3M has kept a constant stream of new products flowing to consumers. The remaining two articles discuss how various types and forms of positioning and repositioning strategy can benefit marketers.

Pricing Strategy. Few elements of the total strategy of the "marketing mix" demand so much managerial and

social attention as pricing. There is a good deal of public misunderstanding about the ability of marketing managers to control prices, and even greater misunderstanding about how pricing policies are determined. New products present especially difficult problems in terms of both costs and pricing. The costs for developing a new product are usually very high, and if a product is truly new, it cannot be priced competitively, for it has no competitors.

"Middle-Price Brands Come Under Siege" begins this subsection by revealing how mid-priced products are creatively looking for new ways to break away from the image of being "just average." In the next article, John Quelch looks at pricing strategy in selling premium products. "How to Compete on Price" discusses the importance of not competing solely on the basis of price. The last article in this subsection reflects on how many consumers have become perplexed by some retail stores' pricing tactics.

Distribution Strategy. For many enterprises, the largest marketing costs result from closing the gap in space and time between producer and consumer. In no other area of marketing is efficiency so eagerly sought. Physical distribution seems to be the one area where significant cost savings can be achieved. The costs of physical distribution are tied closely with decisions made about the number, the size, and the diversity of marketing intermediaries between producer and consumer.

In the first article in this subsection, Peter Drucker discusses the changing nature of distribution channels. "Real Service" explores some of the reasons for PC Connection becoming the top computer mail-order company. "Retail Revolution" investigates the tremendous growth of specialty retailers in the last decade. "The (Un)Malling of America" describes how retail shopping centers may be heading for a decade of decline. The remaining articles in this subsection exemplify some of the ingredients that successful retailers have emphasized in order to win over customers.

Promotion Strategy. The basic objectives of promotion are to inform, persuade, or remind the consumer to buy a firm's product or pay for the firm's service. Advertising is the most obvious promotional activity. However, in total dollars spent and in cost per person reached, advertising takes second place to personal selling. Sales promotion

supports either personal selling, advertising, or both. Such media as point-of-purchase displays, catalogues, and direct mail place the sales promotion specialist closer to the advertising agency than to the salesperson.

The articles in this subsection cover such topics as the analysis of selecting the best media mix and a scrutiny of the importance, cost, scope, and consumer reaction to advertising.

Looking Ahead: Challenge Questions

In general, the marketing concept states that the key to business success is the satisfaction of customer needs. Some critics believe that too strict an adherence to this principle has damaged American industry by leading to a dearth of true innovation, particularly in the area of product development. What emphasis do you think should be put on the product in relation to the other elements of the marketing mix?

Most ethical questions seem to arise in regard to the promotional component of the marketing mix. Both techniques of personal selling and misuses of advertising receive substantial criticism from the general public. Do you feel that this strong criticism of some forms of personal selling and advertising is fair? Why? What are some recent examples of personal selling and advertising that justify the public's criticism?

What role, if any, do you think the quality of a product plays in making a business competitive in consumer markets? What role does price play? Would you rather market a higher-priced, better-quality product or one that was the lowest priced?

What do you envision will be the major problems or challenges retailers will face in the next decade? How should retailers deal with them?

Given the rapidly increasing costs of personal selling, what role do you think it will play as a strategy in the marketing mix in the 1990s? What other promotion strategies will play increased or decreased roles in the next decade?

SEIZE TOMORROW'S MARKETS

Eight Steps to Master Your Entrepreneurial Advantage

JEFFREY LENER

Jeffrey Lener is a business writer who specializes in entrepreneurial opportunities.

You exist for one reason alone: to capture and care for your customers. After all, without them, you're nowhere.

For entrepreneurs, survival is getting tougher by the day. A generation of cynical, fickle consumers has reduced brand loyalty to a slogan of the past. Giant competitors are cloning your best ideas, and nabbing your customers with lower prices and more add-on services.

But you have a secret strength to draw on: marketing.

Marketing puts you on the offensive, enabling you to pounce on every opportunity to get your product into the hands of buyers.

Thinking like a marketer, you'll never again look at your company in quite the same way. That includes everything from distribution and packaging to advertising and product development. You'll fine-tune your operations to create what Harvard's Theodore Levitt, author of *The Marketing Imagination,* calls "a tightly integrated effort to discover, create, arouse, and satisfy customer needs."

The market-driven start-up is guaranteed to be ahead of the pack. It knows that savvy marketing turns each strategic decision into an occasion to learn about and serve its customer base. By relying on marketing, you can:

■ Develop new product ideas that sell because they are inspired by customer needs;

■ Position a product to stand out in a crowded environment;

■ Uncover the most important clues to an effective image, including design and packaging;

■ Find the best distribution route to the buyer;

■ Take full advantage of advertising and public relations—chances to tell potential customers exactly how your product suits their needs;

■ Encourage strong relationships through excellent customer service.

As an entrepreneurial company, you have a distinct advantage over large, muscle-bound corporations: Smaller and more flexible, you can be more innovative about approaching consumers, and quickly spot opportunities your large competitors can't fathom. SUCCESS describes the eight vital steps in a marketing program.

=== STEP 1 ===

Define Your Market

Begin your marketing program even before you write your business plan. Once you crystallize your target, your thinking will be sharper — and investors more receptive. The key is defining your market.

Start by considering three crucial checkpoints offered by Alan P. Kelman, principal of National Analysts, a division of the New York consultancy, Booz Allen & Hamilton Inc.:

■ *What business are you really in?*

■ *Who are your customers?*

■ *Why should they buy from you?*

Segmenting your market is critical. It takes legwork, but needn't be costly. Make a list of suppliers, distributors, and researchers — inside the industry and out. Pick their brains. Find out what your prospects have in common. Do they have enough money to justify your entry?

At the same time, remember that if your market

is everybody, it's really nobody. Consider the example of Chrissellene Petropoulos, an opera singer who launched Huggler International. Selling the knitted Huggler scarf — a type of bib-cum-turtleneck neck warmer — she initially defined her market as anyone with a throat. Sales only took off after she pinpointed skiers and cold-weather sports enthusiasts.

Once you've defined your market, you'll find the road to financing smoother. Venture capitalists will want your market quantified. "I want to know who the competition is and what the market size is," reports David Best, a general partner at Oak Investment Partners, a Menlo Park, Calif., venture firm.

STEP 2
Position Your Product

A great product is seldom enough to put you on the map. You've got to make consumers believe that what you're selling is better than what they're buying now.

Pickles are a case in point. Claussen, a division of Philip Morris' Oscar Mayer Foods Corp., knew that when it came to freshness, most consumers were unimpressed by supermarket pickles. After all, the jars sat around for months. So, the Madison, Wisc.-based firm positioned its product as a refrigerated alternative. Demand boomed.

Identify product differences that consumers care about. Your taste tests may indeed prove that your pickles are better. But if you cannot communicate a *significant* difference, pickle lovers won't bite. For Claussen, touting crispness sold that significance. Their ads featured a pair of hands in racing gloves, with a headline reading: "Test Drive A Pickle." A photograph compared a crisp Claussen pickle snapping in half beside a rubbery competitor. "You've got to identify benefits that are relevant to people," observes Joel Baumwoll, managing partner of Baumwoll & Tannen Associates, a New York marketing consultancy, who worked on the Claussen account.

Once you've found a unique position, hammer it home. Claussen stressed crispness in every aspect of its marketing — from advertising and packaging to selling. "Not many entrepreneurs realize that they have got to get their message across with the kind of frequency that's necessary to penetrate the market," says Baumwoll.

STEP 3
Rev Up Your Research

With the right research, you'll find gold. "It'll help you understand how a market is structured, and allow someone with creativity to see opportunities," says Frank

Feinberg, vice president at Concepts, the business development group of Young & Rubicam.

Market analysis dramatically reduces trial and error. "We can accelerate the process and change the odds," promises National Analysts' Kelman. "With upfront research, you can pinpoint the prospective target, identify necessary product modifications, and design the pricing, promotion, and distribution strategies."

Effective research involves three distinct steps.

1) Gather very specific information on your prospective customers. Scrutinize the market. How big is it? Is there a promising niche?

2) Gauge customer reaction through qualitative feedback. That means talking to people about your product. Some entrepreneurs cold call prospective buyers and ask for their responses. Others seek out special prospects and arrange focus groups to learn more about them. Petropoulos, Huggler's CEO, gave her neck warmers to everyone from grandmothers to construction workers, asking for feedback.

3) With the intelligence you've gathered, you're ready to seek quantitative data through personal interviews with at least several hundred respondents. A host of companies will conduct such surveys on a project basis. You can find them through the American Marketing Association in New York or directories of research firms. Be sure to check references.

Remember, though, that research is a tool, not a goal. "Don't sit back and expect the research reports to tell you what to do," warns Feinberg. "People come up with ideas — data tables don't."

STEP 4
Have a PR Plan

Public relations is an important part of your marketing plan. Advertising provides power, immediacy, and reach. But it also can produce waste, overkill, and staggering costs. Public relations is usually less expensive and *can* be more effective.

When Cellmark Diagnostics Inc., in Germantown, Md., needed to spread the word about its DNA fingerprinting, "We used PR to get broader exposure first," says John W. Huss, vice president. As it found its targets — paternity testing and criminal investigations — "we invested advertising money."

Lazzari Fuel Co. initially marketed its mesquite charcoal as a fuel. But mesquite adds a unique, aromatic flavor. When Lazzari positioned it as an ingredient instead, sales soared.
— From Growing a Business, *by Paul Hawken*

MASTERMINDING TIME
Federal Express founder Frederick Smith knew long before others that he had discovered an irresistible niche: saving customers time.

Federal Express's slogan — "when it absolutely, positively has to be there overnight" — became part of the business parlance.

Today Federal Express even has freestanding mailboxes on the streets.

DISTRIBUTION REVOLUTION
Until 1970, women bought their hose in department stores.

Hanes Hosiery changed all that, introducing L'Eggs in supermarkets and drugstores.

L'Eggs' debut gave mass merchandisers the confidence to sell a host of other nonhousehold items.

"When a customer enters my store, forget me. He is king."
— *John Wanamaker*

"The future belongs to those who see possibilities before they become obvious."
— *The Marketing Imagination*

Case Study 1:

Let Customers Decide

Great marketing ideas come from customers with an unmet need, not inventors with a "neat" idea. Robert J. Paluck and Steven J. Wallach are two entrepreneurs who listened to their customers — and made a fortune as a result.

The two saw an opportunity in a small, but totally unserved, niche: scientists and engineers on tight budgets who needed very sophisticated computers.

Before they launched Convex Computer Corp. in 1982, there were only two options: paying anywhere from $10 million to $20 million for a Cray Research supercomputer or settling for far less powerful minicomputers from Digital Equipment, priced at $500,000. Convex's $1 million machine created a brand new middle market. "The beauty of our marketing concept was that we could describe it in two words: mini Cray," explains Paluck, chairman of the Richardson, Tex., company.

Paluck and Wallach let their prospects dictate design. The result: a mid-priced machine relying on familiar software. Buyers had no trouble understanding the virtues of a Convex.

That focus has kept Convex in front. Last year, revenues hit $105 million.

Look for a firm that works with start-ups on a project basis and is familiar with key magazines, says Heidi Mason, CEO of Acuity Inc., a Mountain View, Calif., marketing consultancy. Be sure to find out how much manpower they're willing to commit to your cause: Expect a minimum of one supervisor and one account executive in the early stages, advises Mason, and at least three people if you're shelling out as much as $150,000. Make sure they're the same folks you interview. Ask about billing: Fees based on time and materials, as opposed to a monthly sum, usually work in your favor. Demand a responsive reporting system, since frequent feedback is vital.

The average cost for a PR launch is around $60,000 for start-ups, says Mason. To get the most out of publicity efforts, count on rolling up your own sleeves and committing time to interviews, speeches, and networking.

STEP 5

Find the Best Ad Agency

For high impact, nothing beats advertising. An agency can put many resources at your disposal that you couldn't get otherwise. If it does the job right, an agency will oversee every stage of a campaign to create a cohesive product image and the maximum market impact.

To get the most out of your advertising, pick your agency with care. Remember: When Federal Express, MCI, and Apple Computer started, the right ad agency played a key role.

To find the right firm, work backward, says Susan Gianinno, executive vice president at Young

---

Why would Sears, Roebuck and Co., with its store credit card the most widely held in America, introduce a competing card called Discover? Sears's data base already included the names, addresses, and credit histories of more than 44 million households. The company knew it had found a natural way to expand further in financial services.
— From Does It Pay to Advertise?, *by John Philip Jones*

& Rubicam. "See who is in the marketplace in your category and getting results," she says. Find out what agency they are using, "then screen for compatibility."

Select an agency that can deliver a range of functions, from strategy and account management to creativity, media, and research capability.

Watch your budget, and don't get involved with hotshots you can't afford. "If you've only got $100,000 to spend, you'd better look for a small, local outfit," says Alvin Achenbaum, chairman of Canter, Achenbaum, Associates, a New York marketing consultancy.

You don't always have to hire the whole company. Often you can work with parts of agencies on a contingency or project basis — a freelance-style approach that's known as "unbundled" advertising. For example, you can hire one agency for your creative product, another for media.

Pay special attention to direct mail, an area which generates tremendous business for many start-ups. Take a few tips from Jay Conrad Levinson, author of *Guerrilla Marketing Attack*: Keep a

Case Study 2:

Grapevine Marketing

Word-of-mouth marketing can make you rich. It's free, and personal recommendations have clout. Just ask George D. Butterfield, head of a $15 million consumer adventure company.

Butterfield & Robinson has leveraged its reputation into a systematic moneymaker: It relies almost entirely on customer referrals to fill its 200-plus biking and walking tours abroad.

Butterfield co-founded the Toronto-based company in 1966. His first trip produced numerous referrals. Then he multiplied those recommendations, targeting groups whose repeat business formed the strength of B&R.

First, he invited friends of students who went on his trip to see slides: "Then once the networking system started, we were off and running."

B&R expanded rapidly, going after special-interest groups, such as art museums, galleries, and wildlife societies. But the company still profits more from satisfied customers than expensive media plans: It focuses its entire $450,000 marketing budget on a spectacular, four-color brochure. And referrals still generate approximately 75 percent of its clients.

mailing list right from the very beginning, taking painstaking efforts to maintain and expand it; supplement direct-mail letters with coupons and postcards; once you've got more than 10,000 names on your list, consider a full-color catalog.

═══ STEP 6 ═══

Build a Total Image

For consumers, one thing sets apart two nearly identical products: image.

Image can't be achieved by advertising alone. You have to consider package design, labeling, name, logo, trademark, and reputation — an array of elements that comprise the aura of brand identity.

Think of packaging as the ultimate ad, capable of creating exactly the right impression during a shopper's split-second shelf scanning. "The package design can come close to eclipsing the actual product inside," says Alan Taylor, managing director of Landor Associates, New York. That impact can be assessed qualitatively, through focus groups, and quantitatively, by tracking test-market aisles with cameras and using tachistoscopes — lab devices that measure how well the eye is attracted to the packaging.

Product names are also critical. Occasionally, piggybacking someone else's success can work. When Lever Brothers challenged Procter & Gamble's Tide, it chose to call its detergent Surf, effectively "borrowing a share of the consumer's perception of Tide," says Taylor.

Credibility and service are vital components of any growing company's image. Your sales force is perhaps the most powerful marketing tool available to you, notes Levinson in his book. Make sure they understand the responsibility of contact time with the customer, when every second of every encounter is a marketing opportunity. Train them to continually ask themselves: How can I market other items? Be of better service? Intensify this relationship?

═══ STEP 7 ═══

Find the Best Channel

Robert Taylor, chairman of Minnetonka Inc., started selling The Incredible Soap Machine, a pump liquid soap, through department stores as a holiday gift item. When customers started coming back for refills, Taylor rethought the whole enterprise. Renaming the product Softsoap, he decided to sell it through mass markets — drugstores and supermarkets. Within two years, sales of Softsoap jumped 16-fold to $80 million.

The key to proper distribution is knowing exactly what business you're in and what customer you're serving. Survey your market. Find out how and where prospects prefer to buy, and what they require in the way of delivery and support. If you make software for the personal computer, for example, you can use retailers and value-added resellers or strike an alliance with a hardware vendor. It all depends on your aim and resources.

Make your distribution decisions an integral part of your business plan.

=== STEP 8 ===

Revitalize Sales of An Existing Brand

A relationship is like a shark, Woody Allen pointed out in *Annie Hall*. It has to constantly move forward, or else it dies. The same is true for all products. "You have to perpetually track the attitudes of the core user and the dynamics of the market," advises marketing consultant Baumwoll.

Take, for example, Cocoribe, a rum product that was essentially a dead shark when Jim Beam Brands acquired it from National Distillers. "We knew we had no future with what was currently there," says Ralph Hallquist, vice president of marketing. Through market studies it discovered that the romance of the tropics played well, but the trade name and graphics turned rum drinkers off to the product.

Reviving the brand called for a complete overhaul. Rechristened San Tropique, the new bottle bore the silhouette of a sailboat on a beach with a silver starlit moon set in a midnight blue sky. "It was almost unrecognizable as the same product," says Hallquist. Early sales of the revitalized product have left Cocoribe in the sand, he says.

"There is a residue of feelings toward brands that are built up over time, based on experience and exposure to advertising and packaging," Baumwoll says. When repackaging or repositioning an existing brand, you have to identify those feelings, and isolate the personality of the brand. "Then you want to build on that, so that you're consistent with the strengths of the brand," he says. An example to avoid: taking a product known for mildness, say a deodorant or floor cleaner, and repositioning it as extra strength.

With these eight steps, you'll uncover your customer's needs, and turn them into the heartbeat of your enterprise.

Enduring Brands Hold Their Allure By Sticking Close to Their Roots

Marlboro Cowboy, Gerber Baby Approach Customers Selectively

Ronald Alsop

Staff Reporter of The Wall Street Journal

To a supermarket shopper, a package of Oreo cookies, a jar of Planters nuts and a box of Nabisco Shredded Wheat are worth about $7.75. To Kohlberg Kravis Roberts & Co., they are worth a fortune.

The buy-out firm paid $25 billion this year to acquire RJR Nabisco Inc., the parent of those and a shopping cart full of other famous brand names. The RJR deal, along with the recent multibillion-dollar takeovers of Kraft Inc. and Pillsbury Co., shows just how precious long-lived brand names have become.

While 80% of new products are destined to fail today, enduring brands like Coca-Cola, Levi's, Budweiser and Hershey just seem to grow stronger, thanks to a winning combination of marketing savvy and product quality, plus a close emotional bond forged with consumers through years of successful advertising.

It is hard to assign a precise value to old, well-respected brand names, but there is little doubt of their financial worth. Some research studies indicate that brands that dominate their markets are 50% more profitable than their nearest competitors. "There isn't enough money in the world to create another brand like Coke or Marlboro," says Stewart Owen, research director at Landor Associates, a San Francisco design and identity consulting firm.

Enduring consumer brands come to represent much more than the product they are stamped on. They actually become part of American pop culture and take on a life of their own. "Brands become extended families and friends to some people," says Carol Moog, a psychologist and advertising consultant in Bala-Cynwyd, Pa.

How do old-time brands manage to stay so important? There isn't any surefire, magic recipe. Every brand and every product market has its own special dynamics. But a look at four of the strongest consumer brands in America—Marlboro, Levi's, Gerber and Coca-Cola—shows some striking similarities about winning products. What is especially notable about these brands is how they have all remained true to their roots. The brands are blessed with distinctive images that they adhere to in advertising and promotions, whether it is the cuddly Gerber baby or the rugged Marlboro cowboy.

Sure, there have been slip-ups—Coca-Cola's disastrous flavor reformulation in 1985, for instance, and Gerber's brief test of Singles dinners, which looked like baby food for adults and bombed in test markets. Yet for the most part, these brands haven't strayed much from the basic marketing strategies that made them stars.

MARLBORO

The Marlboro cowboy is still making the competition eat dust. One out of every four cigarettes smoked in America is a Marlboro, and the brand's market share keeps growing.

Philip Morris Cos. sold 138.8 billion Marlboro cigarettes in the U.S. last year, a 3% increase from 134.6 billion in 1987—at a time when sales of all tobacco brands combined have been declining by about 2% a year.

"Over time, Marlboro could well account for one out of every three cigarettes smoked in America," says John Maxwell, a tobacco analyst at Wheat, First Securities in Richmond, Va.

What keeps the cowboy riding tall? Perhaps more than for any other consumer brand, Marlboro's advertising and promotions help keep it smoking. The ubiquitous cowboy is used throughout the world to plug Marlboro, except in countries that don't permit people to appear in cigarette ads. As for promotions, Philip Morris sticks with the macho image, sponsoring auto races, skiing competitions and country-music concerts. "Marlboro is brilliant in its marketing consistency," says Ms. Moog, the psychologist.

But Marlboro wasn't always such a hit. In fact, it underwent a sex change of sorts. This most macho of cigarettes was once a women's brand. That's right, it was the Virginia Slims of the Roaring '20s. Marlboro was marketed with a rose tip so that the red imprint of women's lipstick wouldn't show. Its advertising slogan: "Mild as May."

But Marlboro never achieved great success as a feminine brand, partly because women didn't smoke as much in those days. "It wasn't ladylike to smoke in public," recalls Joseph Cullman, chairman emeritus of Philip Morris.

Unlike most brands, Marlboro got a second shot at fame. With filtered cigarettes coming on strong in the 1950s, Philip Morris desperately needed to come up with its own filter-tip brand. Rather than start with a new name, the company decided to gamble on repositioning lackluster Marlboro. Working with legendary ad man Leo Burnett, Philip Morris developed the trademark red and white package graphics, an innovative flip-top box and the cowboy image. "We decided to use Marlboro on the new cigarette because it's a very classy name," says Mr. Cullman.

Philip Morris insists on authenticity in its Marlboro advertising. It sends talent scouts out to Western ranches sizing up the local cowboys for the next Marlboro man—someone virile and handsome, but not male-model perfect. "It's more legitimate to use real cowboys to convey the Marlboro heritage," says Ellen Merlo, vice president of marketing services at Philip Morris. "They know how to sit on a horse and ride in a realistic manner."

In the late 1950s and early 1960s, Philip Morris also used other macho figures in its ads, including professional football players, and it featured singer Julie London crooning "You get a lot to like with a Marlboro" in some commercials. But by the 1960s, senior executives decided to focus single-mindedly on the cowboy. That may have been the best decision Philip Morris ever made. Not only did the romance of the West prove appealing to both men and women in the U.S. and most other countries, but it also was easy to transfer to billboard and print-only advertising when cigarette commercials were banned on television and radio.

In fact, cigarette industry analysts believe that the broadcast ad ban actually helped Marlboro become the dominant cigarette brand. Other brands' campaigns weren't as strongly embedded in consumers' minds as the Marlboro cowboy and thus suffered from the broadcast blackout. By the mid-1970s, Marlboro had galloped ahead of Winston to become America's No. 1 cigarette brand.

Marlboro isn't without its Achilles' heel, though. It has failed to make much of a dent in the sizable menthol market despite repeated attempts. In 1988 it developed a major new marketing campaign for Marlboro Menthols, playing off Marlboro's Old West image with ads showing white horses and cool, green water—but no cowboys. Thus far, however, the menthol line's market share stands at only about 0.6%, compared with the full Marlboro line's 25% share.

COCA-COLA

Coke really is it. In virtually every study of favorite consumer brands, the winner is always the cola that John S. Pemberton concocted in an Atlanta pharmacy back in 1886.

If anyone needed convincing of Coke's consumer mystique, it came in 1985, when people raised a ruckus over the change in the taste of their soft drink. And even the embarrassing reformulation fiasco doesn't appear to have done any serious long-term damage to the brand's image. Some analysts believe that consumers now are more zealous Coke fans than ever since the company admitted its error and brought back the original flavor as Coke Classic. It was a victory for the consumer—and for Coke.

"Brands like Coke are extremely jealous of their No. 1 position and react quickly to any problem or challenge," says Marc Particelli, senior vice president of Booz, Allen & Hamilton, a management consulting firm in New York. "You can't kill them with a stick."

Coke sales multiplied steadily through the years, aided by such innovations as the six-bottle cardboard carton in the 1920s that allowed people to take home more Coke conveniently. But the most revolutionary marketing moves didn't happen until the 1980s. Through most of its history, the company had conservatively guarded the brand name and the formula. But then came a burst of new products—Diet Coke, Cherry Coke, Caffeine-Free Coke, New Coke, even Coca-Cola clothing—all within the last decade.

New Coke proved as much a failure as Diet Coke was a blockbuster success. Despite the mixed results, though, soft-drink industry analysts generally applaud Coke's new aggressiveness in exploiting its sterling name and locking up more supermarket-shelf, vending-machine and fountain space with a bigger selection of Coke brands.

"Coke was kind of a sleeping giant until it took the offensive more in the late 1980s," says Michael Bellas, president of Beverage Marketing Corp., a New York consulting firm. "They were

really late in coming out with a diet version of Coke."

With all the brands bearing the Coke name combined, the company now claims about 33% of soft-drink sales, compared with the Pepsi brands' combined share of about 26%. And few people expect Coke to be unseated as the leading soft drink, given its mighty marketing muscle.

Its formidable bottler network has hammerlock control over many outlets, particularly vending machines and fountain dispensers in movie theaters, fast-food restaurants and sports stadiums. Now, the company is hoping to get special soft-drink dispensers into offices to supplant the traditional coffee maker. It even created a special can in 1985 so that astronauts could sip Coke in the weightlessness of Earth orbit. "Whether you're at a little League game or the Olympics, Coke will be there," boasts Donald Keough, Coca-Cola Co.'s president. "In fact, you can be pretty sure that if you go to prison, you'll find Coca-Cola."

Coke advertising and promotions also are everywhere. The company has negotiated exclusive soft-drink sponsorship rights to many of the most prestigious and widely watched events ranging from the Olympics to the Academy Awards. It even stocked coolers with Diet Coke and put them in the limousines ferrying the glitterati to this year's Academy Awards show.

Perhaps more than any other brand, Coke has made the most of an all-American image. That apple-pie and motherhood feeling comes through consistently in the upbeat jingles and the wholesome, fresh-faced people in its commercials. The slogan may have changed from "The Pause That Refreshes" in 1929 to the current "Can't Beat the Feeling," but Coke ads still deal with the same heartwarming, if saccharine, themes as a teen-ager's first love and a child's relationship with his grandfather.

"Coke has always tried to be part of the bright side of life with timely and memorable images," says Mr. Keough. "The coming of TV commercials had a lot to do with deepening people's affections for Coke."

Coke is as much a hit internationally as at home. It is sold in more than 150 countries and achieved its global status partly because of soldiers' hankering for Coke on the battlefronts of Europe and the Pacific during World War II. Coke set up some 64 bottling plants near combat areas. Besides lifting troop morale, the World War II expansion gave the local residents of many foreign lands their first taste of Coke and positioned the company for a big postwar international push.

Still, Coke isn't as invincible as its powerhouse brand image might suggest. "While Coke has a strong position in consumers' minds, its sales aren't so strong," says Al Ries, a marketing consultant in Greenwich, Conn. "Many No. 1 brands outsell No. 2 by a two-to-one margin, but Coke doesn't outsell Pepsi by that much."

PepsiCo Inc. constantly keeps the pressure on, and in the estimation of some marketing experts, it is doing creatively superior advertising and one-upping Coke on big marketing events like the sponsorship of the best-selling home videocassette "E.T. The Extra-Terrestrial" last Christmas.

"Coke's market-share numbers may still look good, but it's in jeopardy," says Jerry Welsh, who runs Welsh Marketing Associates, a New York marketing consulting firm. "Pepsi clearly has the momentum."

GERBER

"Babies Are Our Business . . . Our Only Business." Certainly one of the most recognizable ad slogans of all time, that line made Gerber one of the most revered brands ever. It became the gold standard of baby food and through the years managed to fight off some 70 competitors, including such big names as Libby, Del Monte and Campbell. Only Heinz and Nestle's Beech-Nut brand survive today as significant rivals.

Daniel Gerber created processed baby food after his wife complained about having to strain peas by hand at home for their children. The product hit store shelves in 1928, priced at 15 cents a can, and a group of Gerber salesmen took to the nation's roadways in cars that played "Rock-a-bye, Baby" on their horns.

Today Gerber Products Co. is more than just a baby-food maker. It also sells such products as life insurance, and the slogan has been shortened to simply "Babies Are Our Business." But baby food is still the company's bread and butter.

Given the special nature of its product, Gerber has no choice but to market aggressively, year in and year out. After all, it hangs on to its customers for only a year or two and must always keep busy cultivating new parents and babies. To some degree, Gerber can ride on its past heritage, as new generations of grandmothers keep recommending Gerber to new generations of parents. Indeed, Gerber claims that two out of three Americans under the age of 40 have eaten its baby food.

But Gerber executives don't take much for granted. Gerber constantly tries to reinforce its caring image with parents through such techniques as a toll-free consumer hotline. The company also distributes brochures to pediatricians in hopes that they will pass them on to parents who will view them as an unofficial medical endorsement. And Gerber buys lists of names of new mothers gleaned from newspaper birth announcements and hospital records and sends promotional material to them within weeks of their return home.

While Gerber periodically changes the ingredients in its baby foods and adds new flavors such as this year's broccoli-carrots-cheese dish, it still uses the same baby face that it has featured on its package labels since 1938, after an artist submitted the winning drawing in a Gerber baby-picture contest. Gerber's advertising also still features adorable infants. A few years ago the company departed from beautiful babes—in ads that instead showed beautiful peas and apples to illustrate that Gerber baby food is "natural." But the ads were a flop and the company quickly reverted to cooing babes in its ads.

Gerber does change some things to keep up with the times. This year, for instance, it is selling microwave feeding bowls and a computer software program for monitoring baby's diet and physical growth.

While image is important in soft drinks, cigarettes and fashion, it is invaluable in a product like baby food. Parents are extremely sensitive about what they feed that new bundle of joy, and a name like Gerber is immensely reassuring. Gerber executives learned just how delicate the brand's image is in 1986 when consumers reported finding shards of glass in some jars of its baby food. The company tried to reassure the public that there were no problems in its manufacturing plants and adamantly refused to have Gerber baby food withdrawn form grocery-store shelves.

But some consumers obviously weren't satisfied by Gerber's response. Gerber's market share slumped to 52% in March 1986 from 66% before the February glass scare. "Not pulling our baby food off the shelf gave the appearance that we aren't a caring company," says Robert Johnston, president of the Gerber Products division.

To try to repair the damage, Gerber mailed more than two million letters to consumers explaining that the company was doing all it could to get to the root of the glass scare. The company chairman also appeared in a TV commercial declaring that Gerber is a responsible

company. Market share has since re-bounded, and more, to about 72%.

Gerber's strong identification with strained baby food is a mixed blessing as it tries to increase its sales by expanding into food products for older consumers. When it diversified into adult food in the 1970s, people rejected its Singles by Gerber dinners as glorified baby food with fancier flavors like beef burgundy and wine. "Unfortunately," Mr. Johnston says, "we put Singles in glass jars that resembled baby-food containers."

Undaunted, Gerber is going after older consumers again. This time around, however, it is being more careful. For example, for its new Fruit Classics line of applesauce snacks for older kids and adults, the company has relegated the Gerber name to fine print on the packaging.

"School-age children would never take the applesauce in their lunch with the Gerber name in big letters on the container," says Mr. Johnston. "They'd be too afraid they'd be teased about being a baby."

LEVI'S

When Levi Strauss stitched his first pair of "waist-high overalls" in 1853, he simply thought he had come up with durable work pants for California gold prospectors. Never did the Bavarian immigrant dream that a century later the pants would become a symbol of rebellion to 1950s teen-agers, the uniform of the baby-boom generation in the 1960s, even a coveted black-market product in the Soviet Union.

Although Levi Strauss & Co.'s jeans date back more than 100 years, it was only in this century that they became a mass-marketed brand. Until the 1930s when Easterners started visiting dude ranches and liked the pants they saw the local cowpokes wearing, Levi's remained essentially a regional Western product. Today, of course, Levi's is a world-wide brand synonymous with blue jeans. A pair is even enshrined in the Smithsonian Institution.

For the most part, the look of Levi's jeans has remained the same. Changes in the garment have been minor and have been made only out of necessity. For example, copper rivets were removed from Levi's in 1937, but only after many complaints that they scratched school desks and saddles.

While rooted in the Old West, Levi's image transcends the cowboy culture. It represents individuality, which was reinforced in the 1950s when maverick movie stars James Dean and Marlon Brando wore Levi's and in the 1960s when they became a symbol of the country's anti-establishment, anti-war mood. "Consumers feel people who don't sell out are Levi's kind of guys," says Barbara Pauly, management supervisor on the Levi's account at the Foote, Cone & Belding ad agency in San Francisco. When her agency asks consumers which celebrities today they would associate with Levi's, people name Bruce Willis, Clint Eastwood and other stars with an iconoclastic image.

Whenever Levi's has tried to extend its name to premium-priced pants, it has usually failed. "People at Levi's assumed the brand stood for clothing, but it really doesn't," says Mr. Owen of Landor Associates. "It stands for no-nonsense clothing."

Levi's considered buying the rights to a fashion designer's name during the designer-jeans craze of the early 1980s, but wisely decided to wait out what proved to be largely a fad, not a trend.

However, Levi's isn't immune to the faddishness of the apparel business. Take the Levi's 501 button-fly jeans commercials, which show teen-agers hanging out on city streets and feature bluesy music. Although the ads have been a big hit since they were introduced in 1984 (sales of 501 jeans jumped 50% in 1985), the ads will be replaced with a new campaign this summer. "It was difficult to decide when to end the 501 Blues campaign, but it's important to keep your image fresh in the fashion business," says Ms. Pauly.

She says the new ads won't talk about value or durability or promise that Levi's will make you sexier. "They have to be hip and cool, but also real," says Ms. Pauly. We have tested and killed ad campaigns because they presented phony situations or overpromised that Levi's would help you get the girl."

Levi's greatest challenge may lie ahead, in the 1990s. As the huge baby-boom generation begins to enter middle age and chooses other types of casual pants, Levi's faces a shrinking market for jeans. Its first response is a series of television commercials with men in their late 30s and early 40s that tout looser-fitting jeans for fuller, more mature bodies. The tag line in the commercials: "Life is full of simple pleasures like the comfort of Levi's jeans. Or had you forgotten?"

Strengthen brands with 8 essential elements

Allan J. Magrath

Expert columnist Allan Magrath is director of marketing services at the Canadian headquarters of one of America's largest diversified multinationals in London, Ont.

Brands are the life force of marketing. A powerful brand increases the financial value of a firm, as any recent takeover clearly demonstrates.

When Nestle wanted a strong position in the confectionary market, it paid double the market value for Rowntree's shares to get hold of its toffee, Kit Kat, and other brands.

Brands instill confidence in customers who then demonstrate purchase loyalty and a disposition to try brand extensions. Black & Decker proved this by transferring its brand power from do-it-yourself tools to General Electric's former housewares division.

And a solid brand often nets its owner preferential shelf space and trade terms from resellers because they know the brand's volume movement will provide reliable inventory turns at premium prices—with few markdowns.

This is the winning financial formula distributors, dealers, and retailers dream about at night.

Toys R Us, for example, was quick to list Sony Corp.'s My First Sony, a line of five electronic music makers from cassette players to boom-box stereos in brightly colored plastic. The "toy" audio products were a sellout at Christmas that year among the 4-12 year olds whose parents trusted the Sony name for quality.

When marketers work to create a brand, the goal should be first to figure out what they wish the brand to stand for and then to set their creative talents to work on eight visual or auditory associations that reinforce the brand's identity.

1. A good name

Procter & Gamble's Head & Shoulders shampoo for dandruff is an example of a good brand name. Vaseline Intensive Care Lotion for hands is another. And Visa is a good name for a credit card with global use.

Each of these names conveys associations critical to understanding the point of difference, the uniqueness of the product or service.

2. The brand's logo

Instantly recognizable logos that actually improve upon the identity of the brand are Coca-Cola in soft drinks, Rolex in watches, and Ikea in furniture retailing.

A marketer should always ask, "How can I create a logo for the brand with communication impact?"

3. Color

Campbell Soup's red and white label, Kodak's yellow film box, Visa's blue and gold stripe, Purina's checkerboard square, and 3M's Scotch brand red and green plaids are instantly recognizable—even without the brand names of the firms.

Colors provide recognizable cues, important at point of sale and vital in brand reinforcement advertising.

They also produce emotions and associations that reinforce a brand's image. Visa uses banker colors to convey the image it desires—that of a solid network of financial institutions standing behind its card.

4. A symbol

Planters has Mr. Peanut, Kellogg has Tony the Tiger, Maytag has its lonely repairman, Philip Morris has its Marlboro Man, and Prudential has its Rock of Gibraltar.

Symbols give brands a signature and help visually convey the image the company wants associated with its offer. And, if the symbol is used wisely, it can be a powerful standalone for the brand, as is the case with Ralph Lauren's horse, Lacoste's alligator, and McDonald's golden arches.

5. Packaging

Distinctive packaging can provide a competitive edge. This was, and still is, the case for Chiclets, Life Savers, L'eggs pantyhose, and even Coca-Cola's old bottle, which is a collector's item in some circles.

The package that Old Spice cologne and after-shave comes in is as recognizable as the brand itself.

6. Shape

Dove soap's shape is just as distinctive as that of the Concorde airliner. Any artist merely has to draw the outline of a Porsche or Rolls-Royce for a consumer to recognize the car's nameplate. Disney World is instantly recognizable by the shape of the Magic Kingdom's castle.

A marketer may not always be able to design a distinctive shape into the product or service, but it's very useful to consider the possibility.

Braun, the German maker of razors and other personal appliances uses design shape—ignored by many of its competitors—as a key branding element.

7. A slogan

A slogan can back up a brand name powerfully and add clarity to the

Reprinted from *Marketing News*, January 8, 1990, p. 36, published by the American Marketing Association, Chicago, IL 60606.

value-added which the brand is meant to represent.

Pepsi used its "Pepsi Generation" slogan for a long time and then switched to "The choice of a new generation." This was an excellent bridge from a slogan that needed updating from the "go-go" '60s image to the cooler, more style-conscious '80s.

Toyota's "Oh, What a Feeling" positions its vehicles as quality cars which are fun to own and drive. And slogans also can help reinforce a brand's promise, as Federal Express does with its "When it absolutely, positively has to be there overnight" service promise.

8. Music

Merely play the whistling tune that accompanies Old Spice commercials and you can recognize the brand with your eyes shut.

Beneficial Finance gave a signature to its ads for years with a distinctive jingle. And Miller beer and Budweiser have fought some memorable brand-share battles using jingles such as "When it's time to relax" and "This Bud's for you."

Music brings an added sensory dimension to branding—a tug at the heart strings and the ability to evoke a variety of feelings, from nostalgia and sentiment to excitement.

There are, of course, other branding elements which have been used successfully, such as a paid spokesperson or a company's employees featured in ads.

But these techniques tend to be isolated more to a brand's TV advertising, while the eight proven branding tools have more varied use possibilities, including packaging, signage, customer literature, sales promotion materials, trade show booths, billboards, premiums, and giveaways.

Many of these eight elements can be used in concert with one another, as long as they work together to underscore the brand's top-of-mind, sought-after positioning.

In my next column, I will discuss how brands can be fortified or diluted over time with smart or dumb tactics.

MASTERS OF INNOVATION

HOW 3M KEEPS ITS NEW PRODUCTS COMING

It was 1922. Minnesota Mining & Manufacturing inventor Francis G. Okie was dreaming up ways to boost sales of sandpaper, then the company's premiere product, when a novel thought struck him. Why not sell sandpaper to men as a replacement for razor blades? Why would they risk the nicks of a sharp instrument when they could rub their cheeks smooth instead?

The idea never caught on, of course. The surprise is that Okie, who continued to sand his own face, could champion such a patently wacky scheme and keep his job. But unlike most companies then—or now—3M Co. demonstrated a wide tolerance for new ideas, believing that unfettered creative thinking would pay off in the end. Indeed, Okie's hits made up for his misses: He developed a waterproof sandpaper that became a staple of the auto industry because it produced a better exterior finish and created less dust than conventional papers. It was 3M's first blockbuster.

Through the decades, 3M has managed to keep its creative spirit alive. The result is a company that spins out new products faster and better than just about anyone. It boasts an impressive catalog of more than 60,000 products, from Post-it notes to heart-lung machines. What's more, 32% of 3M's $10.6 billion in 1988 sales came from products introduced within the past five years. Antistatic videotape, translucent dental braces, synthetic ligaments for damaged knees, and heavy-duty reflective sheeting for construction-site signs are just a few of the highly profitable new products that contributed to record earnings of $1.15 billion in 1988.

At a time when many big U.S. corporations are trying to untangle themselves from bureaucracy, 3M stands apart as a smooth-running innovation machine. Along with a handful of other companies that might be called the Innovation Elite—Merck, Hewlett-Packard, and Rubbermaid among them—3M is celebrated year after year in the rankings of most-respected companies. Business schools across the country make 3M a case study in new-product development, and management gurus trumpet 3M's methods. Peter Drucker's *Innovation and Entrepreneurship* is peppered with 3M tales. A star of the bestseller *In Search of Excellence*, 3M remains a favorite of coauthor Thomas J. Peters. "It is far more entrepreneurial than any $10 billion company I've come across," he says, "and probably more entrepreneurial than a majority of those one-tenth its size."

The publicity has attracted representatives of dozens of companies from around the world to tour 3M headquarters near St. Paul, Minn., in search of ideas and inspiration. While such companies as Monsanto Co. and United Technologies Corp. have adopted some of 3M's methods, it's hard to emulate a culture that has been percolating since the turn of the century.

LOSE SOME. So how does 3M do it? One way is to encourage inventive zealots like Francis Okie. The business of innovation can be a numbers game—the more tries, the more likely there will be hits. The scarcity of corporate rules at 3M leaves room for plenty of experimentation—and failure. Okie's failure is as legendary among 3Mers as his blockbuster. Salaries and promotions are tied to the successful shepherding of new products from inception to commercialization. One big carrot: The fanatical 3Mer who champions a new product out the door then gets the chance to manage it as if it were his or her own business.

Since the bias is toward creating new products, anything that gets in the way, whether it's turf fights, overplanning, or the "not-invented-here" syndrome, is quickly stamped out. Divisions are kept small, on average about $200 million in sales, and they are expected to share knowledge and manpower. In fact, informal information-sharing sessions spring up willy-nilly at 3M—in the scores of laboratories and small meeting rooms or in the hallways. And it's not unusual for customers to be involved in these brainstorming klatches.

PEER REVIEW. That's not to say that corporate restraint is nonexistent. 3Mers tend to be self-policing. Sure, there are financial measures that a new-product team must meet to proceed to different stages of development, but the real control lies in constant peer review and feedback.

The cultural rules work—and go a long way toward explaining why an old-line manufacturing company, whose base products are sandpaper and tape, has become a master at innovation. And a highly profitable one at that. Earnings spurted 25% in 1988 from a year earlier. It wasn't always so. The company hit a rocky stretch in the early 1980s. But stepped-up research spending and some skillful cost-cutting by Chairman and Chief Executive Allen F. Jacobson have revived all of 3M's critical financial ratios.

A 3M lifer and Scotch-tape veteran, Jake Jacobson took over the top job in 1985 and laid out his J-35 program. That's J as in Jake, and 35 as in 35% cuts in labor and manufacturing costs—to be accomplished by 1990. 3M is well on its way to reaching those goals, and the push has already improved the bottom line. Last year return on capital climbed almost three points, to 27.6%, and return on equity had a similar rise, to 21.6%. Jacobson has clamped down on costs without harming his company's ability to churn out new products one whit.

MOTLEY CREW. 3M was founded not by scientists or inventors but by a doctor, a lawyer, two railroad executives, and a

Reprinted from *Business Week*, April 10, 1989, pp. 58-63, by special permission. Copyright © 1989 by McGraw-Hill, Inc.

meat-market manager. At the turn of the century the five Minnesotans bought a plot of heavily forested land on the frigid shores of Lake Superior, northeast of Duluth. They planned to mine corundum, an abrasive used by sandpaper manufacturers to make the paper scratchy. The five entrepreneurs drummed up new investors, bought machinery, hired workers, and started mining. Only then did they discover that their corundum, alas, wasn't corundum at all but a worthless mineral that the sandpaper industry wanted no part of.

The company tried selling its own sandpaper, using corundum shipped in from the East, but got battered by the competition. How perfect: The company that tolerates failure was founded on a colossal one. 3M was forced to innovate or die. Most of the original investors got swept out of the picture, and the remaining 3Mers set about inventing. First, the company introduced a popular abrasive cloth for metal finishing. Then Okie struck gold with his Wetordry sandpaper. They drew inspiration from William L. McKnight, who is revered to this day as the spiritual father of the company. He started out as an assistant bookkeeper and worked his way up through sales. His approach, unusual for its day, has stuck with the company. Rather than make his pitch to a company's purchasing agent, McKnight talked his way onto the factory floor to demonstrate his products to the workers who used them. After he became chairman and chief executive, he penned a manifesto that said, in part: "If management is intolerant and destructively critical when mistakes are made, I think it kills initiative."

LOYAL LIFERS. That kind of thinking breeds loyalty and management stability. The company rarely hires from the outside, and never at the senior level. Jacobson, 62, a chemical engineer, started out in the tape lab in 1947. And all his lieutenants are lifers, too. The turnover rate among managers and other professionals averages less than 4%. "It's just not possible to really understand this company until you've been around for a long while," says Jerry E. Robertson, head of the Life Sciences Sector.

Don't let 3M's dull exterior fool you. The St. Paul campus, home of company headquarters and most of the research labs, is an expanse of brick buildings with a high-rise glass tower that could have been designed by a kid with an Erector set. But inside is an army of engineers and technical experts and platoons of marketers just raring to innovate.

Here's how it typically works: A 3Mer comes up with an idea for a new product. He or she forms an action team by recruiting full-time members from technical

areas, manufacturing, marketing, sales, and maybe finance. The team designs the product and figures out how to produce and market it. Then it develops new uses and line extensions. All members of the team are promoted and get raises as the project goes from hurdle to hurdle. When sales grow to $5 million, for instance, the product's originator becomes a project manager, at $20 million to $30 million, a department manager, and in the $75 million range, a division manager. There's a separate track for scientists who don't want to manage.

MANY PATHS. As a result, 3M is big but acts small. There are 42 divisions, so ladders to the top are all over the place. Jacobson reached the pinnacle by cleaning up old-line operations, while his predecessor, Lewis W. Lehr, invented a surgical tape and then rode the company's burgeoning health care business all the way to the chairman's post.

So what are the corporate guidelines? A prime one is the 25% rule, which requires that a quarter of a division's sales come from products introduced within the past five years. Meeting the 25% test is a crucial yardstick at bonus time, so managers take it seriously. When Robert J. Hershock took over the occupational health division in 1982, it was utterly dependent on an aging product category, disposable face masks. By 1985 his new-product percentage had deteriorated to a mere 12%.

That set off alarms. He and his crew had to come up with plenty of new products—and they had to do it in 18 to 24 months, half the normal time. Using technology similar to the division's face-mask filters, Hershock's action teams created a bevy of products. One team came up with a sheet that drinks up the grease from microwaved bacon. Another devised a super-absorbent packing material that was widely welcomed by handlers of blood samples. The idea came from a team member who had read a newspaper article about postal workers who were panicked by the AIDS epidemic. The division's new-product sales are back above 25%.

Then there's the 15% rule. That one allows virtually anyone at the company to spend up to 15% of the workweek on anything he or she wants to, as long as it's product-related. The practice is called "bootlegging," and its most famous innovation is the ubiquitous yellow Post-it note. Arthur L. Fry's division was busy with other projects, so he invoked the 15% rule to create the adhesive for Post-its. The idea came out of Fry's desire to find a way to keep the bookmark from falling out of his hymn book. Post-its are now a major 3M consumer business,

3M'S PUSH FOR PRODUCTS AND PROFIT

MORE RESEARCH SPENDING...

R&D AS A PERCENTAGE OF SALES

TOTAL SALES '88: $10.6 BILLION
TOTAL PROFIT: $1.15 BILLION

'80 '81 '82 '83 '84 '85 '86 '87 '88

▲ PERCENT

...HELPS THE BOTTOM LINE

ANNUAL GROWTH RATE

'80 '81 '82 '83 '84 '85 '86 '87 '88

▲ PERCENTAGE CHANGE IN EARNINGS PER SHARE

DATA: 3M CO.

INSPIRATION FROM THE PLANT FLOOR

When I worked as a tape slitter at 3M, we called them The Ties. They were the buttoned-up members of the 3M Co. quality control team who would occasionally venture onto the grimy factory floor.

"They were the bad guys," says Leo Vernon, who runs a slitting machine that converts huge rolls of tape into the small ones you buy in the store. "They used to tell you rather than listen to you, assuming they even spoke to you in the first place." I worked alongside Vernon 15 years ago, running my own machine, slitting masking tape so I could come up with college tuition. 3M paid me well and, by the standards of the day, treated me well. But despite all the talk I had heard about 3M and innovation, nobody ever asked me for ideas on how to do my job better—least of all the guys from quality control.

That was 1973. Today, 3M's tape business is under assault from Japanese and European manufacturers. Over the years, while researchers at headquarters in St. Paul spewed out new products, innovation in 3M's factories lagged. By the early 1980s costs were out of control, and quality wasn't up to snuff. Productivity became a top priority for Chairman and CEO Allen F. Jacobson, who worked his way up through the tape division. By 1990, he aims to cut labor and manufacturing costs by 35% each.

ON A ROLL. The edict forced major change at 3M's far-flung factories. At its tape plant in Bedford Park, a Chicago suburb, Vernon is in charge of his own quality now. "The difference," he says, "is night and day."

The manufacturing process has been completely overhauled. Tape is made by coating a backing with adhesive and creating a giant roll about the size of an office desk. These "jumbos" are then taken to slitting machines. Until recently, all tape at the plant—masking tape, industrial tapes, closure tape for diapers—was coated in one area and transported for slitting to the other end of the factory. The coating and slitting functions had separate supervisors, and they didn't always communicate well. Production rates weren't coordinated, and hundreds of jumbos were stockpiled throughout the plant.

Now slitters are placed near the coaters, and management duties are determined by product line, not function—that is, a supervisor will be in charge of masking tape, not just coating or slitting. The new setup puts a lot more responsibility on the shoulders of individual workers. A slitting operator is expected to identify quality problems immediately so he or she can have the coater stopped after only two or three bad jumbos are produced, rather than the dozens botched in the past. As a result, inventory has been trimmed dramatically. And manufacturing time has improved by two-thirds.

The workers with whom I talked appreciate the new responsibilities. I had hated feeling like an automaton when I worked in the 3M plant, but it's an entirely different story these days for my former colleagues. They don't miss The Ties at all.

By Russell Mitchell in Bedford Park, Ill.

---

with revenues estimated at as much as $300 million.

CULTURAL HABITS. A new-product venture isn't necessarily limited by a particular market's size, either. Take Scotch tape. It was invented in 1929 for an industrial customer who used it to seal insulation in an airtight shipping package. Who could have known that it would grow into an estimated $750 million business someday?

Another recent example: The market for 3M chemist Tony F. Flannery's new product, a filter used to clean lubricants in metalworking shops, was a mere $1 million. But Flannery got the go-ahead to dabble with it anyway. He hooked up with a customer, PPG Industries Inc., which sells paint-primer systems to auto makers. The filters they were using to strain out impurities weren't doing the job. Flannery made prototypes of filter bags using a fibrous 3M material. They not only turned out to be bang-up primer filters, but the new bags are also being used to filter beer, water, edible oils, machine oil, and paint. Flannery figures that the filters could become a $20 million business in a few years.

Getting close to the customer is not just a goal at 3M—it's an ingrained cultural trait. Back in the 1920s, 3M inventor Richard G. Drew noticed that painters on automobile assembly lines had trouble keeping borders straight on the two-tone cars popular at the time. He went back to the lab and invented masking tape.

IN-HOUSE GRANTS. Even with 3M's emphasis on innovation, new ideas do fall through the cracks. In 1983 some employees complained that worthwhile projects were still going unnoticed despite the 15% rule. Guaranteed free time doesn't guarantee that there will be money to build a prototype. So the company created Genesis grants, which give researchers up to $50,000 to carry their projects past the idea stage. A panel of technical experts and scientists awards as many as 90 grants each year.

One recipient was Sanford Cobb, an optics specialist at 3M. In 1983 a bulb went on in his head at a scientific conference when he ran across something called light pipe technology. Plastic is inlaid with nearly microscopic prisms so it can reflect light for long distances with little loss of energy.

Cobb knew the heavy acrylic used in the original invention was impractical because it would be difficult to mold, but he figured he could use 3M technology to make a light pipe out of a flexible plastic film. Because 3M isn't in the lighting business, though, Cobb couldn't find a division manager willing to fork over prototype money. So he applied for a Genesis grant. He got it, and made his idea work.

CITY LIGHTS. 3M licensed the basic technology from the inventor, and now its light pipes are used in products offered by several divisions. One use is in large highway signs. The new ones feature two 400-watt bulbs, replacing 60 to 70 fluorescent tubes. Manufacturers of explosives use light pipes to illuminate their most volatile areas. And the top of One Liberty Plaza, the new office tower dominating Philadelphia's skyline, is decorated with a light-piping design. Cobb's development is part of a major new technology program at 3M, with potential annual revenues amounting to hundreds of millions of dollars.

It's a surprise, given 3M's strong predilection toward divisional autonomy, that its technology gets spread around. But 3M is a company of backscratchers, eager to help fellow employees in the knowledge that they'll get help when they need it in return. For example, when the nonwoven-fiber experts got together with the lab folks at abrasives, the result was Scotch-Brite scrubbing sponges. A Technology Council made up of researchers from the various divisions regularly gets together to exchange information.

The result of all this interconnection is an organic system in which the whole really is greater than the sum of its parts. It's no coincidence that 3M is never mentioned as a possible breakup candidate. Bust it apart, sever the interconnections, and 3M's energy would likely die. Even if a raider decided to leave it

CORPORATE INNOVATORS: HOW THEY DO IT

3M RELIES ON A FEW SIMPLE RULES . . .

Keep divisions small.   Division managers must know each staffer's first name. When a division gets too big, perhaps reaching $250 to $300 million in sales, it is split up

Tolerate failure.   By encouraging plenty of experimentation and risk-taking, there are more chances for a new-product hit. The goal: Divisions must derive 25% of sales from products introduced in the past five years. The target may be boosted to 30%

Motivate the champions.   When a 3Mer comes up with a product idea, he or she recruits an action team to develop it. Salaries and promotions are tied to the product's progress. The champion has a chance to someday run his or her own product group or division

Stay close to the customer.   Researchers, marketers, and managers visit with customers and routinely invite them to help brainstorm product ideas

Share the wealth.   Technology, wherever it's developed, belongs to everyone

Don't kill a project.   If an idea can't find a home in one of 3M's divisions, a staffer can devote 15% of his or her time to prove it is workable. For those who need seed money, as many as 90 Genesis grants of $50,000 are awarded each year

. . . WHILE OTHER COMPANIES HAVE THEIR OWN APPROACHES

RUBBERMAID   30% of sales must come from products developed in the past five years. Looks for fresh design ideas anywhere; now trying to apply the Ford Taurus-style soft look to garbage cans. A recent success: stackable plastic outdoor chairs

HEWLETT-PACKARD   Researchers urged to spend 10% of time on own pet projects; 24-hour access to labs and equipment; keeps divisions small to rally the kind of spirit that produces big winners such as its LaserJet laser printer

DOW CORNING   Forms research partnerships with its customers to develop new products such as reformulations of Armor-All car polishes and Helene Curtis hair sprays

MERCK   Gives researchers time and resources to pursue high-risk, high-payoff products. After a major scientific journal said work on anticholesterol agents like Mevacor would likely be fruitless, Merck kept at it. The drug is a potential blockbuster

GENERAL ELECTRIC   Jointly develops products with customers. Its plastics unit created with BMW the first body panels made with thermoplastics for the carmaker's Z1 two-seater

JOHNSON & JOHNSON   The freedom to fail is a built-in cultural prerogative. Lots of autonomous operating units spur innovations such as its Acuvue disposable contact lenses

BLACK & DECKER   Turnaround built partly on new-product push. Advisory councils get ideas from customers. Some new hot sellers: the Cordless Screwdriver and ThunderVolt, a cordless powertool that packs enough punch for heavy-duty construction work

DATA: COMPANY REPORTS

Jacobson is also starting to insist that 3M's divisions develop bigger-ticket products. The company has been taking core technologies and coming up with hundreds of variations. But those market niches can be pretty skinny—often only a few million dollars or so. Now the company's strategists are focusing on 45 new product areas, each with $50 million in annual sales potential three to five years out. One example: A staple gun that replaces pins for broken bones. A 50% new-product success rate would contribute $1.2 billion in sales by 1994 from this program alone.

SINCERE FLATTERY. Jacobson's latest achievements have yet to be reflected in 3M's stock price, which has been hovering in the 60s since the 1987 crash. Analysts are concerned that despite the company's diversification into health care, it still makes about 40% of its sales to the industrial sector, so it could get socked in a recession. And 3M is still considered vulnerable in floppy disks and videotape and related media, which account for about $800 million in sales. The unit has been locked in a bruising battle with the Japanese for years, and lost an estimated $50 million in 1987. While those products finally became profitable in last year's fourth quarter as a result of cost-cutting and wider distribution, the area could remain a trouble spot. "It's a fragile turnaround," says analyst B. Alex Henderson at Prudential Bache Securities Inc.

Other companies would love to have 3M's problems if its successes came with them. Indeed, 3M constantly finds itself playing host to companies trying to figure out how to be more creative. Monsanto has set up a technology council modeled on 3M's, and United Technologies has embarked on an effort to share resources among its not-so-united operations. Eight years ago, Rubbermaid Inc. began insisting that 30% of its sales come from products developed in the previous five years.

While other companies may pick up ideas piecemeal from 3M, it would be impossible for any big corporation to swallow the concept whole. "We were fortunate enough to get the philosophy in there before we started to grow, rather than trying to create it after we got big," says Lester C. Krogh, who heads research and development. 3M has a simple formula: Find the Francis Okies, and don't get in their way. But for managers of other companies, large and small, that's often easier said than done.

By Russell Mitchell in St. Paul, Minn.

intact, an unfamiliar hand at the helm might send the company off course. The possibility of a raid on 3M was taken a bit more seriously in the early 1980s, when financial performance slipped as the result of a strong dollar and skimping on R&D in the 1970s.

Jacobson's cost-cutting has done wonders for 3M. But his next challenge is formidable. The company's fortunes tend to track the domestic economy, so with a slowdown on the horizon, he must now find ways to spur growth. For one, he wants to expand internationally, boosting overseas sales from 42% of revenues to 50% by 1992. It may be slow going, however. Just as Jacobson was about to win a beachhead for a plethora of 3M products by buying the sponge unit of France's Chargeurs, the French government blocked the sale on antitrust grounds.

Sales Lost Their Vim? Try Repackaging

More Marketers Alter the Look, Skip Over Ads

ALECIA SWASY

Staff Reporter of THE WALL STREET JOURNAL

Bland packaging can sour even the sweetest-tasting product, and Just Born Inc. knows it.

The Bethlehem, Pa., candy company found that shoppers skipped over its Hot Tamales, Jelly Jos and Mike and Ike treats because of their old-fashioned black-and-white packages. So last year, the company introduced a new package featuring a colorful cast of animated grapes and cherries—and sales soared 25%.

"Kids say we went from dull and boring to definitely awesome" without a single product change or advertisement, says a company marketing official.

Package redesign is nothing new, but lately it has become more popular. Companies, especially small ones without deep pockets, are finding it's a cheaper alternative to expensive ad campaigns. Some even say it's more effective. Markets are increasingly splintered, what with myriad television channels and magazines diluting the effects of advertising. As a result, it's that much more important for a product to have strong appeal on the store shelf, where standing out from the clutter is an eternal struggle.

"Packaging is the last five seconds of marketing," says John Lister, executive vice president of Lister Butler Inc., a New York consulting firm whose package redesign work has risen 20% this year. Redesign is becoming "a more prudent invest-ment as conventional advertising becomes less effective," he says.

But it isn't just a small-company trend. For big advertisers, an eye-catching design can complement ad campaigns: TV commercials typically feature the package for at least half of air time.

While costs of redesign range widely, it's almost always cheaper than the multi-millions spent on ad campaigns. Reshaping a bottle might run as much as $300,000 because of alterations in production equipment. But new graphics on the label or a better photograph, the simplest and most common changes, may cost just a few thousand.

> '**P**ACKAGING IS THE LAST** five seconds of marketing,' says one consultant, whose redesign work has risen 20% this year. Still, many established brands are reluctant to tinker, worried that a new look could alienate loyal customers.

Many established brands are reluctant to tinker, worried that a new look could alienate loyal customers, even though consultants say negative reactions are uncommon. Convincing a pack of managers to agree on a new design can also take time. And unlike advertising blitzes, the results aren't instant. It can take a few years to see the full impact of a new package, especially if it's part of a complete product overhaul.

But when it works, it often works well. Stroh Brewery Co. turned to a new package after market research showed that its white beer cans "didn't stand out" against competitors, says Peter J. Cline, senior vice president of sales and marketing for the mid-sized brewer. Now the cans and bottle labels are bright blue. Sales of Stroh's long-neck bottles are up, especially to first-time buyers, he says, and distribution has been expanded as a result.

Even private-label brands, the Plain Janes of marketing with their stark store-name labels, are opting for face lifts as a way to boost market share without extra advertising. Kroger Co., a Cincinnati-based grocery store chain, redesigned store-brand packages after evaluating their poor sales performance. Now, newly repackaged products are competing with national brands. Kroger's Deluxe ice cream sales grew 20% this year after the type was enlarged and a label photo was enhanced.

With new competitors arriving daily, most companies want products to look in step with the times. Valvoline Oil Co. recently introduced a new package for its motor oil after consumer focus groups said the old package looked dated. The changes were simple, but the process was involved. Valvoline considered more than 40 variations before deciding merely to increase the type size on the oil's grade and add more color to the label. The company says it's too early to tell if sales are affected.

The box for Wheatena, a century-old brand of hot cereal, was redesigned last year to give it a more modern look. An old-fashioned Pennsylvania Dutch style cereal bowl on the front was replaced with a picture of a striped bowl and modern spoon. Uhlmann Co., which has since sold the brand to American Home Products, also played up Wheatena's bran and wheat germ contents on the label to attract fiber fanatics. Sales of the cereal jumped 25% in Florida test markets a couple of months after the new package hit the shelves, without any advertising or promotions.

Procter & Gamble Co.'s Clearasil acne medication now gets a packaging change every few years, rather than once a decade. "Teens tend to buy the newest product on the market," says Ronald Peterson, managing partner of Peterson & Blyth Associates Inc. Peterson & Blyth, the New York company that designed the latest package, says redesign work now accounts for 70% of its business, up from 50% last year.

While rare, negative reactions to new packages do occur. During the summer of 1988, Adolph Coors Co. angered loyal drinkers by changing the label on its beer to read "Original Draft' instead of "Banquet Beer." Some customers claimed the beer tasted different. So, just six months after adding the slogan, the company dumped it. "The last thing you want is a customer to think you've changed the formula when you change the package," says one consultant.

Because of that fear, few companies are that aggressive with new packaging. S.C. Johnson & Son Inc., a Racine, Wis., household products company, hadn't altered the packaging on its Future floor wax since 1960, partially out of concern that customers wouldn't recognize a new bottle. When the company finally decided to make a change this summer, it was a subtle one. The word Future is black instead of white and the background is a brighter shade of purple. "We wanted to cut through the increasing clutter, but keep what the consumers recognize," says Dean Lindsay, a principal of Kornick Lindsay Inc., the Chicago package-design firm that worked with S.C. Johnson.

"In most cases, the client is more inclined to be conservative because they want to protect a franchise that can take only so much fiddling," says Mr. Lindsay. "You're treading a fine line."

That's why Campbell Soup Co. doesn't expect to touch it's familiar red and white color scheme even though it plans to substitute paper labels with lithographs painted directly on cans in a few years. The company says the labeling change is partly to cut back on trash and partly for image. Says Melvin L. Druin, vice president of packaging at Campbell: "Printed cans provide a more upscale product to the consumer."

The Fine Art of Positioning

There is more to positioning than clever slogans and slick ad campaigns.

Edward DiMingo

Edward DiMingo is Director of Corporate Communications for Infotron Systems Corporation in Cherry Hill, New Jersey.

Despite the wealth of literature published during the last two decades on the topic, positioning is still the subject of much confusion. There is a clear distinction between true market positioning and its logical antecedent—psychological positioning. Yet, few strategic planners are familiar with how one grows out of the other and how both work in tandem to achieve a common marketing goal.

If done properly, the complex process demands the kind of tough, disciplined analysis and planning that strains every data-gathering, organizational, and interpretative tool of even the most sophisticated marketing teams. If confusion and errors creep in, however, something that looks like the language of positioning frequently turns out to be just the language of language.

Examples abound. When New York City's Chemical Bank ran its now-famous print campaign, "When her needs are financial, her reaction is Chemical," a small bank in another state (let's call it the Elm Street Bank) ran this ad: "When her needs are financial, her reaction is the Elm Street Bank." Luckily, a few forgiving readers noted it as an intentional parody.

And when another company tried to portray its product as "the Cadillac of the industry" (using a premium strategy for something closer to an Edsel), it put the product in deep trouble from day 1. Because the product was so grossly misrepresented, it lost credibility quickly and never recovered.

Although a slogan may portray (i.e., communicate an image of) the company or product, to be successful, it must grow out of valid positioning homework; otherwise, this image is usually more illusion than reality, more hype than honesty. Clever slogans, slick logos, weighty promises, and synthesized phrases are not sufficient to sell products to customers who have their own reasons to buy. If customers do buy on the basis of some benefit that is promised but not fulfilled by the product, they make the mistake only once.

Positioning goes well beyond slogans and image making. Any company that strives to be different merely by looking different is staking its future on a shaky foundation. True positioning is the process of distinguishing a company or product from competitors along real dimensions—products or corporate values that are meaningful to customers—to become the preferred company or product in a market. Positioning helps customers know the real differences among competing products so that they can choose the one that is of most value to them.

Two Sides of the Positioning Coin

To clear up the confusion surrounding positioning, strategic planners need to understand how the two flip sides of the positioning coin—market and psychological positioning—work individually and together.

The first side of the positioning coin—market positioning—is the process of identifying and selecting a market or segment that represents business potential, targeting vulnerable competitors, and devising a strategy to compete. Essentially, the process involves determining the criteria for competitive success—knowing what the market wants and needs, identifying company and competitors' strengths and weaknesses, and assessing abilities to meet market requirements better than a company's competitors do.

Psychological positioning, the second side of the positioning coin, involves forging a distinctive corporate or product identity closely based on market positioning factors and then using the tools of communication (e.g., advertising, public relations, point of sale, and collateral material) to move the prospect toward a buying decision. This second type of positioning, the next logical step, translates market-determined values into the clear, focused language and visual images that install a product into its own niche in the

consumer's mind. And if it's done well, of course, it will also install the product into the consumer's home or workplace.

"Fly the friendly skies," for example, did not just pop into print. United Airlines breathed life into that thought—an abstract thought with the muscle to literally move people—after extensive passenger research had suggested friendly service as a way to separate the airline from the crowd. Its success is a result of the airline's well-designed campaign to integrate market and psychological positioning.

Market Positioning

The dynamics of market positioning are happening all the time and never in the neat sequence in which they appear below. In reality, the following steps take place partly sequentially and partly simultaneously, always requiring step-by-step review and revision.

Analyze Market Opportunities for Your Corporation

The market positioning process begins with developing an attractive set of relevant opportunities based on corporate purpose, objectives, and growth strategies. In essence, a market opportunity is an area in which a company feels it is likely to enjoy a differential advantage over the competition.

For instance, consider the following hypothetical case. A manager is handling marketing for a large manufacturer of vinyl products used by the construction industry. His mission is to identify and evaluate opportunities in the $2.5 billion floor-covering market (a logical extension of his core business), select a particular opportunity, and develop a specific positioning strategy for his company's market entry.

The market manager begins by determining the sales potential of the new market, its growth rate, buyers and buying influences (where they are and when and how they buy), suppliers and supplier influences, costs to make and sell, prices, profit margins, intensity of competition, market dynamics, and channels of distribution.

One way to do this is to develop a chart that lists the new market's critical success factors and provides qualitative and quantitative information alongside each factor. The factors can be rated low, medium or high.

These factors include market size, market growth, barriers to entry (scale economies, experience curves, capital, and brand loyalty), the negotiating power of buyers (size and concentration as well as switching costs), supplier power (the availability of raw materials as well as bargaining power), price sensitivity, environmental factors (economic, social, legal, cyclical, and seasonal), and profitability.

Select a Market and Target Specific Subgroups

Since a market is typically filled with diverse customer groups and needs, segmentation is the next logical step. Subdividing the market into distinct subsets of customers is an important move toward fine-tuning a positioning strategy.

At this point, it is particularly important to examine the needs and preferences of the segment in light of the current competitive offerings and to determine the extent of customer satisfaction and competitor vulnerability. Doing so can make it easier to decide which customers and competitors to go after—and which ones to avoid.

In the floor-covering market example, two logical ways to segment the market are by product (e.g., ceramic tile, brick/stone, and sheet-vinyl) and by purchaser (e.g., residential, institutional, or commercial). If the marketing manager is attracted to the residential sheet-vinyl segment, he can further subdivide that segment into (1) new and replacement floor covering by residential contractors and (2) do-it-yourself (DIY) replacement.

Let's assume that the manager decides to focus on the DIY market. He then creates a hierarchy of variables that affect a purchase decision in that segment. In this case, research tells him that ease of installation and upkeep are the two most important attributes DIYs look for in sheet-vinyl floor covering. This information enables him to plot out the DIY's

preferences on a product space map, along with the positions of, and shares owned by, competitors. He can then use this map to identify which specific customer group within the DIY market his company should target (which market "space" to occupy).

Devise a Competitive Strategy

The entire concept of strategic market positioning hinges on doing a better job of serving the chosen market than competitors do. To achieve this, a company must focus primarily on identifying its competitors' weaknesses and capitalizing on its own strengths to differentiate an offer.

☐ *Analyze business strengths.* A company that uncompromisingly analyzes business strengths—both its own and those of its competitors—is better able to decide whether it is really in a position to seize a market opportunity.

One caution is in order: In any self-audit, there is a real tendency to view the corporation and the outside world myopically. Building a sustainable competitive advantage demands a clear assessment of what a company has to offer relative to what its competitors are offering.

Setting up a matrix is one way to objectify a company's competitive strengths and weaknesses—it is a good indicator of whether any gaps exist between a company and its competition and of how big those gaps are.

This matrix would rank the following business strengths for a company versus each of its competitors on a scale of 1 to 5: market share, profitability, breadth of product/market coverage, corporate profile, financial strength, cost position, product differentiation, relative capability in important functional areas (i.e., marketing and sales, research, and engineering), quality of management, accessibility to markets, distribution advantages, technological factors, company reputation, and likelihood of sustainable competitive advantage (market and competitive responsiveness).

☐ *Differentiate an offer.* As competition in a market intensifies, products begin to look more and more alike, making it hard

Positioning Armstrong in the Floor-Covering Market

The floor-covering example in this article is based on the experiences of Armstrong World Industries, a company that successfully positioned its sheet-vinyl floor-covering products in the DIY market. Although women were found to drive the purchase decision in the residential floor-covering DIY market, Armstrong found that men do the actual installation.

Through its research, the company discovered a simple fact of floor-covering life—fear of the first cut. This was further confirmed when Armstrong researchers asked people who examined but walked away from an in-store display the reason they had not purchased the product. Nearly 60 percent cited fear of botching the job.

As a result, Armstrong decided to adopt a differentiation strategy based on its ability to combat this fear. Thus, the "You'll be brilliant" campaign was born, coupled with the introduction of the "Trim and Fit" kit. When the small retail markup on the kit provided no incentive to retailers to push the kit concept, Armstrong introduced its "fail safe" guarantee—make a mistake, and the company replaces the floor covering at no cost. Suddenly, the biggest barrier to the purchase of the product was substantially removed. The campaign was so successful that Armstrong extended the creative approach into point of sale with banners, permanent and temporary displays, and even a toll-free number to provide installation tips.

By effectively translating market positioning values into the clear, focused language of psychological positioning, Armstrong went to market with a strong one-two punch. The company used its financial strength, cost position, and manufacturing innovation to differentiate its product. With its strong dealer network and corporate reputation, Armstrong established an offer which gave it a sustainable competitive advantage.

Go on, cut. You'll be brilliant. Armstrong guarantees it.

A "fail safe" promise made in Armstrong ads aimed at do-it-yourselfers.

for buyers to know that differences exist. Differentiation should be thought of less as a specific product and more as an offer—a benefit bundle or value package involving product, price, distribution, and the entire mix of a company's supporting capabilities and services.

Differentiation is possible everywhere and is limited only by a company's ability to use its unique competencies as customer problem-solving tools. If competitive distinction cannot be achieved through a new and innovative product (and many times, this is impossible), the range of other possibilities is endless, including everything from timely response to inquiries to help in design and application, delivery, warranties and return policies, price and payment conditions, service and maintenance, salesperson skill, reordering responsiveness, process technology, or a strong distribution network.

One problem with many differentiation

strategies today is inflexibility. These strategies often lack provisions for the possibility of competitive response and, once in place, cannot adapt to a changing marketplace. Customer needs change, so companies need to keep changing their differential advantage to anticipate the moves and stay ahead of the competitive pack.

Practical Applications

In the floor-covering example, the large market cluster in the cheap-goods end of the market is crowded with four competitors. Although some sales might still be eked out, the competition is too intense, and entry there is a poor choice.

Two other competitors appear strongly entrenched in a niche between the average and cheap-goods sectors. These large companies are battling it out for share in the average-quality sector, where they define the market to be (or where their limitations force them to be). One appears to have a slight edge in both ease of installation and upkeep. The other company's product is slightly less functional but essentially undifferentiated from the first and an exceptionally well-known brand with a loyal customer following.

There does exist, however, a group of potential DIYs who want more than the existing competitors are currently providing—they want easier upkeep and easier installation. This hole should be the manager's primary market position to target because his self-audit showed that his company has what it takes to differentiate a product in this area. In addition to having the potential for product and selling channel differentiation, his research suggests that he can strengthen his offer by building it around a strong warranty and return policy.

Filling this gap with such an ideal offer could give his company instant leadership. In doing so, it might choose to stay put in this segment—with one product, a limited selection, or a full line—or it might later decide to use its position as a launching pad for invading the larger market.

Psychological Positioning

Once market positioning steps are completed, it is time to call in the copywriters and let loose the art directors. What a company says and how it says it is the bottom line of psychological positioning. The content of market positioning informs psychological positioning; it is the glue that holds everything together to create an identity, a message, a look.

Psychological positioning grows out of market positioning. If the market position is based on a product-quality differentia-

tion, this discernible difference must be communicated through an integrated, consistent strategy involving packaging, brand name, product appearance, advertising, public relations, and all kinds of sales promotions from point-of-purchase displays to special events. An image of the product begins to emerge from the product name, the look, and the packaging design, all of which should strive to convey the benefits the consumer will derive from the product. The rest of the communications program completes the picture, strengthening, reinforcing, and enhancing that image and message.

Psychological positioning means selling the product. Its role is to change behavior, to create enough interest in a product to encourage a trial purchase. It is also the underpinning of a communications campaign, the goal of which is to instill in the prospect's mind a vivid picture of three elements: who the company is, what the product does, and what to expect from the purchase.

A successful communications campaign guides potential customers through a hierarchy of attitudes and effects: Awareness leads to comprehension, comprehension leads to a favorable attitude, a favorable attitude leads to interest, interest leads to intention, and intention leads to purchase.

Conclusion

A positioning strategy, in effect, defines the ground on which competitive battles are fought. Winning is a test of how well a company learns the needs of its customers, designs and makes products to fit those needs, communicates all the benefits the customer will derive from using the products, and finally, delivers everything it promises. When a company does this better, it tilts the battle in its favor.

Middle-Price Brands Come Under Siege

KATHLEEN DEVENY
Staff Reporter of THE WALL STREET JOURNAL

To be mainstream used to be a blessing for products. Now, it's becoming the curse of the mundane.

Solid, middle-of-the-road names such as Sears, Holiday Inn and Smirnoff, are struggling against a slew of new competitors that strike from two sides—above and below. Encircled by rivals offering either more luxurious goods or just plain cheaper ones, midpriced products are finding their market shares dwindling and looking for ways to break away from the image of being "just average."

"Getting stuck in the middle is a terrible fate," says Laurel Cutler, vice chairman of New York advertising agency FCB/Leber Katz Partners. "It's the phenomenon of being a mass brand as the market splinters."

To wit: Swanky stores such as Neiman-Marcus and budget outlets such as Wal-Mart Stores Inc. are prospering, while the bread-and-butter **Sears, Roebuck** & Co. flounders. Haagen Dazs, Ben & Jerry's and other "super premium" ice creams are thriving—as are grocers' own bargain labels—while basic brands such as Kraft General Foods Corp.'s Sealtest are struggling to hold their ground. Travelers want either cheap lodging at chains such as Day's Inn or to sleep in the lap of luxury, leaving adequate but unexciting hoteliers such as Ramada Inn and Holiday Inn in the lurch.

"The mainstream brands of old are increasingly under pressure from both ends of the spectrum," says John Quelch, a professor at Harvard Business School who specializes in consumer marketing.

Adds Ms. Cutler, "There's no future for products everyone likes a little."

The murky-middle problem has some roots in demographics. The population growth of the 1940s through 1960s that established mass-market brands has slowed. And while markets have stopped growing, competition has exploded: The number of items stocked at grocery stores has soared from a few thousand 30 years ago to over 40,000 at large supermarkets today.

But the problem goes beyond just population and competition. Since the early 1970s, families have hardly managed to boost incomes. For baby boomers starting out, that's made upward mobility more difficult—hence the need for bargains.

At the same time, it's also made them insecure, argues Frank Levy, an economist with the University of Maryland's School of Public Affairs. Feeling their economic status is precarious, middle-class consumers have become loath to identify with middle-road products, often wrapping themselves in prestige brands. "Status anxiety makes niche marketing very attractive," Mr. Levy says.

This emphasis on image—not to mention a foreign invasion—has put Smirnoff vodka on the defensive. The domestic brand, a product of **Grand Metropolitan PLC**'s Heublein Inc., sells for a moderate $6 to $9 a bottle and faces growing competition from a horde of imported, heavily advertised rivals, led by **Carillon Importers** Ltd.'s Absolut. Last year, U.S. sales of all high-priced imported vodkas, including Stolichnaya, Finlandia, Icy and Tanqueray Sterling, rose more than 20%.

Smirnoff remains the nation's best-selling vodka, but unit sales barely grew at all last year, according to Al Sanchez, manager of research and statistics for Jobson Publishing Corp.'s alcoholic beverage unit. To keep from slipping, Smirnoff has been attempting to strengthen its image of quality by raising prices and running ads with a more upscale look. The company is also pursuing a counterattack, pressing for more sales overseas.

If a middle-price product can't sell on prestige, it has to compete on value. To make Sealtest stand out from store-brand ice creams, Paul Litwack, marketing director for frozen desserts at Kraft, has borrowed some tactics from fancier brands. It recently added a layer of cellophane inside the carton—like the one found in Breyers, a sister brand—to slow formation of ice crystals. Kraft, a unit of **Philip Morris** Cos., also made the package's graphics cleaner and more modern. The idea is to keep the price the same, about $2.99 a half gallon, but come across to consumers as a better value. Still, the product remains in that not-cheap, not-expensive limbo. Says Mr. Litwack: "It's a very tough category."

An average image also haunts retailers **J.C. Penney** Co. and Sears, both of which have seen their middle-income customers defect to discount outlets or trendier specialty stores. Both chains are scrambling to revitalize sales by trying to project an image that's a step up from vanilla. They are stocking more national-brand goods and running slicker, more stylish ads to herald the change.

Sears maintains its program has been successful in strengthening its image with consumers. Unfortunately, perceptions die hard. Despite its much-ballyhooed name-brand strategy, Sears's profits are flagging. "Sears doesn't stand for anything customers aspire to," says John Lister, executive vice president at Lister Butler Inc., a New York image consultant.

Technology has worked against some middle marketers by giving a boost to cheap rivals. Seiko Corp. of America, a unit of **Hattori Seiko** Co., introduced quartz technology in 1969. In no time, Seiko was faced with threatening, low-priced competition from **Timex** Corp., **Swatch Watch** Corp. and other companies that could use highly precise quartz technology in timepieces selling for under $50. "There's no reason to spend more than $100 on a watch unless you're looking for diamonds and gold," says C. Michael Jacobi, vice president of marketing and sales at Timex.

Then, with the advent of the yuppie mentality, status-oozing Rolex and Patek-Philippe watches took a bite from the top.

Seiko has responded by expanding its lines beyond the middle. It now sells the pricey Lassale and the inexpensive Lorus. It's also trying to blend fashion with its traditional claim of superior technology. A snappy $325 analog model, for example, shows the time in 21 different cities.

Although Seiko maintains it has hung on to about half of the midpriced segment, the business "has been no bed of roses," says Joe Whall, a Seiko spokesman.

"It's hard for middle-segment watches to compete either on elegance or on price," says Robert Schmidt, chairman of Levine, Huntley, Schmidt & Beaver Inc., the agency that, in 1987, created some stylish ads for midpriced **Citizen Watch** Co. set to the music of Louis Armstrong and Al Jolson. "We used style to make people feel good about wearing them." He says sales of the brand, virtually unknown at the time, soared to two million units annually, from a scant 200,000.

Despite the success of the ads, Citizen discontinued them last year and switched agencies. Now, the brand seems to have lost its momentum. Executives at Citizen couldn't be reached for comment.

For some, it finally gets to the point where the middle market just isn't worth it. **Marriott** Corp. tried to string its Bob's Big Boy, Allie's and Wag's coffee shops into a single, national chain of casual restaurants. It was a nebulous niche that few consumers wanted: The restaurants weren't as cheap or as appealing to children as fast food. Nor could they please adults with a nice dining-out atmosphere. Last December, the hotel chain announced plans to quit the restaurant business.

"We were sandwiched in the middle," a Marriott spokesman says. "It would have been too costly to establish a new national brand."

In the hotel industry, where chains have spread rapidly, companies are trying to extend their reach both into cheaper accommodations and higher-priced ones. **Holiday** Corp.'s Holiday Inns, which no longer has the casual family traveler all to itself, has added a more upscale entry called Holiday Inns Crowne Plaza. Ramada Inn now operates a low-frills property called Rodeway Inns and a posher chain called Renaissance.

Prime Motor Inns Corp., which operates Ramada's U.S. franchise system and owns or franchises such chains as Howard Johnson, maintains there is still opportunity to serve middle-market customers. The trick, it says, is to distinguish itself from mid-range competitors. So Prime has begun building suite hotels, called AmeriSuites and Plaza-Suite Hotels. Chris Browne, senior vice president of marketing and reservations for Prime's franchise systems division, says the company scrimped on common areas and nixed room service in order to offer rooms with amenities such as two phones, a microwave and a refrigerator, all at the same price as Holiday Inns.

Prime predicts an industry shakeout, and expects to survive. Until then, he says, "If you sit still and do nothing, you'll be devoured."

The middle isn't nearly as amorphous for many packaged-goods makers, where there is often less opportunity to develop prestige brands. But few marketers would dispute that their business is more complex and more competitive than ever. Concludes Joel Weiner, a former senior vice president at Kraft General Foods: "It's a combat zone, and even strong brands are employing battle tactics to hold their share."

Marketing the Premium Product

From gourmet ice cream to luxury imported cars, increasing attention is being paid to the development and marketing of premium products targeted at the upper end of the price performance pyramid. However, despite the current wave of enthusiasm, marketers should not conclude that launching premium products is a sure way to improve profit margins.

John A. Quelch

James A. Quelch is an associate professor at the Harvard University Graduate School of Business Administration. Coauthor of seven books on marketing and consumer behavior, he is a frequent contributor to Business Horizons.

In this day when everything from mustard to diapers to cheese is readily available in an upscale version, what explains the growing trend to marketing the premium product? What are the characteristics of product categories susceptible to premium marketing? How can mainstream marketers respond to the threat—or opportunity—of expanding premium segments in the markets they serve? What strategic risks and growth challenges face the traditional established premium marketer? And how can a company become a successful premium marketer?

THE GROWTH OF PREMIUM MARKETING

In many product-markets, a premium segment is either emerging or growing in size and importance. Many factors are contributing to this trend.

As the rate of population growth in the U.S. has slowed, many mainstream marketers have become more interested in creating, expanding, or penetrating premium market segments. First, they hope to achieve higher unit margins on equivalent volume as existing consumers are persuaded to trade up. Second, because further segmentation typically means that some consumer needs are being addressed more closely, they hope for a growth in total category volume.

According to a point of view that is becoming more widely held, the only strategy for success in the low price end of many product-markets is a high-volume, low-cost production approach that is vulnerable to foreign competition. Therefore, the risks of entry at the low end of the market are seen as greater than the costs of acquiring or developing premium brand franchises to enter the premium end of the market. In addition, the premium marketer controls the price umbrella in the market and is less vulnerable than the mainstream marketer to the low-cost producer. Adding to the interest in premium marketing are the many examples of entrepreneurs who have successfully pursued niche strategies in the premium segments of their respective markets.

In many product-markets, therefore, the mass market appears to be waning. Mass-market brands are being flanked by private label and generic substitutes at the low price end of the

From *Business Horizons*, May/June 1987, pp. 38-45. Copyright, 1987, by the Foundation for the School of Business at Indiana University. Reprinted by permission.

"Although the characteristics of what is meant by 'premium' vary by category, premium brands are typically of excellent quality, high priced, selectively distributed through the highest quality channels, and advertised parsimoniously."

market and by premium products at the high price end of the market.

The retailing environment is also experiencing increased segmentation, with the simultaneous growth of off-price retailers and premium quality specialty stores. In those markets experiencing little or no volume growth, retailer interest is high in premium products that can boost average profit margins. The application of direct product profitability to merchandise selection has further enhanced retailer attention to premium products.

Market research services such as VALS and PRIZM have been developed to segment the population on demographic and psychographic variables and to classify zip codes by dominant segment. When added to media fragmentation and the growth of direct marketing, these segmentation schemes permit the aspirational and achiever segments that are often the principal targets of the premium marketer to be identified and targeted.

Average growth in disposable income is exceeding the costs of acquiring those new products—such as videocassette recorders and microwave ovens—that are the badges of the conspicuous consumer. Increasingly, conspicuous consumers differentiate themselves not by what they own but by the quality of what they own. A growing segment of the population appears to aspire to a premium life-style; Grey Advertising has identified 15.3 percent of all adults as Ultra Consumers.[1] Several magazines stand ready to specify the activities and acquisitions that such a life-style should involve.

Increased population mobility enhances the need to own and use products that are widely recognized for their premium quality. As Thorstein Veblen wrote almost ninety years ago in his *Theory of the Leisure Class*:

> In order to impress transient observers and to retain one's self-complacency under their observation, the signature of one's pecuniary strength should be written in characters which he who runs may read.[2]

Demographic trends, particularly the increasing number of working women and two-income households, have encouraged the emergence of premium segments in product-markets where the premium position was previously occupied by home-made products. A decrease in cookie-making at home prompted Nabisco, Frito-Lay, and Procter & Gamble to introduce convenient, ready-made, premium-quality cookies. Likewise, those working women who allegedly feel guilty that they do not have the time to prepare an evening meal from scratch are willing to pay $6 or more for the convenience of premium frozen entrees such as Stouffer's Lean Cuisine.

The end of double-digit inflation in the U.S. has helped to stabilize prices. Consumers are better able to make meaningful price comparisons so that price is once again being used as an indicator of quality. Such a trend tends to favor the premium marketer.

PROFILING THE PREMIUM PRODUCT

Although the characteristics of what is meant by "premium" vary by category, premium brands are typically of excellent quality, high priced, selectively distributed through the highest quality channels, and advertised parsimoniously.

Excellent quality is a sine qua non, and it is important that the premium marketer maintains and develops leadership in quality. This leadership will usually be based on technical superiority in those product categories where functional attributes and price-performance comparisons drive consumer decision making.

In categories where psychic benefits dominate decision making, the cultivation of a prestige image will often be the basis of leadership. Image leadership is derived partly from the relative exclusivity that a premium price and distribution channel give to the item, but it can be reinforced by a well-selected brand name, logo, and packaging, and by communicating the product's heritage, place of origin, or the personality behind it. All of these factors were attended to in the marketing of Perrier as "nature's soft drink."

When a premium product commands both technical and image leadership—for example, a Rolls Royce automobile—it typically enjoys both a significant comparative advantage and a defensible niche.

The premium segment can exist in almost any product category. Consumers willing to pay higher prices for premium products typically view them as one or more of the following:
- Affordable indulgences (Haagen Dazs ice cream);
- Tasteful gifts (Coach handbags);
- Smart investments (Maytag laundry appliances); or
- Status symbols (Mercedes Benz cars).

Some product categories, however, seem to be more susceptible to premium marketing than others. Although coffee and beer are both

"Increasingly, we find traditional premium products being challenged by nouveau premium products, often higher priced and destined either to supplant their aging rivals or to be mere fads."

beverages, premium marketing strategies have been more successful to date for beer than for coffee. Why?

In the first place, coffee is a mundane, everyday item, more of a commodity. Beer is more of an indulgence. As such, it is more open to appeals to the taste of the self-styled connoisseur.

In a social situation, moreover, the brand of beer a consumer chooses is clearly visible. The choice is a social statement. Coffee, by contrast, is usually served anonymously from a pot.

Furthermore, the consumer is heavily involved in preparing a cup of coffee. Right down to adding too much or too little cream and sugar, it is quite possible for the consumer to make a bad cup from good-quality instant or ground coffee. On the other hand, beer is consumed straight from the bottle; the manufacturer's quality reaches the consumer intact.

When, however, coffee is served in social situations, there is higher risk; therefore, a consumer is more likely to use a premium brand. The percentage of market sales likely to be accounted for by premium brands of coffee is less than that for beer.

In assessing the evolution of the premium segment in any product category, it is well to bear in mind several important points.

• **The meaning of "premium" may vary from one market segment to another.** Older Americans regard Cadillac as a premium automobile; younger Americans are more likely to mention Mercedes or BMW. Increasingly, we find traditional premium products being challenged by nouveau premium products, often higher priced and destined either to supplant their aging rivals or to be mere fads. Will Calvin Klein's Obsession fragrance, though lacking demon-

strable technical superiority and any historical heritage, supplant Chanel No. 5 as the premier perfume? Or will it fade into oblivion after a couple of seasons?

• **The meaning of "premium" may change over time** as consumer lifestyles and technologies evolve. Often, the mainstream marketer interested in obtaining a slice of the premium segment will attempt to change the criteria for what is regarded as premium. By making electronic features an important benefit to consumers purchasing major appliances, General Electric displaced KitchenAid as the premium brand of dishwashers. Conversely, the premium marketers with the greatest longevity are often found in categories characterized by little change in technologies and consumer needs—for example, jewelry and silver flatware.

• **The premium segment may be perceived as delivering different levels of "premiumness."** In product-markets where the premium segment grows in size, a distinction is frequently drawn between premium and *super*premium products. This phenomenon is evident, for example, in the beer market, where Heineken might now be considered merely a premium brand while Samuel Adams might be characterized as *super*premium.

• Sometimes, **the premium product will not, by one standard of judgment, be technically superior.** Hand-blown glassware, for example, is more likely to have irregularities than machine-made glassware. These irregularities do not, however, detract from the product's functionality; paradoxically, the flaws are visual indicators that the glassware is hand-crafted and, therefore, more expensive.

MAINSTREAM MARKETERS MOVING UP

What strategic options are open to the mainstream marketer facing the challenge of increasing consumer interest in premium entries? There are five options which are not necessarily mutually exclusive:

1. Introduce a premium version of the existing mainstream brand;

2. Introduce or acquire a brand with a name unconnected to that of the existing mainstream brand;

3. Trade up a loyal base of consumers from a mainstream franchise when these satisfied customers make repeat purchases;

4. Change the consumer's definition of "premium" to weaken the franchise of existing premium brands; or

5. Redouble marketing efforts for the mainstream brand.

Introduce a Premium Version of a Mainstream Brand

Introducing a premium version of a mainstream brand is typically cheaper and faster than launching a new brand. Shell SU2000 gasoline, Ramada Renaissance hotels, and Maxwell House Master Blend coffee are three examples of this approach.

Because the new entry capitalizes on the already developed consumer recognition for the mainstream brand, it is not difficult to obtain consumer and trade interest. In addition, a premium entry can, if so promoted, cast a halo of quality across the entire brand franchise. However, despite these advantages, problems may arise.

• Stretching the existing brand name can dilute the clarity of its po-

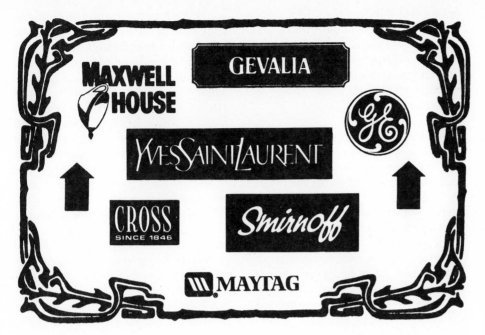

sitioning in an increasingly segmented market.

• Advertising justification for the higher price of the premium entry may detract from the quality of the mainstream entries in a product line. General Electric faced this problem when it introduced its PermaTuf tub liner (with a ten-year warranty) only on its higher priced dishwashers.

• The premium version of a mainstream brand cannot compete convincingly with premium brands that have no poor relations in the mainstream. While the Corvette may help sell other Chevrolets, the image of those other products limits the Corvette's ability to compete convincingly against Porsche.

• Trade channels may not distinguish between the premium version and the mainstream brand. General Foods' attempt to position Maxwell House Master Blend as a premium item was thwarted when the trade aggressively price-promoted the premium product just as it did regular Maxwell House.

• If a manufacturer is selling different quality products through distribution channels of varying quality, all under the same brand franchise, there is a constant temptation to let the premium entry be sold through the lower quality distribution channels.

• If growth of the premium segment proves to be short-lived, the strength of the mainstream franchise will have been unreasonably jeopardized.

• The interests of the premium entry are often subordinated to those of the mainstream brand. The premium entry is not considered important enough to receive special management or sales force attention and is therefore presented to the trade and, ultimately, to the consumer in the same fashion as a mainstream brand. Even though the sales growth rate of the premium product may be superior, the dominant consideration is to protect current sales of the mainstream brands.

Introduce or Acquire a New Brand

The second option, to introduce or acquire a new brand, represents more commitment to the premium segment. It often involves a separate organization independent of the mainstream franchise. This option is especially appropriate when the perceptual gap between the mainstream brand and the premium segment is too great for the first option to stand a chance. A new premium brand can be internally developed or obtained through acquisition or a licensing arrangement. Some examples:

• Holiday Inns have developed a new chain, Embassy Suites, to tackle the premium end of the hotel market.

• Huffy, the bicycle manufacturer, established a joint venture with Raleigh, the U.K. bicycle producer, to secure a piece of the premium segment of the market rather than trying to upgrade consumer perceptions of its existing franchise.

• The Shulton division of American Cyanamid, marketer of Old Spice, the leading medium-priced line of men's toiletries, licensed the right to use the Pierre Cardin name on an upscale line of fragrances. Licensing an established designer brand requires less investment than developing a new premium brand from scratch, but the licensee has little control over how the designer's image will evolve.

• After its experience with Maxwell House Master Blend, General Foods is tackling the premium coffee market with not one but several new brands. Masters Collection is targeted at consumers who equate coffee quality with raw beans, while the Gevalia line of Swedish coffees, distributed by direct mail, appeals to those who see quality embodied in a foreign heritage.

The multiple brand approach is more appropriate than the first option for increasingly segmented markets. Although more costly up front, the mainstream franchise is not put at risk.

In addition, a company has more strategic flexibility. Marketing resources can be allocated among several brands serving different segments as evolving market circumstances dictate.

Finally, participation in multiple segments permits the marketer to exert some control over the relative growth of each. Anheuser-Busch, for example, originally positioned Michelob as a special-occasion beer for weekend use, simultaneously conveying a premium image while influencing the size of the premium segment.

Trade Up Loyal Customer Base

A third option is to penetrate the premium segment of a market by offering premium products under a mainstream brand to an existing base of loyal and satisfied consumers who have purchased mainstream products and are looking to trade up.

Using this approach, Japanese manufacturers of motorcycles and other consumer products have demonstrated that a mainstream brand franchise can be extended into the premium segment in the case of more functional, technical products. Harley-Davidson and the other traditional motorcycle manufacturers had retreated to the high-priced end of the market, expecting to be able to defend it. Indeed, they erroneously regarded the premium segment as a separate market. However, they discovered that, although the size of the premium segment expanded with consumers trading up from smaller motorcycles, many of these consumers wanted the same features (such as electronic ignition rather than kick-starting) that they had become used to on their smaller Japanese bikes. In this case, features and performance proved more important than an exclusive brand name in determining who controlled the premium segment.

Change Consumer's Definition of "Premium"

A fourth option is to try to upgrade the image of a mainstream brand. Marketers can give an upgrade program its best chance of success by trying to change the criteria that consumers use to determine the degree of "premiumness" offered by different brands in the market.

General Electric's leadership in applying electronics technology to dishwashers, which existing premium manufacturers such as KitchenAid did not have the resources to imitate rapidly, has enabled G.E. to upgrade its image from that of a middle-of-the-road manufacturer. Electronic controls rather than a hefty stainless steel tub are now the signature of the premium dishwasher. Because brand images, like prices, are harder to raise than lower, G.E.'s success is especially impressive.

However, such upward stretching of a brand name may well be easier in the case of products that are purchased primarily for functional rather than psychic benefits. It is also worth

noting that G.E.'s control of the Hotpoint brand gave it additional strategic flexibility in upgrading the G.E. franchise; Hotpoint dishwashers could further penetrate the low-price end of the market as the G.E. image improved.

Concentrate on Mainstream Brand

A fifth option open to the mainstream marketer is to do nothing to endorse the legitimacy of the premium segment. The marketer can encourage the trade to dismiss the premium segment as faddish, small, and unlikely to grow, and it can emphasize the quality and value of its mainstream brands. Given the evolution of most markets towards price-quality segmentation and the strategic benefits of multisegment representation, this strategy seems risky.

Mainstream manufacturers are being pressured by competition from above and below. Scripto, for example, lost market share both to a low-cost producer, Bic, and to manufacturers of premium-quality pens such as Cross. Although the middle portion of the market to which Scripto continued to cling was not destroyed, it was seriously eroded in size as the market segmented.

PREMIUM MARKETERS UNDER PRESSURE

While mainstream marketers are at risk if they do not respond to premium brand competition, the premium market has its pitfalls. In product categories driven by functional benefits, the premium marketer is typically vulnerable to attack from below. In categories driven by psychic benefits, the principal risk is attack from above. The two most common failings of the premium marketer are being too conservative and too aggressive.

Too Conservative

Many premium marketers are family-owned businesses with a historical commitment to quality. It may be easier for them to be dedicated to quality through durability than it is for the publicly held company, which is often

accused of perpetrating built-in obsolescence in the interests of sales. Not being under shareholder pressure for growth, these family businesses may prefer to continue their low profile. Their view is that expansion would attract attention and competition. Even though healthy competition would expand the total size of the premium segment, such companies often would sooner remain isolated in the small triangle at the top of the market pyramid.

Such an approach is fine so long as a niche is defensible. When it is not, mainstream marketers attempting to penetrate and grow the premium segment may raise the level of marketing expenditures in the segment and so put the traditional premium marketer under pressure. Here are three examples:

• Distillers, a well-known U.K. manufacturer of premium-quality whiskey and other alcoholic beverages, was recently under takeover pressure from Argyll, a marketer of lower priced brands. One of Argyll's principal arguments to shareholders was that Distillers, by being too conservative, permitted the market share of premium brands such as Black and White and Johnnie Walker to erode while the premium segment as a whole was being expanded by new competition.

• By permitting G.E. to change the definition of "premium" in the dishwasher category to emphasize electronics, KitchenAid lost its command of the premium segment. Being a premium niche player, KitchenAid, like Harley-Davidson, lacked sufficient resources to invest in the new technology. It is now being acquired by Whirlpool, a mainstream brand, which regards KitchenAid as a vehicle for entry into the premium segment.

• Stride Rite has long been the premium quality manufacturer of shoes and sneakers for infants and young children. However, increasingly, younger children want to behave and dress like their older siblings or like adults, with the result that the premium marketers that serve these age groups, facing heavy competition in their own segments, are pressing against and eroding Stride Rite's niche. Unable to extend the Stride Rite franchise to older age groups, the company has responded by acquiring premium-quality shoe manufacturers serving these other market segments.

Too Aggressive

The adage "familiarity breeds contempt" is often the nemesis of the marketer of a premium brand. Many of the premium products of yesterday—Bulova watches, Izod shirts, Smirnoff vodka—are the standard products of today and lack a clear position in their respective markets.

Pressure on the premium marketer frequently comes from distribution channels wanting to upgrade their store images by carrying premium brands. Pressure for sales growth prompts the development of products and services at lower price points to broaden the appeal of the franchise. Such an approach is often justified on the grounds that it will attract into the brand franchise customers who can afford the low-priced item. The idea is that these consumers will trade up later to more expensive products.

In practice, however, such franchise expansion implies a loss of exclusivity that opens the door for a new competitive superpremium brand. Even when sales growth is accompanied by an improvement in quality, the very fact that more people have access to the brand detracts from its "premiumness."

This chain of events is especially likely to afflict premium products in categories where psychic and status benefits are prominent in the purchase decision-making process. For example, Cadillac hurt its reputation and failed to attract younger buyers with its compact Cimarron, a thinly disguised but much more expensive Chevrolet Cavalier. The numbers of Mercedes now on U.S. roads, combined with the introduction of the lower-priced 190 series, are thought to have helped Jaguar establish itself as a strong premium brand on the basis of greater exclusivity. A recent Jaguar advertisement states: "From a heritage of coachbuilders to kings and the sporting aristocracy of Europe comes the most exclusive Jaguar sedan you can own."

Other markets are even more vulnerable to superpremium entries. The premium hotel, for example, depends heavily on the quality of the fixed plant. This plant naturally deteriorates over time. A hotel's location, which is unchangeable, may also lose its appeal. These facts threaten any hotel chain's ability to maintain a premium position, independent of the growth rate of the chain. Thus, over the years, Sheraton has successively been supplanted as the premium hotel chain by Hilton, Hyatt, and Intercontinental.

Coping Strategies

What strategies can a premium marketer follow that will permit growth but, at the same time, minimize degradation of the brand franchise?

Multiple Lines. Hartmann Luggage offers four lines of different quality at different price points. For this strategy to succeed, the differences between the lines must be clearly visible, and the logic of the price-quality relationships must be comprehensible to both consumer and the trade. Hartmann has been able to maintain its premium position while expanding the size of the segment. At the same time it has created a barrier to entry by making multiple lines the price of admission to that segment.

Sequential Featuring. Major fashion houses frequently distinguish between their premium-priced collections, displayed at the New York and Paris fashion shows and sold to a limited number of wealthy clients, and their classification merchandise: lower priced, with a broader appeal, and incorporating the features of last year's collections. In this industry, the profits derived from classification sales subsidize the development of collections, which cast a premium halo over the classification merchandise, for which, in turn, a premium price can be charged.

Selective Broadening. The status associated with using a premium brand often depends upon its being recognized by those not having access to it. Almost anyone in the U.S. can afford a Polo T-shirt. Rather than detracting from the premium quality of Ralph Lauren's Polo franchise, recognition of the Polo player logo en-

hances the status of those who can afford his more expensive lines of clothing.

Signature Brands. A premium marketer typically cannot grow by introducing a mainstream brand under a different name. Premium marketers lack the resources to invest in developing such new franchises. In addition, the interest of mainstream distribution channels is in the existing premium brand rather than some new brand with no established consumer appeal. Faced with these circumstances, the premium marketer may compromise by introducing a signature brand (for example, Zips sneakers by Stride-Rite). The objective is to exploit the halo benefits of the premium name while minimizing possible image damage.

Licensing. Rather than growing by pushing down the price pyramid in the product-markets where they currently operate, premium marketers and designers such as Yves St. Laurent are increasingly licensing use of their brand names to premium manufacturers in other product categories. As long as quality control can be maintained so that the licensed products reinforce rather than detract from the brand image, the premium marketer can grow laterally rather than vertically and not jeopardize the exclusivity of its franchise.[3]

Global Marketing. A global growth approach is similar to the previous strategy. The premium marketer targets the same premium segments in international markets that it currently targets in the domestic market. In many product-markets, increasing international travel and communications have led to a convergence across international boundaries in consumer values and their definitions of what is premium.[4] This convergence is often more evident in the premium than in the mainstream segment of product-markets. The size of the premium segment for Dupont cigarette lighters, which cost more than $300, may not be especially attractive in any one national market, but the global aggregate of multiple national premium segments may well be.

Retail Outlets. Many premium marketers offer consumers a multiple product line of premium-quality items that represent a complete life-style concept. Sales growth is achieved by adding new products under the concept umbrella.

Often, however, the premium marketer finds that its product line is not fully presented or properly merchandised at the point of sale, no matter how carefully selected the retail outlets are. A premium product can easily lose its image for quality if it is lost among mainstream brands on a cluttered shelf. Hence, forward integration becomes a vehicle for the premium marketer to achieve both sales growth and merchandising control.

Many marketers of psychically grounded premium products—for example, Polo Fashions, Haagen-Dazs, and Crabtree and Evelyn—are placing greater emphasis on establishing specialty stores dedicated exclusively to the sale of their own product lines and the life-style concepts associated with them. Such stores also act as advertising vehicles and boost sales of a premium marketer's products through other, nonexclusive channels.

STAYING ON TOP

What actions can the established premium marketer take to defend and solidify its niche? Obviously, it is necessary to establish a powerful, communicable, and defensible comparative advantage. In addition, several prescriptions may be helpful.

Pursue an internally consistent marketing strategy. Premium marketers must ensure that all elements of the marketing mix—premium-quality product and positioning, premium pricing, selective distribution, and selective communications—are continually in concert.

Maintain quality leadership. The premium marketer must closely monitor the meaning of "premium" to consumers in its target segments and beyond. The marketer must strive to

ensure that "premium" continues to be defined on criteria that enable it to stay on top. However, to defend its position, the premium marketer must constantly challenge itself to improve the quality of its products. Mere exclusivity without quality leadership is a recipe for failure.

Cultivate a heritage. Although few Reebok athletic shoes are now manufactured in the U.K., part of the firm's advertising and public relations campaign focuses on the British founder of the company and the values of technical excellence and quality manufacture which he brought to the design and workmanship of Reebok shoes.

Develop quality indicators. Performance warranties, competitive awards, expensive packaging, and brand logos are increasingly being used by actual and aspiring premium marketers to enhance the quality image of their brands. In an effort to upgrade its mainstream image, Gallo is advertising the awards its wines have received from connoisseurs and claims to offer "all the best a wine can be."

A NOTE OF CAUTION

Interest in the premium segments of most product-markets is likely to continue. Attracted by higher unit margins and the promise of greater strategic flexibility, mainstream marketers will seek to penetrate and grow the premium segment. For them, the key issue is not *whether* to enter but *how* to enter in order to succeed.

Their efforts will place established premium marketers under pressure. Some will not be able to defend their niches and will fade from view or be acquired. Others will seek growth in ways that do not jeopardize their established brand images. Some may trade down on the grounds that taking the offensive against the mainstream marketer is the best form of defense, even though this will leave them vulnerable at the high end of

the market pyramid to the entry of superpremium brands.

One important caveat is in order. Marketers should be wary of devoting too much attention to the premium segment at the expense of other emerging segments (for example, retired persons) that may offer greater sales and profit potential. Just because they themselves are among the mere three percent of U.S. households in 1985 with incomes over $75,000, marketing decision makers may be tempted to attribute more importance to the premium segment than it deserves. Too many marketing executives look in their mirrors and think they see America.

If marketers become narrowly focused, marketing itself will be in danger of becoming a niche phenomenon. Satisfying the needs of the mass market will then be conceded to manufacturing-driven low-cost producers, Japanese and Korean manufacturers, and mass retailers (like WalMart) who are close enough to the marketplace to develop appealing private-label products that will erode brand franchises even further.

If premium marketing becomes too glamorous and attracts a disproportionate share of our best marketing talent, the average American consumer will be the loser.

---

1. "Puttin' on the Glitz," *Grey Matter*, 57:1, 1986.

2. Thorstein Veblen, *The Theory of the Leisure Class* (Boston: Houghton Mifflin Co. edition, 1975), p. 72.

3. See John A. Quelch, "How to Build a Product Licensing Program," *Harvard Business Review*, May-June 1985: 186.

4. See Theodore Levitt, "The Globalization of Markets," *Harvard Business Review*, May-June 1983: 92-102.

HOW TO COMPETE ON PRICE

The accepted wisdom is you can't do it anymore—but it's wrong

Paul B. Brown

The marketing gurus are getting better. Their accepted wisdom these days is that you no can longer compete solely on price. Customers—either retail or wholesale—need more, they say: service, speedy delivery, marketing support. Competing on price is passé.

There is some truth to the experts' observations. But not much.

It's fair to say price is now probably the least effective arrow in your marketing quiver. Jaded consumers don't believe words like "manufacturer's list price," "discount," or even "sale" anymore. Heck, you don't believe them when *you're* out shopping, so why should anyone else?

But this doesn't mean that you can't compete on price. You can. But you have to be smart about it. For one thing, you can't be inconsistent. If you're cheap one day, expensive the next, and in the middle every other Thursday, you'll just confuse people. (Does Sears come to mind?) And you can't get around that problem by holding sales or giving rebates. All that does—as Detroit's carmakers have learned the hard way—is condition people to wait for the sale (or rebate) before they buy.

No, if you are going to compete on price, it must drive every other decision you make.

It does at Jan Bell Marketing Inc., a jewelry distributor.

Price and price only fuels the Sunrise, Fla.-based company, which gets most of its $181 million in revenues from selling private-label jewelry to the nation's wholesale clubs. Jan Bell's gold chains and earrings, tennis bracelets, and rings wholesale for about a third of what other manufacturers charge.

To understand how Jan Bell is able to sell for less and still make more—it turned in 8.8% net profit margins last year, compared with the 5% recorded by other jewelry manufacturers—you need to examine everything the company does to produce its jewelry. It's not one big idea that allows it to pull off this pricing strategy. Rather, at each step along the way Jan Bell does at least one small thing that allows it to cut costs.

Begin your examination with how the company buys its raw materials. Not surprisingly, purchases are made in bulk, but it's important to note when and how those bulks are bought. For one thing, Jan Bell buys its gold, diamonds, and other precious stones direct from the source. There are no middlemen marking up the goods.

For another, it always pays cash. (Four public offerings, which have raised a total of $137 million, have helped there.) "If you don't ask your suppliers to be your banker, they're willing to shave somewhere between **3% and 5% off the purchase price,**" says company cofounder and cochairman Isaac Arguetty.

And unlike most other jewelry manufacturers, Jan Bell spends that cash throughout the year. Since most retailers buy jewelry in the fourth quarter—in anticipation of the holidays—manufacturers usually start to buy their raw material somewhere around August or September. "We're probably able to save 10% or 15% by being in the market year round," says cofounder and cochairman Alan H. Lipton.

But you can't buy early and still keep costs down if you're forced to carry a lot of inventory. So Jan Bell immediately converts its gold and diamonds into jewelry that will sell quickly—a gold chain that can be given at confirmations; a diamond bracelet that's perfect for just about every imaginable occasion. "We're going for tonnage," says Lipton. There are no one-of-a-kind $25,000 necklaces sitting in the company vault collecting dust—and carrying costs.

But Cartier, Tiffany, and their kith and kin *like* to display expensive and unique jewelry. So Jan Bell's decision to produce high-volume items limits its market. Some 80% of company revenues come from the likes of Sam's Wholesale Club and Pace Membership Warehouse.

Those places pride themselves on buying cheaply—since they, too, compete on price. To meet its customers' pricing requirements and still turn a profit, Jan Bell needs to have minimal overhead—and does. Selling and general and administrative expenses are 4.4% of revenues, less than half of what they were five years ago, and are probably among the lowest in the country.

To further help keep costs down, Jan Bell

EVERYDAY LOW PRICES
Here is the real way to create them

General Motors can't compete on price. Neither, it seems, can your local department store. Jan Bell Marketing Inc. can. Here's how:

■ **Price governs everything.** The decision to sell at the lowest possible cost controls every decision the company makes—from buying (in bulk) to advertising (it doesn't; it adds to costs) to the kinds of people it sells to (retailers who operate on low margins).

■ **Subcontract wherever possible.** The lower your fixed costs, the higher your margins can be. Jan Bell contracts out most of its assembly work.

■ **But know your costs.** Jan Bell doesn't contract out everything. It makes a representative sampling of its line. That way it knows what each item really costs, and exactly what contractors should charge.

■ **You can't get fancy.** If you are competing on price, you can't afford to have inventory sitting around. That means your line must be designed to move quickly. Leave the carefully aged filet mignon to somebody else; sell hamburger.

---

contracts out almost all of its assembly work. Almost, but not all. About 8% is done in house. "By doing some of the work ourselves, we know what it costs to produce the product," says Arguetty. "This way we know exactly what outside contractors should be charging us."

Jan Bell has no huge inventories or trucking fleets to maintain. The finished goods its contractors produce are logged in, inspected, and shipped out by Federal Express within 48 hours of their arrival, since production is based on anticipated sales to the price clubs. Should raw materials start stacking up, they're offered to other jewelry manufacturers—at cost plus 15%.

The result of the slavish devotion to price is a six-year-old company whose sales and earnings have increased steadily since its founding. In 1989 Jan Bell reported income of $16 million, up 55% on sales that rose 51%.

The question is how long can you keep turning out those results, especially when your strategy of being the lowest-cost supplier leaves little room for error. General Motors can afford to give $2,000 (or more) back on a $20,000 car that isn't moving. If you're working on tiny margins, you can't.

And with more and more retailers deciding to fight on battlefields other than price, Jan Bell's market—like that of any other company, retail or wholesale, that competes

on price—grows more limited by the day. Indeed, The Price Co. recently told Jan Bell it intends to reevaluate its jewelry business, and Costco Wholesale, another major customer, is looking to set up its own jewelry-buying division. To expand its market, Jan Bell now has turnkey retailing programs at Sears Outlet Division stores, Toys "R" Us, Kids "R" Us, and Staples.

In short, the gurus came close. Pricing is not, as they would have you believe, an impossible marketing strategy. Just a very tricky one. But Jan Bell's staggering growth in compound annual sales (65%) and earnings (86%) since 1984 shows it can be done—if you are totally committed to it.

As Retailers' Sales Crop Up Everywhere, Regulators Wonder if the Price Is Right

Teri Agins
Staff Reporter of The Wall Street Journal

It seems everything is on sale these days, and regulatory officials aren't buying it.

The number of sales and markdowns at retail stores has exploded in recent years, leaving consumers perplexed about pricing tactics and wondering whether they are really getting bargains. Responding to a rising tide of consumer complaints, regulators are closing in.

"The key issue is how do you go about judging whether a sale price has market validity," says Steven Cole, vice president of the Council of Better Business Bureaus. "Was [the regular price] a good faith price or a fictitious one set up just for the purpose of having a future sale?" The council has been meeting with a group of big retailers and attorneys general from six states to come up with new advertising standards.

One of the most closely watched regulatory changes is coming in Massachusetts. This May, the state will put into effect a law that regulators consider among the toughest to govern retailers on matters such as price comparison claims, price and quality disclosure, and the availability of merchandise advertised as marked down. Also under the rule, sales advertised in retail catalogs, which are printed months in advance, must disclose that the so-called original price is really only a reference price and not necessarily the actual former selling price.

Campeau Accelerates Trend

Sales have become more suspect simply because they're so commonplace. Once confined mostly to end-of-the season clearances, markdowns now are a year-round promotional tactic. The trend snowballed as competition intensified between department stores and off-price retailers, which have been gaining market share in recent years.

Markdowns seem to be occurring faster and faster. Last month, Spiegel Inc. mailed out its spring catalog filled with seasonal fashions, including a floral sundress "you'll wear long after dark." The price: $68. Just a couple of weeks later, Spiegel sent out another catalog featuring the very same floral sundress. The price: $54—on sale.

Many industry watchers considered this past Christmas season perhaps the most promotional ever. That's partly because of troubled Campeau Corp., which slashed prices at its department stores to generate cash, prompting other stores to follow suit. "Campeau was the catalyst and had other stores insecure enough to follow, which exaggerated that trend," says Bruce Missett, an analyst at Oppenheimer & Co. As a result, many analysts say stores are hurting their profit margins because they've gone so overboard with sales.

While shoppers bagged plenty of bargains during the holiday season, they were wary. "I caught almost all of my Christmas gifts on sale," says Martelle Shaw, a Long Island, N.Y., teacher who treated herself to a raccoon coat marked down 50%. But she was suspicious: "I don't really think all of those sales were for real."

There's also a feeling of frustration among consumers. "All the price cutting has made people anxious that they aren't getting the absolute best price," says Leo Shapiro, chairman of a retail consulting firm that interviewed 300 Chicago-area shoppers after Christmas. He says 82% of those shoppers believed they could probably have found even better deals "if they had just looked a little harder."

For their part, regulators aren't so sure all advertised bargains are such good deals. Last December, the New York state attorney general filed suit against Sears, Roebuck & Co., charging that the company's "everyday low price" strategy has created a "false impression" that Sears' prices represent significant discounts from former prices. Sears, which adopted the policy to try to kick the habit of constant sales, has denied the charges.

A similar lawsuit was filed by New York City's Department of Consumer Affairs against Newmark & Lewis Inc., a consumer electronics chain based in Hicksville, N.Y., that also adopted a so-called lower-pricing strategy last year. Newmark & Lewis has denied the charges that it engaged in deceptive advertising.

Last August, three St. Louis furniture stores agreed to pay $352,000 in restitution to consumers under settlements negotiated by the Missouri attorney general's office. The state alleged that the stores had boosted the manufacturer's suggested retail price when advertising their sale prices. Under the settlement, about 2,500 consumers were refunded, on average, about $150 each on furniture they had purchased earlier from the stores.

Industry watchers are anxiously awaiting the outcome of a suit that Colorado filed against May Department Stores Inc.'s May D&F unit. Among the allegations in that case, which is slated to go to trial in May, the Colorado attorney general charged that May D&F misled consumers on offering sale prices for a limited time only, when such prices are offered "continuously throughout most calendar periods." The state also alleged that May used preprinted price tags with inflated regular prices, which "deceptively convey the impression" that those prices were "genuine regular selling prices." A May spokesman declined to comment on the suit.

Determining value has gotten tougher

lately because stores are selling more private-label merchandise, often putting them on sale at 50% off or more. Even though a shirt with a store's own label looks like a great deal when marked down, the retailer still makes a healthy profit, says George Hechtman, a partner at McMillan & Doolittle, retail industry consultants. Unfortunately, private-label sales make comparison-shopping almost impossible. "With Liz Claiborne you know what it is worth by shopping at different stores," says Mr. Missett, the Oppenheimer analyst. "But with private-label merchandise you have no standard to judge by."

The same kind of problems can occur with discount stores specializing in electronic goods like stereos and VCRs. Their advertising dares customers to find lower prices on comparable merchandise, when in fact in some cases the goods were specially made for the store, so identical items don't exist elsewhere.

Some stores say they are backing off on sales as a marketing strategy. Dayton Hudson Corp. says that last year it cut storewide sales promotions by a third.

The Minneapolis-based chain says the move has allowed it to focus on selling its full-price merchandise. And Toys "R" Us Inc. says that because it constantly adjusts prices, it doesn't need to advertise sales to generate traffic.

But industry sources believe most retailers continue to play the markdown game because customers have come to expect discounts on everything. "Once you start doing this, you're on a treadmill," says Robert Buchanan, an analyst with Alex. Brown & Sons. "And I don't see how they're going to get off."

Manage by Walking Around—Outside

Peter Drucker

Mr. Drucker is a professor of social sciences at the Claremont Graduate School in California.

Everyone knows how fast technology is changing. Everyone knows about markets becoming global and about shifts in the work force and in demographics. But few people pay attention to changing distribution channels. Yet, how goods and services get to customers and where customers buy are changing fully as fast as technology, markets and demography. And they are changing fast all over the world.

The bulk of consumer electronics—radios, TVs, VCRs, calculators—were sold in Britain 15 years ago by thousands of independent, locally owned "mom-and-pop" shops. Today the bulk of these goods is sold by four national chains. The mom-and-pop shop had to carry major manufacturers' brands and relied on the manufacturers' advertising. The four big chains carry their own private brands and do their own advertising.

In the U.S. office furniture—chairs, desks, filing cabinets—was bought 15 years ago in specialized office-furniture stores. Increasingly these goods are now being bought in discount stores and "buying clubs."

The recent Japanese promise to repeal the law that protects their mom-and-pop shops and keeps out big stores and chains, has been hailed as a great American victory. But in Japan's metropolitan areas (where 60% of the population live and shop), a majority of the mom & pop shops have already been converted into franchises of huge chains such as 7/Eleven or Mister Donut.

Six or seven years ago, mutual funds were distributed in the U.S. through two channels: Indirectly, through brokerage houses and directly, through TV advertising. These two channels still carry something like three-fifths of all mutual funds sold. But one of the big mutual-fund groups (which six years ago sold exclusively through brokers) now sells 15% of its products through regional banks, 15% through insurance agencies and another 15% through professional and trade associations.

Independent Outsiders

The hospital became a major market only 25 years ago. But then the hospital itself bought the goods it used. Now a steadily growing share is bought by independent outsiders to whom the hospital contracts mainte-nance, patients' feeding, billing, physical therapy, the pharmacy, X-ray, the medical lab and so on.

Increasingly, even large users do not themselves buy their computers. They are bought instead by computer management firms that design, buy, install and run their clients' information systems. A major computer maker, Digital Equipment Corp., now has its own computer-management subsidiary.

Where customers buy is changing fast too.

Many major department store chains are in serious trouble. Some once great stores—Bonwit Teller, for instance, or B. Altman, only recently New York's fashion leaders—are going out of business. Others, such as Bloomingdale's, are in bankruptcy. But one chain, Seattle-based Nordstrom, has been doing well. The department stores that are in trouble are all organized and run as downtown stores with suburban branches. Nordstrom has only suburban stores. We may be seeing the first result of the slow but steady move of office work out of downtown and into the suburbs where the office workers live.

The big "wire houses," the New York-based stockbrokers such as Merrill Lynch and Shearson Lehman, did exceptionally well only a few years ago. Now they are losing sales and profits. But some large "regional" houses (i.e., brokers not headquartered in New York) such as A. G. Edwards in St. Louis, are doing fine. And so are some "institutional brokers" such as New York-based Sanford Bernstein.

The wire houses serve both the "retail customer"—the individual investor—and the "wholesale customer"—the pension funds. A. G. Edwards serves primarily the retail market, Sanford Bernstein exclusively the institutional market. Traditionally large stockbrokers were successful in serving both markets. But in no other line of business, do retail customers and wholesale customers shop in the same place. Are the securities markets now segmenting themselves the way every other market has?

Changes in distributive channels may not matter much to GNP and macro-economics. But they should be a major concern of every business and every industry. Yet they are very difficult to predict. What's worse: They do not show up in reports and statistics until they have gone very far. They are what statisticians call "changes at the margin." And by the time such changes become statistically significant, it is usually too late to adapt to them, let alone to exploit them as opportunities.

The one way to be abreast of them is to go out and look for these changes. Here again are a few examples:

Alfred P. Sloan built General Motors into the world's premier manufacturing company, in the '20s and '30s, by actually working with customers. Once every three months he would disappear from Detroit without telling any one where he was going. The next morning he would show up at a dealer's lot in Memphis or Albany, would introduce himself and would ask the dealer's permission to work as a salesman for a

---

Drucker on Management

Changes in distributive channels may not matter much to GNP and macro-economics. But they should be a major concern of every business and every industry.

---

couple of days or as an assistant service manager. During that week he would work like this in two more dealerships in two other cities. The following Monday he'd be back in Detroit, firing off memoranda on changing customer behavior and changing customer preferences, on dealer service and on company service to the dealer, on market trends and style trends.

GM in those years had the most up-to-date and comprehensive customer research in American industry. And yet—at least so I was told by the then head of customer research at GM—Sloan, by actually working in the field spotted more and more important trends than did customer research, and spotted them earlier.

The late Karl Bays made American Hospital Corp. the leader in its industry during the 1970s. He himself credited his success largely to his going out into the field. Twice a year he would take for two weeks each the place of a salesman on vacation. When the salesman came back, Bays said (with a twinkle in his eye) "the customer always complained about the incompetence of his replacement and about the dumb questions I asked." But selling, Bays said, was not the point of the exercise; learning was.

Another variant: two men who together took over a small and lackluster chain of fashion shops in the mid-'50s built it into one of America's retail giants. For 30 years, until their retirement, each spent every Saturday in a

---

different shopping mall. They did not visit their own stores. They spent the day in other companies' stores—some fashion stores, some book shops, some stores for household goods and so on, watching shoppers, watching sales people, chatting with store managers. And they insisted that every one of their senior executives do likewise, including the lawyer, the controller and the vice president for personnel.

As a result, the company foresaw in the early '60s the coming of the "youth culture" and built or re-modelled stores to attract teen-agers. A few years later, when every one talked of the "greening of America," the company realized that the youth culture was passe and changed merchandise and stores to attract the young adult. And another 10 years later, well before 1980, the company saw and understood the emergence of the two-earner family.

Dumb Questions

To be able to anticipate changes in distributive channels and in where customers buy (and how, which is equally important), one has to be in the marketplace, has to watch customers, and non-customers, has to ask "dumb questions." It is almost 40 years since I first advised executives to "walk around"—that is, to get out of their offices, visit and talk to their associates in the company. This was the right advice then; now it is the wrong thing to do, and a waste of the executive's scarcest resource, his time. For now we know how to build upward information into the organization. To depend on walking around actually may lull executives into a false sense of security; it may make them believe that they have information when all they have is what their subordinates wanted them to hear.

The right advice to executives now is to walk outside.

► STORY ◄
PROPOSAL

I wanted to write about a company—a *mail-order* company—that has become one of the fastest-growing businesses in America, with room in the margins to finance more than $100 million worth of growth. Its customer-service practices—reliability, courtesy, support—have set new industry standards. This stuff is so basic, the question we should be asking is why we *all* don't treat our customers this way.   —*R.A.M.*

REAL SERVICE

Can providing customer service as outstanding as PC Connection's really be this simple?

ROBERT A. MAMIS

Most up-country enterprises don't make unusual demands on rural utilities. Certainly Patricia Gallup and David Hall had no idea *theirs* was going to. Back in 1982 they meant only to get into something that would keep them ensconced in their tiny New Hampshire town, safely tucked away from the trappings of bona fide commerce. Mail order happened to fit the bill nicely.

Pretty soon, though, the ancient electric and telephone lines along the 20-mile stretch of road that meanders to PC Connection's facility in Marlow, N.H., had to be entirely redone, brittle wire by rickety pole. How else could the two founders hope to run the mighty IBM AS/400 computer and complex Rolm PBX that their micro and handset inadvertently had turned into? By the time the upgrading was finished, their original $8,000 investment had undergone a startling upgrade of its own: from sales of $233,000 in '82 to an estimated $120 million for '88.

No one grows 183% a year in mail order these days merely by slashing prices and waiting for the postman to knock (or, more accurately, for the phone to ring). Not when you're dealing with the fussy microcomputer crowd. Ask any of the scores of companies that went broke trying. If the odds were stacked heavily in favor of failure in

mail order, what did the winner have going that was different?

"Plain common sense," Gallup discloses, most of which came from the owners having been customers themselves. "Living up here, we *had* to buy through mail order. In the past, when mail-order customers got super rake-off prices, they expected to pay at the other end. We wanted to dispel people's fears about ordering over the phone, so we started right in offering a high level of customer support."

They succeeded. Now, their customers expect not only to be raked off, but to be granted such theretofore unlikely favors as prompt delivery, accurate order filling, honest billing, reasonable freight charges, seller-endorsed product reliability, current merchandise, generous warranties, promptly answered phones, deep inventory, knowledgeable salespeople, and aid when the thing doesn't work right. In other words, blandishments other companies try to avoid because there isn't enough room in 10%-over-cost pricing to pay for them.

To launch the nation's first mail-order business exclusively devoted to the then-six-months-old IBM personal computer, Gallup (who was 28) and Hall (who was 32) formed a customer-support staff of two: themselves. They dispensed pre-, during-, and post-sale information freely, and for

free. Any caller could ring up with any question at any time and get a courteous hearing. Today the staff is considerably larger and its largesse less revolutionary, but back then it was unheard of for *any* company in the microcomputer industry, let alone mail order, to accept an outside call for help without first screening for the serial number and date of purchase of the product. "A lot of the things we've done," Gallup's modesty allows, "have improved the quality of service."

Doling out intensive instruction about complex problems shrinks generically tight mail-order margins even tighter; after all, consumers don't pester customer service at Frederick's of Hollywood to find out how to use *its* goods. Yet it's standard policy at PC Connection Inc. (PCC, from here on) that for each product offered there is at least one person on staff who thoroughly understands how it works. If you own a spreadsheet program that is printing out smiley-face gibberish, just call PCC's toll-free line, and a trained person will troubleshoot the problem over the phone—even if you got the disks in a plain brown wrapper from some guy with a pushcart.

Doesn't that mean PCC may be handholding the buyer of a product that another reseller has already squeezed the profit out of? Sure—how else do you build volume?

As far as customer-affairs director Peter Haas is concerned, the best call to PCC is one that begins, "I bought this somewhere else, but ..." Concludes Haas: "We just made ourselves a new customer."

Being out among the lonesome pines as they are, you'd think PCC officers wouldn't be all that fussy about who handles the phones. On the contrary, they're so demanding that only one of every 30 applicants who makes it to the interview stage is offered a job. Only college graduates are considered for positions in sales to begin with, the theory being that at least they'll possess a modicum of communications skills and have an inkling of where the other 49 states are located. "We don't just fill a slot, we hire the right person," emphasizes personnel director Gallup, who checks out candidates' backgrounds as carefully as if they had been nominated for secretary of defense. Why such scrutiny? Because "they're creating customer contact."

There has to be something to the notion, judging from a recent poll undertaken by a leading microcomputer magazine in which PCC absolutely schneidered the competition. Among computer mail-order companies, PCC was rated tops in providing customer service, outpolling the next four contenders combined. PCC also handily won the reputation category, receiving 54% of the vote compared with a mere 19% for the runner-up, and it was uncontested in the three remaining categories: price, available stock, and variety.

Also in 1988, another microcomputer publication ranked PC Connection its number-one-read advertiser, well ahead of flossy, big-name spreads from Lotus Development, Ashton-Tate, NEC, and Toshiba. PCC intersperses typical product listings with corporate-image ads so slick that magazines that once relegated them to the back pages with the rest of the six-point-type crowd now give PCC run of the book. One reason the ads are so well read is that some actually are meant to be. Among the company's first was a double-page spread headlined: "If One More Person Asks Me a Question About Multifunction Boards, I'll Write an Ad." Somebody must have asked, because the text went on to detail answers to the most frequent technical queries the PCC staff got by phone. "It's the type of expenditure that comes back to you in sales," PCC's president and chief administrative officer Gallup says, "even if you can't measure it."

For all their pollable loyalty, though, mail shoppers are a fickle lot who don't bond with some impersonal logo simply out of past favors. To keep them ringing the switchboard at PCC (and at MacConnection, a division formed in 1984 to deal exclusively with Macintosh-oriented accessories) requires hands-on attentiveness beyond self-deprecating ads ("Only a five-day drive from Silicon Valley," reads another).

THE FOUNDERS		
	Patricia Gallup	David Hall
Age at founding	28	32
Hours worked per week, 1982	80+	80+
Hours worked per week, 1989	65+	65+
Percentage of company owned	50%	50%
Business function	President, personnel director	CEO, treasurer
Education	University of Connecticut	University of New Hampshire
Degree/major subject	B.A./ prehistorical anthropology	None/ chemical engineering
Home before moving to New Hampshire	Mansfield Center, Conn.	Amityville, N.Y.

Thus, in an age when mail merchants still abuse their customers by expecting them to wait six weeks for delivery (and nonetheless charging their credit cards immediately), CEO Hall spirits merchandise to his customers the next *day*.

Traditional mail-order operations selling traditional lines of goods don't approach PCC's turnaround time mostly because

When computer users want something, they want it fast. PCC is so swift that even if an order is phoned in as late as 7:59 p.m., the goods are on doorsteps as far away as California by next day's close.

they don't need to, Hall says. "Their customers don't expect to get products tomorrow. But when computer users order something, usually it's because they need it to solve immediate problems. Speed is what they expect." PCC's internal systems are so swift that even if an order is phoned into New Hampshire as late as 7:59 the night before, the goods are on doorsteps as far away as California by next day's close. Not at the double-digit price of some carrier's blue-ribbon treatment, either, but at a flat $3 for the entire order.

Yet even PCC's own in-house professionals had advised Hall it couldn't be done. No expert himself, of course Hall insisted it could. "A buck a pound the world around" became his rallying cry. He invited five next-day carriers—UPS, Federal Express, Emory, Purolator, and Airborne—to take a crack at it for a couple of weeks each. "They all laughed and said they couldn't even come close," Hall recalls. But when he described some schemes for cost reduc-

tion, "the price came into the realm of possibility, and they started getting psyched about it." When the dust settled, Airborne had gotten the contract.

In one step-saver, PCC packers cram the individual cartons into specially curved containers that conform to the inside of a cargo carrier, so they can be moved from the warehouse to the plane without further handling. Whatever spill-over can't be carried on Airborne's flight from Manchester, N.H., to its private hub in Ohio is trucked to Boston—a one-hour stint. When they get to Ohio, the packages are shipped the world around (though not yet for a buck a pound).

PC Connection's phone-handling course is so thorough that, to sharpen the conversational skills of new customer-service trainees, in one simulation session the instructor feigns foreign dialects in case a customer with a hard-to-understand accent dials in. The trainees also are exposed to other aspects of the mail-order trade during a four- to six-month apprenticeship, including two blue-collared weeks working in the warehouse picking and packing orders so that they will appreciate the potential for error when an order is entered incorrectly.

PCC's entry wages, which start in the low twenties, are competitive with those in Boston, 120 miles away—a factor that has helped keep turnover low. But, president and personnel director Patricia Gallup acknowledges, maintaining service standards has become more demanding than it was four years ago, especially in the competitive New England market. Because of the local labor crunch (unemployment in 1988 was 1.6%), activity on the PCC sales floor is nonstop, and burnout has become a genuine concern.

As a reward to salespeople who put in a lot of overtime during the normal 9:00 a.m. to 9:00 p.m. order-taking day, PCC dangles substantial gifts. Many of the incentive items, such as canoes and tools, are ordered from another renowned mail-order specialist, L. L. Bean, just up the road in the neighboring state of Maine. PC Connection—sometimes called the L. L. Bean of computers—purchased so much gear this year that Bean rang back warily, concerned that PCC might be thinking of going into competition.

PCC's computerized system compiles weight and destination information and transmits it directly to Airborne's computers. At the moment the truck leaves the warehouse in New Hampshire, Airborne's people in Ohio know exactly how much fuel to put in each of that night's planes. "We definitely set new standards of delivery," crows Hall, who, to make sure no potential savings had been overlooked, has calculated the cost of PCC's owning its own planes.

PCC constantly receives letters of amazed appreciation from customers who get merchandise faster from PCC than they could have from the corner computer store. A medical-equipment distributor in Pennsylvania wrote last winter that he had received an urgent request for intricate price proposals that had to arrive at a distant hospital convention by noon the next day. It seemed impossible, since Federal Express had already closed. A last hope for a stiff commission was to acquire a fax device for his Macintosh—but pronto. PCC's time-stamp shows that the order was received at 7:54 p.m. and that the plug-in board was packed and ready to be picked up at 9:07 p.m. The salesman's records show that he received said item at 9:00 the next morning and that he faxed the quote by 10:30. Total freight: $3. Exactly what Sears, Roebuck would have charged for express freight to Pennsylvania—in 1902.

But Hall, a formidable worrier, isn't resting easy. "Now that we've shown them how," he frets, "they can do it for the competition, too." To keep also-rans at bay, by the time they gear up to guarantee next-day delivery of an order phoned in by 8:00 p.m., Hall intends to have pushed his own deadline ahead to 9:00 and eventually to midnight. And now that the heavy-duty overhead wires are in, he is shooting for a one-ring answering response, followed by a one-minute order-taking interlude. "Once they decide they want something," Hall has determined, "no one likes to wait on the phone just to ask for it." (That's not entirely true. PCC's music-on-hold is so appealing that one customer whose serenade was interrupted by a live voice asked to be put back on hold until the piece was over.)

The ante may climb further still: PCC shells out extra for polystyrene packing "peanuts" that have been rendered static-free, so that they won't cling to the recipient on arrival. At that, fake goobers may not be good enough for the environmentalist in him: Hall is considering spending yet more for edible clusters of popcorn, which will be disposed of the way nature intended.

In the shallow trenches of deep discounting, it's daunting enough to pay for the likes of popcorn and peanuts while swallowing minuscule margins. But giving away a videocassette and at the same time amortizing its production is, to most minds, unthinkable. Yet a PCC-recorded cassette is what buyers of certain accessories are finding in

THE COMPANY	
Founded	February 1982
Primary line	Sells software and computer equipment by mail
Secondary line	Video production
Sales, 1982	$233,000
Sales, 1988	$120 million (estimated)
Six-year compound annual sales growth	183% (estimated)
No. of employees, 1988	210
Sales per employee, 1988	$571,000 (estimated)

shipments this year. The tapes document fussy procedures that, like fussy children, are meant to be seen, not heard. In a taped demonstration of how to install a hard-disk drive, a PCC tech-staffer spends 20 minutes mucking around in the bowels of a computer, yanking cables and screws with the relish of a butcher eviscerating a turkey.

"It wasn't a luxury, it was a necessity," insists Hall of the $2 million he's plowed into constructing a top-of-the-line television production and broadcast facility. Expensive, maybe, but when such costs are applied against the increasing massiveness of PCC's sales base they become manageable, Hall argues, not one to give a P&L unwarranted scrutiny if nothing's broken. Besides, he expects that not only will the output of the new division, PCTV, cut its parent's customer-relations costs, but it will generate income as well.

The arithmetic goes roughly like this: a $3-or-so instruction tape frees up perhaps 15 minutes for a $20-an-hour technical-support person, who otherwise would be hassled repeatedly on the phone with the same predictable questions. Balance: $2 in the company's favor, applied by a growing business to not having to put the next technical-support person on the payroll so soon. PCC will eventually broadcast via satellite, saving on the cost of videocassettes, and a good part of the company's internal apprenticeship and product training will be prepackaged on video, saving on teaching costs as well.

On at least one demonstration video so far, PCTV has sold part of the airtime to the manufacturer of the product involved, who uses it to talk up some of its other products, just like on commercial TV. Until recently, a vendor-reseller relationship as cozy as that was as unlikely as a Tyson-Givens wedding anniversary. Indeed, from its inception in the late '70s, computer-equipment mail order was well out of the mainstream, and manufacturers aimed to pin it there by refusing to let mail-order houses carry their wares, ostensibly on the grounds that sellers by mail couldn't provide aftermarket technical support. However, Hall observes, the moral high road didn't stop some manufacturers from stooping to buy stuff for themselves at discount. "Mail or-

der is sleazy," they would preach, and in an aside to PCC would add, "but can you give us a good price on a hard drive?"

How times—and the exigencies of the market—have changed. As late as 1987, Lotus Development deauthorized any dealer caught leeching out Lotus products to mail-order aspirants like Gallup and Hall. PCC wasn't fully authorized to carry Lotus products until early '89. (Previously, PCC had to get its Lotus products from gray-market dealers, who turned them over at a few dollars' profit.) By the end of '88, however, Lotus and PCC were chummily working out co-op advertising agreements.

Thanks in part to its indescribable buying power (PCC accounts for "several percentage points" of giant Microsoft's domestic software and peripheral equipment sales, Hall hints), the company has been able to pressure hard-nosed manufacturers such as Lotus to drop copy protection from their software and to ameliorate vendors' cruel insistence that goods be bought in quantity rather than as needed by merchants struggling to balance inventory against cash flow. And it was at PCC's not-too-subtle suggestion (any company that refused would be banned from its latest MacConnection catalog) that a considerable number of previously reluctant manufacturers were inspired to back their products with their own money-back, no-questions-asked guarantees.

But perhaps the best testament to the solidity of PCC's place on the mail-order map is that vendors now trek all the way to Marlow to peddle their lines. Gallup and Hall are preparing eight rooms in the inn for reps to bunk in—including any who may have spurned them in the past.

The reason PCC grew so fast with no outside investment, Hall claims demurely, is that "selling microcomputer peripherals was so easy it was like a black hole—you could throw any product in, and buyers would make it disappear." Yet other stars in the mail-order universe were favored by the same phenomenon, and *they* disappeared instead—this in an industry sector estimated to have grown from $1.5 billion in 1986 to $2 billion in 1989. Nor are any more competitors likely to crop up. When Gallup and Hall began in '82 with a ninth-of-a-page ad, a full page in a computer magazine cost but $1,000. Seven years later, in 1989, the same full-page ad costs $19,000, and PCC runs up to eight pages at a crack in several each month.

Despite its already giddy ascent, PCC could be climbing yet higher, given more space, time, and people. A couple of years ago PCC sold high-ticket computer systems as well as peripherals, and wasn't doing a bad job of it until—on a minor technicality—the FCC banned some PC clones, including PCC's house brand, from the market. Hall never bothered going back into CPUs, all else being equal. "But I could," he warns anyone watching anxiously for a downtick, "if things started to slow." That's not happening just yet, it seems. In February 1989 PCC broke ground for a 120,000-square-foot facility—the most significant industrial construction in Marlow since the sawmill in 1819.

Would-be competitors also must face up to the fact that not only do PCC's vendor contracts protect it from getting caught with a surplus of a product when an updated version is released, but it can buy a vendor's overstock advantageously because of its ability to jump into a volume deal with fast cash. When one manufacturer recently put a large quantity of a certain piece of software on the block at a bargain price, PCC plunked down several hundred thousand dollars for the entire lot, cornering an unbeatable retail price for months to come. And it earns the lowest fee schedules on credit-card charges, having driven the rate down by sheer sales volume. (Hall still stubbornly resists using American Ex-

press, because Amex still stubbornly resists lowering its rate.)

As formidable a volume shopper as PCC has come to be among manufacturers and distributors, its margin schedules do not necessarily dictate best buys for customers. Some intrepid competitors have tried to compete solely on price—an arena where PCC may be vulnerable—but without measurable success. (Indeed, two of PCC's staunchest competitors, both we'll-beat-any-price merchandisers, went under last year). That's because PCC's solid reputation turns its occasionally higher pricing structure into advantage. "There have been items we've gotten really good terms on," admits Gallup, "but we've never gone strictly on price; it's always because it's something we think people would want to use." For PCC repeaters, it's evidently worth a few more dollars now and again not to have to ask themselves after they get it, why was PCC selling *this* awful thing?

In lieu of rock-bottom prices, other thoughtful concessions are aimed at buyer fancies beyond the coffee mugs and pocketknives that PCC gives for customer con-

stancy. For one, Hall dislikes nickel-and-dime add-ons, such as mail order's hoary "handling" charge; not only does PCC not tack them on, but if someone telephones in an order for an item that is quickly found and easily shipped—a replacement knob, for instance—it's postaged and handled gratis.

PCC's payment to many of its vendors is one day net. Not because the company hadn't been discharging credit obligations, says Gallup, "but because it's good for us. Sometimes manufacturers can't keep up with demand for products, and we're making sure we're on the top of their list. We want them to ship to us right away because they know they're going to get their money right away." To accommodate customers should a product be out of stock for a short time, PCC writes the invoice at the current price. Should that price be lowered when the new lot comes in, policy dictates that the difference be automatically refunded. Even if the amount is as scant as a cent, the computer dutifully disgorges a check. "The bank thinks we're nuts," admits Hall, "but I see it as cheap advertising."

THE DELICATE BALANCE
Growing a company in a nongrowing town

For seven years now, PC Connection (PCC) has hired mostly within a 40-mile radius; therefore, few newcomers have moved in to strain the modest services of Marlow, N.H.

But you can't blame the populace for becoming a bit edgy. Who wouldn't, what with PCC's ground breaking for a $5-million commercial edifice that will centralize all its operations within the tiny municipality? To be sure, the company has pledged to make the building as unobtrusive as 120,000 square feet can be made, siting it well off the road, screening it with trees, and camouflaging it to blend with the bucolic background. Then again, when it comes to an aggressively expanding seven-year-old business versus an idyllic two-centuries-old town, guess which stands to lose.

In this case, though, PCC cofounders Patricia Gallup and David Hall have pledged themselves to planned growth. A hard-to-sell concept, perhaps, but one Marlovians can appreciate: history is repeating itself, and it wasn't that bad the first time around.

Indeed, PCC isn't the first enterprise to practice mail order in Marlow. For more than 70 years, starting in 1833, the Farley family posted printers' inks from the 155-year-old Victorian homestead that PCC now owns and is in the

process of restoring. Besides, reports Tracy Messer, the company's in-house historian, PCC isn't even Marlow's first high-tech endeavor. In the 1890s the Granite State Evaporator Co. introduced a sap boiler that stood maple sugaring on its ear. Adding in the then-active sawmill (also owned and rehabbed by PCC today), industry was so brisk in the eighteenth century that town officials tried to direct the region's proposed railroad line through Marlow, rather than see it squandered on a southerly track.

Again the road of commerce is leading to little Marlow (population: barely 600), and it will be bearing more vans and semis than ever. But there are quid pro quos. In 1988 PCC accounted for some 15% of Marlow's tax revenues, even though its employees have added only three students to the town's schools. (There have been 34 marriages involving PCC employees, so that statistic is apt to change.) PCC already has donated six computers to the school and another to town government, has repaired the crumbling dam outside its headquarters to create a swimming hole, has proposed building a baseball field, and is supporting a group of local musicians.

Not every benefit is as tangible: stirred by pride after Messer mounted a show of antique photographs documenting Mar-

low in the old days, townspeople began fixing up houses that had hardly been touched since. For its part, PCC features both the old photographs and old, real-life Marlovians in colorful ads that highlight the attractions of country living.

PCC has acquired an additional 100 acres on which it plans to build housing for employees, triggering concerns that Marlow may turn into macadam. "But we're not developers," protests PCC customer-affairs director Peter Haas, a former exurbanite who happens also to be chairman of the planning board of the next town. "The pattern to *really* worry about is a developer coming along, buying up a nice piece of farmland, and making a big profit selling three-acre lots to New Yorkers who can't believe how low the prices are. Then the developer takes off, leaving it to the community to cope with the demand for services." PC Connection, of course, is staying and helping. One way: each house the company builds is to be on an average of 10 acres of land, twice what the zoning requires.

Though PCC is growing at a furious pace, would it have become yet stronger in a more accessible locale? "Possibly," grants president Gallup. "But the main thing is, we want to live here, and the people who work for us want to live here, and that's why it has been worthwhile to have to overcome the obstacles."

A noncommissioned sales environment is another important ingredient of customer satisfaction. Hall has determined. As a retail shopper, he has been insulted once too often by computer-store clerks eschewing software shoppers in pursuit of the real money in hardware. Besides, in PCC's open setting, a salesperson on commission might be tempted to undercut another's overheard quotes. A strictly salaried force, on the other hand, is willing either to work patiently with callers or pass them on to specialists who can better help them. Sometimes customers themselves are attuned to the commission standard: "Shall I ask for you by name?" PCC salespeople often are asked. But when Hall considered assigning a permanent sales representative to each corporate account, invariably the customers answered: "That's not necessary, everyone is as good as everyone else."

Being noncommissioned, a salesperson's efficiency can't be pinned down through conventional methods, especially since the PCC staff is encouraged to lavish not-necessarily-productive time on callers. As a stand-in for sales-per-employee analyses, a supervisor roams the aisles listening in on sales approaches, and errant sellers are coached into better techniques. Gumshoeing may be rather distasteful, Hall admits; then again, the snooper is apt to pick up a tip from the snoopee, who may have developed a twist that everyone can share.

In furtherance of PCC's one-for-all attitude, Hall has set up an internal system of "spifs"—the trade term for cash premiums offered by vendors to retail salespeople for surpassing certain dollar volumes on given products. The idea is that if a salesperson knows there's a spif behind it, he or she will push that product over competing products. Hall, however, gathers the vendors' spifs into a blind pool, so salespeople won't be swayed by particular products. Sometimes, though, a spif is assigned to a specific set of products, such as when tax-preparation software began getting brisk play in February; Hall detected oh-no-not-another-tax-call grumblings from the sales floor, and

Thanks in part to PCC's buying power, hard-nosed manufacturers have dropped copy protection from their software and now back their products with their own guarantees.

soothed them by announcing a special spif for any tax program sold.

The effort to maintain service standards is far more demanding now than a few years back, Gallup acknowledges, if only because the pace of staffing is starting to slip behind PCC's torrid growth. In a chronically tight labor pool (in 1988 the unemployment rate in Cheshire County, N.H., was a meager 1.6%), PCC has been mounting recruitment programs that self-consciously extol the virtues of small-town isolation. "There are colder places to work than Marlow," one solicitation wryly points out, citing the Arctic and the Klondike as more challenging climes. In truth, Marlow's winter is apt to be nearly as rigorous, so PCC includes four studded snow tires and a set of icebreaker windshield wipers among its benefits. Another appealing notion, Gallup offers tentatively, is that at lunchtime you can grab a quick ski.

In case those perks don't do the trick, Gallup and Hall are casting a more potent lure: a 100-acre plot of farmland on which they plan to build 10 houses, liberally spaced to avoid a company-town look. The houses are to be partially financed by PCC and sold at a modest cost-plus increment to

employees who might otherwise not be able to afford their own.

Even after posting their first $100 million, PCC's two owners have yet to exhibit the familiar signs of fast-growth complacency that would place the next hundred million in jeopardy. "We never wait until we have a problem to come up with a solution," Gallup insists. "We come up with a solution before we have a problem." PCC has every returned product physically probed, for fear its reappearance may be signaling an about-to-widen headache. And Hall indefatigably reads every letter that comes in, lest he miss a hint of disaffection.

Especially evident problems, such as when Eastman Kodak suddenly downrated PCC in its supplier ratings, go right to customer-affairs director Haas. Getting to the bottom of this unacceptable turn of events, Haas rang up Kodak to find out what the problem was. You put packing slips *inside* your boxes, Kodak complained. "What's wrong with that—don't you have to open the box to get at what's inside?" the perplexed Haas asked. Well, our receiving dock looks like a freight terminal gone mad, Kodak explained, and we can't afford to have to slice open the box, burrow through the packing material to find the slip, get the PO number, close up the box, and hope it makes it to the end-user without disappearing altogether.

Hmm, Haas pondered, the same thing is probably irritating any number of customers, only they haven't mentioned it. Now, PCC packers stick corporate-account packing slips on the outside. "I enjoy calls like that," he cheerfully confides. "They're opportunities to make someone happy."

Couldn't PCC consider *not* making people so happy, and settle into the unhurried up-country rhythm its founders originally intended? No way. To stay competitive in the mail-order business these days, you have to hold the undivided attention of manufacturers, and there's only one way to do that: move a lot of product. And Gallup and Hall know there's only one way to do *that*. □

RETAIL REVOLUTION

Specialty Retailers Gain Ground On Mass Merchandisers

TOP 10 SPECIALTY CHAINS
SOURCE: STORES MAGAZINE, AUGUST 1987

	Type	(000,000) Sales	Total Units
1. The Limited	Apparel	$3,143	2,682
2. Mervyn's	Apparel	2,862	175
3. Radio Shack	Electronics	2,700	4795
4. Toys "R" Us	Toys	2,445	295
5. Marshall's	Apparel	1,410	261
6. Petrie Stores	Apparel	1,198	1,478
7. Circuit City	Electronics	1,011	87
8. T.J. Maxx	Apparel	1,010	226
9. Zales	Jewelry	939	1,216
10. Volume Shoe	Shoes	934	2,210

The incredible success of specialty stores like The Limited has given the retail industry a whole new twist.

Erika Kotite

Looking for something special? It seems most Americans are, judging from the tremendous success of specialty retailing over the last eight years. The shift from huge, multi-level department stores to smaller, streamlined stores with a closely defined inventory has been so rapid you could almost sit in a mall and *watch* it happen. And the trend doesn't stop with clothing—everything from toys to hardware, to products associated with a certain hobby or interest, is marketable as a specialty item.

Returning to the age of the small, select store may seem to be a regression after the convenience of department stores and the low prices at high-volume discount outlets, but the statistics quickly prove otherwise. Specialty clothing outlets have taken millions of dollars in sales from de-

partment stores in the last few years. And between 1982 and 1985, specialty store sales grew 60 percent faster than did department store sales. Just take a look at what's happening in the marketplace—giants like Ohrbach's and Gimbels have closed their doors, while specialty shops like The Limited and Banana Republic seem to open new stores every day.

One of the biggest factors contributing to this trend is, of course, the increasing number of working women. Shopping is no longer a leisurely process for the woman who works 40 hours a week. Now, she wants to enter a store, find what she wants quickly, and leave. A specialty store takes the "by guess and by gosh" out of shopping, so it saves most people a lot of time. Stores like Alcott & Andrews (upscale executive women's clothing

and casual wear), The Limited (all-American women's sportswear mixed with a splash of exotica), and Esprit (colorful mix-and-match clothing) are all good examples of how selling a narrower selection of *themed* clothing can bring the customers in droves.

Kurt Barnard, publisher of *Barnard's Retail Marketing Report* in New York City, cites another important reason for the success of specialty retailing. Just as children in the '40s and '50s practically grew up in department stores, children in the '80s identify themselves more closely with specialty stores. "Kids today are growing up with the specialty store 'habit,' if you will," he says. "They see these stores as a familiar part of the shopping environment as *the* place to go." Or, as a recent article in *Newsweek* put it, the age of

"McFashion" is in, and kids are drawn by smaller "express" stores the same way they're attracted to fast food.

Another reason for the success of specialty retailing is that it makes targeting customers easier. Large department stores are hampered by their enormous inventory needs and their tendency towards mass purchasing. "The department-store approach generally was that if you had enough merchandise, enough people will [eventually] buy it," says Dorothy Metcalfe, chairman of the merchandise marketing department at the Fashion Institute of Design and Merchandising in Los Angeles. "The marketing department [of department stores] used to consist of one or two people in the back of a freight elevator who did surveys once a year. Now, however, they have to really get into marketing as a [critical] function of business."

Specialty stores are structured around a deep merchandise selection instead of a wide one. "The line is very narrow, but the selection within that line is very great," explains Barnard. The time it takes for department stores to react to fashion changes is greater than that for smaller, specialized stores. And in the apparel industry, timing is everything.

Specialization has meant that entrepreneurs can start a business with a minimum of floor space and a more reasonable outlay of cash for their start-up inventory. In addition, since fewer types of items are stocked, larger volumes are purchased from the same supplier, thus possibly lowering costs. In other words, House of Almonds is going to buy a lot more wholesale chocolate-covered almonds than the local department store's candy department.

There's Good News and Bad News

The darker side of specialization is that sometimes, too much of a good thing is . . . well, not good. There *is* such a thing as overspecialization, and some retailers have succumbed to the temptation. Made giddy by the instant success of flavored popcorn, torn sweatshirts, or quickie auto repairs, many retailers learned the hard way that most fads die quickly, and they are left holding the bag.

For instance, take a look at The Gap. The store began in 1969, when Don Fisher saw a need for a place to find a good selection of Levis and other low-cost casual clothing. The concept worked well for over 10 years, until the early '80s, when competition increased and the demand for low-cost jeans, denim jackets, and sweats began to decrease. Sales slipped a little further every year.

The Gap's story does have a happy ending, however. The company undertook a major merchandising overhaul in 1985, replacing the store's previous denim-and-clearance-sale style with crayon-colored shetland sweaters, 100-percent-cotton T-shirts, and safari-style pants and jackets. In 1983, The Gap purchased Banana Republic, a khaki-dominated clothing company with a safari theme. Recently, the company started an upscale sportswear outlet called Hemisphere. All this averted the obsolescence that could have occurred if the corporation hadn't been aware of the changing marketplace.

The point here is that specialty store owners have to be more careful than most retailers to keep track of their customers' tastes.

What Works and What Doesn't?

What made Mrs. Field's Cookies a household word? Why is Benetton succeeding where so many others have failed? The answer is probably a combination of excellent market research, good timing, and good luck. According to Kurt Barnard, the secret is not so much the product as the packaging. "Generally speaking, we see people opening up stores with rather novel concepts," he says. "And it is not only the merchandise that makes the difference; it is how the store *presents* itself." In other words, you have to stand out to make it.

Another way a new concept in specialty retailing becomes a hit is simple—there is a need that is not being filled. Somebody comes along, tries to buy something that isn't available, and starts selling it themselves. Dorothy Metcalfe cites The Forgotten Woman as a perfect example. "[The founder] went to buy something and couldn't find it," she explains. "So she made a business out of [large-size women's apparel]."

Many stores are capitalizing on the appeal of novelties to attract customers. For example, Udderly Perfect, in Manhattan Beach, California, sells only cow paraphernalia; another shop in Massachusetts sells only purple products. There are successful teddy-bear stores, pipe and tobacco stores, left-handed stores, and pig novelty stores. Some of these are tested concepts; most, however, are the result of something the owner has always wanted to do. If you are an inveterate knitter, chances are you'll open up a yarn shop, not a hardware store. Just make sure that the area you locate in will support a yarn shop, and that there isn't too much competition.

You should also be aware of what businesses are hot right now. According to Barnard, houseware stores are doing very well. This includes closet organizer stores, pottery stores, and linen stores. Fancy food is also a big category. The proliferation of delicatessens and fresh-vegetable salad bars in the United States has led to an increase in gourmet, ethnic, and natural food stores. Specialty bakeries selling cookies, muffins, and cinnamon rolls are doing a brisk business. Women's apparel is a big specialty category, but it's also extremely competitive. You are up against the big guys mentioned earlier—The Gap, The Limited, Benetton, and others—all with established names, huge buying potential, and multi-million-dollar marketing budgets.

The apparel industry is far from saturated, however. It just takes a little innovation and good timing to succeed. A recent winning entry into the mainstream women's apparel industry is large-size women's clothing. There are 35 million American women who are size 14 and up in this country, and in 1986, they spent about $10 billion dollars on high-quality clothing. There is also room for more large-size lingerie and accessories. And the petite-size market, especially on the upscale end, hasn't yet been saturated.

A recent wave of mergers and acquisitions in the retail industry has affected specialty stores. The big chains are getting bigger and more powerful, swallowing up huge amounts of prime retail space and the market share. But in spite of this trend, Americans are still going into specialty retailing as independent operators, and making money at it.

THE (UN)MALLING
OF AMERICA

*The Great Shopping Mall Shakeout
of the 1990s is just beginning*

Francesca Turchiano

*Francesca Turchiano is president of In-
Fact, a consulting firm in New York City.*

Shopping centers are a mega-industry on the brink of a mega-decline. As many as 20 percent of the regional shopping centers now operating in the U.S. will close by 2000, and the declines will continue into the 21st century. The survivors will pay close attention to the expectations of their customers. The doomed will stick to business as usual.

Most of us grew up with the holy trinity of regional shopping centers, suburbs, and automobiles. A typical regional shopping center is an enclosed mall that contains 400,000 square feet or more of selling space and two department stores on 100 acres. It serves a market of at least 150,000 people. During the past decade, regional shopping centers have faced direct competition from many sources, including newer superregional malls that are triple their size.

A major shakeout among regional shopping centers could do more than release a lot of valuable real estate. Pension funds, insurance companies, and foreign investors have sunk billions of dollars into the industry, and they plan to multiply their present stake. *Institutional Investor* recently noted that $10 billion of pension fund money alone is allocated to real estate every year, and an estimated one-third of that goes into shopping centers. Moreover, almost 9 million people, or 8 percent of the U.S. labor force,

worked in 30,600 shopping centers in 1987. These centers generated $586 billion in sales, or 13 percent of the country's gross national product.

A convergence of controllable and uncontrollable events is causing profits to shrink in much of the shopping center industry. These events include the fragmentation of consumer markets, the high cost of removing asbestos from older malls, the shopping preferences of working women, the high cost of adequate security, the rise of first-rate catalog stores, the growing acceptance of electronic retailing, and the shortage of entry-level workers in most regions of the country. But the main causes of the coming contraction are these: marketing myopia, the department store debacle, an aging population, and shopping fatigue.

MARKETING MYOPIA

"Marketing myopia" is a term coined in a now-classic *Harvard Business Review* article by Theodore Levitt. It is easy to diagnose. Organizations suffering from it never make customers their first priority. Numbers drive these businesses. Rates of return, operating efficiencies, and profit margins take precedence over understanding and satisfying customers.

The physical evidence of marketing myopia is highly visible to most mall shoppers. It takes the form of poor housekeeping, confusing signs, stores

that appear too upscale or downscale, outdated mall directories, and too many redundant clothing stores. The cause of the problem is financially oriented owners and managers who do not bring marketing know-how to the management of their centers.

To compete and prosper in the retail environment of the 21st century, shopping center management groups must see each of their centers as a single superstore—an integrated entity that competes with all other channels of distribution. Each center needs to be designed, leased, and marketed in a way that its target audience will find compelling and its competitors will find hard to duplicate.

THE DEPARTMENT STORE DEBACLE

For decades, an anchor store was the big draw to the big mall. Many shoppers didn't know the name of the mall they were visiting, but they did know the name of the department store that was drawing them there. During the past decade, however, the foundations of many department stores have weakened. After a period of foreign ownership, chains like Bonwit Teller, Bloomingdale's, Saks Fifth Avenue, and Marshall Field are either bankrupt or for sale. Other department stores, like Macy's, face a draining debt repayment schedule. Still others have changed names and owners one or more times, confusing customers along the way. Two giants, Sears and Montgomery Ward, are entrenched as general merchants in an era that strongly favors specialists.

More important, many shoppers see department stores as stale and unexciting. Proprietary research, social trend research, and department store sales data all give evidence that the industry has not kept pace with changing consumer markets. In a quest to bolster profits, many department stores have stressed operating efficiency. They have cut back on sales help, store maintenance, effective merchandise displays, and other elements that contribute to a positive shopping experience. By choosing operating efficiency over marketing effectiveness, many department stores have given busy consumers good reason to shop elsewhere or to shop less. Shoppers' enjoyment of browsing has dropped during the past five years, according to the Roper Organization. Less browsing translates into less buying. The shakeout among department stores will continue, and it will cause a falling-domino effect across the shopping center industry.

AN AGING POPULATION

Every shopping center owner and manager should understand the growing impact of the older adult market and its economic power. People aged 50 and older control at least half of the nation's discretionary income. Yet few shopping centers know how to respond to an aging population.

Five intangible attributes are sure selling points to mature consumers: security, quality, comfort and convenience, socialization, and recognition, according to Donnelley Marketing's 1989 study of the mature market. Value is also an important motivator. With the exception of security, the intangible qualities sought by older adults are not easily found in a shopping center environment. For example, rest rooms are often difficult to find; mall seating is often sparse to deter

teens from loitering; mall directories are often out of date and printed in small type; and salespeople are often underpaid, undertrained, unfriendly, and impersonal. A tenant mix that is often weighted toward apparel and other merchandise aimed at younger women doesn't help either.

If regional shopping centers do not develop programs to attract and retain older shoppers, they can expect many more customers to defect to armchair shopping. Regional malls cannot take the older population for granted. Many of the 63 million adults who are now aged 50 or older will gravitate to the newer "power centers." These are unenclosed shopping centers anchored by "category killer" stores, such as Toys "R" Us, Circuit City, or Staples. "Category killers" carry an exhaustive supply of merchandise in specific categories. They act as magnets for many shoppers because they stress convenience, low prices, and depth of merchandise selection. Off-price centers, which stress branded goods at bargain prices in secure and friendly environments, will cut mall crowds even further.

SHOPPING FATIGUE

"Shop Till You Drop" was the motto of many consumers during the 1980s. It soon may be replaced by a very different one: "Fashion Free and Proud of It." This is currently the battle cry adopted by one small town whose residents are protesting a proposed new shopping center.

Research published by the *Wall Street Journal* last fall revealed that many Americans plan to curtail their acquisitiveness. Three-quarters of those surveyed said they had fulfilled most, if not all, of their material needs. The *Journal* called this attitude "shopping fatigue."

The majority of Americans may now want to clear their closets and shop for new experiences, not new merchandise. They're frustrated with high prices, mediocre quality, and the lack of cus-

tomer service. Shopping to them is an unpleasant chore. A labor shortage and a bifurcation in the work force add fuel to this negative attitude toward shopping. There are too few entry-level workers to fill the job slots at shopping centers, and a widening communication gap exists between the selling personnel and the buying public. Without serious sales training, these two trends will continue to translate into poor or no service at the store level.

Poor service may have been tolerated in the past, but it isn't now. Consumers feel pressed for time. They have many other shopping options, and they will bypass poorly run malls in favor of less stressful alternatives.

The best shopping centers will survive and prosper in the 1990s by providing their customers with the merchandise, services, and experiences they seek. In ethnically diverse markets, mall directories and signs will be multilingual. In markets with large older populations, directories will be in large type. In markets with significant Asian populations, more small-size apparel will be available. In markets with significant black populations, hair care, cosmetics, hosiery, and other lines of merchandise will be available in color assortments that make sense for that segment of the population. In family-oriented markets, a wide assortment of low-priced children's apparel will be available. In communities with many older people, a wide assortment of spoil-the-grandchild items will be available. The needs of shoppers, not financial managers, will dictate what businesses and services are available at the mall.

Shopping center owners and managers must make a commitment to understanding the people who live and work in each center's trade area. They need to divide the population into commercially meaningful segments and determine which groups to target. They then need to renovate, lease, and market the mall to capture a larger share of the expenditures made by their target groups. Tomorrow's survivors will market the mall as if it were one irresistible product.

Preparing For The New Consumer Era

REVAMPED RETAIL

GAYLE SATO

Gayle Sato is a writer in Manhattan Beach, California, who frequently writes on business topics.

You can still grab a healthy share of the $1.71 trillion retail industry, but not without some effort. Now more than ever, smarts count over the counter. The spending spree of the 1980s is over. Here come the '90s—and if current trends are any indication of what's to come, retailers are going to have to get smart to stay ahead of the game. Last year, retail sales posted the smallest gain in seven years, a measly 5 percent, according to the Department of Commerce.

Meanwhile, competition is keener. The buying bonanza of the last decade has left its mark. Consumers now have more places to spend their disposable income than ever: at scores of stores, on personal services, on vacations and travel, and through mail order catalogs—and that's just the beginning. Making yourself heard above the din can be difficult in today's business climate, especially with consumers touting a new philosophy of saving, not spending.

To capture a share of the more thoughtfully spent consumer dollar, the retailer of the '90s will have to be wily.

Though solutions are highly individual and trends are diverse, two overriding themes seem to be emerging. On the one hand, consumers demand convenience. They do not want to hop from place to place or stand in line for what seems like days just to make a simple purchase. On the other hand, they want to be romanced. They're looking for innovation, quality, ambience and that personal touch.

On both counts, the standards are high. And on both counts, savvy retailers are delivering just what the customers order. While it's too soon to tell what the '90s will bring, it is not too early to see how today's retailers are preparing for the decade to come. With that in mind, here's what's hot in the marketplace.

A MATTER OF CONVENIENCE

Convenience isn't a new issue in retailing, but it is more important than ever. Why? As a nation, we've learned to worship convenience. Witness the success of microwave dinners, maid services, and mail order. "With more and more women working, anything that makes shopping easier, faster, and more convenient is a plus," says Rosalind Wells, chief economist at the National Retail Federation.

Convenience starts with the basics. "Customers want to get in and out of a store quickly. They don't want to queue up behind 20 other people," says Joseph Carideo, retail partner at Thorndike Deland Associates, a New York City executive search firm. "If people can get what they want fast, they'll consider the shopping experience positive."

Beyond the basics, retailers have instituted all sorts of creative innovations—from delivery services to in-house personal shoppers to talking electronic scanners. Retail stores have come a long way in terms of convenience, but you haven't seen everything yet.

Convenience is forcing retailers to rethink old notions about competition. According to the old school of thought, small retailers avoided competitors like the plague. But Tustin, California, retailer West Allen did just the opposite when he opened Charter West Bedroom Centre last year. Charter West is located in a "power center," a shopping center that specializes in one type of store—in this case, home furnishings. Charter West shares quarters with a contemporary furniture warehouse, a water-bed shop, a clock shop, and about 10 other home-related businesses. The idea here is strength in numbers. People might not drive 20 miles to visit a single furniture showroom, but if they can see five different stores in just one trip . . .

"Power centers are meant to draw customers from a long distance," explains Allen. "This center draws people from 15 miles away or more. In the furniture business, that helps. If we were in the cleaning business, we could count on the same customers coming in every month. But how often do people buy furniture? A small neighborhood market isn't enough for us to draw our customers from."

Power centers are really just a variation of the old concept of clustering. Clustering occurs whenever similar businesses group together. The art galleries of Soho and the ethnic shops of San Francisco's Chinatown are two classic examples. Advocates of clustering predict that more and more businesses will flock to such centers, whether they're planned "power malls" or informal neighborhood groupings.

And old notions about separating yourself from competitors will give way to the new priority of convenience. "My competition [isn't just furniture retailers]; it's also the guy who's selling electronics or boats or vacation packages," argues Allen. "We're all trying to get a share of the consumer's dollar." If locating next to indirect competitors makes Charter West more convenient, Allen says, the benefits outweigh any potential drawbacks. "The retailers here are all in the same category, but they aren't selling the same things," he says. "I'm not going to sell to everyone, no matter what—I knew that going in. I just want my share."

PUTTING THEMSELVES IN THE MAIL

Allen is not alone in his search for new ways to play up the convenience factor. Yet his solution—finding a competitive location—doesn't work for everyone. Thirteen years ago, Cheri Faith Woodard and her husband, Martin, opened their own store, The Faith Mountain Co., in Sperryville, Virginia. They planned to sell herbs, dried flowers, and country wares to tourists from nearby Washington, DC. The site they found, an 18th-century house where "everything was

crooked," seemed an ideal showcase for their goods.

The problem was that their rural location wasn't as accessible as the average suburban mall. "Sperryville is a tourist town," explains Cheri, "so the retail business is really only good for six months out of the year. That wasn't enough to pay our bills."

The Woodards faced an exaggerated version of a problem many small retailers encounter. Shops that aren't located in the almighty mall must somehow accommodate a clientele that doesn't have time to run from shop to shop. They must also contend with the increasing threat of mail order, that epitome of convenience shopping. Service is usually the remedy. Some stores offer free delivery or shipping—extras that are easy enough to set up. The Woodards went a step further: They launched their own catalog in 1980.

Cheri admits that getting into mail order was a drastic measure, but she also says mail order and retailing complement each other well. "The catalog is a great advertising vehicle," she notes. "People are constantly coming into the store and saying, 'I was going through your catalog and decided I had to come by.'" Similarly, the retail store provides the opportunity to interact directly with customers and to liquidate merchandise that doesn't sell through the catalog.

Furthermore, mail order operations made it possible for Faith Mountain to survive. The companies 1989 sales are an estimated $4 million—largely due to their catalog business. "When we started the store, I thought I would just open my doors and people wouldn't be able to stay away, but it didn't work out that way," Cheri says. "We've had to make changes. If we didn't have the catalog, we wouldn't be in business."

THAT SOMETHING EXTRA

Starting a mail order business is not a requirement for every retailer. But showing the kind of verve the Woodards exhibited is. Successful retailing requires a willingness to go the extra mile to deliver something exceptional, something different, something inspiring. Sometimes, the answer is improving service, as the Woodards did. Other times, standing out is a subtler matter.

At Peet's Coffee & Tea in Berkeley, California, the focus is on the product. "As with most processed foodstuffs, the quality of coffee starts with the growing," explains Jerry Baldwin, Peet's principal owner. "Our sources are very highly developed; our green [unroasted] coffee buyer, Jim Reynolds, travels around the world checking out coffee. Our head coffee roaster has been with the company for 10 years, and we think he has a real talent for developing the flavor of the beans. We deliver to our stores at least three or four times a week, so you never get two-week-old coffee at Peet's. It's always fresh."

Admittedly, this is a lot of trouble to go through for plain old coffee. But then, this coffee is nothing like plain to the regulars at Peet's nine locations. On weekends, customers line up around the block at the original Berkeley shop, fighting with locals for parking and warding off the cold with sample cups of the daily brew. It has been this way ever since the day Alfred Peet opened his doors in 1966—even though specialty coffee was almost unheard of then, and even though it is available widely in supermarkets now. "People continue to come back," says Baldwin, "and it must be because our coffee tastes better. I can't imagine why else."

As competition heats up, such slavish devotion to individuality won't be an indulgence, but a necessity. If not with quality, tomorrow's retailers will set themselves apart with unusual lines of merchandise. For some, this means cultivating a particular focus—women's accessories, specialty neckties, designer socks, and space-saving storage devices are just a few of the new specialties vying for consumer attention.

A notable example is Units, a Dallas-based chain operation that sets conventional boutique shopping on its ear. Units manufactures and markets its own brand of women's clothing, designed to be simple, comfortable, and affordable. The interchangeable pieces are cut to fit a whopping 6-to-18 size range, and made mostly from a poly-cotton knit fabric that doesn't wrinkle or require dry cleaning. Units has 200 locations in the United States, Canada, Great Britain and Mexico.

And the easy-to-wear clothing line is a hit. "We're becoming a mainstay in people's closets," says Units media relations manager Cynthia Sutton. "Units has been very smart in responding to what customers want, and that's where retailing is going in the '90s."

SHOPPING AS AN EVENT

Finding exceptional products to sell is just part of the romancing process. Retail is by all means a practical pursuit, yet romance is also an issue. What do we mean by romance? Increasingly, American consumers want to be courted. They want retailers to surprise, entice and entertain them.

According to Joseph Coates, a future researcher at JF Coates Inc., in Washington, DC, shopping has become much more than an errand. "Shopping is not a physical exercise, but should be an intellectual, social and spiritual experience," he said in a recent address to the National Retail Federation. "That is the only way to neutralize the time-wasting elements of shopping. True, we shop in part to acquire something, but for many of us, the great appeal is something to do, a hobby or recreation."

Ah, the fun factor. It's why stores that make shopping an event have it all over catalogs and the home shopping networks. To understand this phenomenon, think of a Sharper Image store. You can buy most of their items through their catalog, yet the stores are almost always packed with curious customers. Anyone who's been there knows why: There are a million things to look at, pick up, and play with—and there is always something new. A good store appeals to the senses. It has the look, feel, smell, and sound of a good time.

Carideo warns retailers not to get carried away with theatrics ("If it doesn't produce sales, don't do it"), and of course, he's right. Yet even small touches can make a difference. Woodard keeps an herb garden next to her shop. "People from the city just love it," she says. "It's very idyllic." Peet's exudes an aroma that can be inhaled at a healthy distance. "Even if you hate coffee," asked one customer, "how can you resist the smell?"

This element of intrigue is a continuing project. "You have to be a smart enough merchandiser to keep your concept fresh," says Carideo. "Think about stores like The Limited or The Gap. They always look exciting, they never look drab. That is the heart of retail: always making the customer want to buy your products."

That isn't easy to do over the long haul. After four years in the retailing business, Units' greatest challenge is moving from novelty to staple. "We've gone from trying to show the uniqueness of the product to trying to adapt to the needs of our customers," says Sutton. The approach is aggressive: Customer requests for everything from business attire to print fabrics to pockets are immediately addressed. Customers appreciate the responsiveness; and although Units will not disclose exact sales figures, the company's sales continue to grow.

"We don't expect women to buy only Units clothing," Sutton says, "but we'd like them to keep thinking of our clothing as a part of their wardrobes."

GETTING IT ALL TOGETHER

So runs the story for today's retailers. Whether business is booming or in a slump, most hold out some hope that the '90s will be a prosperous decade.

Clearly, it will not be without challenges—both national and individual. For West Allen, 1989 wasn't a storybook year. "It was not a good time to start a furniture business," he admits. "The furniture industry had one of the slowest years that they had experienced in some time. We've been operating in a center that hasn't been fully developed, and the freeway outside the center has been under construction." All things considered, though, Allen feels he's on track now and projects 1990 revenues of over $1 million. "We're still here," he says. "We have a good idea where the business is going and how we're going to get there."

For those who have the resources and the smarts to pave their own way, retailing promises to be a good opportunity in the '90s. Though the standards for convenience and panache are high, retailing remains a simple option (that's simple, mind you, not easy). You buy goods and you sell them. "The business itself hasn't changed in centuries," says Peet's Baldwin. "It's the level of execution that matters."

Home Depot's Do-It-Yourself Powerhouse

Michael J. McCarthy

Staff Reporter of The Wall Street Journal

ATLANTA — When **Home Depot** Inc. opened its first home-improvement stores in the Northeast last year, it took the uncommon and expensive step of relocating dozens of people to head departments such as plumbing and paint.

Why bother to move hourly employees hundreds of miles to sell cans of paint? The company wanted the new stores to be headed by employees bred in the Home Depot culture, people who "bleed orange," a term of honor derived from store workers' orange aprons.

With a culture that stresses candor among employees and a commitment to service that transcends lip service, Home Depot has remodeled the more than $100 billion home-improvement industry and become one of the nation's fastest-growing retailers. In sales per square foot, an important measure of retail performance, Home Depot's $303 figure last year beat out the likes of **Sears, Roebuck & Co.**, **K mart Corp.** and **Wal-Mart Stores** Inc.

Enamored with such numbers, Wall Street has pushed up Home Depot's stock price about 77% this year—a jump that comes despite a cloudier industry outlook and regrouping efforts by competitors.

Spartan Warehouses

Home Depot has become the largest home-repair chain in the business by winning over customers first with broad selection and low prices. In each of its 126 stores in the South and on the East and West coasts, Home Depot sells more than 30,000 fix-it items, triple the number for typical hardware stores. In its spartan warehouses with ceiling rafters and concrete floors, the company has been able to slash costs, undercutting hardware stores by 20% and matching or beating its warehouse competitors.

More important, though, is the company's slavish attention to service, sometimes won by playing hardball with manufacturers. Using its volume-buying clout, Home Depot demands that the makers of products, such as certain light fixtures and gas grills, rewrite instructions it deems incomprehensible. It has strong-armed vendors into putting bar codes on such unwieldy items as plywood and wood dowels to speed up checkout lines. And it hires former electricians and tradespeople to ensure that shoppers get skilled advice.

"Trying to wed two conflicting strategies—low-cost structure with broad assortment and a high level of customer service—is arguably one of the most difficult retail concepts to pull off," says David Bolotsky, an analyst with Goldman, Sachs &

Co. "Home Depot is further along the learning curve than anyone else."

That curve, though, has had its share of rough spots. Five years ago, rapid expansion hurt the company. Stretched too thin, management was forced to curtail new-store openings and to sell off some properties after earnings took a dive. "That was a tremendous strain," concedes Bernard Marcus, Home Depot's 61-year-old chairman and chief executive officer.

Earnings have rebounded since then. In its year ended Jan. 28, Home Depot's net income jumped 46% to $112 million, or $1.42 a share, and sales climbed 38% to $2.76 billion, the most in the industry. With those numbers behind it, the company believes its current plan to triple in size to about 365 stores by 1995 is manageable.

Maybe. Sales in the home-improvement market are slowing. Partly as a result of a softer housing market, home-repair industry sales are expected to climb only 1% to 6% annually in the next five years, compared with the 7% to 15% surges in much of the 1980s, according to Management Horizons, a Price Waterhouse consulting unit that tracks the retail industry.

Competitors Imitate Success

In the meantime, Home Depot has forced some retailers to copy its warehouse format. K mart, for one, developed

Builders Square, a warehouse chain that has grown to 145 stores since the mid-1980s. But analysts believe Builders Square, despite having more stores, is weaker in service, selection and presentation of products.

Competitors also have begun playing on Home Depot's weaknesses. Some building-material chains, such as **Lowe's Cos.**, North Wilkesboro, N.C., are pursuing sales to small contractors, an important clientele that Home Depot recently has been trying to target more. Some smaller hardware chains have adopted a convenience-store orientation, eschewing discounts and selection while opening more stores to become more accessible to shoppers.

Still other stores, including Builders Square, are trying to steal sales from Home Depot by offering professional installation services for items such as gutters and roof shingles. This type of service, which Home Depot says it has begun to experiment with, is particularly well suited for a growing number of consumers termed buy-it-yourselfers. They purchase products such as kitchen cabinets for bargain prices at home centers, then hire someone to do the installation.

Founders' Openness

The stores that have had the most trouble responding to Home Depot are independent stores lacking strong roots in their

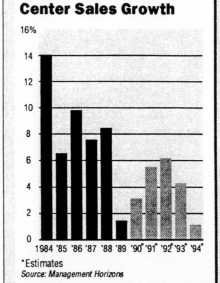

Fixing Up Home Sweet Home

Home-Improvement Center Sales Growth

[Bar chart showing home-improvement center sales growth from 1984 to '94. Y-axis ranges from 0 to 16%. Values decline from a peak of about 14% in 1984 to lower levels, with estimates ('90–'94) shown in lighter shading.]

*Estimates
Source: Management Horizons

Top Do-It-Yourself Projects

The percentages of 6,000 homeowners who completed the following projects in the past year.

Project	%
Interior Painting	25.0%
Exterior Painting	13.0
Wallpapering	13.0
Door/Window Replacement	12.0
Carpet Installation	11.4
Shelving	11.0
Floor/Ceiling Tile Installation	8.0
Roofing	7.0
Insulation	6.0
Patio/Deck Installation	6.0

Source: Home Improvement Research Institute

communities. "Right now, when Home Depot goes into an area, they just cut up and spit out the independents," says Walter Stoeppelwerth, a remodeling consultant in Bethesda, Md.

Much of Home Depot's success comes from the culture it's developed. Mr. Marcus and President Arthur Blank, the pair who founded the company in 1978, encourage a fierce competitiveness. At sales meetings, managers cheer cartoons of Homer, Home Depot's handyman mascot, visiting competitors in hospital beds and unplugging their life-support systems.

The founders also take pains to encourage a high level of candor in the company. Once each quarter, the executives answer impromptu questions from any of Home Depot's army of 20,000 employees in orange aprons on a live talk-and-rally session beamed by satellite to the stores.

At a February meeting, store managers got to poke fun at the company's merchandise buyers in a contest to pick the worst product of the year. Entries included an electric heater that wouldn't shut off, a ceiling fan that shook and hummed, and a flimsy paint tray that sagged when paint was poured into it.

The buyers weren't overly ashamed, though, because Home Depot puts a premium on experimentation. No adherent to the "if it ain't broke, don't fix it" philosophy, the company is constantly tinkering with its merchandise mix. Going beyond the faucets and cabinets that it already offers for kitchen remodeling, for example, the company has begun to test sales of refrigerators and stoves.

Home Depot also takes steps to prevent dilution of its culture. Store managers, who typically earn a $45,000 base salary, are never hired from outside. The highest entry-level position in the stores is assistant manager. Once the assistant learns the culture and proves he's adept at training others, he may advance to store manager. Mr. Marcus and Mr. Blank, who spend about 40% of their time visiting stores, are personally involved in training every manager—a practice likely to be strained by the company's rapid growth.

Training for store workers stresses taking care of customers first, then stocking shelves. That way, the stocking becomes the interruption, instead of the other way around. Sometimes, however, workers become so busy with shoppers that pallets of merchandise sit untended, blocking aisles—a problem that Mr. Marcus acknowledges. Among other things, the company is studying the use of special night crews to stock shelves.

Having highly trained, ready-to-serve salespeople helps Home Depot in its mission to give novice do-it-yourselfers the confidence to try increasingly complex and expensive projects. "Most of us aren't plumbers," says Leonard Berry, director of Texas A&M University's Retailing Studies Center. "Home Depot helps you through the mystery of home upkeep."

It did for Robert and Phyllis Witherington, bankers by day, home tinkerers by night. They were recently in a Home Depot in Kennesaw, Ga., outside Atlanta, buying some paint for their garage. Mr. Witherington mentioned to the paint salesman that his front porch steps were in disrepair. The salesman directed Mr. Witherington to a display with several types of concrete and pamphlets on concrete repair. Knowing they can find solid advice and the proper materials for projects, the Witheringtons are now planning a complex and costly job—expanding their deck.

What's Right, What's Wrong With Each Medium

Tom Eisenhart

Selecting the right media tools to promote your messages requires careful consideration of all the available options. Here's an evaluation of the strengths and weaknesses of media most commonly used by business marketers.

Note that the definition of media has been narrowed to include only "impersonal" forms of communication. Excluded are the more personalized communication tools such as telemarketing and trade shows.

Specialized Business Publications

Pros: Widely used by business marketers, specialized business publications are considered the most efficient way to meet both reach and frequency goals.

"Trade magazines are probably the most cost-effective way to reach customers—provided they are well targeted," says Donald Purtill, group communications director in Eaton Corp.'s Truck Components Division.

Because they cover vertical markets, marketers can pinpoint types of buyers and specifiers with little waste compared to most other media. Those readers usually have a greater identification and loyalty to magazines serving their market than general business magazines.

Specialized business publications also offer reader service options other media do not. Because of an increasing push toward rate negotiation, those magazines have stepped up their merchandising activities for advertisers. And specialized publications often provide special editorial editions or sections to improve the chances advertisers can direct their message to select readers. Annual directories, another advertising option, are often available.

Cons: Some marketers find specialized business publications' audiences are not narrow enough for the markets they want to reach. The problem is compounded because few of these magazines offer regional, industry or job function editions. So some advertisers turn to direct mail, for example, to reach more specific audiences.

Some business markets are flooded with publications. That can dilute advertisers' messages, making it difficult to build awareness.

Also, advertisers have long been concerned that advertising in specialized business publications had little or no effect on their sales or profits. Yet a 1987 study by the Advertising Research Foundation and the Association of Business Publishers indicated that more advertising means greater sales and can result in higher profits.

Technology is available to personalize ads, but few publications have added that capability because of cost. Magazines need a very sophisticated data base to be able to select certain readers for an advertiser's message.

Direct Mail

Pros: Direct mail's biggest asset is its ability to zero in on specific business audiences—by Standard Industrial Classification (SIC), job title, company size, zip code and other business demographics. "Direct mail can target a niche market much better than trade (publications)," says Eaton's Mr. Purtill.

Direct mail produces easily measured results such as leads or sales. And the medium is very flexible: Marketers can create packages of different sizes and quality—and mail those as frequently as desired. With new technology, the messages in those packages are personalized to the receiver.

Timeliness is another advantage of direct mail. Mailers can use it to introduce price changes and new products, for example. Direct mail also works well in tandem with other media such as print and broadcast. It can reinforce messages from those media while offering additional details.

Cons: When the costs of paper, printing, lists and postage are added, direct mail is more expensive than many other media. Mr. Purtill estimates that on average, it costs his division about $1 to reach each prospect via direct mail vs. about 15 cents per prospect in trade advertising.

A direct mail campaign also requires substantial—and carefully planned—lead time for production and mailing.

Clutter is another problem, reducing a mailing's impact. "We have engineers in our (targeted) industry who receive a ton of this," says Steven Ulett, advertising director at Penstock Inc., Sunnyvale, Calif. "They will take the time to read a technical article rather than reading a brochure." In other words, a prospect is more motivated to read a publication rather than a promotional mailing.

The huge increase in mail volume has created an additional drawback. Some companies now discard promo-

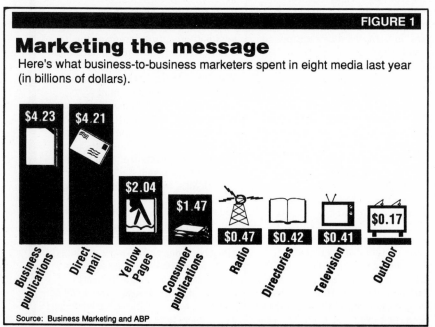

FIGURE 1

Marketing the message

Here's what business-to-business marketers spent in eight media last year (in billions of dollars).

$4.23 — Business publications
$4.21 — Direct mail
$2.04 — Yellow Pages
$1.47 — Consumer publications
$0.47 — Radio
$0.42 — Directories
$0.41 — Television
$0.17 — Outdoor

Source: Business Marketing and ABP

HOLLY SEGUINE

From *Business Marketing*, April 1990, pp. 40-41, 44-47. Reprinted by permission.

tional mail pieces before the mail reaches the recipient.

Directories

Pros: Industrial directories perform a "point-of-purchase" function. Buyers and specifiers see a company's ad at the point they're making a purchase decision or specifying a product. According to Thomas Register of American Manufacturers, New York, buyers initiate 97% of all industrial purchases; 54% regularly use buying guides and directories to select potential new sources.

Directories also have a long shelf life—company departments tend to pass along old directories to other departments, subsidiaries or companies when they purchase new ones. So advertisers' pass-along coverage and exposure expands as well. With the widespread use of microcomputers,

---

OEM Product: Awareness With a Media Blend

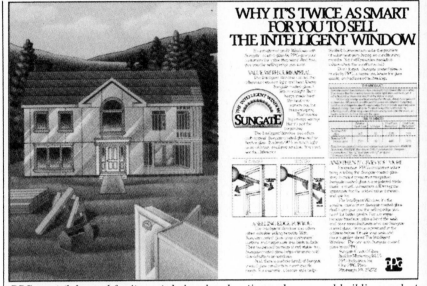

When PPG Industries Inc. introduced an energy-efficient coated glass for the construction industry in 1984, window manufacturers reacted cooly.

Despite its benefits over conventional glass, window makers and glass unit insulators hesitated carrying the product because of weak end-user demand. Specially coated glass, such as PPG's Sungate, was new to the industry.

PPG's solution? Create demand by educating end-users through print advertisements. And at the same time build product awareness among manufacturers, distributors and builders through a combination of print ads and direct mail.

"The pull-through strategy worked best for our (manufacturing) customers," says Christopher W. Umble, director of marketing communications for PPG's glass group.

The glass group, which produces Sungate, accounted for about 40% of PPG's 1989 sales of $5.7 billion. The Pittsburgh-based company also makes coatings and resins, chemicals and medical electronic instruments.

To educate end-users, PPG ran ads in consumer magazines, such as *Reader's Digest* and *Better Homes & Gardens*. In addition to describing product benefits, some ads encouraged end-users to check out Sungate at their local distributors. If a distributor agreed to display Sungate point-of-purchase materials, PPG listed its name, address and phone number in regionally targeted ads.

"When end-users went to their distributors they would see the same material and graphics, and see the link between" the ad and the point-of-purchase display, Mr. Umble says. "It gave distributors a selling tool and an education."

At the same time, PPG advertised in specialized business magazines to create awareness among manufacturers, as well as builders and remodelers who have direct contact with end-users. Ads geared

PPG created demand for its coated glass by educating end-users and building product awareness among manufacturers, distributors and builders.

toward builders and remodelers mentioned how PPG was trying to promote Sungate to end-users. Those ads also encouraged builders and remodelers to find out more about Sungate from their distributors.

In addition, PPG used videotapes to promote Sungate to builders. Builders, in turn, used those tapes to sell to end-users.

PPG also used direct mail to reach manufacturers, builders and remodelers. Those campaigns complemented the company's print ads. For example, direct mail pieces aimed at manufacturers promoted product benefits. Those geared toward builders and remodelers promoted the value-added aspect of Sungate windows for their customers—the end-users.

As end-user demand grew, PPG altered its advertising programs. In some large markets, local newspaper ads listing distributors replaced regional consumer magazine ads. Eventually, those ads listed only a toll-free phone number that end-users could call to get a list of distributors in their area, or to request product information.

"As the product grew in acceptance, listing thousands of distributors became burdensome," Mr. Umble says. "There were too many distributors to afford dealer-listing advertising."

Now, PPG's current advertising goal is to generate inquiries for its manufacturing customers, such as Century Windows and Wenco Windows. It has dropped its print advertising and direct mail campaigns aimed at manufacturers, and replaced them with a cooperative advertising program. However, PPG continues to advertise in specialized business magazines to reach builders and remodelers, and consumer magazines to reach end-users.

And PPG plans to drop its pull-through advertising strategy altogether once specially coated glass becomes an industry standard.

"At some point end-users will have trouble buying a window that isn't coated," Mr. Umble says. "There will be no reason to do pull-through advertising if consumers have no option."

some directories are now conveniently available on-line or on diskette.

Cons: Deciding which directory in which to place ads is difficult because thousands are produced in North America. "There are a lot of suspect directories," says William Loos, sales manager at wire and cable maker Loos and Co., Pomfret, Conn. He says certain directories in some industries are respected and well-known. But he explains that because it's so easy to become a directory publisher, new ones pop up all the time.

Because they're consulted only when a specifier or buyer makes a decision, directories can't build awareness. Also, the cost is high to advertise in some large directories because they are divided into so many sections that multiple ad placements usually must be made.

Yellow Pages Directories

Pros: The Yellow Pages is a "directional medium." Marketers who advertise in them reach people when they are ready to buy. "We perceive the Yellow Pages as a retail store where people find us," says William Hudson, director of marketing for Ryder Truck Rental Inc., Miami.

And because the directories are so popular, many marketers consider the directories a "must buy." In some business markets, prospects use the Yellow Pages to narrow their choice of vendors.

By placing cooperative ads with dealers and distributors, marketers can stretch their marketing dollars.

Cons: Since the Regional Bell Operating Companies no longer have a monopoly over Yellow Pages, the number of directories has proliferated. That makes advertisers' choices more difficult and dilutes the effectiveness of their ads. Magnifying the problem is a lack of circulation audits among directories. For example, the Business Publications Audit of Circulation Inc., a major Yellow Pages auditor, reported last year that it lost 57% of its Yellow Pages publisher members in the previous year. Only 49 Yellow Pages publishers, representing about 85 directories, are now BPA members.

Because directories require ad materials well in advance, advertisers are limited as to the type of information they can put in ads. "You are committed for a year-and-a-half" once the directory is printed, says Jean Coppenbardger, manager of corporate communications for MobilComm, a paging company in Ridgeland, Miss.

General Business Publications

Pros: These publications, including *BusinessWeek*, *Forbes*, *Fortune* and *Industry Week*, offer advertisers a broad reach of readers in middle- to top-management positions. Their frequency provides flexibility to generate awareness and to keep campaigns timely.

"It's a good environment . . . well suited for any corporate message," says Earl Medintz, VP-associate media director at Campbell-Mithun-Esty, Minneapolis.

With some general business magazines, marketers can zero in on certain types of managers. For example, *Inc.* and *Entrepreneur* are aimed at small-business owners.

Cons: On a cost per thousand basis, general business magazines' usefulness is generally limited to corporate advertisers and companies in the tele-

---

Business Consumable: 3M Prefers Print

At 3M Co., nothing beats the printed word for advertising computer flexible diskettes.

Because floppy disks are purchased frequently, St. Paul, Minn.-based 3M uses a variety of print media to reach its two primary audiences: distributors and end-users.

"Print seems to be the best environment for our ads," says James W. Roepke, marketing communications manager for 3M's memory technologies group. "It's a cost-effective way to reach our customers often."

3M sells most of its floppy disks through distributors, such as computer retail stores and office supply stores. It also sells a few through discount retail chains, such as K mart.

Floppy disks are sold through 3M's memory technologies group, one of the company's largest business units. Its best-sellers: 3.5-inch and 5.25-inch diskettes.

To reach distributors, 3M uses specialized business magazines, such as *Office Products Dealer*. By promoting product benefits, 3M hopes to persuade dealers to carry its diskettes. As an added incentive, a cooperative Yellow Pages ad program lists authorized distributors.

At the same time, ads in other publications attempt to drum up end-user demand. For example, 3M advertises in specialized computer magazines, such as *Personal Computing*, to reach what it calls "power users"—educated business computer users. And it occasionally advertises in general business

3M's end-user ads convey a 'high-performance message.' To tie in with the 1988 Olympics, 3M showed 'winners' from its own arena—the laboratory.

magazines, such as *Fortune* and *BusinessWeek*, to promote its brand name to corporate managers and "predispose them to 3M products," Mr. Roepke says.

In general, end-user ads convey a "high-performance message," Mr. Roepke adds. "The ads tell users how they can perform better with 3M products."

For timely messages or new product introductions, 3M often turns to *The Wall Street Journal*. To tie in with the 1988 Olympics, 3M ran ads in the *Journal* that showed "winners" from its own arena—the laboratory.

"We wanted to show the quality of people behind our products," Mr. Roepke says. "It gave us a lot of impressions quickly."

communications, office equipment, computer, air freight and other service industries. Other marketers might find that specialized business publications reach decision-makers more efficiently.

The growing popularity of business magazines and the corresponding increase in advertising volume has created problems for marketers trying to break through the clutter.

Mr. Medintz notes their reach is limited; the publications aren't necessarily "must reads" for plant managers, MIS directors or other functional department heads.

Regional Business Publications

Pros: Unlike metropolitan newspapers, regional business publications deliver a narrower band of readers specifically interested in business subjects. Those readers are primarily in top- and middle-management or professional positions who make corporate purchasing decisions.

Also, these publications frequently contain sections focusing on specialized subjects, such as telecommunications, which allow marketers to reach prospects in certain industries. National companies find regional publications a good environment for cooperative advertising with dealers and distributors.

Cons: For marketers who need extended reach, regional publications may not offer large enough circulations. Because they tend to be published weekly or less frequently, advertisers who need to generate greater awareness may need newspaper advertising's greater frequency.

Regional publications, like general business publications, also lack breakouts by industry or job function, for example. "(They) reach the business community, but don't target any specific markets," says Lynda Rudge, sales manager for Midco Inc., a Chicago-based telecommunications company.

Card Decks

Pros: Card deck producers and many specialized business publications offer card decks and card booklets, a more recent innovation. The decks are an inexpensive and quick way to generate sales or leads. Like other direct response media, they also allow marketers to precisely measure what a sale or lead costs.

Unlike a solo direct mailing, advertising in a card deck is inexpensive because advertisers share postage, printing, list and administrative costs. The typical 3½-inch x 5½-inch postcards take little time or money to produce. Card decks also offer split runs —an inexpensive way to test different creative messages.

Cons: Readers flipping through card decks spend little time reviewing each card. With 15 square inches to work with, postcards leave little room for graphics, copy, offer, order form and reply vehicle. Typically, decks are not used for complex or big-ticket products and services.

Another problem is that some card deck lists aren't that specific. Gordon Savoie, chairman of Skyline Displays Inc., St. Paul, Minn., says his firm can

---

Services: Image in Print and Media

Jupiter Realty Services Inc. uses a mixture of print advertising and direct mail to build its corporate image, as well as its business.

The 3-year-old firm manages various real estate properties, such as office buildings and shopping centers, and provides brokerage services for office, retail and industrial use. Chicago-based Jupiter conducts business in several states outside Illinois, including Wisconsin, Michigan, Texas, California and Florida. The company sells its services to clients through a direct sales force.

Jupiter initially attempted to build its corporate identity by advertising in regional business magazines, such as *Crain's Chicago Business*, BUSINESS MARKETING's sister publication. At the same time, it advertised in specialized business publications—such as *National Real Estate Investor*—to promote its services to real estate owners. Jupiter also occasionally zeroes in on specific client segments by advertising in specialized local papers, such as the *Law Bulletin*.

As business has grown, Jupiter has started to rely more heavily on direct mail to zero in on specific customer groups. Most direct mail

The Issue is Trust

You have thousands of real estate brokers or asset managers from whom to choose. Many are experienced. However, the key element in selecting a real estate professional is trust.

Jupiter Realty Services shares with its clients an incomparable depth of experience in brokerage, property and asset management, and development for office, retail and industrial use.

JUPITER REALTY SERVICES, INC.
Chicago/Dallas/Detroit/Los Angeles
919 North Michigan Avenue, Suite 2000
Chicago, Illinois 60611   312. 944. 2800

Jupiter built its corporate identity by advertising in regional business magazines.

campaigns promote the company's successful building projects. For example, if Jupiter relocates a law firm, it promotes that fact to other lawyers through direct mail.

To reach other customer groups, Jupiter has put together several direct mail campaigns featuring articles it has placed in various specialized business publications. An article submitted to *Managers* magazine became a direct mail piece for insurance agency managers. A story in *Real Estate Finance Journal* was sent to institutional investors and developers.

Some of Jupiter's direct mail campaigns include videotapes describing the features and benefits of certain properties. For example, a videotape describing a major office building in downtown Chicago was sent to select prospects.

To back up its direct mail campaigns and print ads, Jupiter advertises in local Yellow Pages and uses a form of outdoor advertising. Whenever it manages or leases space in a building, it installs an outdoor sign promoting its services to passers-by. "You never know where you're going to reach somebody," says Jeff Schomisch, Jupiter's executive vice president.

reach more specific audiences with direct mail than with card decks or in-flight magazines. Other marketers believe that clutter in decks has become a bigger nuisance.

Newspapers

Pros: Because of their frequency and variety of ad space formats available, advertisers can include numerous details on product and services in newspaper advertising. In many cases, daily newspapers offer national advertisers an excellent opportunity to run cooperative advertisements with dealers or distributors. Also, some newspapers offer zoned editions that allow business marketers to zero in on certain locales.

Financial newspapers, such as *The Wall Street Journal* and *Barron's*, reach the financial community and top corporate executives. Those newspapers typically provide a good editorial environment for corporate advertising and investor relation campaigns.

Cons: In many large cities, circulation of daily newspapers has decreased, while the cost of advertising has increased, forcing marketers to pay a steadily rising cost per thousand. The higher costs are an especially acute problem for business marketers, who are already paying for a great deal of wasted circulation. As metropolitan dailies have folded, marketers have fewer options.

It's also difficult to achieve ad dominance in newspapers. "To (create) an attractive, eye-catching ad and be in consistently, the cost is prohibitive," says Robert Bembenek, director of sales and marketing for Active Homes Corp., a Marlette, Mich., manufacturer of modular homes.

In addition, people now spend less time with newspapers, meaning marketers may be getting less frequency and reach than they paid for.

Advertising in financial newspapers, such as general business publications, is often only practical for the largest national advertisers. The lack of color in those newspapers also limits creativity.

Outdoor

Pros: A truly local medium, outdoor is effective for marketers trying to reach audiences on a geographic basis. Its constant presence, larger-than-life size, colorful graphics and simplicity let advertisers create impact with their messages. That en-

hances top-of-mind awareness and builds name recognition.

A fast-growing branch of outdoor advertising, called "out-of-home advertising" gives business marketers more options for planning ads. Those locations—including buses, trains, airports and phone booths—can reach hard-to-get business travelers. Some business marketers find that out-of-home ads in key locations during trade shows are an effective way to attract attention to their booths.

Cons: Besides generating awareness, outdoor's use is limited. "You can't put much on outdoor. You only have a few seconds" to make an impression, says Maury Eikner, media director at Good Advertising Inc., Memphis, Tenn. So the medium doesn't work for marketers who need to explain complicated product or service benefits.

For many business marketers, outdoor probably isn't as focused as other media.

Radio

Pros: A local medium like outdoor, radio provides good reach for business marketers, especially during morning and evening drive time. Because radio is often the first source of news for people, advertisers can schedule their messages around the business news updates.

At the office, 61% of adults have a radio and 53% of those listen to it while they work, according to a survey conducted for the Radio Advertising Bureau, New York. So marketers can also boost the frequency of their message during the business day.

Because radio stations select a certain programming format, such as news or adult contemporary, listeners tend to be loyal to a few stations. Marketers can narrow their choices to stations that appeal to middle- or upper-management-type prospects. And as a sound-only medium, advertisers can use creative approaches to capture listeners' imaginations. Advertisers can also make last-minute copy changes.

Cons: For many business marketers, radio is too expensive. "You're paying for a lot of people you don't want," says Barbara Thompson, media supervisor at DDB Needham Worldwide Inc., Los Angeles. She adds that radio stations offer little audience information.

Besides drive time, it's difficult to get reach and frequency any other time of day. Because radio is a background medium, listeners aren't fo-

cused on the messages. Ms. Thompson also notes, "You can't do a lot of copy points. You only have 60 seconds."

Television

Pros: Television is a reach medium, useful for building awareness quickly. It's also a powerful medium, with its unequaled combination of sight, sound, motion and emotion. Frequently, TV is most often used for corporate image building or generating awareness of office equipment, microcomputers and business services.

With the arrival of cable TV, marketers have found that certain financial, news and sports programs are attractive environments and efficient media buys, compared to more expensive network TV. To keep costs down and extend reach, some marketers buy a cable schedule and then buy spots from local network affiliates.

Cons: Expense and wasted viewership are TV's two biggest drawbacks. "The cost of time and commercial production continues to escalate," says Norman Brust, VP-corporate advertising at Contel Inc., Atlanta. "If you use TV, you'd better expect a 10% to 15% inflation rate."

"TV is never going to sell you anything," adds Robert E. Lee, senior VP-marketing and communications at Konica Business Machines USA Inc., Windsor, Conn. "We use it to create awareness."

Consumer Magazines

Pros: Generally, consumer magazines are favored by business marketers in the office equipment, computer and business services industries to raise awareness. Some companies also place corporate ad campaigns in those publications to build their images. In either case, consumer magazines can help achieve broad reach among upscale readers who populate middle- and upper-management positions.

They tend to be less cluttered with ads from business-to-business companies—unlike general and specialized business publications. To narrow their scope, some consumer magazines offer business and regional editions.

Beyond those strengths, ads in general magazines catch readers in a different frame of mind, according to Edward C. MacEwen, vice president of corporate communications at GTE Corp., Stamford, Conn. "Their mindset is different than (it would be) in reading business publications," he says, explaining why GTE selects magazines such as *Smithsonian* for its corporate campaign.

Cons: Considering circulation waste, consumer magazines are very expensive. Beyond a narrow range of products and companies, the costs are too great for most marketers. Also, marketers complain that clutter from other advertisers dilutes their messages.

Diskette Ads

Pros: One of the newest media forms, diskette ads are a novel variation on direct mail brochures. Because they are so new, they generate higher response rates than typical mailings.

Diskette ad mailings get a better response because they are interactive; typically, an advertiser includes capabilities that lets recipients design product configurations or perform a cost-benefit analysis. "It forces you to become interactive with the advertising," says Scott Silk, director of marketing-alternative channels at Unisys Corp., Blue Bell, Pa. He adds that while it's more expensive to produce the diskette, that's offset by not having to pay for the printing expense of a brochure.

Cons: This medium is only effective for groups such as MIS directors and telecommunications managers that frequently use microcomputers. Also, marketers have to know what diskette format their prospects or customers use. Mr. Silk says that as more companies produce the diskette the novelty has begun to wear off, resulting in lower response rates.

Is the Mix Balanced Just Right?

Every advertiser should tailor his or her media mix to the unique needs of the product or service they're selling. Customer behavior, promotion timing, market and distribution structure, competitive activity, cost and, of course, the campaign's objectives, are leading factors affecting media choices.

For example, business marketers often don't take competitive advertising weight into account. They should, particularly when advertising is a critical factor to a product or service success.

In consumer package goods markets where advertising can be the most important marketing tool, for instance, advertisers frequently measure their "share of voice" alongside their share of market, the "voice" being total category ad spending.

A voice share significantly different from a market share suggests that other elements such as ad creativity or distribution strength heavily influence market activity as well. Some business markets operate much like package goods, making comparative ad spending an important planning consideration.

Regardless of the relative importance of advertising in the marketing mix, advertisers should evaluate their media campaigns with all external and internal influencing factors in mind.

Checklist Help

Among the many checklists experts have developed over the years is the 18 criteria offered by James Morris-Lee. He provides a useful starting point for tailoring a media mix. (Mr. Morris-Lee, a partner at the Pennington, N.J., marketing communications firm of Morris-Lee & Tilden Inc., published his list in BUSINESS MARKETING, August 1987.)

1. Cost per thousand (CPM): Direct mail has a high CPM, while fractional-page space ads and direct response cards have a lower cost per thousand.

2. Total cost: Four-color literature and trade show space, exhibit, travel entertainment, meals and lodging generally represent significant expenses in a marketing communications budget.

3. Length of message: Of all media, direct mail comes closest to approximating the length of message of a personal sales call.

4. Completeness of message: Here too, direct mail has a decided advantage in telling the whole story about a product or service.

5. Life of message: The high retention value of some kinds of sales literature gives it a longevity advantage. Some media provide messages that will be referred to often or sit in files for years.

6. Degree of follow-up needed: Trade show inquiries, for example, require a greater degree of follow-up than other leads because of the high cost of acquiring them, and because of generally casual, on-the-spot prospect qualification that occurs at a show.

7. Repetitiveness: Space advertising usually requires a great deal of repetition to ensure that you've reached the principal target market enough times for your message to have an effect.

8. Targetability: Direct mail has an advantage because of its ability to single out only those prospects we wish to receive the message.

9. Dispersion: Space advertising has a high degree of dispersion, while direct mail can pinpoint individual prospects.

10. Penetration: The high targetability of direct mail also makes it a better choice for penetrating key markets.

11. Demographic match: Unless special demographic or geographic editions of business publications are available, direct mail, with its data base sorting capabilities, best meets this criterion.

12. Psychographic match: Direct mail also best satisfies this factor whenever psychographically matched lists are available. But note that a business publication's editorial approach may preselect certain types of readers, psychographically as well as demographically.

13. Ergographic match: Both direct mail and space ads in vertical-market trade publications deliver a message to prospects in specific job categories.

14. Production difficulty: Because they must function as "leave-behind" pieces to speak for the product when buyers make their choice, inquiry fulfillment packages justifiably can be elaborate, difficult productions.

15. Production costs: Both trade shows and inquiry fulfillment packages generally have high production costs compared to other media.

16. Notice required: If four-color photography is involved, product literature generally requires long production lead times.

17. Codability: Direct mail permits easy encoding of responses by source, list, industrial classification, job title function, etc.

18. Impact of message: The credibility of publicity in the trade press gives it great impact. Dramatic, four-color advertising also is a high-impact vehicle.

—The Editors

ADVERTISING: IN DIRE STRAITS

While hardly on its
last legs, advertising still can't
do what it used to.

Hunter Hastings

Hunter Hastings is CEO of Ryan Management Group based in Westport, Connecticut.

Advertising has traditionally been viewed as the sine qua non of marketing. Up to now, good advertising—creative, persuasive, communicative—not only could make consumers aware but also could increase distribution, support pricing strategies, and win first-time and repeat customers. A great advertising campaign was the single answer to all marketing problems.

Today, however, advertising can't do what it used to do. At best, advertising is only a partial answer to the new marketing dynamics of the 1990s. In fact, spending too much money advertising a new product can be fatal.

Perhaps the most significant shortcoming of modern advertising is its inability to provide detail. Today, because of consumers' short attention spans and the overabundance of advertising messages, it is reckless to attempt to get more information across in an ad than brand name and product category. This is particularly hard on new products, which prospective consumers don't yet know anything about.

Worse, the media are often going after market segments different from those advertising is targeted toward. Marketers seek audiences that are defined by attitudes and situations, while the media look for populations defined by demographics, psychographics, and hobbies. There is often little common ground between the marketing target and the available media. Take older consumers, for example. Because they're often home with the TV turned on, we are told that we can best reach them through prime time television. Yet the content of sitcoms and other network shows is rarely geared toward their interests and concerns.

Research shows that consumers are now following new and different cues when they decide what to buy. Many of them are making decisions based on in-store advertising and position at the point of purchase. Others are basing their choices on peer group acceptance, buying brands that they see their friends using or that have been recommended by someone whose opinion they respect. In many cases, what they have seen through the media is irrelevant.

Consumers are more suspicious, more discerning. Young people, for instance, are often distrustful of advertising and will frequently avoid conventionally advertised goods, considering the advertising an attempt by outsiders to impose their views upon them. At the other end of the demographic spectrum, aging baby boomers are changing their buying criteria. No longer will their decisions be driven by imagery. Rather, they will be wooed by the information provided on the package and by the recommendations of experts, whether the American Association of Retired Persons, their doctors, or respected peers.

A school of New Marketing is emerging to respond to the consumer dynamics of the '90s. The same levels of thought, analysis, and skill that in the past marketers applied only to advertising are now being put to use in promotion, public relations, special events, licensing, trade spending, sales, and merchandising. Fundamental to the New Marketing is the notion that advertising is not the only creative way to communicate with consumers. The best evidence of this is the emergence of promotion as a way to attract attention to new products. New products can be promoted through purchased shelf space and displays in stores as well as through samples or coupons. Promotion based on trial is especially effective for products that have a terrific taste or are in some way superior to the competition.

So far, only companies marketing relatively small brands with limited resources have followed the promotion-only route, but often with spectacular success. These companies realize that it is more effective to single-mindedly pursue one marketing strategy than to make a small marketing budget even less effective by splitting it up among the conventional mix of marketing tools. Marketing for Smartfoods popcorn, for instance, was originally based entirely on sampling, package design, and word-of-mouth recommendation. This marketing strategy made Smartfoods a $20 million regional brand, giving it a sound foundation on which to begin its recent nationwide advertising and marketing campaign.

There are also certain categories and brands for which distribution can do a better job of selling a product than can advertising. Certain groups of consumers develop a positive perception of a brand simply because it is available in the "right" outlets. This is particularly true for beverages. When Perrier was first marketed in the United States, it was carefully introduced into fine restaurants and other so-called thought-leader locations. Because of its availability in the right places, Perrier was adopted by an upscale group, and success followed. As it gained popularity and moved from an elitist drink to a more broadly accepted beverage, the brand was able to widen its distribution. The discovery of traces of benzene in Perrier last February enabled rival waters to take over some of Perrier's loyal market with ease; whether or not they will remain popular now that Perrier is back is yet to be seen.

The distribution strategy has also worked for hair-care and pet-food products. Many hair-care brands have built their reputations by being distributed first through salons. Jhirmak, Redken, Paul Mitchell Systems, and Nexus have all become $100 million brands by using this strategy. In pet foods, Iams and Hills Science Diet were originally distributed exclusively through pet professionals such as breeders, veterinarians, and specialty pet-food store proprietors. Marketing money was spent on presence at dog shows rather than on advertising. These products have since competed successfully with supermarket brands.

New Marketers are beginning to transplant the distribution-by-experts strategy to supermarkets. Retailers such as Sainsbury in Britain have achieved a position of authority in consumers' minds that is analogous to the role of the veterinarian to the pet lover. Unlike American supermarket chains, Sainsbury has created its own label of food products with quality equal to or even superior to manufacturers' brands, with presentation to match. Brands that are promoted along with Sainsbury products enjoy the endorsement of the retailer as well.

Supermarkets that have added fresh bakeries, produce grown in situ on hydroponic frames, and freshly prepared take-out food have created an environment in which brands that contribute to the new shopping experience can prosper. Manufacturers' brands that are displayed in a manner complementary to popular new supermarket departments or that tie in with retailer promotions in the produce or fresh foods sections will increasingly fare well. Those who see the new retailer initiatives as a threat to packaged food sales may find themselves wasting valuable resources on advertising as a defensive measure.

The capability of modern public relations has been vastly underestimated, especially its potential for introducing new products or services that don't lend themselves readily to advertising. Think, for example, of brands that have emerged from the world of motor racing. Expensive performance tires such as Goodrich T/A radials, brand-name oils such as Quaker State and Pennzoil, and even such esoterica as STP gas treatment are commonly used by weekend mechanics and everyday drivers because of their association with prominent race car drivers and teams. Public relations has more credibility in marketing the product than advertising. Once public relations has expanded use of the product from the specialist arena to the broad market, ads are often used to expand market share.

Public relations marketing has also served in making Mondavi wines a household name. Early publicity for the wines shunned advertising and instead was intensely personal: Robert Mondavi himself met with wine aficionados. Once these professionals started using and talking about the product, ordinary wine drinkers began to buy it. In fact, the single most effective piece of publicity for Mondavi was a joint venture with the Rothschilds to create a wine under a new label, "Opus." If the Rothschilds were prepared to endorse Mondavi, the wine consumer needed to ask no more.

Newman's Own brand has also become a roaring success as a result of public relations. The proposition that Paul Newman himself actually developed and still uses the gourmet pasta sauce, salad dressing, popcorn, and lemonade has been too much for consumers to resist. The fact that charities are beneficiaries of the profits made from the products also gives the brand a "green" character, a quality that is increasingly appealing to consumers, and which is much better communicated through public relations than through advertising.

A presence among highly visible people—professional athletes, entertainers, prominent businessmen—is more convincing than all the advertising in the world to the right target audience. Sometimes, the advertising-oriented thinkers choose to create the connection artificially and then advertise it, as was the case with the Pepsi-Michael Jackson ads or the K-Mart-Martha Stewart ads. Increasingly, such advertising will fail. Not only can the advertising be mimicked by competitors, but, more importantly, the association with the personality will lose credibility with the audience simply because it *is* advertised.

In the future, advertising will come to communicate not the individual character and benefits of single products and services, but the more general value and appeal of a particular company or brand. Single products and services will instead be marketed exclusively via promotion and merchandising. This technique can be called brand equity expansion.

Today's best example is Weight Watchers. Weight Watchers promotes a system by which consumers can lose weight and gain the fitness, shape, and healthy life style they want. The system includes clinics and courses and all kinds of foods, snacks, beverages, and condiments. Currently, Weight Watchers is primarily advertising its clinics and frozen entrées. Yet the whole franchise is growing in many more directions than merely those parts that are advertised. Weight Watchers can introduce new products and variations without advertising them because its name instantly legitimizes the new products. All Weight Watchers has to do is provide in-store merchandising, which will make consumers aware of the product, and, in certain cases, provide some trial incentives.

Brand equity expansion represents a whole new way of thinking about what a brand is and the role it plays with consumers. With this new thinking comes a new appreciation for what advertising can and can't do in marketing a new product. If a corporation already has a brand that has meaning for consumers, that meaning can often be extended to cover the new product, in which case it is redundant to tell the consumer a second time about the assets of the brand. In many cases, it will be sufficient to simply invite the consumer who already uses the brand to try its new form by using trial incentives. Advertising may play a key role in building parent brand equity; conversely, it may have no role whatsoever in introducing wave after wave of new products that live and flourish under the parent's umbrella.

Advertising can no longer play the all-powerful marketing role that it traditionally has. Promotion, public relations, endorsement, distribution, and other new tools are better able to generate consumer awareness. Advertising still has a role to play as a part of a bigger and more flexible ensemble of players, but in many cases it will deliver its best performance in a supporting role, and sometimes it will not even appear.

Companies need to be rigorous in their analysis of when advertising is less appropriate than other options. This may be a kind of qualitative analysis—for example, in instances in which consumers will be better persuaded by a trial usage of the product than an advertising message—or a kind of quantitative analysis—such as when the marketing budget prohibits sufficient advertising or cannot match the advertising power of an entrenched competitor. Given the right kind of picture of the target audience and its attitudes, habits, and practices, companies can classify the way in which the audience can be most effectively reached. They will then be able to develop a marketing plan that is truly tailored not just to the target audiences of specialized media plans, but to target attitudes, target situations, and target trial susceptibilities.

Ads of the '80s: the Loved and the Losers

Joanne Lipman

A television commercial flies by in 30 seconds. A magazine ad disappears with the turn of a page. What, if any, ads from the 1980s are people likely to remember after the decade is over and done?

The Wall Street Journal informally polled some of the ad industry's top  executives for their opinions on the best—and the worse—that Madison Avenue has cranked out in the past 10 years. Certainly the exceedingly popular animated California raisins commercial will live on. And the "Where's the Beef?" series for Wendy's International even entered pop parlance.

But, according to executives, many others were noteworthy. The results of the poll, while surely not scientific, make some interesting points. For starters, it was the same agency that scored most often on both the praise list and the pan list. Chiat/Day/Mojo, an innovative risk-taker, came up with three of the best, but also two of the worst. Secondly, the most memorable ads weren't all on television; a print campaign and a billboard qualified, too. And perhaps most important, despite the fears that mega-mergers would kill creativity, a number of the kudos-winning campaigns came from the biggest merged and remerged agencies, including units of conglomerates Omnicom and WPP Group.

Here then, is a peek at the decade's pinnacles and pits. And the best campaigns were . . .

APPLE COMPUTER. The computer company's "1984" commercial, shown during the 1984 Super Bowl, was the most frequently cited best-of-show. The ads played off of Orwell's forecast for the future. Chiat/Day created the campaign, but lost the client. Keith Reinhard, chairman of DDB Needham, calls the "1984" campaign perhaps "the single best piece of advertising in the decade."

PEPSI. The soft drink company was cited for two '80s campaigns: its commercials featuring Michael J. Fox, and "archaeology," which depicted archaeology students of the future puzzling over a Coke bottle while drinking Pepsi. Both were created by Omnicom unit BBDO.

GALLO. The wine company's campaign from the early '80s was a strong contender. That campaign, created by Hal Riney & Partners, included richly photographed depictions of weddings and other earthy scenes, all tinged in a rosy glow, backed by emotional music, and narrated by the sonorous Mr. Riney himself.

The Gallo ads touched off a slew of copycat advertising—and the most ardent follower appears to have been Mr. Riney himself. He no longer handles Gallo, but his subsequent ads for Perrier and Blue Cross/Blue Shield all look and sound like the Gallo work.

AMERICAN EXPRESS. By far, the most frequently cited print campaign was the "portraits" series using Annie Leibovitz photos of celebrity "cardmembers," from Tom Seaver to Jessica Tandy and Hume Cronyn. Created by WPP Group's Ogilvy & Mather, the campaign capped American Express's already successful "Don't leave home without it" effort.

NIKE. Two campaigns, from different ad agencies, got glowing mentions. The current "Just Do It" campaign—which features, for example, athlete Bo Jackson with musician Bo Diddley—was created by Wieden & Kennedy. Then there were the early '80s billboards of beautifully photographed athletes, created by Chiat/Day. That campaign was "visually incredible," reflecting "a new [television] generation who saw everything that way," says Marvin Sloves, chairman of Scali McCabe Sloves.

Some other campaigns rate honorable mention. President Reagan's "Morning in America" election campaign, created by a group of ad executives known as "the Tuesday Team," made him into the first politician in history to be sold like cereal. Federal Express's "Fast Talker" ad also gets some plaudits. And yet another Chiat/Day campaign, while local, made a big splash: the Nynex yellow pages ads featuring humorous literal translations of yellow pages listings. (In one ad, a crowd of chic, self-absorbed snobs are making hollow cocktail-party chatter. The picture then cuts to the phone book heading for "Vanity Cases.")

Some of our judges couldn't resist naming their own work, even though they were asked not to. Mr. Reinhard of DDB Needham singles out Spuds MacKenzie for Bud Light as well as the moody "The Night Belongs to Michelob" TV campaign, and the

Michelin spots using babies playing in tires. Jerry Della Femina, chairman of Della Femina McNamee WCRS, says Joe Isuzu, the smarmy lying Isuzu pitchman "is the campaign of this decade for us." Joe Mack, chairman and chief executive of Saatchi & Saatchi Advertising in New York, nominates his "Where's the Beef?"

Ralph Ammirati, of Ammirati & Puris, singles out his agency's "World News, Club Med Style," a commercial for Club Med, along with an ad calling the BMW convertible "The Ultimate Tanning Machine." And George Lois, chairman of Lois/GGK, insists that his agency's "I Want My MTV" is "the ad campaign of the decade, and I would win that debate with anybody who's half alive and understands our culture."

The executives were only slightly less enthusiastic when tearing into what they see as the decade's worst:

BURGER KING. The disastrous "Herb the Nerd" campaign from J. Walter Thompson was a clear loser. While Burger King has had a lot of awful campaigns this decade ("We Do It Like You Do It" comes to mind), this series, which centered on a hopelessly out-of-it guy who never ate at Burger King, stood out for sheer ridiculousness and lack of consumer acceptance. Thompson no longer handles the account.

REEBOK. The weird U.B.U. campaign that featured people acting crazy while a voiceover recited Ralph Waldo Emerson tied for worst. Created by Chiat/Day, it was quickly abandoned, and Reebok now runs performance-oriented commercials from the same agency.

Seeing the Reebok ad, "I just felt the shoe must be really dopey," says

Martin Puris of Ammirati & Puris.

NISSAN. The second black mark on Chiat/Day's record was its yuppie-engineer "Built for the Human Race" series of ads. The campaign was short-lived, allowing Chiat/Day to redeem itself with a different campaign using the same slogan.

INFINITI. Rarely has a new campaign for a new product annoyed so many, so quickly. Created by Hill Holliday Conners Cosmopulos, the ads are zen-inspired nature scenes of things like pussy willows and rocks. "It will come back to haunt us all in advertising," says Mr. Della Femina. "When you play games with a client's money, it trivializes the client's business. It says people can just throw money down the drain and show pictures of lakes." The Infiniti ads continue to run.

WANG. The Wang commercials a few years back were packed with mystifying computer jargon. Although the spots were initially hailed as breaking through the ad clutter, many found them irksome. The campaign, created by Hill Holliday, was "yuppie computer talk" and "by far the worst" of the decade, Mr. Della Femina insists.

Some executives also said nix to a style of ad: The shaky-camera commercial. The offenders are legion, and any one of them qualifies. Director Leslie Dektor originated the format, which gives a jittery, horror-movie feel to commercials, with ads including a 1987 American Telephone & Telegraph campaign that hinted at the dire possibilities for your career if you didn't use AT&T. Soon it seemed almost everybody was hopping onto the angst-advertising bandwagon.

Cold War Commercial

CBS and ABC have refused to run a television ad for Drixoral cold medicine that features pictures of President Bush and Soviet leader Gorbachev, according to executives of the ad agency that created the spot.

Last night, executives of the agency, Messner Vetere Berger Carey Schmetterer, said the networks had requested letters of approval from the White House to run the ad. Traditionally, the White House has discouraged use of the president's likeness in advertising.

The agency said the networks hadn't heard back from the White House and decided not to run the spot on the basis of their standards. CBS, according to the agency, told the New York shop it thought the commercial appeared to be too much of a product endorsement on the part of the political officials. The ad was scheduled to run on both networks today.

Officials of CBS and ABC couldn't be reached for comment.

NBC plans to run the ad, according to the agency. Newspapers, including USA Today and the New York Times, also haven't changed plans to run the print ad, according to the agency. Drixoral is made by Schering-Plough Corp.

The TV commercial declares, "In the new year, may the only cold war in the world be the one being fought by us." It shows a picture of the two world leaders shaking hands at the Malta summit.

Ron Berger, one of the agency's partners, said the shop never attempted to obtain approval from the White House.

Global Marketing

It is certain that marketing with a global perspective will continue to be a strategic element of U.S. business in the 1990s and beyond. The United States is both the world's largest exporter and largest importer. In 1987, U.S. exports totaled just over $250 billion—about ten percent of total world exports. During the same period, American imports were nearly $450 billion—just under ten percent of total world imports.

Whether or not they wish to be, all marketers are now part of the international marketing system. For some, the end of the era of domestic markets may have come too soon, but that era is over. Today it is necessary to recognize the strengths and weaknesses of our own marketing practices as compared to those abroad. The multinational corporations have long recognized this need, but now all marketers must acknowledge it.

International marketing differs from domestic marketing in that the parties to its transactions live in different political units. It is the "international" element of international marketing that distinguishes it from domestic marketing—not differences in managerial techniques. The growth of global business among multinational corporations has raised new questions about the role of their headquarters. It has even caused some to speculate whether marketing operations should be performed abroad rather than in the United States.

The key to applying the marketing concept is understanding the consumer. Increasing levels of consumer sophistication are evident in all of the world's most profitable markets. Managers are required to adopt new points of view in order to accommodate increasingly complex consumer wants and needs. The markets of the 1990s will show further integration on a worldwide scale. In these emerging markets, "conventional textbook approaches" can cause numerous problems; the new marketing perspective called for by the circumstances of the 1990s will require a long-range view that looks from the basics of exchange and their applications in new settings.

The selections presented here were chosen to provide an overview of world economic factors, competitive positioning, and increasing globalization of markets—issues to which each and every marketer must become sensitive. "Strategic Options for Global Market Players" presents key considerations for developing and positioning a product in the global market. James Bolt's article suggests 10 criteria for successful global competition. "Beware the Pitfalls of Global Marketing" addresses how shortcomings in marketing strategy can fell a good product. In the next article, the author shows how the Japanese believe that you do not have to hit a home run with every product to stay ahead of the market. "Myth and Marketing in Japan," discloses some important ways in which the Japanese market has rapidly changed. The last article in this section, "Distribution: The Key to Success Overseas," summarizes some basic factors that need to be considered when selecting a global market distributor.

Looking Ahead: Challenge Questions

What are some of the economic, cultural, and political obstacles that an organization seeking to become global in its markets must consider?

Do you believe that an adherence to the "marketing concept" is the right way to approach international markets?

With reference to the "Beware the Pitfalls of Global Markets" article, what are some examples of situations you are familiar with where shortcomings in marketing strategy have felled a good product?

What trends are taking place today that would suggest whether global markets will grow or decline?

Unit 4

Strategic Options for Global Market Players

By developing a product that meets worldwide requirements and positioning that product to capitalize on local needs, companies can capture new markets with good potential for growth.

Edward R. Koepfler

Edward R. Koepfler is Vice President of Strategic Markets System for Software Associates, Inc., in Chicago.

There exists today a window of opportunity for U.S. firms to enter emerging markets in other countries. It is based on growing demand, favorable exchange rates, and productivity gains already realized by U.S. manufacturers but not yet established among foreign competitors.

But the window can close quickly as the worldwide economy becomes more closely integrated and foreign firms gain strength, technological sophistication, and market presence, causing U.S. companies to lose their worldwide competitiveness. The devaluating U.S. dollar, combined with high production costs in the United States and lower costs abroad will contribute to this changing business environment.

For example, in the newly industrialized countries of the Far East, the standard of living has risen to the point where traditional wage rate advantages are quickly disappearing. With economic annual growth rates of 8 percent to 10 percent, these are among the fastest growing industrialized countries in the world and are rapidly becoming a new set of emerging markets for consumer and industrial products. Their growth alone should make these countries a top strategic priority for U.S. firms—not just as sources of inexpensive labor, as has been the case in the past—but as potential for new sales and profits.

Europe, too, offers growing market potential. The freeing of the European Common Market in 1992 will open Europe into a far larger and more diverse marketplace than it has been. Marketers are advised to think of Europe 1992 as many unique countries within a single continent, rather than as a collective entity.

Similarly, a recent free trade agreement opens the door wider for U.S. companies to enter the Canadian marketplace. Though Canada is a close neighbor geographically, its culture and business attitudes can be far from what U.S. firms think of as "American" and should be approached in a different manner.

Adopt a Global Perspective

To be most successful in the global marketplace, a firm must view itself in a global context, rather than as a U.S. firm doing business abroad. The global marketplace actually is a vast market with many smaller national or regional submarkets, each with its own business and social cultures, attitudes, and protocol built over centuries. The global marketer must adapt his business practices to suit these differences while still preserving the basic integrity of his products and services.

Aggressive companies must recognize global markets early in the game and be actively involved in developing those markets. If a company, its products,

Four Keys for Global Growth

The following are essentials for global growth.

1. **Identify potential markets early.** Become actively involved in stimulating market demand early on.

2. **Analyze current and future regional markets.** Think long-term, and assess the strategic potential of each region in terms of five-, ten-, and twenty-year time frames.

3. **Maintain firsthand knowledge of the market.** This is the most effective way to do business. For each market, select on-site management with an in-depth understanding of the local culture, and give that management decision-making authority.

4. **Form partnerships.** Make a commitment to form strategic partnerships that will achieve the goals of increased earnings and success for all parties involved.

and its services are present as the market starts to unfold, that company has a good chance of becoming dominant in that market. If not, the company may forfeit its presence in that market forever.

U.S.-based firms are realizing that, like the Japanese in the United States, they can successfully sell their products and services on a global basis. They can thus satisfy overseas demands and capture a part of emerging markets by stimulating—or even creating—demand. By developing a product that meets worldwide requirements and positioning that product to capitalize on local needs, companies can conquer new markets with good potential for growth. (See accompanying box for key strategies for global growth.)

How to "Create" a Market

Creating a market is a pragmatic process. Put simply, it involves identifying a previously unidentified need and satisfying it.

How does a company begin to analyze a market for its strategic growth potential? First, take a look at how related industries are growing in that country. Are there firms in fields similar to yours already in existence? Are they successful? Why or why not? Do such companies possess expansion potential? In your research, consider the demographics and trends of that country and how such factors may open new doors for your products.

In Japan, for example, packaged application software products were, by U.S. standards, a rare commodity even two years ago. But because of the prevalence of computers, there was good market potential but no existing market because this type of software had not yet been introduced in Japan.

The key for application software developers was to educate the Japanese business community about the benefits of packaged application software. They then developed software that met the specific needs of Japanese business and industry and, in effect, stimulated demand. It was then that a market was born.

System Software Associates, Inc. (SSA), based in Chicago, Illinois, is one example of a company that followed this strategy. It was founded on a global growth strategy and essentially has created new markets. SSA develops and markets an integrated application software system for use on IBM midrange computers. The company recognized that business operations of potential clients were similar worldwide. Therefore, SSA's family of products was designed to have a worldwide application. Today, the $62 million company has more than 50 percent sales outside the United States.

Global marketing means approaching

business decisions from both a U.S.-based and a global perspective. The U.S. perspective occasionally accounts for regional differences, but more typically it treats all market prospects as identical. In the global perspective, variations in market size and composition, demographics, language, and culture must also be considered.

Product positioning, sales protocol, and the average sales cycle vary from country to country and from region to region. The aggressive, U.S. selling style would not work well in Japan, for example, where a committee makes a slow, deliberate analysis before making purchase decisions.

Whatever and wherever the products or services are being sold, a company must meet several common challenges for a global business strategy to succeed. These challenges fall under the categories of language, marketplace barriers, and finding the right strategic alliance to strengthen market presence.

Speak the Local Language

Language is tricky. In some parts of the world, particularly the Commonwealth countries, English is the accepted business language. In other areas this is not the case. Whether business is conducted in English or the country's native tongue, each area has its own colloquialisms and idioms that make an outsider easy to recognize.

A nonnative business professional may know the language where he or she works but not understand the nuances and idiosyncracies necessary to communicate effectively in that country. Consider the United States: The phrase "How are y'all doing?" might be common in Atlanta business circles but certainly not in New York or Chicago. The same is true abroad where American English may not be the English—or the language—that businesspeople speak.

A global strategy must "fit" products and services to the language and practices of each market. For example, computer software developers may translate the product's screens, commands, and currency functions in order to suit the cultural business requirements. Support-

ing documentation and training materials also must be translated. In doing so, however, the quality and functionality of the product and service must never be compromised.

Overcome Marketplace Barriers

In the newly industrialized countries of the Far East, there is open admiration of U.S. business. Many established U.S. firms have demonstrated their long-term commitment to those markets by investing money, people, plants, and equipment. These investments make a strong statement recognized by the local population that will utimately drive sales, profitability, and recruiting efforts.

In other regions, including parts of Europe, a pro-U.S. attitude is not as prevalent. In either type of environment, the company and its decision makers must have a local market mentality backed by meaningful demonstrations of their long-term commitment.

Form Strategic Partnerships

Getting "plugged into the system" in many foreign markets—whether established or emerging—requires forming business relationships with existing local distribution/sales channels and professionals with established business contacts. Strategic partnerships can help U.S. companies gain acceptance in foreign markets. Distributors, direct sales/joint ventures, or "affiliates," are three common ways that firms enter foreign markets. Each option has pros and cons which companies should consider.

Distributors

Distributors typically are the least expensive option, but they also offer the original equipment manufacturer (OEM) the least control over its market destiny. The distributor buys and then resells a company's product, but it does not serve as a direct representative or extension of the producer company. The distributor typically sells several companies' products, so there is minimal loyalty on the part of the distributor or manufacturer.

The distributor generally has the right to set pricing for the manufacturer's product, which may lead to underpricing the product and downgrading the company's image in the market. The distributor also does not guarantee the level of service that the original manufacturer may offer its customers domestically.

Some firms use distributors as a cost-effective way to test new markets without making a long-term commitment or substantial investment. If the market shows good potential, the company may terminate its relationship with the distributor and take over the market structure already built during the test.

A Direct Sales Force

A direct sales force is the most costly way to enter a market, but it grants the U.S. firm the most control of product pricing, positioning, and support. In countries such as Brazil, U.S.-based companies are not allowed to establish their own autonomous sales forces; instead, they must enter that market by forming a joint venture with a native firm. This firm may then eventually become a subsidiary of the U.S. firm.

While it offers more corporate control, the direct sales option does have a major disadvantage in foreign markets. The direct sales force of a U.S.-based firm typically is American and, therefore, is perceived as a group of strangers doing business in a strange land. They may not understand the culture and expectations of the foreign country, and might lack the close, local network of business contacts. The need to understand the native language and culture, plus the desire to offer service within the same geographic proximity, is the reason some companies choose to build relationships with alliances who are native to the market region. For SSA, this means developing and maintaining a worldwide network of independent companies to sell, service, and support its product line on an ex-

clusive basis. Such distribution channels are known as SSA "affiliates."

Affiliates

Affiliates are native firms that operate as representatives in non-U.S. markets. The company provides affiliates with the SSA product, complete training, and consulting. The affiliate relationship, exclusive to the SSA product, is close and long-term, which enables both partners to grow together and modify operations as market conditions change over time.

While the affiliate profits by generating revenues through new product introductions, the OEM can simultaneously keep close tabs on the territory to ensure that it will continue to be a stable, lucrative market for years to come. In order to maintain this essential contact, corporate representatives from the United States should meet with each affiliate face-to-face at least twice per month.

Unlike a distributor, the OEM maintains control by setting guidelines for pricing, positioning, and support of its products in each market, to assure consistency throughout the world and create a unified identity for the supplier and its products. The affiliate offers the local business flavor and inroads to the foreign market that should be addressed in strategic market expansion plans, as well as the flexibility to adapt the company's "global" policies to local customs and business conventions.

For example, SSA recently opened an office in Singapore with an affiliate who is from Singapore and, thus, knows the Chinese language, heritage, and accepted business formalities. As a native of China, this affiliate can also be effective in the Hong Kong and Taiwan markets. Business in these countries is done with the highest-ranking official of an organization. As a result, sales are typically initiated and closed between the owner of the affiliate company and the owner of the customer company.

An affiliate relationship works best when the parent company finds organizations in target market areas with a shared vision of success and similar management style. A common commitment to operational goals is key to building a sound strategic relationship.

While companies should set up guidelines for their partners to assure global consistency of product positioning, pricing, and service, they must allow their affiliates a significant degree of flexibility and decision-making authority. This confidence comes from the shared vision and trust that are established up front during the initial affiliate selection process.

Also implicit in the affiliate alliance is a loyalty factor which states: (1) Do not compete directly with your partners and (2) do not allow competition among partners within a given marketplace. Affiliate partnerships are not merely a method to test the market or to gain an initial product presence; they are long-term relationships in which each partner shares in the success of the other.

Secure Vital Business Resources

Before seeking a business partner or entering a new market, make sure that critical resources and conditions exist in the market. An educated work force, established financial institutions, media and telecommunications services, and government support of business are crucial market components. In addition, the business partner you select must have a basic knowledge of how to run a business that fits into your company's view of management.

One prime concern when entering foreign markets is protection of the product. More and more countries are implementing their own patent, trade-

mark, and copyright legislation in order to mimic the U.S. laws on copyright protection. You must have some legal recourse to protect your product. It is far easier for an affiliate who is a national to deal with legal issues in his own country, rather than for a U.S. firm, as an outsider.

Clearly, an internal connection in a foreign market will help U.S. firms enter foreign markets and gain market share. The ability to understand and handle local language, culture, and business attitudes is critical for success in the global marketplace. This is an ability that few U.S. business professionals can master easily, and it is better suited to affiliates or partners in each market who are native to the area.

The process also works in reverse. Think about a foreign firm trying to enter the U.S. market without understanding the language and business environment. Like the global market, the United States is comprised of many markets, each with a slightly different culture that influences business. Urban, rural, East, West, Midwest, and Southern United States are examples. What works for a business in New York City may not go over well in Omaha.

So, any company trying to be a player in the global market would be wise to remember that the "global" market is, in fact, many individual markets, each with its own nuances. Although time and distance are smaller obstacles than they once were, a company still must address differences in language, culture, and business customs within each market it enters. Decision making and management from a strictly U.S. perspective are now too narrow to be successful in the global game.

Global Competitors: Some Criteria for Success

Companies that want to succeed on a worldwide scale need to have a management that takes a world view, supports its overseas operations, pays close attention to the political winds, and uses local nationals whenever possible.

James F. Bolt

James F. Bolt is founder and president of Executive Development Associates, a consulting firm based in Westport, Conn. that specializes in the development of customized executive education programs. This paper was developed for use in an executive education program designed for a Fortune 200-sized firm aimed at preparing its executives for global competition.

N o set of criteria has ever been developed to assess what makes a corporation a successful global competitor. No magic formula or convenient road map for the international executive exists.

That conclusion, reached after conversations with experts at academic and research organizations, is hardly surprising. No two global competitors are alike. The combinations of management styles, products, markets, strategies, countries, plants, and myriad other factors are virtually limitless. What works for one corporation might be disastrous for another. Some years ago, Pieter Kuin, then vice-chancellor of the International Academy of Management and a past president of Unilever, N. V., wrote in the *Harvard Business Review* that "the magic of multinational management lies not so much in perfection of methods or excellence of men as in developing *respect* for other nationalities and cultures and for the *determination* to succeed in foreign markets."[1] This observation is as valid today as it was more than a decade ago.

Yet, some broad criteria, the ones most-often cited as necessary for a successful global competitor and most-often evident in large corporations that have succeeded in the global business arena, can be isolated. These criteria can be broken, somewhat arbitrarily, into ten separate statements.

1. Successful global competitors perceive themselves as multinational, understand that perception's implications for their business, and are led by a management that is comfortable in the world arena.

"The common denominator is that each of these highly successful global competitors altered the dynamics of its industry and pulled away from the other major players."

If there is one key criterion for successful global competitors, it is this one. In virtually all corporations, global success is dependent on a corporate leadership that sees the world as a global village. Successful leaders all seem to understand that there are two distinct breeds of multinational corporations—the multi-domestic corporation and the truly global corporation.

The multi-domestic company pursues different strategies in each of its foreign markets. Each overseas subsidiary is essentially autonomous. In this type of arrangement, "a company's management tries to operate effectively across a series of worldwide positions with diverse product requirements, growth rates, competitive environments and political risks. The company prefers that local managers do whatever is necessary to succeed in R&D, production, marketing, and distribution, but holds them responsible for results."[2]

In effect, the company competes with local competitors on a market-by-market basis. Many successful American companies operate this way: Procter & Gamble in household products, Honeywell in controls, Alcoa in aluminum, and General Foods in consumer foods, for example.

The global company, on the other hand, pits its entire resources against its competition in a highly integrated way. Foreign subsidiaries and divisions are largely interdependent in both operations and strategy. Says one expert:

> In a global business, management competes worldwide against a small number of other multinationals in the world market. Strategy is centralized, and various aspects of operations are decentralized or centralized as economics and effectiveness dictate. The company seeks to respond to particular local market needs, while avoiding a compromise of efficiency of the overall global system.[3]

Many multinationals are moving in this direction. Those who have already arrived include IBM in computers; Caterpillar in large construction equipment; Timex, Seiko and Citizen in watches; and General Electric, Siemens, and Mitsubishi in heavy electrical equipment.

The important thing is that successful global competitors have carefully considered the difference between multi-domestic and global. Corporate leadership can show that it is serious by making sure that someone at the top is knowledgeable about and comfortable in the world arena. A Conference Board study some years ago found that the companies with foreign operations doing well invariably were led by chief executive officers who were "uncommonly well read, well traveled and took a very broad view of the world and the role of business in that world."[4]

2. Successful global competitors develop an integrated and innovative global strategy that makes it very difficult and costly for other companies to compete.

Perhaps the best evidence for this criterion was amassed by Thomas Hout, Vice President of the Boston Consulting Group; Michael E. Porter, professor at the Harvard Business School; and Eileen Rudden, Manager of the Boston Consulting Group's Boston office.[5]

The three authors argue that most successful global competitors "perceive competition as global and formulate strategy on an integrated worldwide basis." They develop "a strategic innovation to change the rules of the competitive game in its particular industry. The innovation acts as a lever to support the development of an integrated global system." The authors cite three cases to illustrate this point—Caterpillar, whose strategic innovation was in manufacturing; L. M. Ericsson, of Sweden, whose breakthrough was in technology; and Honda, where the innovative strategic thrust was in marketing.

The common denominator is that each of these highly successful global competitors altered the dynamics of its industry and pulled away from the other major players. Caterpillar achieved economies of scale through commonality of design. The competition could not match Caterpillar in either costs or profits. Consequently, the competition could not make the large investments required to catch up.

Ericsson, by developing a unique modular technology, created a cost advantage. Its global strategy turned electronics from a threat to Ericsson into a barrier to its competitors.

Honda unlocked the potential for economies of scale in production, marketing, and distribution through aggressive marketing. The only thing left for the competition was the small-volume specialty market.

In each case, there existed within the industry the potential for a world-

"Successful global competitors have embraced the new phenomenon; they now sell standardized products in similar ways across increasingly larger portions of the planet."

wide system of products and markets. A company with an integrated global strategy (something all three companies had) could exploit that situation, which these three did.

3. Successful global competitors aggressively and effectively implement their worldwide strategy, and they back it with large investments.

That leads conveniently to our third criterion for success on the global stage: the determination and the ability to back the strategy with substantial long-term investments. The Caterpillar experience is a case in point. Caterpillar is the only Western company that matches its major competitor, Komatsu, in capital spending per employee. In fact, Caterpillar's overall capital spending is more than three times that of its Japanese competitor. And Caterpillar does not divert resources into other businesses or otherwise dissipate its financial advantage. With almost single-minded purpose, it pumps huge proportions of its profits back into its base business and dares the competition to try to match it.[6]

In *Competitive Strategy: Techniques for Analyzing Industries and Competitors*, Michael E. Porter points out that successful global competitors not only are willing to invest heavily, but (perhaps even more important) they are also willing to wait long periods of time before these investments pay off.[7] Porter adds that implementing such strategies takes time. The result, he says, can be major investment projects with zero or even a negative return on investment for periods that would be thought unacceptable a few years ago.

A case in point is the experience of Xerox Corporation. In the mid-1970s, the company's Japanese subsidiary, Fuji Xerox, fell on hard times. The oil shock hurt Japan's economy severely. Ricoh introduced a highly successful line of inexpensive, low-volume copiers. Xerox sales in the Far East plummeted, and the partnership reached a crossroads.

Had Xerox considered Fuji Xerox to be a basically Japanese subsidiary doing business only in that part of the world, it probably would have opted to scale back operations. But Xerox took a global approach, realizing that the partnership could be a powerful weapon in its worldwide battle with the Japanese. The company made large investments in technology, product development, and manufacturing capacity.

Although the investment did not become profitable for five years, it has since paid for itself many times over. Fuji Xerox is now the leader in its market. More important, Fuji Xerox supplies low-volume copiers for Xerox to market in much of the world—including the United States.[8]

4. Successful global competitors understand that technological innovation is no longer confined to the United States, and they have developed systems for tapping technological innovation abroad.

Another key factor in the battle for supremacy in international markets is technological innovation. In the late 1950s, more than 80 percent of the world's major innovations came from the United States. That percentage has steadily declined, and today less than half of the world's innovations can legitimately lay claim to the "made in America" slogan.[9]

How do the more successful global competitors respond to challenges on the worldwide technological front? Robert Ronstadt, associate professor of management at Babson College, and Robert J. Kramer, project director at Business International Corporation, sought to find answers in their landmark study three years ago. Their analysis was based on interviews with more than 50 American, European, and Japanese managers of multinationals, a mail survey of 240 corporations around the world, and data covering more than 100 foreign-based R&D investments.[10]

Their data suggests that those companies who have done well in the international technological arena do some or all of the following:

• **Scanning and monitoring.** This includes reading journals and patent reports; meeting with foreign scientists and technical experts through conferences and seminars, and serving on advisory panels and study teams sponsored by the government and professional associations.

• **Connections with academia and research organizations.** Successful global enterprises actively pursue work-related projects with foreign academics, and they often make these associations with faculty members formal by using consulting agreements.

• **Programs to increase the company's visibility.** Many technological bonanzas go to companies with the right reputation. One common method of attracting attention is providing information to computer data banks that facilitate communication between prospective purchasers and vendors.

• **Cooperative research projects.** Many successful global enterprises enter into research projects with each other to broaden their contacts, reduce expenses, diminish the risk for each partner, or forestall the market entry of a competitor.

• **Acquiring or merging with foreign companies that have extensive innovative capabilities.** The two re-

"The international division provides the easiest way to concentrate scarce managerial expertise for international operations. Worldwide product divisions provide the widest scope and latitude for individual decision making and risk taking."

searchers found that the acquired company's innovative capability is not the primary reason for the merger. Nevertheless, significant technology may be acquired that can enhance an organization's ability to innovate abroad.

● **Acquisition of external technology by licensing.** A corporation may license in a technological innovation from another country, license out its own technology to others in the hope of getting access to improvements made by the licensee, or exchange its technology for another company's by cross-licensing.

Ronstadt and Kramer emphasize that "company owned R&D labs located overseas provide the best opportunities for managers to internationalize their scanning operations and obtain foreign innovations or new technology... U.S. multinationals have spent untold time and money establishing extensive operations and resources abroad. The time has come for greater utilization of these resources—not just as sales outlets for domestic or foreign products but as sources of innovation in technology and management that will aid in the resurgence of U.S. industry and the world economy."[11]

5. Successful global competitors operate as though the world were one large market, not a series of individual countries.

Daniel J. Boorstin characterizes our age as driven by "the Republic of technology whose supreme law...is convergence, the tendency for everything to become more like everything else."[12] In business, this trend has pushed markets toward global commonality. Successful global competi-

tors have embraced the new phenomenon; they now sell standardized products in similar ways across increasingly larger portions of the planet.

Writing in the *Harvard Business Review*, Theodore Levitt says:

The transforming winds whipped up by the proletarianization of communication and travel enter every crevice of life. Commercially, nothing confirms this as much as the success of McDonald's from the Champs Elysees to the Ginza, of Coca-Cola in Bahrain and Pepsi-Cola in Moscow.[13]

The implications for all global competitors—consumer-goods producers and high-technology companies—are profound. American corporations, in particular, have built their success largely on giving their customers *precisely* what they say they want, even if that means higher costs. That philosophy has led many corporations to overreact to different national and regional tastes, preferences, and needs. There is powerful new evidence that this road is doomed to failure. Lynn W. Phillips, Dae Chang, and Robert D. Buzzell, in their as yet unpublished Harvard Business School working paper, document that this notion of being all things to all people dramatically drives cost up and quality down.[14]

Successful global competitors, on the other hand, have remembered Henry Ford and the Model T. They stress simplification and standardization. Much of the success of the Japanese is based on this approach. It is significant that Japanese companies operate almost entirely without the kinds of marketing departments and

market research so prevalent in the West. John F. Welch, Jr., the chairman of General Electric, puts it this way: "The Japanese have discovered the one great thing all markets have in common—an overwhelming desire for dependable, world-standard modernity in all things, at aggressively low prices."[15]

This new reality is difficult for many American managers to comprehend. It runs counter to the methods that they have been taught and that have proven successful in the past. But companies that do not adapt to the new global realities lose to those that do adapt.

"Corporations geared to this new reality," according to Levitt, "benefit from enormous economies of scale in production, distribution, marketing, and management. By translating these benefits into reduced world prices, they can decimate competitors that still live in the disabling grip of old assumptions about how the world works."[16]

6. Successful global competitors have developed an organizational structure that is well thought out and unique.

Of all the subjects our research covered, the question of organization was the most vexing. There is simply no clear answer. If one examines the organization charts of most global competitors, it becomes clear that "there is no one way in which international companies organize their domestic and foreign activities."[17]

Most United States-based multinationals have at one time or another established international divisions to manage their overseas operations. As they grew, these same companies also sprouted several product-oriented di-

"Many multinationals who now have relatively good foreign representation among their senior executives began that process by placing a foreign manager in the hierarchy of personnel."

visions at home. In many cases, the result was a structural conflict between the geographic orientation of the international division and the product orientation of the domestic operations.

It is not surprising, therefore, that the international division has proved to be a transitory organization for many global competitors. As growth mushroomed in these companies, many of them abandoned their international divisions as such. J. William Widing, Jr., one-time vice president of Harbridge House, has identified three alternative structures that are most often used:

• Worldwide product divisions, each responsible for selling its own products throughout the world.

• Divisions responsible for all products sold within a certain geographic area.

• A matrix consisting of either of these arrangements with a centralized functional staff, or a combination of area operations and worldwide product management.[18]

The literature on organization and multinationals is extensive. Much of it is opinion and conjecture. Still, some broad guidelines do emerge. Among them are the following:

• Corporations using the worldwide-product-division structure have grown about 50 percent faster than those using the area-division structure. Whether there is a cause-and-effect relationship is debatable, but there seems to be at least a preference for worldwide product divisions in situations involving rapid growth.

• The greater the diversity of product lines, the more likely it is that an American company will manage its foreign business through worldwide product divisions.

• The availability and depth of management resources is also important. The international division pro-

vides the easiest way to concentrate scarce managerial expertise for international operations. Worldwide product divisions provide the widest scope and latitude for individual decision making and risk taking. A geographic structure requires a large number of broad-gauged managers with considerable general management experience.

• Geographic divisions can concentrate most efficiently on developing close relationships with national and local governments. Worldwide product divisions do not fare as well in this regard.

• Although the relative cost of operation varies, the matrix form tends to be the most expensive. It focuses extra attention on functional considerations and thus requires more staff personnel. Area divisions usually have the leanest staffs and, therefore, the lowest operating costs.

These and other guidelines are just that. "Organizational structure and reporting relationships present subtle problems for a global strategy," according to Hout, Porter, and Rudden. "Effective strategy control argues for a central product-line organization. Effective local responsiveness argues for a geographic organization with local autonomy. A global strategy argues for a product-line organization that has the ultimate authority, because without it the company cannot gain system-wide benefits. Nevertheless, the company still must balance product and area needs. In short, there is no simple solution."[19]

Echoing this sentiment, Levitt writes that "there is no one reliably right answer—no one formula by which to get it....What works well for one company or one place may fail for another in precisely the same place, depending on the capabilities, histories, regulations, resources, and even the cultures of both."[20]

7. Successful global competitors have a system that keeps them informed of political changes abroad and the implications for their business.

The world in which multinationals must operate is fraught with risk. Says Thomas A. Shreeve, a political analyst with the United States Department of State and a research associate at the Harvard Business School, "A new political party in power—or the new head of an old governing coali-

tion—can easily decide to change the fundamentals for operating and investing by altering the regulation of licensing, for example, or so changing foreign equity restrictions, local participation requirements, or the basis of corporate taxation."[21]

Most successful global competitors have some system that attempts to read the winds of political change. As early as 1969, Gulf Oil formed an international policy analysis unit to keep senior executives apprised of political developments on a daily basis. Dow Chemical, General Motors, IBM, most large banks, and virtually all oil companies have people dedicated exclusively to political analysis.

But few multinational corporations seem satisfied with the way their systems function. Part of the problem is that most systems are designed to track dramatic events, such as the overthrow of a government or the taking of hostages. These types of

"Any corporation seeking to expand globally would do well to ask itself how well it measures up to the Peters-Waterman criteria for excellence. At the very least, they provide some useful food for thought."

events do not need to be monitored because they quickly become public knowledge, and because once they happen there is little the corporation can do. Corporations need systems that pay attention to small details that, when pieced together, provide advance information of what is likely to happen.

8. Successful global competitors recognize the need to make their management team international and have a system in place to accomplish the goal.

Most senior executives in large multinational corporations profess their commitment to bringing foreign managers into their inner circles. Yet, when one looks at the hierarchies of large global competitors, "the gap between their stated aims to have truly multinational executive personnel and the practice of actually having them is great....And in the face of pressures from without and from within, it is becoming obvious that solving this human problem incurred in developing MNCs will be critical to the success of the enterprise in question."[22]

The crux of the problem seems to be a matter of attitude, not policy. For example, in determining who will receive incentive compensation, who will get a foreign assignment, or who has high management potential, the home-country executive is likely to rely on his own perception of who is the most competent and trustworthy, his compatriot down the hall or a foreigner thousands of miles away who he rarely sees. Given that choice, a variety of cultural and social biases often dictate the selection.[23]

Not surprisingly, then, most multinationals have a poor track record in integrating their management teams. One survey of 150 of the largest global competitors found that barely 1 percent of the senior headquarters positions were filled by foreign nationals, despite the fact that the average income generated by overseas operations was at least 20 percent of the companies' total income.[24]

Another survey found that "executives we questioned in several successful companies closely associate paying greater attention to foreign nationals with improvement of corporate performance."[25] This same study, which was conducted by Howard V. Perlmutter, chairman of the Multinational Enterprise Unit at the Wharton School of Business and Daniel A. Heenan , then vice president for manpower planning and development at First National City Bank, identified four critical areas which need attention.

The first is headquarters and foreign service assignments. As one observer puts it: "They all love to talk about the Brazilian in London and the Indian in Belgium. But all that talk is for public consumption...the ultimate responsibilities still lie with the Americans." Those who have broken this pattern usually have done so with a two-pronged approach: a manpower-resource planning system that is dedicated to identifying and moving people across national boundaries, and a company godfather who is responsible for a handful of senior foreign executives. This role is normally reserved "for a person of considerable stature and influence in headquarters whose role is to ensure that people on overseas assignments are neither forgotten nor allowed to neglect the growth of their functional skills."[26] IBM is the most-often-cited example of this two-pronged approach.

The second critical area that needs to be addressed is compensation. Even today, only a handful of global competitors maintain truly multinational compensation programs for their managers. In many instances, foreigners with identical credentials and jobs receive one-half to one-third the total compensation package of their American counterparts. One expert explains the problem this way: "Without pay practices that offer equal

monetary incentives for all managers, companies run the risk of not attracting and retaining high quality professionals."[27]

A third key area is managerial inventories. The manpower lists from which candidates are assigned to key overseas and headquarters positions tend to be exclusive. While American expatriate managers are invariably included in these worldwide inventories, foreign nationals are not. If the manpower-planning lists contain only Americans, it should not be surprising that only Americans are found in prime international positions.

The fourth key area is performance-appraisal techniques. The Perlmutter-Heenan study found that the most successful global competitors had "adopted a worldwide performance appraisal system that assesses a manager's functional and administrative abilities plus his skills to operate in a global setting. The MNC executives we talked with suggest blending the best evaluative techniques from all over the world."[28]

Our research indicated that many multinationals who now have relatively good foreign representation among their senior executives began that process by placing a foreign manager in the hierarchy of personnel. That person tends to act as a catalyst and conscience when key operating assignments open up.

9. Successful global competitors give their outside directors an active role in the affairs of the company.

More and more multinationals are appointing local nationals to their foreign subsidiaries' boards of directors. Much of this trend is in response to foreign legislation that demands it. But the more sophisticated and successful global competitors realize that "the outside director who is also a citizen of the host country can play an important role in developing an atmosphere of trust in which they will be able to operate with a reasonable degree of freedom."[29]

Writing in the *Harvard Business Review*, Samuel C. Johnson and Richard M. Thomson offer some sage advice: "The chief executive of the MNC should not delegate to others the selection of outside directors and the invitation to serve. His personal involvement will indicate the significance he ascribes to the position."[30]

Tasks the outside board members perform that are most often considered positive contributions include the following:

- Becoming familiar with the operation of the business and keeping abreast of local economic, legal, and political developments, so he or she can anticipate changes affecting business not only in his or her home country, but in the entire region or continent as well.
- Making certain that the subsidiary follows objectives and policies established by the parent and communicated to him or her through memoranda and discussions with the corporation's officers.
- Counseling the parent company regarding local compensation standards, trade-union regulations, an other personnel matters.
- Periodically appraising the performance of the subsidiary's management (primarily through review of its financial reports).
- Counseling the subsidiary's management on its relations with financial institutions, governmental bodies, and the public.
- Offering advice and counsel on broad political and social trends that may have a significant impact on long-range planning.
- Helping to insure that the subsidiary behaves as a responsible member of the community.

Successful global competitors seem to have two things in common in their use of local nationals on their boards of directors. First, they are selected by the chief executive officer and have his confidence, support, and trust. Second, they are not just figureheads. They are effective contributors. Says one source: "If he (the outside director) is doing his job properly, he will have his hands full. The onus is on him to be vigorous and informed. The responsibility of the parent company is to listen and react."[31]

10. Successful global competitors are well-managed.

This may seem self-evident, but it bears mention. It would be foolhardy to think that a corporation could successfully expand beyond its own national borders if its domestic management house was not in order.

There are numerous ways of course, to assess a corporation's management effectiveness—not the least of which are healthy financial statements that show relative freedom from debt and consistent revenue and profit growth. We have elected to include here for the basis of discussion the eight attributes which best-selling authors Thomas J. Peters and Robert H. Waterman, Jr. used in *In Search of Excellence.* They are:

- **A bias for action.** While these companies may be analytical in their approach to decision making, they are not paralyzed.
- **Close to the customer.** They learn from the people they serve. Many of the innovative companies got their best product ideas from customers. That comes from listening, intently and regularly.
- **Autonomy and entrepreneurship.** The innovative companies develop many leaders and many innovators throughout the organization.
- **Productivity through people.** Excellent companies treat the rank and file as the root of quality and productivity gain. They do not have we/they labor attitudes.
- **Hands-on, value driven.** The basic philosophy of an organization has far more to do with its achievements then do technological or economic resources.
- **Stick to the knitting.** The odds for excellent performance strongly favor those companies that stay reasonably close to businesses they know.
- **Simple form, lean staff.** The underlying structural forms in the excellent companies are elegantly simple. Top-level staffs are lean; it is not uncommon to find a corporate staff of fewer than 100 people running multi-billion-dollar enterprises.
- **Simultaneous loose-tight properties.** The excellent companies are both centralized and decentralized.[32]

Any corporation seeking to expand globally would do well to ask itself how well it measures up to the Peters-Waterman criteria for excellence. At the very least, they provide some useful food for thought.

As we said at the outset, these ten criteria for global successful competitiveness are somewhat arbitrary. Each reader could probably add to the list or refine it. Nevertheless, any corporation seeking to expand globally can help itself succeed by taking inventory against these ten criteria.

1. Pieter Kuin, "The Magic of Multinational Management," *Harvard Business Review,* November-December 1972, p. 89.

2. Thomas Hout, Michael E. Porter, and Eileen Rudden, "How Global Companies Win Out," *Harvard Business Review,* September-October 1982, p. 103.

3. Hout, Porter, and Rudden (see note 2).

4. *Organization and Central of International Operations* (New York: The Conference Board, 1978), p. 8.

5. Hout, Porter, and Rudden (see note 2), pp. 98-108.

6. Hout, Porter, and Rudden (see note 2).

7. Michael E. Porter, *Competitive Strategy: Techniques For Analyzing Industries and Competitors* (New York: Free Press, 1980).

8. Jeff Kennard, "An American Expatriates'

View of Japanese Business," *Agenda: A Journal For Xerox Managers*, March 1983, pp. 4-10.

9. Robert Ronstadt and Robert J. Kramer. "Getting the Most Out of Innovation Abroad," *Harvard Business Review*, March-April 1982, p. 94.

10. Ronstadt and Kramer (see note 9), pp. 94-99.

11. Ronstadt and Kramer (see note 9), p. 99.

12. Daniel J. Boorstin, *The Americans.* (New York: Random House, 1973), p. 284.

13. Theodore Levitt, "The Globalization of Markets," *Harvard Business Review*, May-June 1983, p. 93.

14. Lynn W. Phillips, Dae Chang, and Robert D. Buzzell, "Product Quality: Cost Production and Business Performance—A Test of Some Key Hypotheses," *Harvard Business School Working Paper No. 83-13*.

15. John F. Welch, Jr., *Speech to the Foreign Policy Association*, New York City, November 28, 1983.

16. Levitt (see note 13), p. 92.

17. Joseph La Palombara and Stephen Blank, *Multinational Corporations In Comparative Perspective*, (New York: "The Conference Board, 1979).

18. J. William Widing, Jr., "Reorganizing Your Worldwide Business," Harvard Business Review, May-June 1973, p. 156.

19. Hout, Porter, and Rudden (see note 2), p. 107.

20. Levitt (see note 13), p. 100.

21. Thomas W. Shreeve, "Be Prepared For Political Changes Abroad," *Harvard Business Review*, July-August 1984, p. 111.

22. Howard V. Perlmutter and David A. Heenan, "How Multinational Should Your Top Managers Be?" *Harvard Business Review*, November-December 1974, p. 123.

23. Howard V. Perlmutter, "The Tortuous Evolution of the Multinational Corporation," *Columbia Journal of World Business*, January-February 1969, p. 9.

24. Perlmutter and Heenan (see note 22), p. 124.

25. Perlmutter and Heenan (see note 22), p. 124.

26. David A. Heenan, "The Corporate Expatriate," *Columbia Journal of World Business*, May-June 1970, p. 49.

27. David Young, "Fair Compensation For Expatriates," *Harvard Business Review*, July-August 1973, p. 117.

28. Perlmutter and Heenan (see note 22), p. 130.

29. *The Changing Role of the International Executive*, The Conference Board, SBP No. 119, p. 18.

30. Samuel C. Johnson and Richard M. Thomson, "Active Role For Outside Directors of Foreign Subsidiaries," *Harvard Business Review*, September-October 1974, p. 14.

31. Johnson and Thomson (see note 30), p. 14.

32. Thomas J. Peters and Robert H. Waterman, Jr., *In Search of Excellence*, (New York: Harper & Row, 1982), pp. 89-318.

Beware the Pitfalls of Global Marketing

*Shortcomings in a campaign,
like inadequate research and poor follow-up,
can fell a good product.*

Kamran Kashani

Before Kamran Kashani became professor of marketing at the International Management Development Institute (IMEDE) in Lausanne, Switzerland, he worked for Coca-Cola, General Tire, and Continental Can International. He is the author of Managing Global Marketing, *published by PWS-Kent.*

It's fashionable today to enthuse over globalized markets and cite glowing examples of standardized marketing winners around the world. True, some markets *are* globalizing, and more companies are taking advantage of them with signal success. But the rosy reports of these triumphs usually neglect to mention the complexities and risks involved; for every victory in globalization there are probably several failures that aren't broadcast. It's not fashionable to talk about failure.

To get an idea of the complexity and the risks in global marketing, examine the case of Henkel, West Germany's leading industrial and consumer adhesives producer. In 1982, Henkel decided to pump new life into its internationally accepted but stagnating consumer contact-adhesive brand, Pattex. The strategy called for expanding the Pattex brand to include newly introduced products in fast-growing segments of the market. The idea of using Pattex as an um-

brella faced heavy opposition, however, from among Henkel's country subsidiaries worldwide. "People were shaking their heads and saying it can't be done and shouldn't be done," recalls the product manager responsible for the decision.

The subsidiaries' doubts led to a consumer test of the umbrella branding concept in West Germany, Austria, and Benelux. According to the test results, Pattex could be repositioned without hurting sales, and it could enhance the prospects of a broader product range. The highly positive survey responses helped soften local managements' opposition. The

 Why did Henkel's global branding succeed with Pattex and fail with Pritt?

global branding of Pattex as "strong universal bonding" took effect soon after.

Almost from the beginning, the relaunched brand showed good results. Today Pattex is Henkel's top brand in consumer adhesives in Europe and in 20 other countries. Surpassing all management expectations, the new products account for close to one-half of the brand's total sales of approximately 100 million deutsche marks.

Thus encouraged, Henkel's management took a similar step a few months after the relaunch of Pattex. This time the subject of umbrella treatment was Pritt, the company's number one brand around the world in glue sticks. Previously, Henkel had repositioned Pritt from "stick gluing" to "simple all-purpose gluing," but with little success. Nevertheless, the experience with Pattex gave top management reason to hope that a coordinated, standardized package design and communication strategy might do the trick this time.

Besides, the major subsidiaries had changed their tune: they endorsed an internationally harmonized Pritt line. In fact, the champion of the concept was the Benelux unit, one of Henkel's largest. Many executives in headquarters in Düsseldorf also viewed the Pritt decision as the next logical step after Pattex.

What more could central product management possibly ask for?

There was one potential problem, however, with the Pritt plan. A quickly arranged consumer survey in West Germany and Benelux had shown that the harmonized line might still be insufficient to turn the broader Pritt umbrella brand around. While comparative test results indicated some improvement over the current package design, they still put UHU, Pritt's global archrival, ahead along many consumer-perceived dimensions. But Pattex's encouraging performance and the unusually strong support from the leading subsidiaries persuaded the head office to proceed with the harmonized line anyway.

In the months that followed, while Pattex maintained its sales climb, the new strategy failed to im-

> ## The "Learn to Speak Polaroid" campaign made all the right moves.

prove Pritt's ho-hum performance, to everybody's surprise. The brand did not lend support to the lesser products under its umbrella, and their sales continued to stall. Today worldwide sales still hover far below expectations, and Pritt remains a one-product brand standing for stick gluing and not much more.

What explains the success of one program in the face of heavy subsidiary opposition and the failure of the other in spite of warm local support? Henkel management has discovered two reasons. Headquarters let forceful subsidiary officers drown out early warnings based on research about Pritt, and they hastened the decision. It was a case of enthusiasm substituting for hard data. Moreover, when the early results disappointed hopes, the subsidiaries diverted

Pritt's promotion funds to other products in a search for immediate payoff. With no central follow-up, the local units did nothing to make up the lost promotion support.

Accordingly, the Pritt plan got neither the initial scrutiny nor the later subsidiary backup that Pattex had enjoyed. Combined, the two handicaps proved fatal to Pritt's global branding.

Winners and Losers

To ascertain why certain global marketing decisions succeed while others fail, I recently studied 17 cases of marketing standardization at 9 American and European multinationals. Nine of the ventures were successes, but in eight, the companies failed to meet their objectives. This article reports on the findings of the study.

A systematic comparison of the "winners" and "losers" reveals that the differences in outcome often depend on the processes underlying the decision making. In other words, my study shows that the ways global decisions are conceptualized, refined, internally communicated, and, finally, implemented in the company's international network have a great deal to do with their performance.

I have identified five pitfalls that handicap global marketing programs and contribute to their suboptimal performance or even demise. The pitfalls include insufficient use of formal research, tendency to overstandardize, poor follow-up, narrow vision in program coordination, and inflexibility in implementation. I'll take these up in turn.

Insufficient Research. Formal research is of course not alien to marketing decision making, yet many a global program has been kicked off without the benefit of a reality test. Nearly half of the programs examined included no formal research before startup. And most of the companies paid for this omission afterwards.

A case in point was Lego A/S, the Danish toy marketer, which undertook American-style consumer promotions in Japan a few years ago. Earlier, the company had measurably improved its penetration of U.S. households by employing "bonus" packs and gift promotions. Encouraged by that success, it decided to transfer these tactics unaltered to other markets, including Japan, where penetration had stalled. But these lures left Japanese consumers unmoved. Subsequent investigation showed that consumers considered the promotions to be wasteful, expensive, and not very appealing. Similar reactions were recorded in several other countries. Lego's marketers thus got their first lesson on the limitations of the global transferability of sales promotions.

Lego management examined consumer perceptions of promotions only *after* the program had failed. In the words of one headquarters executive close to the decision concerning Japan, "People at the head office in Billund and locally believed so much in the U.S. experience and its transferability that they didn't see any need to test the promotions."

This case typifies managerial complacency toward use of market information. At the extreme, it exhibits itself as "we know what we need to know," an attitude that discounts the necessity of research in the early phases of a program. This blinkered outlook often accompanies an assumption that one market's experience is transferable to others—as though the world has finally converged and market idiosyncracies have disappeared. Even managers' enthusiasm can get in the way of research. Henkel learned this point in its almost casual dismissal of Pritt's consumer survey results.

Shortcutting the early step of research in a decision process is likely to be costly. Of the cases in the sample, nearly two-thirds of the global programs that did not benefit from formal research before launch failed in their mission, while the same proportion of those that relied on research succeeded.

Overstandardization. Paradoxically, without some diversity of practice in the organization, marketing standardization will not work. When a program is burdened with too many standards, local inventiveness and experimentation close to the markets dry up. Local innovation is exactly what a global program needs to keep itself updated and responsive to evolving market conditions.

In the mid-1970s, when Polaroid introduced its pathbreaking SX-70 camera in Europe, the company employed the same advertising strategy—including TV commercials and print ads—it had used in the triumphant launch of the product in the United States. To headquarters in Cambridge, Massachusetts, the camera was a universal product with a universal consumer benefit: the pleasure of instant photography. Therefore, the communication approach should be standard around the world. Well, the product was surely universal, but the television commercials, featuring testimonials from personalities well-known in the United States, like Sir Laurence Olivier, were not necessarily transferable to Europe. At least, that's what Polaroid's executives there thought.

Unperturbed by subsidiaries' concerns, Cambridge set strict guidelines to discourage deviation from the global plan. Even local translations of the English spoken in the commercials had to get approval from the head office. As one senior European executive recalls, "We were treated like kids who have to be controlled every step along the way."

The Europeans were proved to be right. The testimonials by "unknown" personalities left consumers cold. The commercials never achieved much impact in either raising awareness of Polaroid for instant photography or pulling consumers into the stores for a closer look at the camera. Even though the SX-70 later became a winner in Europe, local management believes that the misguided introductory campaign in no way helped its performance.

Fortunately, the lesson was not forgotten a decade later, when Polaroid's European management launched a program of pan-European advertising to reposition Polaroid's instant photography from a "party camera" platform, which had eroded the brand's image and undermined camera prices, to a serious, utilitarian platform. But this time, headquarters didn't assume it had the answer. Instead, it looked for inspiration in the various advertising

Would local managers buy DEC's Europe-wide sales program?

practices of the European subsidiaries. And it found the answer in the strategy of one of the smallest subsidiaries, Switzerland's. With considerable profit, the Swiss unit had promoted the functional uses of instant photography as a way to communicate with family and friends. A pan-European task force charged with setting the advertising strategy tested the concept in major markets. These tests proved that the Swiss strategy was transferable and indeed produced the desired impact.

Thus was born the "Learn to Speak Polaroid" campaign. The two-year European project is considered one of the company's most successful advertising efforts. Subsidiaries outside Europe, including those in Australia and Japan, liked the strategy so much that they adopted it too. The experience is a source of pride for European management and a reaffirmation that "Europe can take care of itself."

What made the SX-70 and "Learn to Speak Polaroid" campaigns decidedly different was the decision-making processes involved. Promoting the SX-70 was a top-down process. But in "Learn to Speak Polaroid," the subsidiaries were offered the opportunity to influence the outcome, and they took it. Furthermore, "Learn..." was a product of the diversity found in the subsidiaries' communication strategies. The task force had the luxury of choosing among several solutions to the problem. It also had the wisdom to test the chosen strategy for confirmation of its impact around Europe.

Finally, and perhaps most important, even after adopting the pan-European program, local management retained the freedom to adapt the campaign to domestic tastes and needs. For example, where tests showed that the "Learn..." tag didn't convey the intended meaning in the local language, the subsidiary was free to change it. The message was more important than the words. Moreover, while the copy and layout for print ads remained fixed throughout Europe, local units could choose their preferred illustrations from a large set of alternatives prepared by the ad agency.

The contrasting outcomes of these two campaigns underscore a point clear to experienced marketers that, for a global program to achieve its aims, the scope of standardization need not be total. Any such program usually can attain its objectives through standardization of a few elements in the marketing mix of a product or service. Never too many elements, however, these are the leverage points around which the rationale for standardization is built.

With Pattex, for instance, the global branding strategy depended on the use of a successful brand for new products, uniform positioning of the entire range, and harmonized package designs. Local units, on the other hand, had authority over a set of decisions including communication strategy, pricing, and distribution channels. They could even decide on the package illustrations pertaining to the uses of adhesives. These matters, though important to the marketing success of Pattex in each country, did not impinge on the rationale or the crucial elements of standardization.

Nor did the flexibility allowed in the execution of "Learn to Speak Polaroid" advertising weaken the campaign. Deviations in execution didn't distract from the common mission; rather, they helped strengthen the effort by bringing local expertise to bear on the details. Overstandardization would have destroyed the incentive for local contribution, a price no global marketing program can afford to pay.

Poor Follow-up. Impressive kickoff meetings, splashy presentations to country heads, and the like are important attention-getters at the start of a campaign. But the momentum will be lost, as in the case of Pritt's promotional support, if these are not followed by lower key yet concrete steps to monitor progress and solve problems as they come along. These post-launch activities can determine whether a program survives the domestic organization's other priorities.

The differing experiences of Digital Equipment Corporation and another U.S.-based computer company, which I will call Business Electronic Systems (BES), are instructive. Not long ago, DEC's European operation installed a standardized sales management program in its 17 regional subsidiaries. Aimed to improve sales force productivity and customer service, the program touched on many aspects of overseeing

the region's 2,500-strong sales force. But as sales operations were traditionally considered a local matter, sales managers were at first predictably unenthusiastic about using the system. It was considered an infringement on their authority.

What gradually sold them on it was the continuity of attention the program got in the two years after its highly visible launch. Through watchful monitoring of progress toward full implementation, coordinating sessions among local sales managers, and periodic messages of reinforcement from top management, sponsors at regional headquarters made sure that the program received priority from subsidiary officials. The coordinating sessions for subsidiary sales managers were particularly helpful, highlighting the payoffs from use of the system and furnishing a forum for dealing with common problems. These sessions proved to be invaluable for taking a creative solution produced in one market and spreading it to the other 16.

At BES, which installed a standardized software-house cooperation program in Europe, the picture was much different. Regional headquarters conceived the program to help penetrate a market segment where BES was weak – small and medium-sized accounts. The program required a big change in sales force operation: no longer in control of the hardware and software package, the sales force had to determine its content jointly with a software house that had access to the smaller accounts. The success of the standardized program depended on how well the sales force carried out its new assignments in BES's eight country and subregional European operations.

Like DEC, BES gave the project a highly visible launch. Top management left no doubt that the software-house cooperation strategy enjoyed its

It took nonconforming managers to make Unilever's household cleaner a success.

wholehearted support. But the program never got the follow-up attention it needed. The responsibility for overseeing the project kept changing hands in the head office. Partly as a result of these switches in management, efforts to monitor progress in the subsidiaries dwindled.

The main problem, however, was the absence of a communication channel for sharing and building on subsidiary experiences. Each unit was obliged to find its own solutions to problems common to many. Hence the wheel was reinvented every time. Moreover, many country sales managers resented having to implement an unpopular program. Some gave up; others reluctantly carried on to the end, which came in three years. The reason: poor performance.

The quality of follow-up is of paramount importance when a global program introduces abrupt changes in local practice. As DEC's example shows, timely follow-up measures can go a long way to ensure subsidiary involvement and compliance. Without such measures, as BES learned, the program can easily succumb to local management's lukewarm interest.

Narrow Vision. A coordinating organization is needed to look after the health of a global marketing program because, as we have seen, a program's success depends so much on what happens after its launch – whether problems in implementation are resolved, and how the program's content is adapted to evolving internal and market conditions.

Two common mechanisms employed to manage a global program through its launch and beyond are those based, respectively, in the headquarters and a "lead market." Under a headquarters mechanism, the formal authority for a program rests with a central line or staff function like worldwide product management, regional management, or international marketing coordination. Under a lead market mechanism, a subsidiary is assigned the responsibility to define and manage a given program for all the participating "follower" countries. The choice of a lead market is usually a function of its expertise or experience with a particular product or service.

Though popular, both approaches have serious weaknesses. Headquarters, by definition removed from the firing line, nevertheless makes decisions that are supposed to keep the program fine-tuned to changing subsidiary market conditions. Similarly, the lead-market structure lacks the global perspective and information sources to coordinate international activities well. That is especially true when the lead market is also the home base for successful products that are globalization candidates. In these cases, management isn't always willing to adopt its "tried and proven" marketing ideas to different conditions prevailing elsewhere in the international organization.

But the main problem with both mechanisms is narrow vision; in each, only a single perspective is represented. As such they are not open to a continuous stream of inputs from local markets. Nor do they provide a forum for debating alternatives or sharing solutions to common problems. As a result, local management often justifiably regards headquarters or lead-market decisions as narrow, insular, top-down, and even dictatorial.

Unilever's experience with its household cleaner Domestos shows how a decision-making structure representing a single view can hamper global market-

ing. In the 1970s, the Anglo-Dutch company targeted Domestos for international expansion and assigned development of a global "reference mix" to the brand's lead market in the United Kingdom, where Domestos had been well established for a long time. But years and several market entries later, top management was still waiting for a repeat elsewhere of the UK's success story. Later analysis identified a key contributor to the problem: the lead market's insistence on a home-brewed recipe of positioning Domestos as a "lavatory germ killer" in markets already crowded with specialized and lower priced competition.

Where the product had won penetration, it had done so largely by deviating from the lead market's guidelines and staking out a whole new product category. In West Germany, Domestos was positioned as an all-purpose sanitary cleaner, and in Australia as a "bathroom plaque remover" – an innovative platform with potential for universal application, as consumers in many markets now show a growing concern with the appearance of their bathrooms.

To avoid the problems inherent in center-based or lead-market mechanisms, Unilever's detergent unit recently opted for a multisubsidiary structure to coordinate brands in Europe. The European Brand Group (EBG) is a decision-making body that includes executives from headquarters and a number of large subsidiaries.

So far, the company's experience with this mixed organization has been encouraging. As an example, EBG was instrumental in developing and launching a lemon-scented version of Vif, Unilever's successful abrasive liquid cleaner, across Europe in record time of a few months. Most important, the introduction outfoxed Procter & Gamble, which was known to be planning a similar move with its Mr. Clean; Vif Lemon won the race to market in every single country. Unilever management hopes that such gains in coordination will reinforce EBG's mandate to "view Europe as one business" and help speed up harmonization of marketing practices around the continent.

Rigid Implementation. Standardized marketing is a means of reaching an end, never an end in itself. When global marketers forget that obvious truth, standardization risks becoming rigid and ultimately self-defeating. Two common manifestations of rigidity are forced adoption and automatic piloting.

Forced adoption is the outcome of a tendency to ignore local units' reservations about implementing a standardized marketing program. Higher level management's typical reaction is to close the exit door on this ground: "After all, what's left of global marketing if the implementation isn't universal?" Theoretically, this is right. And ardent globalizers would argue that local resistance can be expected in any standardized effort and that without some central direction, a program would never get off the ground. But forced compliance rarely delivers the anticipated rewards. Among the programs I studied, every case of forced adoption had eventually flopped.

It is true that a subsidiary's objection may stem from resistance to ideas originating from outside. But local management's reservations may also be based on a sound understanding of its domestic market. When Nestlé launched its innovative cakelike Yes chocolate bar in Europe, the UK organization refused to take the product because a soft bar assertedly

 ## Lego's packaging was just fine for kids, but parents buy toys.

would not appeal to British tastes. Subsequent market tests validated this local opinion. Forced adoption would have led to failure on a large scale.

Whatever the reasons for local opposition, forced compliance destroys any commitment to program implementation. And no global program, no matter how sound, can survive such absence of commitment.

Automatic piloting is symptomatic of inflexible program management in the face of changing market conditions. Lego's costly difficulties in the United States illustrate this problem. The company, whose motto has been "kids are kids and alike around the world," pioneered standardized marketing in its industry and became a truly global enterprise by marketing its educational toys in the same fashion in more than 100 countries.

Recently, however, Lego has encountered stiff competition from look-alike and lower priced rival products from Japan, the United States, and other countries. In the United States, where the competition has been the fiercest, Tyco, a leading competitor, began putting its toys in plastic buckets that could be used for storage after each play. This utilitarian approach contrasted with Lego's elegant see-through cartons standardized worldwide. But American parents seemed to prefer the functional toys-in-a-bucket idea over the cartons. Seeing a potential for serious damage, Lego's alarmed U.S. management sought permission from Denmark to package Lego toys in buckets. The head office flatly refused the request.

The denial was based on seemingly sound arguments. The bucket idea could cheapen Lego's reputation for high quality. Moreover, the Lego bucket would rightly be seen as a "me too" defensive reaction from a renowned innovator. Finally, and perhaps most important, buckets would be a radical deviation from the company's policy of standardized marketing everywhere. Even U.S. consumer survey results comparing buckets favorably with cartons

weren't considered a good enough reason for a change from the global concept.

Two years later, however, headquarters in Billund reversed itself. The impetus was a massive loss of U.S. market share to competitive goods sold in buckets. Soon after, the American subsidiary began marketing some of its toys in a newly designed bucket of its own. Now, to the delight of many in Billund, the buckets are outselling the cartons, and the share erosion has reassuringly halted. (Last Christmas the bucket was introduced worldwide and was a smashing success.) An observer of Lego's about-face in the United States attributed the two-years-late response to automatic piloting on the part of its global marketers.

The Lego story highlights the principle adhered to by some, but ignored by many others, that international conformity to global standards may have to be sacrificed to respond to shifting conditions in particular markets. As one Lego executive put it ruefully, "While kids will always be alike around the world, parents who buy the toys may change their behavior."

Improving the Process

The pitfalls I have examined can all be traced to shortcomings in a global program's decision-making process. But the winners in my sample show that such traps can be avoided. Analysis of them leads to the following observations on ways of upgrading the process and the decisions that result from it.

☐ Market research helps a global marketing program in two ways: by influencing decisions to more accurately reflect the commonalities as well as the differences among subsidiary markets; and by winning support for the program in local organizations when research results are especially encouraging.

Useful research is multisite in geographic coverage and uniform in methodology. The multisite criterion ensures enough local diversity to make the findings valid for the program's international scope. Needless to say, a global marketing program doesn't have to be tested everywhere. Some companies find the inclusion of at least one major subsidiary market and a few others considered representative of the rest sufficient not only for geographic diversity purposes but also for building internal credibility for the results. Uniform methodology, on the other hand, ensures comparability of international research data, which is so often a problem for global marketers. "Without similar methods," one experienced executive noted, "the local organizations can kill a good global program with their own research."

☐ Local initiative and decision making are often the

keys to a program's long-term success. To avoid sterile uniformity at one extreme and a free-for-all at the other, global marketers have to delineate early on the few standards that are essential to attaining a program's objectives and the many that are not. They must insist on compliance with the essential stan-

▌Strike a balance between central control and subsidiary autonomy.

dards. But at the same time, local experimentation with the less critical elements should be allowed and even encouraged. Astute marketers will keep an eye on the local experiments and in due course incorporate the successful innovations into an evolving and dynamic set of global standards.

☐ Effective follow-up – as important as any prelaunch measure – means identifying common problems hampering implementation, spreading creative solutions found by local units, and winning support for the program over parochial priorities. But these tasks don't get performed automatically; they need to be recognized and assigned.

The responsibility for initiating and directing postlaunch activities must therefore be focused by a central program manager or a management team. The chosen individual(s) should possess not only the international overview necessary to administer the program but also negotiating skills for bypassing organizational barriers and building consensus and support for the project. These skills become particularly useful in cases where globalization demands radical departures in local practices.

☐ While the *process* for formulating a program, starting it, and following it through may be driven centrally by, say, program management, decisions on its *content* are best left to the subsidiaries or country or-

ganizations. So an ad hoc decision-making mechanism incorporating a number of subsidiaries offers more openness to local input than one centered at headquarters or in a lead market.

To prevent this process from becoming cumbersome, headquarters should limit the group's membership to a few of the larger and more influential subsidiaries and confine its participants to those local marketing managers with deep knowledge of the issues and the organizational weight to see decisions through to implementation. The experience of a growing number of companies employing such ad hoc mechanisms suggests, not surprisingly, that their effectiveness improves as the participants get practice working together on issues of concern to most member countries. That experience also suggests that thorny problems are best left for resolution after the group has established a track record of successful decisions.

☐ Flexibility should be built into a global program's implementation. That means a willingness on its sponsors' part selectively to sacrifice global standards when local conditions so dictate or to leave open an exit door when local management argues against adoption of a program. In the absence of flexibility, standardized marketing risks becoming an obstacle to competitive advantage.

But what to do in those frequent cases when global marketers and their subsidiary colleagues differ on the standards appropriate in a certain market? A number of companies in my study have a "facts-over-opinions" policy to get around this potentially volatile problem. A subsidiary gains exemption from having to conform in part or altogether if, and only if, careful research confirms its doubts. By letting facts decide each case, the policy helps focus the attention of both sides on the substantive issues and clears the debate of mere opinions – which are so often colored. Implementation of the marketing program then proceeds in an informed but flexible fashion.

HITTING FOR SINGLES

Sheridan M. Tatsuno

Sheridan M. Tatsuno, president of NeoConcepts, a high-technology consulting firm in Fremont, California, is author of *Created in Japan: From Imitators to World-Class Innovators*, from which this article is adapted. © 1989 Harper & Row.

For years, Westerners have conceded that the Japanese are adept at refining products, but have dismissed their refinement techniques as purely imitative. In doing so, Western managers have ignored the imagination and creativity behind these techniques. The Japanese are now applying them to scientific and technological research; the result has been world-class status in high-definition television, next-generation computers, and superconductivity. It may be time for those in the West to take a studied look at the Japanese method of refining ideas.

For the Japanese, creative refinement is not merely product imitation or copying. It is a disciplined method for transforming an idea into something new and valuable, just as cutting and polishing diamonds is an industrial process for creating jewelry. Creative refinement introduces totally new marketing concepts and applications. It is conceptual leapfrog. Sony Corporation, for example, redefined the concept of portable sound by using stereo headphones to develop the Walkman, creating a whole new way of listening to music. No longer do listeners have to sit in an auditorium or living room to enjoy stereo sound. They can bring it with them shopping, jogging, or lounging at the beach. Similarly, Japanese video manufacturers have transformed home movies into a cinematographic experience. By offering superior audiovisual quality and instant feedback, Japanese 8mm video cameras have made Shakespeare's famous line, "All the world's a stage," come alive at family gatherings and special events.

The concept of *kaizen*—constant improvement—is central to understanding Japan's approach to creative refinement. Unlike Western companies, which often seek quantum leaps in technology and productivity, Japanese companies prefer to make small, incremental improvements in their daily operations. They hit for singles and doubles, not the home run or grand slam. Japanese workers are constantly encouraged through the use of quality circles, suggestion boxes, meetings, and consensus decision-making to offer new ideas for reducing costs, increasing quality, simplifying procedures, and developing new products. They are taught that small improvements, no matter how minor or seemingly insignificant, are crucial for the ultimate success of their company. If there is any secret to Japan's economic successes, *kaizen* surely ranks high on the list.

Today, Japan is adapting the concept of *kaizen* to basic research and new technologies. *Kaizen* is now being used to creatively refine ideas, not just products. In the field of personal computing, for example, Toshiba Corporation and other computer makers are rapidly introducing generation after generation of new ideas into their laptop computers. Initially, they introduced liquid crystal display (LCD) screens and built-in printers, then memory storage cards, optical scanners, and ergonomic keyboards, and now voice recognition systems. In the field of high-temperature superconductivity, Japanese researchers are refining new theories and experimenting with various materials in hopes of making new breakthroughs.

The Magic of Miniaturization

A powerful Japanese technique for refining new ideas and technologies is miniaturization. The Japanese are well known for their proclivity for making things ever smaller, which is reflected in their compact, lightweight radios, cameras, televisions, and automobiles. This expertise in miniaturization is highly developed, even when compared with that of other Asian nations. The Chinese, for example, are master carvers of miniature jade and ivory figurines, but unlike the Japanese, they did not incorporate the idea of smallness into their very culture.

The Korean writer O-Young Lee, author of *Smaller is Better: Japan's Mastery of the Miniature*, observes that the Japanese predilection for smallness is not found even in nearby Korea, which was the source of many Japanese traditions: "In Japanese . . . it is not the prefixes for 'huge' but those for 'tiny' that are commonly used.... The round bean (*mame*) is like a condensed representation of the world.... Such words as *mame-bon* (minibook), *mame-jidosha* (minicar), *mame-ningyo* (minidoll), and *mame-zara* (miniplate) all denote objects that are much smaller than normal.... If one explores this concept of miniaturization beyond Japanese folklore into other aspects of Japanese culture, one discovers fascinating realms—of tiny festival dolls, for example, and dwarf trees (*bonsai*). And here one gets a glimpse of what is unique in Japanese culture ... it is not so much Japan's external conditions that drove it toward smallness as an innate propensity toward shrinking things."

The Japanese tradition of miniaturization has been highly valued because of the premium placed on the country's limited resources and space. The Japanese have been able to transform this tradition into a competitive tool. Sharp Corporation's development of hand-held calculators is a good example. In 1964 Sharp introduced the CS-10A desktop electronic calculator, which weighed 55 pounds and cost $2,500. By using integrated circuits, Sharp reduced its Model CS-16A desktop calculator to 8.8 pounds and $1,770 in 1967. By 1972 light-emitting diode (LED) screens reduced the weight of its Model E1-81 to three pounds, bringing the price down to $300. By 1980 the use of energy-efficient chips reduced the weight of the Model EL-826 to less than an ounce and a half. The price had plummeted to $23. Today, Sharp's solar-powered calculators are $4 at any drugstore.

By rapidly miniaturizing its calculators and constantly reducing production costs, Sharp has been able to remain competitive in the calculator market. This is the famous "learning curve" phenomenon in which manufacturing costs decline as production volumes increase. Because it forces manufacturers to reduce the size and number of parts used in new products, miniaturization is a strategic tool for quickly moving up the learning curve.

Miniaturization is also a technique for developing new product concepts. In the early 1980s, for example, Plus Company tried selling portable copiers for use with blackboards. Images and handwriting on a blackboard could be recorded by sliding a hand-held copier over them. The product failed in the marketplace and was dropped for several years, but a group of Plus researchers persisted in developing a new pocket-size copier for business and students. In 1984 Plus introduced the "Copy-Jack," the world's first portable copier, which was shaped like an electric shaver and weighed slightly less than a pound. Matsushita Electric Industrial Company liked the concept and asked Plus to redesign the copier to make it sleeker and less expensive. In June 1985 Matsushita introduced the redesigned Copy-Jack, which caught skeptical retailers completely by surprise. On

Minimarket: Plus Company's portable copier spurred a wave of spin-off products, including miniscanners.

the first day of sales, the 10,000 Copy-Jacks immediately sold out, creating an instant three-month backlog of orders. Other Japanese makers quickly jumped into the minicopier market, setting off a wave of spin-off products. NEC Corporation, Toshiba, and other Japanese computer companies, for example, have connected portable copiers to their personal computers for use as image-scanning "mice." Unexpectedly, minicopiers have opened the door to miniscanners for laptop and portable computers, which, like facsimile machines, will change the way corporations conduct business.

The Strength of Simplicity

If miniaturization is a source of refinement, simplicity is its cultural handmaiden. Whereas Americans and Europeans often develop complex, large-scale solutions to problems, the Japanese constantly pare down and reduce the complexity of products and ideas to the barest minimum. They streamline the design, reduce the number of parts, and simplify the inner workings. The influence of Zen and haiku poetry are often evident in the simplicity and utility of Japanese designs.

Fuji Photo Film Company's disposable camera is an example of how Japanese companies simplify technology to its bare essentials. In 1985 the manager of Fuji Photo Film's consumer photo product division, Keiji Nakayama, headed a team that combined optical technology with industrial design. Their goal was to develop a disposable camera for teenagers and young adults. The camera had to be easy to use and offer high-quality pictures, but they also wanted something that could be sold for less than $12 and that did not look like a high-tech, sophisticated camera, to avoid scaring away some customers. To achieve its goal, the Fuji Photo Film team pared down its camera. A paper-box design was chosen to reduce cost and weight. The lens system was simplified by eliminating the focusing and diaphragm devices.

When the camera was launched in July 1986, Fuji Photo Film's stock rose sharply. Sales took off, outstripping the company's planned annual production of one million units. And most surprising, a customer survey revealed that the biggest users of Fuji Photo Film's disposable cameras were not teenagers but businessmen in their 30s. They wanted something lightweight and simple for their business trips.

Thus, as Fuji Photo Film learned, simplicity is an art in its own right, one that often leads to unexpected results.

Embracing Incompleteness

If simplicity focuses on reducing the complexities of life, the Japanese concept of incompleteness is its cultural opposite, but is no less influential in the transformation of ideas into innovative products and services. Since Japan's feudal period, the notion of leaving something slightly incomplete or partially undone has been a common feature of Japanese art and etiquette. Both the artist's canvas of a large white expanse touched only with a few suggestive brush strokes and the asymmetric incompleteness of a Zen garden convey the notion of unfulfilled possibilities. They elicit creative responses by leaving viewers to "fill in the gaps" using their own imaginations.

An example of the incompleteness philosophy at work is the evolution of the 35mm single-lens reflex camera. During the late 1970s, sales at Japan's leading camera companies sagged as the market for 35mm cameras became saturated. As during previous lulls, many industry watchers thought there was little future in the camera business. Sony had failed with its Mavica optical disk camera, and others fumbled with electronic cameras. But in the early 1980s, Nikon Inc. hit upon the point-and-shoot 35mm camera for amateurs, which triggered a rush of new family-oriented cameras. Then, Canon Inc. hit the market with its best-selling EOS automatic 35mm camera, which immediately made it the leading camera company. That success was followed by Minolta Camera Company's stunning Maxxum 7000 automatic camera, which catalyzed major breakthroughs in electronic systems. Canon, Nikon, Minolta, and other makers added ergonomically designed handgrips, electronic exposures, and other new features to a product that others had considered mature.

This rush of product creativity suggests that because Japanese companies view their products as "incomplete," they are able to dream up new features to transform common items into hot-selling products.

The Value of Visualization

Another technique favored by the Japanese is the depiction of ideas as visual images and the refinement of visual appearances. Their inclination to visualize has deep roots in their language. Whereas Western languages are phonetically and aurally based, the Japanese and Chinese languages are more visually based because of their dependence on complex ideograms to convey meanings. The rigorous process needed to learn the Japanese language characters has the secondary effect of teaching one to recognize complex patterns and think in visual terms. The written language is a form of visual shorthand—very much like stenography or international street signs.

The Japanese are beginning to experiment with visualization techniques to design new products on computer-aided design systems. Daiwa House Industry and Kikusui Homes, for example, have developed "design-your-own-home" computer systems that allow customers to choose the number and size of rooms, the types of building materials, and the quality of various amenities. The software automatically draws the floor plan layout, provides a visual image of the final product, and calculates the final closing costs, mortgage payments, and qualifying income required for the home. Bedrooms, living rooms, kitchens, and other home features are denoted by a few visual icons. Thus designing one's home becomes merely a matter of moving boxes and icons around on a two-dimensional plane, which is then translated into three-dimensional drawings. By automating and visualizing the design process, buyers can choose from a variety of housing designs—as well as come up with their own ideas—without having to invest a lot of time and money.

As personal computers and computer-aided design systems proliferate throughout Japan, new visualization techniques will become increasingly important for training people in research and product design. NEC, for example, is developing four-dimensional workstations capable of simulating three-dimensional objects through the use of moving video. The effectiveness of such machines will rely on the ability of users to visualize the desired end result, an ability in which the Japanese seem to have a cultural headstart.

Tactical Transformation

Japanese culture has also provided Japanese companies with a tradition of transformation—rearranging parts of a setting or system to develop something entirely different. Perhaps the best example is the Japanese house, which traditionally features multifunction rooms. A living room is transformed into a master bedroom by merely shifting sliding screens, putting away collapsible furniture, and pulling out bedding. The dining room turns into the family room by rearranging the furniture, and the bathroom doubles as the laundry room.

Owing to the high cost of land, Japanese companies have adapted this technique to shopping malls and office complexes. The Nakagin capsule tower building in Tokyo, for instance, consists of 140 capsule-shaped rooms that can be rearranged and restacked like building blocks into different shapes as needed. Unlike inflexible buildings that are demolished after several decades of use, such "transformer buildings" can respond to the dynamic ebb and flow of urban businesses.

Because of its commercial potential, the concept of transformation is rapidly spreading throughout Japanese industry. Mattell Corporation's Transformer toy, which can be changed from a sportscar into a robot, is being copied by Japanese carmakers in an attempt to keep pace with rapidly changing consumer tastes. Mazda Motor Corporation's MX-04 concept car, for example, enables the owner to change the car's body style at will. By removing one set of body panels and replacing them with another, car owners may eventually be able to transform their daily runabouts into sporty weekend convertibles.

Signs of Japanese creativity are everywhere. At international trade shows, Japanese companies are trendsetters in industrial design, audio-video equipment, computerized language translation, bullet trains, car navigation systems, advanced robots, and factory automation. New product ideas, such as electronic keyboards, ceramic paper, plastic dancing flowers, and floating factories, are emanating from Tokyo. Japan's surging creativity is not newfound; its roots lie in Japanese language, religion, environment, and management skills. This makes it all the more critical for the West to wake up to the implications of Japan's latest creative endeavors, lest it be left in the dust as Japan blazes a trail of its own into the 21st century.

MYTH AND MARKETING IN JAPAN

BY DAMON DARLIN

Staff Reporter of The Wall Street Journal

TOKYO—American cars don't sell in Japan because Detroit puts the steering wheel on the "wrong" side—or at least that's the usual story.

It's a myth.

The reality: Most Japanese who buy a Mercedes or BMW actually prefer having the steering wheel on the left side. Even Honda quickly sold out of the U.S.-made Accords it recently brought to Japan, despite their wrong-side steering wheels.

This is just a minor example of the marketing myths that surround Japan. These hoary bits of conventional wisdom—on such matters as setting prices and adapting products for local tastes—typically shape foreign executives' thinking on how to do business here. Sometimes, too, they spark behavior that seems odd when viewed from the U.S. Indeed, such advice has served to discourage some American and European companies from even bothering to enter the world's second-largest consumer market.

More and more, however, executives here are recognizing the myths as myths. They see a lot of companies succeeding by flouting the old rules. And such successes are causing others in the foreign marketing community to start questioning their preconceived notions.

"The market is changing quickly here," says Per Norinder, director of Volvo Japan Corp.'s marketing division. "So if you don't see how it is changing, you are lost."

Of course, many of the generalizations now heard about the Japanese market, made up of some 125 million people with an average disposable household income equivalent to more than $38,000 a year, were once true. Moreover, a few of the old saws do still apply. For instance, Japanese consumers *are* perhaps the most quality-conscious in the world—a fact that businesses ignore at their peril. But a closer look at three of the more tenacious myths shows how different things have become.

MYTH 1

FOREIGN PRODUCTS MUST BE PRICED HIGH TO SUCCEED

"That's the fundamental belief of the foreign companies here," says Joel Silverstein, general manager of Brown & Williamson Tobacco Corp., a unit of London-based B.A.T Industries PLC. "That's all I ever heard. Otherwise, why would prices be so high here?"

In 1987, Brown & Williamson took a chance. It dropped the price for a pack of its Kent cigarettes to 220 yen (about $1.67) from 280 yen, lower even than the 250 yen a pack charged by Japan Tobacco Inc., the country's tobacco monopoly. The price cut—the first ever for a major imported consumer product here—was such a striking challenge that it made front-page news in some national Japanese newspapers.

Many people figured that Brown & Williamson would take a bath. "A Japanese trading company was concerned that if you dropped the price you'd sell less," Mr. Silverstein recalls. However, Kent became one of the fastest-selling cigarettes in Japan. Other foreign tobacco companies followed suit, as did Japan Tobacco. Foreign companies' market share zoomed from less than 3% to more than 12%.

Koyo Kanaya, president of Apex Inc., an importer of Western luxury goods, has also ignored the naysayers. When Apex started importing Hublot watches from Switzerland in 1984, it cut the price on one model to 1.2 million yen from the 1.8 million the previous importer had charged. "The watch shops were angry," Mr. Kanaya recalls, adding that some even stopped carrying the watch, claiming its image was ruined. But Apex sold 450 in the first year, he says, almost 150 more than the total of the previous three years.

"You cannot simply price a product high because it is imported," says Mark Bedingham, a senior managing director of Jardine Wine & Spirits, a liquor importer that once did just that. "But that was very much the strategy in the 1970s."

Several years ago, when a dollar bought 260 yen, few U.S. imports were going to be cheaper than comparable Japanese products. Thus, it made economic sense to bring in low-volume, high-margin goods, because demand for them is less sensitive to high prices. Eventually, it became common practice to market mid-range products—whether they were cars or beer—as high-class items.

Buying the Western Way

How a variety of imported products are faring in Japanese markets.*

Schick razor blades: 70% of the safety-blade market.

McDonald's hamburgers: 30% of the fast-food hamburger market (by sales).

Coca-Cola: 30% of the market for carbonated soft drinks.

Pampers: 20% to 22% of the disposable-diaper market.

German cars: 2.6% of the total car market.

U.S. cars: 0.4% of the total car market.

Braun shavers: 40% of the electric-shaver market. (Braun, a German company, is owned by Boston-based Gillette Co.)

Kodak amateur color film: 12% to 15% of the market.

Foreign-made cigarettes: 11.5% of the market (U.S. makers account for most).

*By volume, unless otherwise specified   *Sources: Company executives, market analysts*

With the dollar buying only about 132 yen now, it's easier to bring in cheaper products and compete in the mass market at the same price points as domestic companies. However, old habits die hard.

"We would never recommend a lower price," says Sadafumi Nishina, marketing director for international products at the Japanese ad agency Dentsu Inc.

MYTH 2

FOREIGN PRODUCTS MUST BE ADAPTED TO LOCAL TASTES

List some of the most successful products in Japan, and the truth is readily apparent. Even though many Japanese are convinced that what they get is different, the Coca-Cola, McDonald's hamburgers, M&M candies, Kodak color film, Listerine mouthwash and Kellogg's Corn Flakes available here are—apart from packaging—essentially the same as in the U.S.

It's not surprising that this myth prevails, though, given the prevalence of books that tell the Japanese how special they are. This idea of uniqueness, known as *Nihonjinron*, was behind the argument of a top Japanese politician who, during trade negotiations last year, told U.S. officials that Japanese can't eat beef because their intestines are longer than Americans'. (Actually, beef consumption is rising rapidly in Japan.)

Of course, some factors do have to be taken into account. For instance, most Japanese girls wash their hair daily, so milder shampoos are favored. Because laundry is done in cold, hard water, detergents formulated for such conditions sell best. And sugar is expensive, so using less

in a product makes economic sense.

But many ideas about what the Japanese will and won't accept have proved unfounded. When Yamazaki-Nabisco, the company that makes Nabisco-brand products in Japan, was considering selling Oreo cookies here, the thinking of many managers was, "Black food? No one in Japan would eat it," says Eiji Irino, a managing director. In 1987, the company did it anyway, and Oreos are now the No. 1 cookie in Japan.

Merle Higa, an American executive here, heard similar warnings when she started planning to bring pizza to Japan in the mid-1970s: "People said, 'It will never sell. Japanese think cheese tastes like soap.' " But that sounded too much like the arguments that her father, who helped to bring Pepsi to Japan, heard about cola's tasting too medicinal. Needless to say, both went ahead anyway, and Japan—where cola is now the most popular soft drink—is in the midst of a pizza craze.

MYTH 3

JAPAN IS A HOMOGENEOUS MARKET

To be sure, there is less ethnic, religious and cultural diversity here than in a nation of immigrants such as the U.S. And most Japanese, according to regular polls, consider themselves middle-class. What's more, as recently as 1978, books for foreign companies eyeing the Japanese market included such chapters as "Concentration and Uniformity—the Formation of a Mammoth Homogeneous Market."

But for the most part, the Japanese market is now uniform only compared with the U.S. Market researchers see large dif-

ferences in income levels and life styles here. "The myth is being shattered daily," says Norman A. MacMaster, president of J. Walter Thompson Co. Japan.

Robert Wilk, who runs a market-research firm owned by McCann-Erickson Hakuhodo Inc., has found that the Japanese rich—the top 10% of the population making more than 10 million yen a year—can be divided into five distinct groups. These range from the "overts," who spend heavily, particularly on foreign goods, art and travel, to the "conservatives," who tend to save their money or spend it on such things as their children's education. Studies of women, the elderly and the young have turned up similar findings.

Largely as a result of this knowledge, niche marketing is in full bloom in Japan. Cigarettes are a good example. There are now brands aimed at young men, such as Lucky Strike, and those aimed at older men, such as Kent. There are Capri and Virginia Slims for women. Japan Tobacco also sells a bevy of products aimed at various niches, including Dean for young men and Alex for young women.

Goldstar Co., the giant South Korean manufacturer of home electronics and other products, says that market segmentation in Japan—where it does about $90 million of business a year—is enabling it to invade the country with its lower-priced products. "The market wasn't there before," says Kim Young Jun, managing director of Goldstar's overseas business operations. "There was no demand for the low end, only high-end products. Now there is a market we can get into."

DISTRIBUTION
THE KEY TO SUCCESS OVERSEAS

JACK NADEL

Jack Nadel is the founder of Measured Marketing Services, a $100-million international company involved with both import and export. His AMA-COM book Cracking the Global Market *emphasizes the imperatives behind international trade.*

One of the most vital and powerful parts of the product mix is distribution, and companies that control distribution control almost everything. Merchandise can be distributed in 100 different ways, ranging from selling to importers, to selling direct to consumers. The method is dictated by the product, the consumer target for the product, the margins you want, and your company's capabilities. When it comes to a decision how to distribute, about 50 percent is determined by the product itself, 25 percent is determined by the marketplace and the margins, and 25 percent comes from your own gut feelings.

Theoretically, the more direct your distribution, the better off you are. If you sold directly to the customer—rather than to the importer which sells to distributors which sell to stores which sell to customers—

margins should be better. But this is not necessarily true. There are costs to distribution, and they are borne either by the distributor or you. The only difference is that the distributor is definitely going to take a profit. The question is, will you take a profit for that phase of business if you perform that function?

There must be fair profit on all ends of a business for them to be viable. In the United States, our company is both manufacturer and distributor. Hypothetically, you could say that because we manufacture in Providence, Rhode Island, and distribute in Los Angeles, we could eliminate one profit and benefit the customer. But that ultimately is a bad way to go. If you perform a function, you have to make a profit on that function, or it becomes a dead weight on other divisions in the company. It takes money to set up and distribute, just as it does to manufacture.

This is not profit for profit's sake. Each phase must have a definite function in the marketplace. Indeed, business takes a turn for the worse when people tack on profits for a service or function that is not being performed.

For example, say I were to introduce you to a potential customer, and ask for a commission on all of your business with that customer, and step out. I don't service the customer in any way and perform no further function. I'm really getting a finder's fee. But if I stretch that into a continuing commission, then I'm taking money out of the mix and it eventually will make you noncompetitive. If, instead, I take a one-time finder's fee, I'm performing a function that benefits everyone—and I'm not crippling your competitive capabilities.

There is a legitimate place in the market for finders such as business brokers involved in acquisitions. They serve as matchmakers between buyer and seller. But you can imagine what would happen if the business broker demanded a continuous fee from all business that ensued from that point on?

The Middle East's oil business is an excellent example of this practice carried to an illogical extreme. It's an economy based on a great deal of corruption, bribery, and contacts in high places. ("I'll introduce you to this sheik, but I want 5 percent of every-

From *Management Review*, September 1987, pp. 40–43. Excerpt from "Cracking the Global Market" under the new title *Passport to Prosperity—Tales of a Yankee Trader* by Jack Nadel. © 1987, Jack Nadel. Published by MMS Publishing, 1–800–451–3533.

thing you do from now on.") This worked to some degree when oil cost $30 a barrel, but at $10 a barrel (and even later at $18 a barrel) it can't.

I look for distributors that are going to give me continuing service.

TYPES OF DISTRIBUTION

Distribution costs money and affects margins. Choice among the many alternatives is dictated by the type of item, the margins, and the marketplace. Let's look at the various forms, from the least expensive to the most.

□ A broker is exactly what the name implies. They have no inventory and take no risk. They sell for you or buy for you and make a commission on the transaction. Keeping in mind the risk/profit ratio, this is the lowest margin that has to be sustained in the chain.

□ Importers will take from you and may or may not sell the product before buying it. But they are still taking all the risks of business. If anything goes wrong between the time they contract for the merchandise from you, the exporter, and sell it to their customers—be it a distributor, a jobber, or a consumer—they are taking the business risks. Their markup, therefore, will be much higher. The price of the product when it lands in the foreign country is going to be higher than if you deal through a broker, but distributors remove your risk and guarantee distribution.

□ The third approach is even more direct, it is to bypass the importer and call on the distributor or jobber in the foreign country. In essence, you become your own importer and deliver directly to the distributors.

□ The fourth approach is to eliminate the broker, the importer, and the distributor, and sell directly to the trade. This is what most of the name brands do. In that way you become your own distributor.

Companies evolve through these stages. It's interesting to look at what happened to companies such as Sony or Panasonic. When they originally entered the U.S., they dealt with American importers who handled radios. But as their fame and distribution grew, they left the importers and went to their own exclusive distributors. When the marketplace grew even larger, they went to the final stage and eliminated the distributors. Now they do the whole job themselves. This is why manufacturers' representatives have a common complaint: "The better job we do, the quicker we sell ourselves out of a job." Once they've given the distri-

bution to manufacturers, they are no longer needed.

PRODUCT DICTATES METHOD

The product dictates distribution. What is the product? What is the market? What markups can the product sustain? You shouldn't make the mistake we made a few years ago and distribute radios through pen distributors. They don't know what to do with them. Choosing distributors is as difficult as setting price. Do you take a small markup and go for large volume, or do you take a larger markup and go for smaller volume? If my product is limited and I want to export to 50 countries, then the simplest thing is to sell to importers in those countries and forget about it. There's no way I can create vast demand and satisfy the marketplace. On the other hand, IBM, with its enormous resources and a vast potential market, can't depend on anyone else to do its marketing. It is its own manufacturer, importer, distributor, and sales force.

Entrepreneurs don't have the resources of giant multinational corporations, of course. Individuals bringing products to the marketplace certainly don't have that kind of facility, or muscle, or financing. They must find the shortest, fastest means of distribution. As they improve their position, they can start moving through the distribution alternatives.

THE CASE OF SONY

How Sony became a household name in the U.S. makes for an interesting story. In one of its first attempts to distribute in the United States, Sony approached Bulova. Bulova liked the product and wanted Sony to manufacture it exclusively under the Bulova name. It argued that it took 50 years to create the Bulova name and would sell more radios as Bulova than as Sony.

Sony president Akio Morita turned down the easy sale. He knew in the long term the best thing would be to have a label of his own—one that people would know and learn to trust and want to buy. Of course, he proved himself right.

Soon after he turned down Bulova, Morita again displayed his business acumen. He went to one chain of stores with the first transistor radios. The chain loved the product and asked for quotations on 5,000, 10,000, 25,000, 50,000, and 100,000 radios. Morita thought about it and realized Sony would have to stretch to get the capacity to fill an order for

100,000 radios. Other markets would suffer. Perhaps it was tempting on a short-term basis, but what of the future? What would happen next year?

What did he do? He quoted the buyer prices based on the following: The highest per-unit price was for 100,000, for 50,000 it was a little lower, etc. The best unit price was for a 10,000-unit order—better than the price for 5,000.

The buyer thought Morita was crazy, but wound up buying 10,000 radios—which is exactly what Morita wanted to sell him. Morita didn't do the obvious and go for the quick and easy buck. He went instead for distribution that would give his product life, and would not put all his eggs in one basket, and that would allow him to build production properly. Now that is thinking distribution.

CONTROL

You can find people to make things, to engineer products, to administer finances, but if you don't have the distribution, you have nothing. If you have distribution, you control the product. As a businessman with a choice, I would much rather control distribution than manufacturing.

If I am importing a product and I have distribution for that product—whether I'm selling to jobbers, to stores, or direct—I control it.

How difficult is it for the exporter to replace my distribution? If it is very difficult, I have great control. If it is simple, then I have no control. If I have what is aptly called controlled distribution, then that exporter is vulnerable to me.

When we went into France, we manufactured and shipped directly to the customers. We were, in effect, making the French distributors dependent upon us. When distributors can buy the merchandise anywhere, imprint it themselves, and so on, they are independent of the manufacturer, but suffer certain inefficiencies. When distributors got into our system, in which we manufactured, imprinted and delivered to the customer, they could devote more time to selling, cut overhead, expand markets and make more money. But the one thing they could consider negative was that they were dependent on us.

The need of the distributor is exclusivity; the need of the manufacturer or exporter is diversification.

As an exporter or manufacturer, the less distribution I have, the more vulnerable I am, even if a single dis-

---

"The need of the distributor is exclusivity; the need of the manufacturer or exporter is diversification."

---

tributor gave me all the business I could handle.

Distribution should be as extensive as possible. And the more distribution you are responsible for, the more control you have.

It is wise to remember, however, that you never can control your distributors completely, and the further away from you they are, the more difficult it becomes. If you want your distributor to adhere to a particular marketing strategy, you can build it into your sales contract. However, even with that, you are severely limited in what you can accomplish.

You can specify the market in which you want the product sold and, if you are granting an exclusive or franchise arrangement, the distributor can stand to lose it if he ignores your directions. But in the U.S.— and in some form almost everywhere in the world—there are restraint-of-trade laws. If you buck those you can have a lawsuit on your hands. You should build subtle conditions into your sales contract that enable you to discontinue sales to a particular distributor if it acts in a way that will hurt the product image or market, but it is very difficult to enforce.

The best way to handle these problems is to know who your distributors are and trust in their integrity. If you reach an agreement with them, you will be as assured as you can be that they will fulfill the terms. Even if you are lucky enough to have a distributor like this, however, it still takes great effort, constant supervision or frequent checks to ensure the job is being done.

CHOOSING YOUR DISTRIBUTOR

When I look at distributors, I don't care if they have 20 warehouses and 3,000 salespeople. I want to know if they can sell my product and pay their bills.

There are even times you may not want the biggest and most powerful distributor. Your poor little product might have to scuffle to find a place in his scheme of things. You might be better off finding a hungry company who needs a new and exciting prod-

uct and has the temperament to hustle it aggressively.

Generally, however, when looking for a distributor I assess who has done the biggest job in a comparable item. I don't want to give people on-the-job training on my time and money. I would rather go after a company that has the best track record selling my type of product. If I can't get it, I'll go to the one with the second-best track record, and so on.

When you find your distributor, it's smart to remember that you are not establishing a life-long commitment. The biggest mistake is to say now is forever. You're not stuck with anyone for your entire business life and shouldn't be—either by inference or by contract.

The simplest thing is to sell to an importer on a nonexclusive basis. If he buys, fine. If not, you find someone to replace him.

Most distributors, however, will ask for exclusivity if they think the product has anything going for it. It gives them time to develop the marketplace and, if there's no competition, they have the ingredients for greater profits. As a manufacturer or exporter, I do not want to be vulnerable to one individual, however, unless I have a three- or five-year contract in which he guarantees all the merchandise I want to ship into that area.

There are times when exclusivity is a valuable selling tool.

The scenario could go something like this:
— The distributor asks for an exclusive and you say, "How many will you buy?"
— "I could probably use a lot," he says.
— "I want to know exactly. I'd like to take an order," you say. You never ask for projections or hypothetical numbers. The best and only test is an order. That's a real commitment.
— You negotiate the deal. You look in your charts to see what you can produce and what you'd like to get out of the area. You base the deal upon the fact that in order to have the exclusive each year, the distributor has to fulfill volume commitments. Depending on the product and if it's an

expanding market, he could take 100,000 pieces in the first year, 150,000 pieces in the second, and 200,000 in the third, and so on.

I am satisfied to know that I've escalated my market. The year he doesn't fulfill the quota, he loses the exclusive, and I'm free to sell it elsewhere. That's a fair deal.

You'll find that it usually doesn't happen that quickly, however. More often than not, the distributor or importer will buy 10,000 pieces to test the market. You'll give him a 90-day exclusive to test the market, followed by an order for 100,000 on an exclusive basis, as outlined above.

But everything doesn't have to be absolute. If the distributor can't handle the volume you want, you can give him a limited exclusive. You could give him an exclusive in the Paris area, sell to another company to distribute exclusively in the south of France, another for the central region, and another for the north. Now you have four exclusive distributors by territory in France. And vulnerability is less of a factor because all of your eggs are not in one basket.

MAKING YOUR DISTRIBUTOR WORK HARD FOR YOU

You have convinced a distributor to take your product on. He has committed himself by ordering a certain quantity. Your problem is that he also handles 100 other product lines. How are you going to ensure your product doesn't languish in the catalog, the salesforce wants to sell it, and the distributor will order more?

The first way to get the distributor's attention is with profit. If you can, try to make your product more profitable than other items on the normal product list. To make the distributor work for that profit you might put the discounting on a sliding scale. If he buys $100,000 worth, his discount is 40 percent, but he will get volume rebates when he orders $200,000 worth, or $300,000, or $400,000, etc. So, you are not giving the distributor more than anyone else, but you are encouraging him to sell more. If he sells more, the firm makes an additional profit.

The second element is to make it

as easy as possible for the distributor to sell your product. Provide him with all needed corollary material—from brochures to point-of-sale items, to case histories, good photographs, newspaper veloxes—and anything you can think of that will make it easier for salespeople to make presentations.

It's one of selling's basic rules: make it as easy as possible for someone to buy. Make your ordering system as simple as possible for distributors. Better yet, make it fit their systems, so it's no big deal for them to put the line in.

Now, what about the salesforce? You have made your point with distributors, but they haven't the ability, or desire, or incentive to put it out as strongly to their salesforces. The first and most effective thing to do is try and address salesforces directly, as though they were your own. Give them sales seminars. Show them how to sell the product. And, if pos-sible, bring detail people to the territory to go into the field with the salespeople.

The second thing is to provide salespeople something that will make your product stand out. Maybe it is a special little gift they use in their daily business: a special folder for papers, a special portfolio in which to carry samples, a special order form that makes it easier for to operate, or even something as simple as a good writing pen. But put something in those salespeople's hands to remind them constantly of you and your product.

The third element in the program should be to come up with some kind of incentive over and above their regular salaries, or commissions and bonus. Sometimes it is as simple as money, or points toward an incentive vacation, or points for gifts in a catalog.

These programs are always done with the advice and consent of distributors. If you've already persuaded them that they're going to make more profit on your items, and that it is going to be easier to process than anyone else's lines, they'll be only too willing to let you motivate their sales forces.

Which method of distribution should you choose? If you have an atypical product and investigate the market to find the typical distribution outlets, should you use them? If you go into typical distribution, you may just end up with a typical product.

The marketplace has changed drastically in recent years. New techniques, new hardware, new technology have made merchandising that was formerly impossible entirely possible and profitable. But you are in a highly complex market with more outlets, more people who will buy, more of a marketplace than ever existed, and more competition. Your alternatives are numerous.

Glossary

This glossary of 122 marketing terms is included to provide you with a convenient and ready reference as you encounter general terms in your study of marketing which are unfamiliar or require a review. It is not intended to be comprehensive but taken together with the many definitions included in the articles themselves it should prove to be quite useful.

Advertising Efforts to stimulate sales through the use of mass media displays, direct individual appeals, public displays, give-aways and the like. Although advertising can take many forms, the particular mix of such forms which gets the best results for either a product category or an individual company is often developed to a high level of efficiency. *See* Marketing Mix, Promotion

Anti-Dumping Tariff A tariff penalizing the sale of imported goods at a price lower than they sell for in their country of origin. *See* Imports

† **Barter** The exchange of goods or services between two parties without resort to money. A practice which is becoming more common in international trade.

Brand An identification, name or symbol used to differentiate the products of one company from its competition. A brand may actually consist of any set of individual product characteristics which the consumer associates with only that single product, product line or selling company. *See* Brand Differentiation, Brand Image, Brand Name

Brand Differentiation The degree of consumer discrimination between products on the basis of product brand, or the ability of a company to promote such discrimination.

Brand Image The quality and reliability of a product as perceived by consumers on the basis of its brand reputation or familiarity.

Brand Name That part of the brand of a product which can be and is communicated as a name or equivalent product identification. The brand name is usually that element of a particular brand which triggers the brand consciousness within the consumer.

Buyers Market A condition of a market in which supply exceeds demand, thus putting downward pressure on prices. *See* Sellers Market

Capital Goods Equipment, machinery or tools which are used in the production of, or facilitate the eventual production of, other goods. In general, they are comprised of that portion of industrial goods which are not consumed in the normal course of business.

Caveat Emptor "Let the buyer beware." A principle of law meaning that the purchase of a product is at the buyer's risk with regard to its quality, usefulness and the like. The laws do, however, provide certain minimum protection against fraud and other schemes.

Channels of Distribution The various means employed by a company in distributing its products through wholesalers, distributors, jobbers, retailers and the like. *See* Distribution

Competition The contest by two or more parties for the business of a third party. It is the act of securing business through offering the most favorable deal to one's customer.

Consignment An arrangement in which a seller of goods does not take title to the goods until they are sold. The seller thus has the option of returning them to the supplier or principal if unable to execute the sale.

Consumer The final buyer or user of a product, good or service. Commonly used in reference to individuals rather than industrial, institutional or other classes of consumers.

Consumer Advertising Advertising which is directed at the final purchaser of goods or services.

Consumer Behavior The way in which buyers, individually or collectively, react to marketplace stimuli.

Consumer Goods Those goods which are produced for direct use by individuals and households. *See* Capital Goods, Convenience Goods, Industrial Goods, Shopping Goods, Specialty Goods

Convenience Goods Consumer goods which are purchased at frequent intervals with little regard for price. Such goods are relatively standard in nature and consumers tend to select the most convenient source when shopping. Convenience goods include tobacco, drugs, newspapers and some grocery items. *See* Shopping Goods, Specialty Goods

Cooperative Advertising Advertising of a product by a retailer, dealer, distributor or the like with part of the advertising cost paid by the product's manufacturer.

Copyright A statutory right granted to the creator of a published or artistic work protecting the exclusive prerogative of reproduction for a specific period of time. A relatively simple and inexpensive process, works copyrighted in the United States are afforded reciprocal protection under a copyright agreement.

Demand In general, the need or desire for individual or collective products within a marketplace. *See* Law of Supply and Demand, Supply

† **De-Marketing** The use of marketing techniques to discourage consumption of a particular product or service. For example, when a utility company encourages consumers to turn off lights.

Demography The study of human population densities, distributions and movements.

Direct Mail Promotion Marketing goods to consumers by mailing to them unsolicited promotional material.

Direct Selling A manufacturer's sales efforts directed to the final purchaser or consumer.

Discount The reduction in the price of an item, usually given in return for some benefit such as prompt payment or quantity purchase. It also refers to the difference between a bond's (or other item's) selling price and its face value when it is selling below face value.

Discount House   A retail company which sells goods at prices below those generally prevailing, usually relying on selling large quantities in order to pay overhead expenses and generate sufficient profit.

Discretionary Income   That portion of disposable income, either of an individual or of a nation as a whole, which remains after paying for necessities.

Disposable Income   That portion of income, either of an individual or of a nation as a whole, which remains after payment of personal taxes to the government.

Distribution   The ways by which a company gets its product to the point of purchase by the final consumer. In statistics, the way in which a set of numbers tends to be more or less concentrated in different ranges or categories. Perhaps the most widely known distribution is the classical bell shaped curve, with the largest concentration of numbers at the mid point. *See* Channels of Distribution

Distributor   In general, any person or organization performing the function of product distribution. The term usually excludes retailers but includes wholesalers and dealers who sell to either retailers or industrial consumers.

Dual Distribution   The selling of products to two or more competing distribution networks, or the selling of two brands of nearly identical products through competing distribution networks. An example of the first case is found in the petroleum industry which sells to independent dealers as well as captive retailers. An example of the second case is found in the marketing of products under private label which are also being sold as nationally advertised brands. *See* Channels of Distribution, Distribution

Dumping   The act of selling large amounts of goods or securities without regard to the effect on the marketplace; or the selling of imported goods at a price lower than that charged in the country of origin. *See* Anti-Dumping Tariff

Durable Goods   Products that continue in service for an appreciable length of time such as automobiles or major household appliances. *See* Non-Durable Goods

Exports   Goods produced within a country and subsequently sold in another country. *See* Imports

Fair Trade Laws (Fair Trade Acts)   Statutes which exempt price maintenance agreements between manufacturers and distributors for certain trademarked items. While the use of fair trade agreements is diminishing, the absence of this special legal status would put such agreements in direct conflict with the restraint of trade provisions of the antitrust laws.

Franchise   The right to distribute a company's products or render services under its name, and to retain the resulting profit in exchange for a fee or percentage of sales.

Free on Board (FOB)   Delivered, without charge, to a specific location where ownership changes hands at the expense of the buyer.

Freight Absorption   Payment of transportation costs by the manufacturer or seller, often resulting in a uniform pricing structure.

Imports   A country's buying of goods or services which are manufactured or produced in some other country.

Industrial Goods   Those goods which are destined for use in, or consumption by, commercial businesses. The industrial goods market generally exhibits more uniform and rational buying patterns than the consumer goods market. *See* Capital Goods

Inventory   An asset composed of goods held for sale or raw materials and semi-finished goods held for use in their production.

Inventory Profit   Profit made by a company because it had inventory on hand during a period of rising costs and prices. If a company increases its selling prices as soon as its costs increase, it will realize more than its normal profit on the on-hand inventory which it purchased at historically lower costs.

Inventory Turnover Rate   The rate at which inventory is fully replaced each year. It is normally determined by dividing the cost of goods sold during the year by the average inventory level during the year. Also called stockturn rate.

Invoice   A detailed statement of goods or services provided, usually including a request for payment.

Jobber   One who buys from wholesalers and sells to retailers to eliminate the necessity of one-to-one contact between each wholesaler and retailer. Sometimes used synonymously with wholesaler.

Law of Supply and Demand   Those laws, generally relating to economic theory, which describe the behavior of prices through an understanding of such factors as the economic structure, the nature of products, and specific combinations of the supply and demand levels for products.

Life Cycle   The phases through which a product or business passes during its viable life. There are four generally accepted life cycle phases: (1) development, 2) growth, 3) maturity, and 4) decline. The duration and intensity of each phase depends upon the characteristics of each product or business.

Logo   The symbol or trademark which a company uses to identify itself such as on letterheads, signs or advertising.

Loss Leader   An item which a manufacturer or retailer sells at or below cost in order to either achieve greater market penetration or attract purchasers for other products in the product line.

Market   The potential buyers for a company's product or service; or to sell a product or service to actual buyers. The place where goods and services are exchanged. *See* Marketing, Marketplace

* Market Analysis A sub-division of marketing research which involves the measurement of the extent of a market and the determination of its characteristics.

Marketing The total effort of a company in directing products from manufacturer to final consumer including advertising, selling, packaging, distribution, market research and other such functions.

* Marketing Budget A statement of the planned dollar sales and planned marketing costs for a specified future period.

† Marketing Concept A company belief that the best way to be successful is by identifying the needs and wants of a particular market segment and developing and implementing marketing strategies to satisfy those needs in ways that are more efficient than the competition's.

* Marketing Management The planning, direction and control of the entire marketing activity of a firm or division of a firm, including the formulation of marketing objectives, policies, programs and strategy, and commonly embracing product development, organizing and staffing to carry out plans, supervising marketing operations, and controlling marketing performance.

Marketing Mix The elements of marketing: product, brand, package, price, channels of distribution, advertising and promotion, personal selling, and the like.

* Marketing Planning The work of setting up objectives for marketing activity and of determining and scheduling the steps necessary to achieve such objectives.

Market Orientation A marketing philosophy which emphasizes the dynamics of the marketplace (particularly customer needs) as opposed to the product. *See* Product Orientation

Market Penetration Typically, market penetration refers to the advancement of one's products or services into a particular marketplace or market segment. *See* Market Share

Marketplace In general, the place where the business of a market is conducted. It is the place or circumstances where the buying and selling of goods and services occurs.

* Market Potential (also Market or Total Market) A calculation of maximum possible sales opportunities for all sellers of a good or service during a stated period.

Market Research The generation of empirical and statistical information concerning consumers or purchasers. Market research seeks, for example, to determine how purchasers behave and how they perceive the various characteristics of products.

Market Segment A group or segment of consumers who share some characteristics in common, such as age, sex, income, education, occupation, marital status or geographic location. A company usually directs its marketing effort at specific market segments.

Market Share A product's sales as a percent of all sales of similar products. Market share may also apply to a group of products or to a company in relation to its industry.

Market Skimming Exploiting only the prime market segment of a product's or company's marketplace which is either the most profitable, the least costly to reach, or requires the least amount of available resources.

Market Stimulation The act of increasing sales through the introduction or augmentation of an element of the marketing mix.

Mark Up As it relates to retail selling it is the retailer's expected margin expressed as a percentage of selling price (selling price minus cost divided by selling price). It differs from gross margin in that the latter is an achieved percentage of gain while the former is an intended percentage of gain.

† Mass Marketing Utilizing marketing strategies to attract as many customers from all market segments as possible. Usually involves the mass-production and mass-distribution of a single product; some toothpastes and laundry detergents are examples.

Mass Media Advertising The use of any advertising media whose audience consists of the general population such as with radio, newspaper or television advertising.

Middleman A person or business which buys and sells between manufacturers and consumers or similarly brings together two complementary interests.

Missionary Selling The initial sales efforts by a manufacturer into virgin markets. Typically, the missionary sales person will receive a salary rather than a commission for services.

* Motivation Research A group of techniques developed by the behavioral scientists which are used by marketing researchers to discover factors influencing marketing behavior.

Multinational A company which conducts operations in many countries.

Non-Durable Goods Products that do not last or continue in service for any appreciable length of time. Clothing is an example of non-durable goods.

Obsolescence The decrease in the value of an item which is caused by age, style change or new technology. An item may be obsolete even though it still functions in the way in which it was designed. *See* Planned Obsolescence

Patent A license granted by a government to an inventor giving, for a period of time, exclusive manufacturing rights to the invention. A patent has value and is often included as an asset on a company's balance sheet. In the United States, a patent can be protected for 17 years.

Personal Selling Any form of oral sales presentation or assistance to a customer. Traditionally the cornerstone of selling and promotional activities, it is one of the elements of the marketing mix.

* Physical Distribution The management of the movement and handling of goods from the point of production to the point of consumption or use.

Planned Obsolescence Purposely designing obsolescense into a product. This can be achieved either by incorporating periodic changes which are stylistic rather than functional, or by designing a product with a physical life shorter than its useful life.

Point-of-Purchase Advertising The act of promoting a product at the location of purchase. A point-of-purchase display is designed to impel on-the-spot buying by customers. It is used more extensively in marketing consumer than industrial goods, because ultimate consumers are more susceptible to impulse buying.

Predatory Price Cutting The practice of selling goods or services at or below cost. Predatory price cutting may be employed to increase a company's market share or to sell unwanted merchandise. Note, however, that predatory price cutting does not refer to such selling of seasonal or perishable items.

Price Elasticity An economic concept which attempts to measure the sensitivity of demand for any product to changes in its price. If consumers are relatively sensitive to changes in price (i.e., higher price results in a lower demand for a product), then the demand for such a product is elastic. If, on the other hand, changing price does not affect the quantity purchased, then such a product is said to exhibit an inelastic demand characteristic. *See* Law of Supply and Demand

Price Fixing The illegal attempt by one or several companies to maintain the prices of its products above those that would result from open competition.

* **Price Leader** A firm whose pricing behavior is followed by other companies in the same industry. The price leadership of a firm may be limited to a certain geographical area, as in the oil business, or to certain products or groups of products, as in the steel business.

Price Out To calculate the price or cost of a set of actions; or to lower a price in an effort to drive high priced competition out of a market.

Pricing Policies The manner in which a company determines the prices of its goods or services. Three such methods used are: 1) to apply a standard markup to the cost of goods, 2) to maintain prices in line with competition, and 3) to charge what the market will bear.

Primary Market Demand The demand for goods and services in the market for which they were primarily intended.

Product Anything which a company sells. In the narrowest sense product refers to manufactured items. In popular terminology, however, product can also refer to services, securities and the like.

Product Differentiation The ability or tendency of manufacturers, marketers or consumers to distinguish between seemingly similar products. *See* Brand, Brand Differentiation

Productivity The rate at which production occurs (presumably to generate profit) in a given period of time. Productivity may apply to a laborer, machine, company, industry or even an entire country.

* **Product Line** A group of products that are closely related either because they satisfy a class of need, are used together, are sold to the same customer groups, are marketed through the same type of outlets or fall within given price ranges. Example, carpenters' tools.

* **Product Management** The planning, direction, and control of all phases of the life cycle of products, including the creation or discovery of ideas for new products, the screening of such ideas, the coordination of the work of research and physical development of products, their packaging and branding, their introduction on the market, their market development, their modification, the discovery of new uses for them, their repair and servicing, and their deletion.

Product Market Erosion A decrease in demand for a product or service. Product market erosion might be caused, for example, by the introduction of a similar product which consumers purchase as a substitute.

* **Product Mix** The composite of products offered for sale by a firm or a business unit.

Product Orientation A marketing philosophy which emphasizes the product as opposed to the customer. Such an orientation usually involves efforts to perfect product design, improve production efficiencies, and reduce product cost without heeding the dynamics of the marketplace or changes in the competitive situation. *See* Market Orientation

Promotion The stimulation of sales by inducements or product exposure directed at either the channels of distribution or the final consumer. Promotion can refer to various forms of advertising, trade or consumer discounts, specially advertised discounts or the like. The promotion of a new product might include a combination of several of these. *See* Marketing Mix

Proprietary Product A product which is of such distinction as to be under patent, trademark or copyright protection. Also those products protected by proprietary market positions, such as through strength of distribution channels, production efficiencies, geographic location, etc.

† **Psychographics** Measurable characteristics of given market segments in respect to lifestyles, interests, opinions, needs, values, attitudes, personality traits, etc.

* **Publicity** Non-personal stimulation of demand for a product, service or business unit by planting commercially significant news about it in a published medium or obtaining favorable presentation of it upon radio, television, or stage that is not paid for by the sponsor.

Pull Strategy A marketing strategy whose main thrust is to so strongly influence the final consumer that the demand for a product "pulls" it through the various channels of distribution. Such a strategy is generally accompanied by large advertising expenditures to influence the consumer and relatively low markups to wholesalers and retailers. *See* Push Strategy

Push Strategy   A marketing strategy whose main thrust is to provide sufficient economic incentives to members of the channels of distribution so as to "push" the product through to the consumer. Such a strategy is usually accompanied by high price markups, selective distribution and retail price support by the manufacturer. *See* Pull Strategy

* **Resale Price Maintenance**   Control by a supplier of the selling prices of his branded goods at subsequent stages of distribution by means of contractual agreement under fair trade laws or other devices.

Restraint of Trade   In general, activities which interfere with competitive marketing. Restraint of trade usually refers to illegal activities.

* **Retailing**   The activities involved in selling directly to the ultimate consumer.

* **Sales Forecast**   An estimate of sales, in dollars or physical units for a specified future period under a proposed marketing plan or program and under an assumed set of economic and other forces outside the unit for which the forecast is made. The forecast may be for a specified item of merchandise or for an entire line.

* **Sales Management**   The planning, direction, and control of the personal selling activities of a business unit, including recruiting, selecting, training, equipping, assigning, routing, supervising, paying, and motivating as these tasks apply to the personal sales force.

* **Sales Promotion**   (1.) In a specific sense, those marketing activities, other than personal selling, advertising, and publicity, that stimulate consumer purchasing and dealer effectiveness, such as display, shows and exhibitions, demonstrations, and various non-recurrent selling efforts not in the ordinary routine. (2.) In retailing, all methods of stimulating customer purchasing, including personal selling, advertising, and publicity.

Secondary Market Demand   The demand for goods or services in a market other than that for which they were intended. *See* Primary Market Demand

Selective Distribution   The use of only those means of distributing a product which are either most profitable, easiest to manage or control, or otherwise particularly beneficial or consistent with other marketing, production or financial considerations. *See* Distribution, Market Skimming

Sellers Market   A condition within any market in which the demand for an item is greater than its supply. A market in which the seller maintains a more favorable bargaining position than the buyer. *See* Buyers Market

* **Selling**   The personal or impersonal process of assisting and/or persuading a prospective customer to buy a commodity or a service or to act favorably upon an idea that has commercial significance to the seller.

Services   In general, efforts expended to meet human needs which are primarily direct person to person activities or those activities not associated with the manufacturing or processing of a product, good, commodity or the like.

Shopping Goods   Consumer goods which are purchased only after comparisons are made concerning price, quality, style, suitability and the like. Shopping goods are often purchased infrequently, consumed or used up slowly and are subject to advanced or deferred purchase decisions on the part of the consumer. Such items include, for example, furniture, rugs and shoes. *See* Convenience Goods, Speciality Goods

† **Social Marketing**   The use of marketing strategies to increase the acceptability of an idea (smoking causes cancer); cause (environmental protection); or practice (birth control) within a target market.

Specialty Goods   Consumer goods, usually appealing only to a limited market, for which consumers will make a special purchasing effort. Such items include, for example, stereo components, fancy foods and prestige brand clothes. *See* Convenience Goods, Shopping Goods

† **Target Marketing**   Developing product and promotion strategies for a very well-defined group of potential customers to which a company decides to market goods or services.

Trade Advertising   Advertising directed at the trade which distributes, sells or uses a product.

Trademark (Trade-Mark)   An affixed sign or mark distinguishing articles produced or marketed by one company from those of another. Generally used to protect the goodwill or name of a certain class of goods, trademarks can be registered thus restricting use by others.

* **Ultimate Consumer**   One who buys and/or uses goods or services to satisfy personal or household wants rather than for resale or for use in business, institutional, or industrial operations.

* **Value Added by Marketing**   The part of the value of a product or a service to the consumer or user which results from marketing activities.

Wholesaler   One who makes quantity purchases from manufacturers (or other wholesalers), and sells in smaller quantities to retailers (or other wholesalers). The wholesaler usually handles the products of many different manufacturers and in turn is only one of many suppliers to his customers. Similarly, the wholesaler will operate in a smaller geographic area than the manufacturer but a much larger area than the retailer. The wholesaler will usually rely on a small percentage profit from a large volume of sales, and may be expected to provide various services to the customer which would otherwise not be available.

Sources for the Glossary:

Terms designated by an asterisk (*) were taken from "Marketing Definitions: A Glossary of Marketing Terms," Committee on Definitions of the American Marketing Association.

Definitions for terms designated with a dagger (†) were developed by the Annual Editions staff.

The remaining terms were taken from "The Language of Business" (1975). The complete pocket glossary is available at either single list price or quantity discount price through Cambridge Business Research Inc., 4 Brattle St., Suite 306, Cambridge, MA 02138.

Credits/
Acknowledgments

Cover design by Charles Vitelli

Marketing in the 1990s and Beyond
Facing overview—IBM Corporation.

Research, Markets, and Consumer Behavior
Facing overview—TRW, Inc. 114—Chart, Source: SAMI,
Illustration by Susan Faila.

Developing and Implementing Strategies
Facing overview—The Port of New York Authority photo by L.
Johns.

Global Marketing
Facing overview—United Nations photo by Y. Nagata.

ANNUAL EDITIONS ARTICLE REVIEW FORM

■ NAME: _____ DATE: _____

■ TITLE AND NUMBER OF ARTICLE: _____

■ BRIEFLY STATE THE MAIN IDEA OF THIS ARTICLE: _____

_____

_____

_____

_____

■ LIST THREE IMPORTANT FACTS THAT THE AUTHOR USES TO SUPPORT THE MAIN IDEA:

_____

_____

_____

_____

_____

■ WHAT INFORMATION OR IDEAS DISCUSSED IN THIS ARTICLE ARE ALSO DISCUSSED IN YOUR TEXTBOOK OR OTHER READING YOU HAVE DONE? LIST THE TEXTBOOK CHAPTERS AND PAGE NUMBERS:

_____

_____

_____

_____

_____

_____

■ LIST ANY EXAMPLES OF BIAS OR FAULTY REASONING THAT YOU FOUND IN THE ARTICLE:

_____

_____

_____

_____

■ LIST ANY NEW TERMS/CONCEPTS THAT WERE DISCUSSED IN THE ARTICLE AND WRITE A SHORT DEFINITION:

_____

_____

_____

_____

_____

ANNUAL EDITIONS: MARKETING 91/92
Article Rating Form

Here is an opportunity for you to have direct input into the next revision of this volume. We would like you to rate each of the 57 articles listed below, using the following scale:

1. **Excellent: should definitely be retained**
2. **Above average: should probably be retained**
3. **Below average: should probably be deleted**
4. **Poor: should definitely be deleted**

Your ratings will play a vital part in the next revision. So please mail this prepaid form to us just as soon as you complete it.
Thanks for your help!

Rating	Article	Rating	Article
	1. Portrait of a Changing Consumer		29. U.S. Companies Go for the Gray
	2. Marketing in an Age of Diversity		30. Beyond Consumer Decision Making
	3. Stalking the New Consumer		31. Cueing the Consumer: The Role of Salient Cues in Consumer Perception
	4. What Consumers Want in the 1990s		
	5. Marketing Myopia (With Retrospective Commentary)		32. Shoppers' Blues: The Thrill Is Gone
			33. Seize Tomorrow's Markets
	6. King Customer		34. Enduring Brands Hold Their Allure By Sticking Close to Their Roots
	7. Service = Survival		
	8. How to Handle Customers' Gripes		35. Strengthen Brands With 8 Essential Elements
	9. Guiding Principles for Improving Customer Service		
			36. Masters of Innovation
	10. Sure Ways to Annoy Customers		37. Sales Lost Their Vim? Try Repackaging
	11. Customer Satisfaction		38. The Fine Art of Positioning
	12. What Is Good Service?		39. Middle-Price Brands Come Under Siege
	13. Service Marketing: Image, Branding, and Competition		40. Marketing the Premium Product
			41. How to Compete on Price
	14. Nonprofits Learn How-To's of Marketing		42. As Retailers' Sales Crop Up Everywhere, Regulators Wonder If the Price Is Right
	15. An Ethical Base for Marketing Decision Making		
			43. Manage by Walking Around—Outside
	16. Marketing and Its Discontents		44. Real Service
	17. Some Food Labels Aren't on the Level		45. Retail Revolution
	18. Children's Advertising Grows Up, but Not Everyone Approves		46. The (Un)Malling of America
			47. Revamped Retail
	19. How to Hunt for the Best Source		48. Home Depot's Do-It-Yourself Powerhouse
	20. Market Research the Japanese Way		49. What's Right, What's Wrong With Each Medium
	21. The Selling of Life-Styles		
	22. New Species for Study: Consumers in Action		50. Advertising: In Dire Straits
			51. Ads of the '80s: The Loved and the Losers
	23. Focus Groups Emerging as Important Business-to-Business Market Research Tool		
			52. Strategic Options for Global Market Players
	24. A Symphony of Demographic Change		53. Global Competitors: Some Criteria for Success
	25. Downscale Consumers, Long Neglected, Start to Get Some Respect from Marketers		
			54. Beware the Pitfalls of Global Marketing
			55. Hitting for Singles
	26. Different Folks, Different Strokes		56. Myth and Marketing in Japan
	27. "Real" Consumers Just Aren't Normal		57. Distribution: The Key to Success Overseas
	28. Meet Jane Doe		

(continued on back)

ABOUT YOU

Name_____ Date_____

Are you a teacher? ☐ Or student? ☐

Your School Name _____

Department _____

Address _____

City _____ State _____ Zip _____

School Telephone #_____

YOUR COMMENTS ARE IMPORTANT TO US!

Please fill in the following information:

For which course did you use this book? _____

Did you use a text with this Annual Edition? ☐ yes   ☐ no

The title of the text? _____

What are your general reactions to the Annual Editions concept?

Have you read any particular articles recently that you think should be included in the next edition?

Are there any articles you feel should be replaced in the next edition? Why?

Are there other areas that you feel would utilize an Annual Edition?

May we contact you for editorial input?

May we quote you from above?

ANNUAL EDITIONS: MARKETING 91/92

BUSINESS REPLY MAIL

First Class   Permit No. 84   Guilford, CT

Postage will be paid by addressee

The Dushkin Publishing Group, Inc.
Sluice Dock
DPG **Guilford, Connecticut 06437**

No Postage
Necessary
if Mailed
in the
United States